South.

THE POST

South Africa in Africa

THE POST-APARTHEID ERA

Edited by Adekeye Adebajo,
Adebayo Adedeji and Chris Landsberg

UNIVERSITY OF KwaZulu-Natal PRESS

Published in 2007 by
University of KwaZulu-Natal Press
Private Bag x01
Scottsville 3209
South Africa
books@ukzn.ac.za
www.ukznpress.co.za

Publishing management by

Electric Book Works
87 Station Road
Observatory 7925
Cape Town
South Africa
www.electricbookworks.com

ISBN 978-1-86914-134-9

Set in Minion by William Dicey
Cover design by Pete Lewis
Printed and bound by Interpak Books, Pietermaritzburg

Contents

Part III: Case studies

Contributors

ADEKEYE ADEBAJO is Executive Director of the Centre for Conflict Resolution at the University of Cape Town (UCT), South Africa. He served as Director of the Africa Programme of the New York-based International Peace Academy between 2001–03. During the same period, Dr Adebajo was an Adjunct Professor at Columbia University's School of International and Public Affairs. He previously served on UN missions in South Africa, Western Sahara and Iraq. Dr Adebajo is the author of *Building Peace in West Africa: Liberia, Sierra Leone, and Guinea-Bissau; Liberia's Civil War: Nigeria, ECOMOG, and Regional Security in West Africa;* and co-editor of *Managing Armed Conflicts in the Twenty-First Century; West Africa's Security Challenges: Building Peace in A Troubled Region;* and *A Dialogue of the Deaf: Essays on Africa and the United Nations.* He obtained his doctorate from Oxford University, where he studied as a Rhodes Scholar.

ADEBAYO ADEDEJI has been a proponent and architect of regional integration in Africa since the early 1970s, beginning with the establishment of the Economic Community of West African States (ECOWAS). Between 1971 and 1975, he was Minister of Economic Reconstruction and Development in Nigeria. During his tenure as Executive Secretary of the UN Economic Commission for Africa from 1975 to 1991, Adedeji led the development of the Preferential Trade Agreement (PTA), which later became the Common Market for Eastern and Southern Africa (COMESA). He is the editor of the book *South Africa and Africa: Within or Apart?* and various publications on African political economy, development and security. At present, Professor Adedeji is the director of the African Centre for Development and Strategic Studies (ACDESS), a think-tank based in Ijebu Ode, Nigeria.

AUGUSTA CONCHIGLIA is an experienced journalist and worked as an editor-in-chief for *Le Nouvel Afrique Asie* (Paris). She has worked widely in Europe and Africa, and freelanced for *Il Manifesto* (Rome), *Le Monde Diplomatique* (Paris), and *Radio France Internationale.* She has also done freelance consultancy for the European Commission, producing reports on Southern Africa's political economy. Ms Conchiglia studied Social studies at the University of Rome, Italy, and holds a Masters degree in Sociology from Padua University in Italy.

DEVON CURTIS is a lecturer in the Department of Politics at the University of Cambridge. Her research analyses the limits of power-sharing arrangements following ethnic conflict, and the transitions of rebel movements into political parties in Africa. She is currently completing a book about the peace process in Burundi. Previously, she was a Post-doctoral Research Fellow at the Saltzman Institute of War and Peace Studies at Columbia University, New York and a Pre-doctoral Fellow at the Center for International Security and Cooperation (CISAC) at Stanford University, in California. She has also worked for the Canadian Government, the United Nations Staff College, and the Overseas Development Institute. Dr Curtis received her doctorate in International Relations from the London School of Economics (LSE) in 2004.

RUTH HALL is a researcher at the Programme for Land and Agrarian Studies (PLAAS), a research unit in the School of Government at the University of the Western Cape (UWC), where she conducts research mainly into the progress and problems of the land reform programme in South Africa. Before joining PLAAS, she worked for the Centre for Rural Legal Studies (CRLS), in Stellenbosch, South Africa. She has also done research on land reform policies and practices in South Africa and in India, focusing on land redistribution, political economy and gender equity. She holds a Masters degree in Development Studies from the University of Oxford where she studied as a Rhodes Scholar, an Honours degree in Political Studies from the University of Cape Town, and is currently registered for a doctoral degree in Politics at the University of Oxford.

JUDI HUDSON is an independent consultant working with a range of clients, including the Finmark Trust, the South African Institute of International Affairs and CARE South Africa. Previous clients include the Nelson Mandela Foundation, Shisaka Development Management Services, the South African Revenue Services and the Business Trust. She holds a masters degree in Political Science from the University of Natal, where she also lectured in that subject. Previously a senior research fellow at the Department of War Studies, Kings' College, University of London, Ms Hudson has worked for a number of research and policy think-tanks including the Centre for Policy Studies, the Centre for Development and Enterprise, and the Small Business Project, all based in Johannesburg, South Africa.

IQBAL JHAZBHAY lectures in the University of South Africa's (UNISA) Department of Religious Studies and Arabic and serves on the boards of the Institute for Global Dialogue (IGD) in Midrand, South Africa, the Academy for Self Knowledge in Tshwane, South Africa and the Commission for Religious Affairs of the African National Congress (ANC). He also serves on the editorial board of the *Journal of Global Politics, Economy and Society*. In addition, he edited a special edition of *African Security Review* on the Horn of Africa (2004), and is the author of *Somaliland's Post-War Nation-Building and International Relations, 1991–2006*. He writes on African issues for the ANC policy discussion journal, *Umrabulo*, as well as for South African newspapers, such as the *Sunday Times* and *Mail and Guardian*.

CHRIS LANDSBERG is Director of the Centre for Policy Studies in Johannesburg and a Research Professor at the University of Johannesburg (UJ). He is a co-founder of the Centre for Africa's International Relations at the University of the Witwatersrand, where he is also a Board member. He is author of *The Quiet Diplomacy of Liberation: International Politics and South Africa's Transition*; and co-editor of *From Cape to Congo: Southern Africa's regional Security Challenges*. He obtained his doctorate from Oxford University, where he studied as a Rhodes Scholar.

KHABELE MATLOSA is the Research Director at the Electoral Institute of Southern Africa (EISA), in Johannesburg, South Africa. He holds a PhD in Political Economy from the University of the Western Cape (UWC). He is a member of the Board of Governors of the Centre for Conflict Resolution based at the University of Cape Town. He was one of the experts who produced the Principles for Election Management, Monitoring and Observation in the SADC Region, developed by the Electoral Institute of Southern Africa and the Electoral Commissions Forum (ECF) and subsequently adopted in a regional conference in November 2003. He is the co-editor of the *Journal of African Elections* (JAE) and was commissioned by the African Union, between 2005 and 2006, to develop the Draft African Charter on Democracy, Elections and Governance. He has researched and written widely on various governance and development themes.

SHAUNA MOTTIAR is a researcher for the Centre for Policy Studies, Johannesburg, South Africa. She is a PhD candidate at the University of the Witwatersrand, conducting research on democratic consolidation.

SAM MOYO is the Executive Director of the African Institute for Agrarian Studies based in Harare, Zimbabwe. He has more than 25 years of research experience on rural development issues with a focus on land and natural resources management, civil society organisations, and capacity building and institutional development. He has been involved in writing and editing several publications, with key works being *The Land Question in Zimbabwe*; *Land Reform Under Structural Adjustment in Zimbabwe* and *African Land Questions, the State and Agrarian Transition: Contradictions of Neoliberal Land Reforms*.

ANGELA NDINGA-MUVUMBA is a Senior Researcher at the Centre for Conflict Resolution in Cape Town, and head of its HIV/AIDS and Security project. Before joining CCR, Ms Ndinga-Muvumba served as a Political Officer in the Bureau of the Chairperson of the Africa Union Commission in Addis Ababa, Ethiopia. She worked with the International Peace Academy's Africa Programme between 2001 and 2004. Ms Ndinga-Muvumba has served as a consultant for the UN's HIV/AIDS and Governance Commission as well as for the AU. She holds a Master's degree in International Affairs from Columbia University's School of International and Public Affairs in New York, and has published several scholarly articles and book chapters.

MAXI SCHOEMAN obtained her doctorate from the University of Wales and is currently professor and head of the Department of Political Sciences at the University of Pretoria in South Africa. She has published widely on topics related to regional security, international political economy, and gender issues. She is deputy chairperson of the board of the Institute for Global Dialogue in Midrand, South Africa and serves on the editorial boards of *African Affairs*, *Foreign Policy Analysis*, *Small States,* and *The South African Journal of International Affairs*.

KHEHLA SHUBANE is currently employed at the BusinessMap Foundation, an institution that monitors and conducts research into black economic empowerment. He is part of a team working around BEE issues. Previously he was employed at the Centre for Policy Studies, as well as at the Mandela Foundation, both in Johannesburg, South Africa.

YASMIN SOOKA has been Executive Director of the Foundation for Human Rights in South Africa since January 2001. Prior to joining the Foundation, Ms Sooka was a member of the Truth and Reconciliation Commission in South Africa, serving first for three years as the deputy chair to the Human Rights Violations Committee and then as the chair of the Committee. During 2002 and 2004 she was appointed by the United Nations as an international Commissioner of the Truth and Reconciliation Commission of Sierra Leone.

Acknowledgements

The editors would like to thank all the authors and contributors to this unique three-year project on South Africa's role in Africa in the post-apartheid era. A first-class group of authors have shown remarkable patience, perseverance and professionalism in revising several versions of their chapters in an extremely rigorous review process. The seminar from which the volume emerges was held in Stellenbosch, South Africa, in July and August 2004, and was organised by the Centre for Conflict Resolution at the University of Cape Town, South Africa in collaboration with the Centre for Policy Studies, Johannesburg, South Africa, and the African Centre for Development and Strategic Studies, Ijebu-Ode, Nigeria, as part of continuing efforts to disseminate Pan-African perspectives on this and other important issues related to Africa's international relations. We would like to thank our colleagues at these three institutions for their unflinching support, which ensured the success of this project.

We would also like to express our profound gratitude to the funders of CCR's Africa Programme, who supported this project: the Swiss Agency for Development and Co-operation; the governments of Denmark, the Netherlands, Sweden, Norway and Finland; the United Kingdom's Department for International Development; the Foundation for Human Rights; and the Rockefeller Brothers Fund. We would like to thank the participants at the 2004 Stellenbosch seminar whose discussions and debates helped to shape the project. The editors would also like to thank David Le Page for his exceptional and efficient copy-editing skills; Devon Curtis and Khabele Matlosa for insightful comments on the introduction to the volume; and Noria Mashumba, Dawn Alley, and Elizabeth Myburgh for their editorial, research and organisational support. We thank Glenn Cowley and his colleagues at the University of KwaZulu-Natal Press for their friendly professionalism and total dedication to quality. The editors are also grateful to Arthur Attwell, Parusha Naidoo, and Diane Awerbuck at Electric Book Works for meeting what seemed like an impossible production deadline. Last but not least, we would like to thank our families and friends for their consistent support and understanding as we completed this project.

ADEKEYE ADEBAJO, ADEBAYO ADEDEJI, AND CHRIS LANDSBERG

Terms, acronyms and abbreviations

ACDESS	African Centre for Development and Strategic Studies (Nigeria)
AEC	African Economic Community (proposed)
AICC	African Institute for Corporate Citizenship
ANC	African National Congress (SA)
APRM	African Peer Review Mechanism
ARV	antiretroviral
ASF	African Standby Force (to be established by 2010)
ASGISA	Accelerated and Shared Growth Initiative (SA)
AU	African Union
BCP	Basutoland Congress Party
BEE	black economic empowerment
BNC	Binational Commission (South Africa–Nigeria)
CIA	Central Intelligence Agency (US)
CNDD-FDD	*Conseil National pour la Défense de la Démocratie – Forces de Défense pour la Démocratie* (Burundi)
Codesa	Convention for a Democratic South Africa
Comesa	Common Market for Eastern and Southern Africa
Cosatu	Congress of South African Trade Unions
CSSDCA	Conference for Security, Stability, Development and Cooperation in Africa
DMS	development merchant system
DRC	Democratic Republic of the Congo (formerly Zaire)
DTI	Department of Trade and Industry (SA)
ECA	UN Economic Commission for Africa
ECOMOG	ECOWAS Ceasefire Monitoring Group
ECOWAS	Economic Community of West African States
ECOSOCC	Economic, Social and Cultural Council (of the AU)
EO	Executive Outcomes
EU	European Union

FDI	foreign direct investment
FESTEC	Festival of Arts and Culture (Nigeria, 1977)
FLS	Front Line States
FRODEBU	*Front pour la Démocratie au Burundi*
G8	Group of Eight Industrialised Countries
Gear	Growth, Employment and Redistribution policy (SA)
GDP	gross domestic product
HCB	*Hidroelectrica de Cahora Bassa* (Mozambique)
HDI	Human Development Index (of the UNDP)
HIV/AIDS	human immunodeficiency virus/acquired immune deficiency syndrome
IDC	Industrial Development Corporation (SA)
IGAD	Intergovernmental Authority on Development
IMF	International Monetary Fund
IPA	Interim Political Authority (Lesotho)
ISSDC	Inter-State Security and Defence Committee (SADC)
LCD	Lesotho Congress for Democracy
LPM	Landless People's Movement (SA)
LRAD	Land Redistribution for Agricultural Development (SA)
MAP	Millennium African Recovery Plan
MDGS	Millennium Development Goals (UN)
MONUC	United Nations Organisation Mission in the Democratic Republic of the Congo
MPLA	*Movimento Popular de Libertação de Angola – Partido do Trabalho* (Popular Movement for the Liberation of Angola – Party of Labour)
NACOSA	National Aids Convention of South Africa (early 1990s)
NAI	New African Initiative (replaced MAP and the Omega Plan)
NAM	Non-Aligned Movement
NCP	National Contact Point (OECD mechanism)
NEP	National Empowerment Fund
NEPAD	New Partnership for Africa's Development
OAU	Organisation of African Unity (superseded by the AU in 2002)
ODA	overseas development assistance
OECD	Organisation for Economic Cooperation and Development

OPDS	Organ for Politics, Defence and Security (SADC)
Palipehutu-FNL	*Parti pour la libération du peuple Hutu – Forces Nationales de Libération* (Burundi)
PSC	Peace and Security Council (of the AU)
RDP	Reconstruction and Development Programme (SA)
SAA	South African Airways
SABC	South African Broadcasting Corporation
SACP	South African Communist Party
SACU	Southern African Customs Union
SADC	Southern African Development Community
SAIIA	South African Institute of International Affairs
SANAC	South African National Aids Council
SANDF	South African National Defence Force
SAP	Structural Adjustment Programme (usually World Bank-inspired)
SDI	Spatial Development Initiative
SETA	Sector Education and Training Authority (SA)
SIPO	Strategic Indicative Plan for the Organ (SADC)
SLAG	Settlement/Land Acquisition Grants (SA)
TAC	Treatment Action Campaign (SA)
TB	tuberculosis
TRC	Truth and Reconciliation Commission (SA)
Unctad	United Nations Conference on Trade and Development
UNDP	United Nations Development Programme
Unisa	University of South Africa
UNITA	*União Nacional para a Independência Total de Angola* (Union for the Total Independence of Angola)
UPRONA	*Union pour le Progrès National* (Burundi)
WTO	World Trade Organisation

Introduction

ADEKEYE ADEBAJO, ADEBAYO ADEDEJI
AND CHRIS LANDSBERG

Can a country that has brutalised and exploited its own people, and those of surrounding countries, go on to become a credible champion of human rights, democracy and sustainable development on the African continent, even after a remarkable political transformation? To what extent has South Africa been liberated to play a leading role in Africa, and to what extent is it still crippled not only by the past, but by the widely varying priorities of its 47 million people? How have these dynamics played out in the years since the 'rainbow' nation stepped out of its own shadow in 1994?

This volume offers the beginnings of some answers. It is, in part, a follow-up to Adebayo Adedeji's edited book of a decade ago, *South Africa and Africa: Within or Apart?*[1] The 1996 book was the outcome of a workshop organised in Windhoek, Namibia, by the Nigerian-based African Centre for Development and Strategic Studies (ACDESS) in January 1994.

ACDESS organised a second workshop in January 1996 whose theme was 'South Africa within Africa: Emerging Policy Framework'. This meeting was held in Johannesburg, South Africa, and concluded that more time was required before a discernible corpus of holistic policy frameworks for South Africa's role in Africa could become available. The meeting also concluded that at least ten years was required before a credible and definitive assessment could be undertaken. Such an assessment should seek to analyse the domestic and regional factors required to integrate South Africa into the rest of the continent after decades of isolation under apartheid. This book is partly the result of this vision and is the first publication to assess comprehensively South Africa's role in Africa over the last thirteen years.[2]

SOUTH AFRICA AND AFRICA: WITHIN OR APART?

Given its history since 1910 when the Republic of South Africa was established – particularly since 1948 when apartheid became institutionalised – the country was not only apart from itself but also from the rest of Africa. The illegitimate, racist government in Pretoria saw Africa, and particularly its immediate neighbourhood in Southern Africa as areas for penetration, exploitation and destabilisation. This was the Africa of 'labour reserves' from which – from the nineteenth century – hundreds of thousands of Southern African migrants ventured to South Africa to work in mines, farms and industry for a pittance. This was also the Africa of 'broken-backed' states as apartheid's marauding military bombed Mozambique, Angola, Lesotho, Botswana, Zambia and Zimbabwe in a campaign of awesome destructiveness that eventually resulted in a million deaths and an estimated $60 billion in damages between 1980 and 1988.[3] The collective memory of these actions is still fresh in the minds of regional states.

South Africa's apartheid governments saw themselves culturally and politically as very much part of the West, with the country having been part of the 'white dominions', with Australia, Canada and New Zealand. As Hendrik Verwoerd, one of the key architects of apartheid, put it: 'We look upon ourselves as indispensable to the White World ... We are the link. We are white, but we are in Africa. We link them both, and that lays on us a special duty.'[4] Verwoerd claimed that whites had brought civilisation, economic development, order and education to Africa and that South Africa would determine the continent's destiny. In a similar vein, an earlier South African premier, D.F. Malan, talked of 'preserving Africa for white Christian civilisation.' Long before Thabo Mbeki began promoting a more egalitarian vision for a renewed Africa, these leaders considered themselves 'Renaissance' men, seeking to spread 'enlightenment' to 'ignorant savages' on a 'dark continent'. Such patronising thinking was very much a feature of South African political thought from Cecil Rhodes – the diamond tycoon, imperialist, and premier of Cape colony – to F.W. de Klerk, leaving the black-led governments of Nelson Mandela and Mbeki little choice after 1994 but to engage the region with great humility.

South Africa's biggest trading partners were, and remain largely today, Britain, the United States (US), Germany, France and Japan. But South Africa's trade with the rest of Africa has increased dramatically since the end of apartheid. In some eyes, this has revived fears of the visions of South African leaders like Hendrik Verwoerd and John Vorster who often invoked dreams of a South

African-led Southern African common market and a political Commonwealth. In a perverse appropriation of the term, both leaders actually claimed to be pursuing 'Pan-Africanist' policies. South African premier, Jan Smuts, captured this mercantilist, imperialist spirit well in 1940: 'All Africa may be our proper market if we will but have the vision, and far-sighted policy will be necessary if it is to be realised.'[5]

As earlier noted, the end of the first decade of apartheid was deemed the most appropriate time to undertake a frank assessment of what has been accomplished in South Africa's relations with Africa: how much of the long journey has been covered and how successfully. To undertake this task, the Centre for Conflict Resolution (CCR) in Cape Town, South Africa, along with ACDESS, Nigeria, and the Centre for Policy Studies (CPS) in Johannesburg, collaborated in organising a policy seminar in Stellenbosch, South Africa, in July/August 2004.[6] Eleven of the papers from this seminar have been reviewed, edited, and thoroughly updated, while two additional chapters on South Africa's economic expansion into Africa, and its role in the Great Lakes region and the Horn, were commissioned after the Stellenbosch meeting. This unique volume introduces new voices into debates on South Africa's role in Africa, with seven authors from Lesotho, Zimbabwe, Nigeria (two), Uganda, Canada, and Italy, joining eight South African colleagues to produce chapters; while a South African editor joins two Nigerian editors.

This volume argues that any strategy for addressing South Africa's long-term development must necessarily deal with the country's political and socio-economic structural problems. Without addressing these issues, South Africa will have very little room to manoeuvre, let alone be able to play a leadership role in Africa. Similarly, on the part of other African countries, the fundamental impediments to political stability and economic revitalisation as well as continuing obstacles to the establishment of diversified domestic economies will also be determining factors in the evolution and development of their political and socio-economic relations with South Africa after apartheid. Such relations must be devoid of the domineering and destructive hegemony of South Africa's past if they are to be mutually beneficial, and true partnerships must be forged with other African states.

The thirteen chapters in this volume have, to varying degrees, addressed these issues – taking stock of developments since 1994 and discussing the challenges that still lie ahead. One of the benefits of this book is that some contributors and participants at the Stellenbosch seminar in 2004 had taken part in one or both of the workshops in January 1994 in Windhoek and January 1996 in Johannesburg. There has therefore been some element of continuity in the process. The process is also a dynamic one. Today's South Africa is far from becoming a 'rainbow society'. It faces serious political and socio-economic challenges and widespread and pervasive poverty despite the government's policy of black economic empowerment (BEE).

But South Africa has also made impressive strides since 1994. Human rights and the rule of law have become institutionalised, and human dignity universalised. The economy grew nearly five per cent in 2006. The government reported a surplus for the first time in the country's history in 2007, even as it announced plans to dramatically expand spending on social services infrastructure and a new social security system from R66,6 billion in 2007/08 to R78 billion in 2009/10.[7]

However, post-apartheid South Africa is still waiting to be 'deconstructed', as many of the institutions inherited from the apartheid era are still intact: the economy, universities, think-tanks, and the South African National Defence Force's (SANDF) officer corps. The land problem – in which a five per cent white minority continues to control about 70 per cent of the country's most fertile land while many historically dispossessed blacks remain landless – must still be addressed holistically; the trade union movement and civil society groups are also currently struggling to find a role in a new era in which the liberation movement – the African National Congress (ANC) – which they had fully supported and collaborated with during the struggle, has now become the ruling party. There is a widespread perception that the ANC itself is yet to transform successfully from a liberation movement into a political party. Finally, the neo-liberal economic policies of the Thabo Mbeki government and an obsession with foreign direct investment – dubbed the 'cargo cult' by Chris Landsberg – have exacerbated the skewed income distribution of South Africa rather than cultivated a culture of self-reliance and self-sustainment.

Without doubt, South Africa is yet to shed its dual heritage: the 'skyscraper economy'[8] still co-exists with the subsistence economy. In the 1996 book, *South Africa and Africa: Within or Apart?*, it was noted that the wide disparities between white and black communities in the United States pale into insignificance when compared with the disparities between South Africa's white and black population. If white South Africa were a separate country, it would rank in the Organisation for Economic Cooperation and Development (OECD) league table as 24th in human development terms – just below Italy and Spain but above Portugal. In stark contrast, black South Africa would rank 123rd in the world – very much below Botswana, Gabon, Swaziland, Lesotho and Zimbabwe. Yet South Africa has many attributes of the first world: good infrastructure; world-class corporate bodies and corporate governance; and world-class universities and other tertiary institutions. No wonder President Thabo Mbeki himself talks of 'South Africa of two nations'.

Despite these constraints, South Africa has, during the past thirteen years, established solid credentials to become Africa's leading power. Its role in the establishment of the New Partnership for Africa's Development (NEPAD) and the African Union (AU) and its commitment to promoting peace in Burundi, the Democratic Republic of the Congo (DRC) and Côte d'Ivoire are clear evidence that, since 1994, South Africa is not only *within* but also *for* Africa. But on what terms, it may be asked? As a behemoth or hegemon or partner or just another kid on the block? These are some of the issues that are addressed in this volume, and they will continue to evoke heated debates for many years to come. However, a small minority of people would like South Africa to remain apart from the rest of the continent, as it did during the apartheid era. Such people argue that the rest of sub-Saharan Africa constitutes South Africa's bad neighbourhood and albatross. This reminds one of the invoking of the slogan *swart gevaar* – black peril – during the apartheid era.

Many African governments and people have also expressed unease about what they perceive to be South Africa's protectionist trade and xenophobic immigration policies; they have accused South Africa's leaders of ingratitude after three decades of support for the ANC at enormous cost to their own countries; and they have voiced concerns about the aggressive drive by South Africa's mostly white-dominated corporations in search of new markets north of the Limpopo. The fact that South Africa accounts for 80 per cent of the Southern African Development Community's (SADC) economy and has a nine-to-one favourable trade balance with its smaller neighbours continues to breed envy and resentment. The end of the Cold War diverted western investment to eastern Europe and Asia, leaving South Africa with surplus capital (from the era of international economic sanctions which were imposed in the mid-1980s) that has made it Africa's largest investor. In reaction to these concerns, Thabo Mbeki has consistently stressed that South Africa will engage the region 'as a partner and ally, not as a regional superpower'. In February 2000, South Africa established a $30 million Africa Renaissance and International Co-operation Fund – from slush funds that were being used for destabilisation policies by the apartheid government – to promote democracy, development and security in Africa.

SOUTH AFRICA IN AFRICA: MESSIAH OR MERCANTILIST?

In one of the greatest ironies of the post-Cold War era, South Africa has been transformed from being Africa's most destabilising and destructive power to being its most active peacemaker. After a cautious and tentative Africa policy under Nelson Mandela's presidency between 1994 and 1999, Thabo Mbeki sent about 3 000 peacekeepers to Burundi and the DRC under the auspices of the United Nations (UN). But South Africa's past still continues to haunt its present, and many analysts continue to wonder whether South Africa will play the role of messiah or mercantilist in post-apartheid Africa. Despite the emergence of a black-led government in Tshwane (Pretoria)[9], the fact that South Africa's economy, military, academic and policy institutions remain stubbornly untransformed thirteen years after the end of apartheid further weakens its credibility to be Africa's leading power. This has sometimes denied the country the legitimacy and credibility to play a leadership role on the continent, and led to suspicions that South Africa is pursuing a western-oriented rather than African agenda.

A subregional customs union, established in 1889 and transformed into the Southern African Customs Union (SACU) in 1910, binds South Africa, Botswana, Lesotho and Swaziland (and since 1990, Namibia) to the establishment of a free trade area, but also perfectly symbolises the mercantilist approach that Pretoria historically adopted towards its neighbours. Through SACU, South Africa pursued one-sided trade deals while restricting access to its own markets. South Africa unilaterally determined SACU's tariffs and was responsible for administering all customs, excise, and other duties. Far from promoting industrial development within SACU, South Africa often blocked its neighbours' industrialisation efforts.

In the post-Cold War era, the reluctance of western countries to intervene militarily in African countries after UN debacles in Somalia (1993) and Rwanda (1994), led many observers to question whether potential African hegemons like South Africa could fill the security vacuum. During Nelson Mandela's inauguration in May 1994, US vice-president, Al Gore, urged South Africa to send peacekeepers to Rwanda. Based on a history in which apartheid's leaders defined the country as a European outpost, South Africa still struggles today to shake off an identity as a western Trojan horse in Africa. However, under Mandela, South Africa had a globally revered statesman, one of the most representative political systems on the continent, arguably its strongest army, and Africa's largest economy.

A democratic South Africa joined a reformed SADC in 1994. During Mandela's presidency, the country largely shunned a military role in its sub-region out of fear of arousing allegations of hegemonic domination. As SADC chair, Mandela, however, became embroiled in a spat with Zimbabwe's Robert Mugabe over the structure of the subregional body's Organ on Politics, Defence and Security (OPDS) which Mugabe chaired. Furthermore, South Africa's first major peacekeeping mission was marred by controversy. The country undertook the intervention in Lesotho with Botswana in September 1998, but faced stiff opposition from sections of Lesotho's army and parts of the population. The legitimacy of the intervention as a SADC-sanctioned action was widely questioned. The leadership of the peacekeeping force by white South African officers from the apartheid army (the force commander had been part of South Africa's destructive forces in Angola) further fuelled passions.

Perhaps the most significant event in South Africa's post-apartheid Africa policy was the bruising battle with Nigeria in 1995/1996. After the brutal hanging by General Sani Abacha's regime of Nigerian activist, Ken Saro-Wiwa, and eight of his fellow Ogoni campaigners during the Commonwealth summit in Auckland, New Zealand, in November 1995, a deeply betrayed Mandela called for the imposition of oil sanctions on Nigeria, and advocated the West African Gulliver's expulsion from the Commonwealth. This policy failed spectacularly to gain African support, and South Africa found itself diplomatically isolated. Both Lesotho and Nigeria transformed South Africa's leaders into committed multilateralists and largely explain Thabo Mbeki's policy of 'quiet diplomacy' over Zimbabwe.

Under Mbeki's presidency since 1999, South Africa established solid credentials to become Africa's leading power. Chastened by Mandela's bitter foreign policy experiences, Mbeki consistently sought multilateral solutions to resolving regional conflicts and skilfully used both a strategic partnership with Nigeria[10] and his chair of the African Union between 2002 and 2003 to pursue his goals. Mbeki has also been more prepared than Mandela to send peacekeepers abroad. He was the first chair of the AU and was also chair of the Non-Aligned Movement (NAM); he was the intellectual architect of NEPAD; and under his leadership, South Africa has hosted two high-profile UN conferences on racism and sustainable development, and won the right to host the football world cup in 2010: the first time the event will take place in Africa.

South Africa is becoming an African power, and can aspire to global middle-power status through its current policy of working with key African allies, as well as Brazil and India, in international fora in which South Africa's voice is widely respected. But South Africa's future lies in Africa and its global status can only be achieved by being accepted as a leader on its own continent. South Africa also has many elements of 'soft power' that it can use more effectively to promote its interests and to win friends in Africa. The supreme irony is that while South Africans may be among the most ignorant people about the rest of Africa, much of Africa's elite probably know more about South Africa than about any other country in Africa. South Africa can use *Channel Africa*, which transmits to 33 African countries, to expose Africans further to South Africa and to improve the knowledge of South Africans about the rest of the continent. South African mobile giants, MTN and Vodacom, could connect the entire continent with their mobile phone network; while South African technology and capital could help build the roads, railways, and ports that Africa badly needs for its industrial take-off. South Africa already generates, by some estimates, half of sub-Saharan Africa's electricity needs and is investing in a trans-African electricity grid. South African Airways (SAA) is the most reliable aircraft carrier on the continent.

Post-apartheid South Africa is neither a messiah nor a mercantilist power. It is simply an aspiring middle power seeking to punch above its weight in global politics. With its own massive domestic problems inherited from the inequities of apartheid, South Africa is attempting to reverse these problems through an effective foreign policy that promotes its trade interests abroad and seeks to attract foreign investment to its domestic market. South Africa can also not be a messiah for Africa because it simply lacks the economic and military muscle and political legitimacy to impose its preferences on its own Southern African subregion, let alone on the continent. Mbeki has grasped one basic reality: only by working through other regional states can Tshwane (Pretoria) promote its diplomatic interests within Africa. South Africa is also no longer the mercantilist power it once was under apartheid. The country is gradually loosening its protectionist policies in Southern Africa. South Africa has restructured SACU and SADC to render greater benefits to its other members, and the country is at last now conscious of the urgent need to promote investment and industrialisation policies that benefit its neighbours. But despite Mbeki's efforts to integrate South Africa into the rest of Africa, it is unclear how deeply entrenched these efforts are within South Africa's political and business elite and citizens, and questions have been raised about whether Mbeki's heirs will maintain the commitment to Africa that he has shown.[11]

SOUTH AFRICA'S AFRICAN RENAISSANCE AGENDA

A key aspect of South Africa's foreign policy over the past thirteen years has been its role of peacemaker in Africa, promoter of democratisation on the continent, and a champion of Africa's interests abroad: all part of an African Renaissance agenda. The government of Thabo Mbeki has pursued a largely pragmatic foreign policy with a core concern: the articulation of an ambitious African posture, officially dubbed 'The 'new' African agenda' in search of development, peace, security, governance and economic growth.

South Africa has sought to position itself as a 'middle-ranked' power and its status derives from its geo-political and geo-strategic roles in Africa. Many foreign governments and investors seeking opportunities in Africa regard South Africa as a gateway to the rest of the continent. In the aftermath of its own negotiated settlement in 1994, the new post-apartheid government quickly moved to make the promotion of democratisation in Africa the central tenet of its foreign policy. Under the banner of an 'African Renaissance,' this policy stated that durable solutions to problems in the world 'can only come through the promotion of democracy throughout the world.'[12] Former president Nelson Mandela, in an address to the US Congress in Washington D.C. on 6 October 1994, advocated that '… we should cease to treat tyranny, instability and poverty anywhere on our globe as peripheral to our interests and to our future.' Mandela declared in Washington in October 1994 that 'it is perhaps a common cause among us that everywhere on our globe there is an unmistakable process leading to the entrenchment of democratic systems of government'.

A major theme running through South Africa's foreign policy became the promotion of 'democratic peace'.[13] Under Mandela, South Africa openly subscribed to the idea that democracies do not go to war with each other, and that democracy is fundamentally more peaceful than other forms of government. Mbeki too, even before he became president, was committed to the 'building of stable democratic systems … and [making] a contribution to the challenge of peace, democracy, development and stability in the rest of our continent.'[14] For Mbeki, 'the dream of peace and stability, of democracy and human rights' are all intertwined. South Africa's president has repeatedly noted that Southern Africa must transform into a 'zone of peace' by means of 'building stable democracies.'[15] Mbeki strongly criticised one-party rule and personal dictatorships in Africa. He has cautioned that 'the one party system and military governments will not work'[16] and suggested that Africans must 'rebel' and 'resist all tyranny.'[17] Mbeki has often advocated for governments in Africa to 'derive their authority and legitimacy from the will of the people,' as well as become fully representative of women.[18]

Given its commitment to ending Africa's international marginalisation, South Africa, over the past thirteen years, has actively promoted regional integration and development. In the 1996 *Draft Discussion Document on a Framework for Cooperation with the Countries of the Southern African Region,* South Africa's Department of Foreign Affairs (DFA) stated: 'South Africa should strive to achieve regional economic development by utilising the instrument that is ready at hand, in the form of the Southern African Development Community.' The document further noted that South Africa's vision for the SADC region is one 'of the highest possible degree of economic cooperation, mutual assistance where necessary, and joint planning of regional development initiatives, leading to integration consistent with socio-economic, environmental and political realities.'

South Africa's stance on regional integration favours a 'cautious and step-by-step' approach towards regional development in Southern Africa. The emphasis was thus initially on cooperation rather than full-fledged integration. Policy was based on 'the principles of equity and mutual benefit'; a denunciation of domineering hegemony towards the region; and the belief that an emphasis on partnership and fairness would more effectively achieve the country's foreign policy goals. South Africa put much effort and energy into restructuring SADC,[19] stressing the implementation and operationalisation of protocols on free trade, politics, defence, and security cooperation.[20] Emphasis was also placed on boosting international investor confidence and attracting foreign direct investment to Southern Africa.

Thabo Mbeki played a key role in negotiating the New Partnership for Africa's Development in 2001. NEPAD was an initiative to spur Africa's development after decades of failures as a result of the legacies of colonialism and the Cold War, bad governance, unsound economic policies and management, and destructive conflicts.[21] The NEPAD plan of action identified five critical issues as being essential to bolstering Africa's development efforts:

- Democracy, governance and peace and security;
- economic and corporate governance;
- infrastructure and information technology;
- human resource development (notably health and education); and
- agriculture and market access.[22]

South Africa adopted a strong policy in favour of continental integration and was a key actor in establishing the AU in 2002, with the death of the OAU and the birth of the AU taking place in South Africa's port city of Durban. With South Africa's influence, the AU stressed the need to strengthen its capacities and actions in conflict prevention, management and resolution. Special emphasis was placed on AU missions in Burundi and Sudan's Darfur region and on strengthening the 15-member AU Peace and Security Council (PSC) that was established in July 2004, on which South Africa won one of only five three-year renewable seats. (The other 10 seats are two-year non-renewable.) South Africa is also hosting and has largely funded the AU's Pan-African Parliament (PAP), established in Midrand in March 2004. Some of the areas through which the country has consistently sought to maximise its global prestige and influence were: campaigning against illicit trafficking of light weapons, anti-personnel landmines and child soldiers; and promoting human security. In its foreign policy, and through the AU and NEPAD, South Africa's policymakers have sought to move away from strict notions of militarily-defined state security to a greater emphasis on human security and social justice. South Africa has also been a key player in favour of new modalities for resource mobilisation such as better and more effective levels of aid to Africa. South Africa and its African partners have specifically campaigned for international support to enhance the continent's peace support operations capabilities, and to strengthen the AU's African Standby Force (ASF) which is planned to be established by 2010 around five subregional brigades.

Under Mandela and Mbeki, South Africa's foreign policy has promoted adherence to democratic benchmarks and governance indicators in order to benefit from a renewed focus on African 'ownership'. South Africa was instrumental in setting up an African Peer Review Mechanism (APRM) in 2003 to promote democratic governance in Africa.[23] About 28 countries have signed up to be reviewed in this voluntary, self-monitored system involving governments, the private sector, and civil society actors.

External perceptions of South Africa's conduct have impacted greatly on its policy preferences. A cursory glance at official documentation from the foreign ministry in Tshwane would suggest that the ANC-led government has sought to balance international expectations and its own fear of dominance in the Southern African region. Thus, while many outsiders viewed South Africa as a hegemon – a sort of regional superpower in the subregion and more broadly on the continent – the government, from Mandela to Mbeki, was quick to denounce such ideas. Instead, South Africa's leaders believed that its status and prominence in Africa and in world affairs more generally, would be enhanced not by reinforcing but by downplaying such domineering attitudes. As early as 1996, South Africa's deputy minister of foreign affairs, Aziz Pahad, stated that '… we must carry our relations with the region in a way that is not a big brother relationship. This means that because of our relative strength we don't simply impose ourselves.'[24] Pahad further cautioned: '[t]his does not mean that we are not sensitive to the Big Brother or Big Sister syndrome. However, it also means that South Africa cannot afford to sit on the sidelines. There can be no debate about this issue.'[25] Pahad also noted that African leaders '… have indeed warned that if South Africa continues to hide behind the rhetoric of not wanting to play a leadership role, Africa would indeed suspect a hidden agenda.'[26]

The deliberately cautious approach adopted by South African policymakers towards Southern Africa suggests that the best way to gain status and enhance its reputation is to reassure its neighbours that the country does not harbour any threatening or aggressive intent. South Africa has chosen to portray a strategic and defensive non-threatening military posture as the best way of enhancing security and confidence within Southern Africa and beyond. South Africa's defensive military strategy is also based on both a notion of deterrence and effective military capability. But this stance appeared to be contradicted when South Africa entered into arms deals worth more than R30 billion between 1997 and 1999. These deals involved arms manufacturers in Italy, Britain, Germany and Sweden. In justifying these purchases, South Africa's government argued that, in exchange for purchasing military equipment from these states, their private sector would directly invest in South Africa to the tune of R100 billion. This agreement would thus create jobs to reduce South Africa's unemployment rate of 35–45 per cent. The arms deals unleashed a storm of criticism from civil society groups and some parliamentarians. Many critics argued that South Africa faced no real military threats in the post-apartheid context; that the overhaul of its military may send the wrong message to its smaller neighbours; and that this could trigger a new arms race in Southern Africa. South Africa's purchase of its massive new artillery did indeed trigger anxiety in many regional quarters. Policymakers in Tshwane had to reassure their neighbours that South Africa's new weapons were not intended as a threat to them, but were acquired merely as a means to modernise its armed forces and to promote foreign investment.

While South Africa has been at pains not to be seen as a 'bully' in political, diplomatic and military terms, it has nonetheless continued to be perceived by many as the economic 'bully' in the region. South Africa enjoys skewed trade relations with the rest of the region that have greatly undermined Tshwane's political democratisation project in Africa, by making the country appear to be pursuing parochial economic interests under the guise of democracy. South Africa's economic expansion into the continent has been both private sector-driven and government-promoted. Trade with the rest of Africa increased by a massive 328 per cent between 1993 and 2003. But, this trade was massively skewed in South Africa's favour: out of a total R20,3 billion trade with the SADC members in 1999, R17,7 billion were South African exports to the region. Total trade with the rest of Africa in 2001, excluding the Southern African Customs Union, amounted to US$856 million in imports and US$3,7 billion in exports: an imbalance of nearly 5:1.

Turning from trade to values, South Africa's *Weltanschauung* (worldview) and quest for international influence and prestige are heavily influenced by the experience of its transition from apartheid to democracy. Policy has been predisposed towards 'quiet diplomacy' and preventive diplomacy, notably the settlement of disputes through negotiations. Both the Mandela and Mbeki governments emphasised the need for regional reconciliation following decades of tensions and destabilisation by the apartheid state. Until 1998, the ANC-led government ruled out the military option in international affairs and the preferred strategy was brokering peace pacts among belligerents in conflict situations. Such pacts were often promoted along the lines of South Africa's own Government of National Unity (GNU) of 1994–96.

It is important to highlight some of South Africa's peacemaking efforts in Africa in the last thirteen years. As early as 1994, Nelson Mandela sought to broker an 'inclusive' peace deal in Angola's two decade-old civil war, urging Eduardo dos Santos to seek an 'accommodation' with UNITA (*União Nacional para a Independência Total de Angola*) rebel leader, Jonas Savimbi. Mandela similarly encouraged Savimbi to accept the government under Dos Santos instead of seeking to topple the ruling Popular Movement for the Liberation of Angola (MPLA). In the mountain kingdom of Lesotho, the Mandela government joined Botswana and Zimbabwe in a preventive diplomacy effort in 1994 to encourage elections and to stave off a constitutional crisis. Four years later, South Africa was mandated by the OAU to address the constitutional crisis in the Comoros, while the South African Independent Electoral Commission (IEC) provided assistance and cooperation to the authorities on the island. These two smaller cases of Lesotho and Comoros increased South Africa's confidence in tackling larger cases like Burundi and Congo.

In another display of South Africa's 'peacemaker' philosophy, Thabo Mbeki (then South Africa's deputy president) played an active role in seeking an end to the rebellion against Zairian dictator, Mobutu Sese Seko, in 1997. Mbeki's approach involved an application of inducement strategies to try to nudge the parties towards a settlement. He suggested that, in exchange for a peace agreement, South Africa would make efforts to help rebuild the war-ravaged country through substantial post-conflict reconstruction support. Mandela eventually became involved in an unsuccessful mediation effort with Mobutu and rebel leader, Laurent Kabila, in 1997.

A year later, South Africa refused to send military troops to fight alongside any of the two warring blocs in the Congo: the Zimbabwe-Angola-Namibia-Kabila axis and the Uganda-Rwanda sponsored rebels. Mandela instead pursued an independent line by refusing to side with any of the two blocs and instead opted for a peacemaker role. Since 1999, the Mbeki administration has singled out peace in the DRC as its number one priority. South Africa was instrumental in efforts to ensure a successful Inter-Congolese Dialogue (ICD), which it hosted in Sun City in 2002. Mbeki also played a key role in negotiating the interim government arrangement in the Congo and has consistently called on the international community to help implement the peace process.[27]

In Burundi, South Africa has sought, since 1999, to strengthen the Arusha peace process, and former deputy president, Jacob Zuma, played a key facilitation role in supporting the efforts of Nelson Mandela. Since 2001, one of South Africa's key policies was to promote peace in Burundi by providing an armed protection unit for members of the country's interim government as part of an AU force, while successfully pushing for the deployment of a UN peacekeeping force by 2004.[28] The transition in Burundi was concluded with the election of a democratic government in 2005, though the country remained fragile.

The Zimbabwe issue has attracted more headlines in South Africa's foreign policy than any other issue. Many have noted that this is perhaps due to the presence of a sizable white minority population in the country with historical roots to South Africa and the West. South Africa opted for a strategy of 'quiet diplomacy' towards Harare which many criticised without themselves being able to offer a viable alternative. Mbeki used his strategic relationship with Nigeria's Olusegun Obasanjo to try to cajole Robert Mugabe to accept a negotiated end to the Zimbabwe crisis. South Africa also encouraged peaceful, free and fair elections in March 2002 through the participation of election observers under the auspices of the SADC Parliamentary Forum and the multi-sectoral South Africa Observer Mission (SAOM) until May 2003. Mbeki consistently but unsuccessfully sought a political *rapprochement* between ZANU-PF (Zimbabwe African National Union–Patriotic Force) and the MDC (Movement for Democratic Change) and in order to ensure peace and stability, as well as to engineer an economic recovery in Zimbabwe. Finally, on the Horn of Africa, South Africa has supported and encouraged the Intergovernmental Authority on Development's (IGAD) peace process on Sudan,[29] and is actively involved in post-conflict reconstruction efforts in South Sudan.

CHAPTER OUTLINE

The thirteen chapters in this volume are all academically rigorous as well as policy-relevant, and are written for both scholars and practitioners. We start the volume with three chapters that provide the socio-economic and political context to South Africa's foreign policy in Africa. The first chapter by Adebayo Adedeji, the Nigerian chair of South Africa's peer review mechanism, is titled 'South Africa and Africa's political economy: Looking inside from the outside'. This chapter reviews South Africa's political economy within the broader African context. It considers three key questions: What effort has been put in place to 'deconstruct' South Africa's political economy now that apartheid has been abolished? When will South Africa's leaders launch the process of moving from the 'democratic transition' of the first post-apartheid decade to 'democratic transformation?' Will South Africa's leaders opt for the business-as-usual approach of other African countries once they got rid of colonial rule? This chapter notes that since 1990 – and particularly since May 1994 – South Africa has revealed a clear intention to remain within Africa and to play a proactive leadership role on the continent. Adedeji considers how far South Africa has moved from a role of domineering hegemony to one of partnership in its relationship with other Southern African countries, and notes how far the country has been fully and dynamically reintegrated into the Southern African region.

The chapter also considers the controversies around post-apartheid South Africa's opting for a neoliberal economic strategy, and examines how the country has taken practical responsibility for the regional restructuring required for a neoliberal, export-oriented accumulation process within Southern Africa, and indeed in the rest of Africa. After critiques of the Reconstruction and Development Programme (RDP) – implemented in 1994 – and the Growth, Employment and Redistribution (GEAR) macro-economic strategy – adopted in 1996 – Adedeji makes the case for building an effective and equitable 'developmental state' in South Africa.

In the second chapter, 'Black economic empowerment: Myths and realities', South African scholar Khehla Shubane makes a strong case for black economic empowerment as a necessary means of addressing a history of black dispossession that was a key feature of apartheid as well as other forms of white domination that preceded it. Shubane notes how BEE is but one measure to address apartheid's devastating legacies. While there is still a long way to go to correct these inequalities, Shubane argues that what has been achieved in just over a decade is remarkable. For Shubane, BEE is necessary to deracialise the ownership of significant economic assets, and the initiative is founded on the belief that this is a plan through which South Africa's economy can be effectively grown for the benefit of all its citizens. BEE thus seeks to ensure the participation of all South Africans in the country's economy, and is a basis for normalising the economy and society. Shubane boldly asserts that BEE remains the only practical solution to a complex, practical problem. He offers a robust response to, and seeks to shatter the myths of, the 'many and varied' critics of BEE, including some white share-holders and those who believe that BEE is little more than a 'gravy train' for a 'comprador' class of a politically-connected black bourgeoisie.

In the third chapter, 'Race and reconciliation: *E pluribus unum?*', Yasmin Sooka, a former commissioner in South Africa's Truth and Reconciliation Commission (TRC), addresses issues of race and reconciliation in South Africa. She considers how, near the end of the TRC process, 'cleavages within the nation began to show', despite the fact that, to the international community, it had become necessary for South Africa to present the face of a reconciled nation. Sooka is critical of the fact that it is not white people who have behaved nobly in post-apartheid South Africa, but the blacks who had a 'just cause'. Black South Africans, she argues, continue to take the lead in reconciliation, while many whites continue to suffer from guilt. The author strongly asserts that race remains an intrinsic factor in debates on reconciliation in post-apartheid South Africa. She also provides a critical assessment of the country's TRC process and achievements, even arguing, based on market research, that the work of the commission may have actually exacerbated tensions in society.

Having provided the political and socio-economic context of post-apartheid South Africa, the second section of the book considers the challenges faced by post-apartheid South Africa's foreign policy in the areas of leadership; regional security; corporate economic expansion; land reform; and HIV/AIDS.

In her chapter titled 'South Africa in Africa: Behemoth, hegemon, partner or just another kid on the block?', South African scholar, Maxi Schoeman, addresses the question of where – and how – South Africa fits into Africa. She pays particular attention both to South Africa's role allocation internationally, and more specifically, the role assigned to it by its African counterparts. Schoeman considers how South Africa's role is embodied mainly in the expectations that other states have of the country, and examines how South Africa views its role, particularly in Africa. As the title suggests, Schoeman grapples with the key question: Is South Africa's role in Africa that of a behemoth (a colossus), hegemon, partner, or just another kid on the block? In Schoeman's analysis, South Africa is striving for a hegemonic role in Africa that also includes strong elements of partnership. In some instances, however, South Africa comes across as 'just another kid on the block': behaving just like any other country. The author also considers the activities of South Africa's business community and allegations of the country's role being that of a behemoth promoting its own rabid self-interest. Schoeman encourages South Africa 'to play the role of partner, and for the government to play the role of a hegemon with a well-developed sense of its responsibilities being based on its own long-term interests on a strong and vibrant continent'.

A leading scholar of Southern Africa from Lesotho, Khabele Matlosa, in his chapter 'South Africa and regional security in Southern Africa', assesses contemporary regional security trends, highlighting South Africa's dominant role and outlining possible trends in the next decade following South Africa's second democratic elections in 2004. The chapter emphasises the dominant role of South Africa in the region's evolving security landscape based on the country's politico-economic power *vis-à-vis* its neighbours. Matlosa also highlights South Africa's leadership role, while noting that Tshwane has not exercised its regional dominance through unilateral hegemonic designs for fear of projecting itself as a sub-imperial power whose foreign policy outreach is driven more by self-interest than by regional and continental imperatives. He supports these points with two case studies of South Africa's policies in Lesotho and Zimbabwe.

South African scholar Judi Hudson's chapter, 'South Africa's economic expansion into Africa: neo-colonialism or development?', considers the speed at which South Africa has become the largest investor in the rest of Africa in a short decade, eclipsing even the recent increased interest from non-African investors. She describes this rush as 'one of the biggest economic phenomena of the last decade'. Hudson considers concerns that South Africa's rapid corporate expansion has led to new relations of dependency and exploitation of workers in the African operations of South African companies, and assesses how unequal exchange and terms of trade disproportionately favour South Africa.

Hudson's chapter grapples with six key questions: To what extent has South Africa become the 'big brother' in Africa? How can the country best respond to allegations of being the 'new colonisers'? Is South African capital playing a sub-imperialist role in Africa or is it a 'motor for revival'? What informs the South African perspective as its firms fan out across the continent? To what extent do South African businesses see themselves as 'ambassadors' for South Africa as they move into the continent and is the regional peacemaking role that is being played by South Africa being undercut by the sometimes predatory actions of some of its white-dominated corporations?

Sam Moyo and Ruth Hall, scholars from Zimbabwe and South Africa respectively, deal with the contentious issue of the land question in their chapter 'Conflict and Land Reform in Southern Africa: How exceptional is South Africa?' In situating the South African case in a historical context, both scholars note that 'land reform is an inherently conflictual process'. They consider South Africa's attempts at land reform in the first thirteen years of its democracy, and argue that the process has proved to be slow, with little progress made towards the goals of rural restructuring and poverty alleviation. Suggesting that South Africa's policymakers have not drawn relevant lessons about the limits of market-based land redistribution from other countries in the region, the authors advance new alternative solutions. Moyo and Hall are critical of South Africa's tendencies towards elite capture (dominance of the ruling class and its allies), moderate deracialisation of the land-owning class, and the growth of a small, black commercial farming class in place of wider agrarian reform. They warn of signs of conflicts emerging both from unmet land demands and from the process of land reform itself, as well as the emergence of rural social movements which seek to give voice to rural dissatisfaction. The authors draw comparative lessons from Zimbabwe and Namibia (noting that Zimbabwe transferred more land in its first post-independence decade than South Africa has), and also briefly assess South Africa's land summit of 2005.

The future of South Africa and the continent will be determined by the response to the new security threat of HIV/AIDS. According to the Joint United Nations Programme on HIV/AIDS (UNAIDS), about 75 per cent of all AIDS-related deaths in the world occurred in sub-Saharan Africa in 2004. South Africa has over five million people living with HIV: probably the largest figure in a single country in the world. In their chapter, 'HIV/AIDS and the African Renaissance: South Africa's Achilles heel?', Angela Ndinga-Muvumba and Shauna Mottiar, Ugandan and South African researchers respectively, examine the nature of this new security threat and assess South African, Southern African and continental policies shaping the response to HIV/AIDS. The authors argue that HIV transmission is accelerated by poverty and instability, while simultaneously undermining the family unit and decreasing economic production. HIV/AIDS also has serious implications for military security. As the AU plans to establish an African Standby Force by 2010, peace support operations in Africa will remain heavily dependent on African troops. Yet, armed forces are particularly vulnerable to HIV infection. South Africa's future leadership on peace and security issues is ultimately tied to its domestic challenges on the HIV/AIDS front, particularly since 23 per cent of its military is estimated by the government to be HIV positive.

Ndinga-Muvumba and Mottiar also point out that the seriousness of South Africa's own epidemic calls for a more robust approach and the provision of anti-retroviral treatment (ARVs). Following pressure on the government by domestic civil society and external actors, its ARV rollout promised in November 2003 was reaching close to 250 000 people by March 2007, though civil society argued that poor monitoring and evaluation made this figure difficult to verify.[30] The authors contrast the strong leadership of Senegal and Uganda in the anti-AIDS fight to what they see as South Africa's inept approach. Moving from the national to the subregional and continental levels, Ndinga-Muvumba and Mottiar note that SADC and the AU have put in place their own strategies for mobilising an accelerated response to HIV/AIDS. SADC's *HIV/AIDS Framework and Programme of Action 2003–2007* seeks to harmonise policies and legislation relating to HIV prevention, care, support, and treatment. The AU's *HIV/AIDS Strategic Plan 2005–2007* is to be implemented in partnership with regional economic communities (RECs) such as SADC, the Economic Community of West African States (ECOWAS) and the Intergovernmental Authority on Development. The authors argue that a meaningful response to HIV/AIDS in Africa will be more feasible if governments contribute to initiatives at the national, subregional and continental levels. SADC and the AU will require the full cooperation and ownership of South Africa in order for their plans for combating the pandemic to succeed.

The third and final section of the volume contains five case studies focusing on South Africa's role in the construction of the AU and NEPAD; as well as South Africa's relations with, and roles in, Nigeria; Angola and Mozambique; the Great Lakes; North Africa; and the Horn of Africa. South African analyst, Chris Landsberg's chapter, 'South Africa and the making of the African Union and NEPAD: Mbeki's "progressive African agenda"', examines South Africa's role in crafting the continental public policy landscape over the past thirteen years. The chapter considers Thabo Mbeki's Africa policies, particularly what Mbeki and his continental allies have referred to as the 'African Agenda' or 'African Renaissance'. Landsberg unpacks the 'African Agenda': the new progressive governance agenda in search of development; peace and security; democratic governance and economic growth; as well as the construction of the African Union, the reform of Regional Economic Communities, and NEPAD.

Landsberg also examines the Mbeki government's strategies and tactics, explains how and why this agenda is being pursued, and reveals the sensitivities about South Africa's role, objectives and agenda in Africa. He argues that Mbeki, his government and the ruling ANC all believe in building strategic partnerships with key African states. Mbeki has worked closely with allies like Joaquim Chissano of Mozambique and his successor Armando Guebuza, Olusegun Obasanjo of Nigeria, Abdelaziz Bouteflika of Algeria, Benjamin Mkapa of Tanzania and his successor Jakaya Kikwete, John Kufuor of Ghana, and others, to pursue his 'African Renaissance' plan. Landsberg argues that South Africa is forever watchful not to appear as if it is playing into foreign expectations for it to fulfil the role of 'Africa's policeman'. He argues that, from 1999, South Africa played a key role in the transition of the OAU into the African Union, and also played the major role in articulating and negotiating NEPAD. After analysing more recent criticisms of South Africa's role in promoting NEPAD among African governments, the author concludes by assessing the progress and challenges of South Africa's peer review process that began in 2005.

Nigerian scholar Adekeye Adebajo argues in his chapter, 'South Africa and Nigeria in Africa: An axis of virtue?', that South Africa's most strategic partnership in Africa is with Nigeria. He notes that this partnership has been built around the close personal relationship between Thabo Mbeki and former Nigerian President Olusegun Obasanjo. Mbeki and Obasanjo worked closely in managing African conflicts through the AU, SADC, ECOWAS and the UN. They attempted to promote norms of democratic governance and respect for human rights. Both frequently offered their personal mediation services and 'good offices' for the resolution of African conflicts. While Obasanjo energetically promoted security and democracy in Africa – despite his apparently unsuccessful efforts in 2006 to change the Nigerian constitution to allow a third presidential term – and sought to resolve crises in Liberia, Sierra Leone, Togo and Sudan; Mbeki sought to make peace in the DRC, Burundi, Zimbabwe and Côte d'Ivoire.

Adebajo argues that the relationship between South Africa and Nigeria reached its nadir during the tenure of General Sani Abacha, Nigeria's autocratic leader between 1993 and 1998. Mandela called a SADC summit to take collective action against Nigeria after the hanging of Ken Saro-Wiwa and eight Ogoni activists in November 1995. Even his iconic status failed to rally a single Southern African state to take action against Nigeria. Instead, it was South Africa that was accused by many African leaders of sowing seeds of division in Africa and undermining African solidarity. African efforts to depict South Africa as a western stooge over Nigeria was a painful experience that the country was determined never to repeat. Mbeki was determined not to suffer the same fate over Zimbabwe. The chapter devotes much attention on South Africa–Nigeria relations between 1999 and 2007 under the presidencies of Mbeki and Obasanjo, assessing the Binational Commission (BNC) and growing bilateral trade ties, as well as the strained relationship between Tshwane and Abuja over Côte d'Ivoire; the UN Security Council; and the AU chair.

Italian analyst, Augusta Conchiglia's chapter 'South Africa and its lusophone neighbours: Angola and Mozambique' argues that South Africa's 'repositioning in the continent', though 'spectacular', has 'not been linear'. The temptation to 'use its own political experience as a blueprint for others' has sometimes 'provoked irritation among its African partners'. Conchiglia further argues that this has been particularly true in the case of Angola. In contrast, South Africa's relations with Mozambique – the other lusophone country in Southern Africa – 'have been mutually profitable, sustained by strategic economic and political interests'. Conchiglia thus argues that South Africa's patterns of relations with the two former Portuguese colonies of Angola and Mozambique are 'poles apart'. This chapter considers the reasons why South Africa became more interested in its Mozambican neighbour, since the two have historically been tied together by important strategic interests, particularly in the energy sector. In Angola by contrast, the continuation of that country's civil war after 1992, and apartheid South Africa's support for UNITA triggered suspicions around

South Africa's real intentions in the country. These tensions between Luanda and Tshwane have constituted a major hindrance to South Africa's economic expansion into Angola.

In the twelfth chapter, 'South Africa: "Exporting peace" to the Great Lakes region?', Canadian scholar Devon Curtis assesses the South African 'model' of peacemaking and its applicability to the two cases of Burundi and the DRC in which Tshwane played a leading facilitating role and deployed about 3 000 peacekeepers. The limits of 'exporting' South Africa's negotiated 'government of national unity' abroad are assessed. The chapter offers three broad arguments. First, South African policymakers have championed 'democracy promotion' in Africa as a key foreign policy goal and tend to view conflict resolution through the narrow prism of South Africa's 'negotiated revolution'. Second, the South African approach has often failed to take into account key political economy factors that are specific to the Great Lakes region. Finally, despite the limits of 'exporting' South Africa's own model to Burundi and the DRC, both countries have benefited from some of the transitional strategies employed by South African peacemakers.

The final chapter, 'South Africa's relations with North Africa and the Horn: Bridging a continent', by South African academic, Iqbal Jhazbhay, compares and contrasts South Africa's policies in Morocco, Algeria, Libya, Tunisia and Egypt during the Mandela and Mbeki presidencies. Issues assessed include: self-determination over the Western Sahara; Mandela and Mbeki's personal relationship with Libyan leader, Muammar Qaddafi; human rights and poverty alleviation issues in Tunisia; and South Africa's complex and competitive relationship with Egypt. Jhazbhay argues that opportunities abound, particularly in Algeria and Libya, for South African businesses and the NGO community. He concludes by warning of the dangers of North Africa drifting apart from black Africa and becoming further integrated into the European Union (EU) and the Mediterranean basin.

The chapter also assesses South Africa's role in the Horn of Africa, with a specific focus on Sudan, Eritrea, Ethiopia, Djibouti, Somalia and Somaliland. Jhazbhay assesses South Africa's bilateral economic and capacity-building initiatives in Sudan, and notes that it contributed peacekeepers to an AU force in the country's troubled Darfur region. The author also assesses South Africa's role in Eritrea and growing influence in Ethiopia. South Africa's more low-profile role in Djibouti, Somalia and Somaliland is also examined.

The chapters in the first section of this academically rigorous and policy-

relevant volume provide the socio-economic and political context for understanding South Africa's foreign policy, on the premise that an effective foreign
policy can only be built on a strong domestic base. The second section assesses
key challenges of regional leadership for South Africa involving both traditional
issues of leadership, military and economic power, as well as newer and less
conventional but equally important foreign policy issues of land conflicts and
HIV/AIDS. The final section of the book provides case studies of South Africa's
relations with strategic countries in West, Southern, and North Africa as well as
the Great Lakes and the Horn of Africa. This final section also highlights South
Africa's role in Africa's pre-eminent post-apartheid multilateral institutions:
the African Union and NEPAD. All of these diverse authors generally accept the
necessity of South Africa's leadership role on the continent, while highlighting
the challenges and obstacles to the country fulfilling its ambitious dreams of
leading an African Renaissance.

1

South Africa and Africa's political economy: Looking inside from the outside[1]

ADEBAYO ADEDEJI

In 2007, one country after another in sub-Saharan Africa began to celebrate the golden jubilee of the dawn of political independence. These are the first generation of independent African countries. Beginning with Ghana in March 1957, and Guinea in October 1958, the long walk to freedom gathered momentum in the 1960s, with over thirty countries claiming their independence (seventeen in 1960 alone; ten between 1961 and 1965; and five between 1966 and 1969). The pace slowed down considerably in the 1970s, as the struggle for independence in all but three of the remaining eleven countries led to bloody anti-colonial wars.

The worst affected and war-torn countries were the five lusophone countries (Guinea-Bissau, Angola, Cape Verde, Mozambique, and São Tomé and Príncipe) and the white settler anglophone countries of Rhodesia and South West Africa (now Zimbabwe and Namibia, respectively). While the lusophone colonies achieved independence in the mid-1970s, bloodletting still continued for five years in Rhodesia before it emerged as independent Zimbabwe in April 1980. And South West Africa had to wait until March 1990 before it was transformed into Namibia. This long journey to freedom did not reach its climactic end until May 1994 when a majority-ruled, democratic South Africa was born. Consequently, the entire continent of Africa – from Cape to Cairo – became politically free.

For more than 500 years, Africa has had 'open veins'. As I pointed out in 1994:[2] *Ex Africa semper aliquid novum:* ('Something new always comes out of Africa.') This saying is credited to Pliny the Elder. This *something* that is always new has, in the course of the past five centuries, come to denote slavery, military defeat, partition, colonialism, dependence, economic exploitation and dispossession. So engrossed have Africans been in the long walk to political freedom, that economic empowerment and emancipation have suffered severe neglect. Not surprisingly, therefore, the African economy is still basically underdeveloped, with a sharp bifurcation between the traditional and the modern sectors. African economies are still excessively dependent on external *stimuli* rather than on indigenous factor inputs – without which there can be no sustainable development on the continent.

The failure to deconstruct and reconstruct the inherited colonial economy has had the cumulative effect of exacerbating centuries-old dependence, dispossession and marginalisation. The optimism heralded by the era of political independence has long since evaporated. The ever-recurring armed conflicts and civil wars and the new waves of globalisation in the post-Cold War era have severely accentuated the marginalisation of Africa. The continent is now at the periphery of the periphery. Africa's most serious mistake is the separation of politics from economics. By so doing, the discipline of economics has been cut off from its origins of political philosophy and ethics and has been deprived of its human dimension. The obsessive concern with growth economics to the detriment of a holistic approach to sustainable human development has conveyed the message that people are irrelevant. Instead, what counts are fine theories and technicalities rather than the holistic combination of the political, social, cultural, psychological and institutional factors. The emergence of the development merchant system (DMS) – with its marabouts, soothsayers, and latter-day prophets – has replaced human-centred development.[3]

Whereas the eighteenth and nineteenth century economists – or, more appropriately, political economists – had focused on the creation of wealth for human security and welfare; emphasised the cumulative nature of sustainable development; and linked these umbilically with its context (politics, society, culture, ethics, moral values, and institutional framework), the apostles of the DMS are concerned with only macro-economic aggregates. Perversely, sub-Saharan Africa has been viewed by these neoliberal fundamentalists as having a better opportunity than Asia and Latin America to make rapid progress, because our continent has been perceived to be a *tabula rasa,* having no culture, moral values and ethical principles of its own. Africa, south of the Sahara, would therefore have to rely hook, line and sinker on the cultures, values and ethics of western societies. This lack of development that respects the nature and dynamics of existing African political economy has resulted in many failures in the last five decades.

It is not surprising that attention has now shifted to various new initiatives in order for Africa to claim its future. However, unless and until the continent faces directly all the factors and forces that have inhibited and continue to inhibit its capacity to forge a dynamic socio-economic development and transformation process for its 800 million people, its claims on a successful future will prove illusory and no more than mere wishful thinking and rhetoric. Africans must make up the various deficits, which have, in the course of the past five decades, stood in their way of achieving a socio-economic breakthrough.

In my Washington D.C. lecture of March 1985, I unveiled an analytical framework for analysing the root causes of Africa's development challenges – the *Seven Ds of Africa's Development Problematique* – demography, drought, desertification, dependency, disequilibrium, debt, and destabilisation.[4] The Nigeria-based African Centre for Development and Strategic Studies (ACDESS) conference, of November 1992 in Dakar, Senegal, also identified many other factors that continue to have backwash effects on Africa's struggle for socio-economic progress. These are: lack of people-centred democracy and popular participation in governance; lack of public accountability and transparency; lack of primacy of the rule of law and independent judicial systems; and endemic corruption.[5]

Africa's tragedy is that no serious and comprehensive attempt has been made to address these inhibitive anti-development factors. Instead, in the last two decades, attention has been focused on short-term, quick-fix solutions rather than on the root causes of Africa's *development problematique.* Plans drawn up to redress the imbalances of the inherited colonial economic structures such as the Lagos Plan of Action of 1980 – in which I was centrally involved – and the African Alternative Framework to Structural Adjustment Programme (SAP) for Socio-Economic Recovery and Transformation of 1989 have been left to gather dust. Consequently, economic stagnation has persisted in Africa with poverty becoming endemic. This in turn has led to the spread of civil strife, conflict and war in many countries. Contrary to popular belief, Africa's conflicts do not stem from ethnic diversity. Rather, they are prompted by poverty and driven by underdevelopment. Ethnic diversity is only an excuse and a distraction. Inevitably, the unfolding future has continued to be haunted by the past and the present.

There is no doubt that the failure to confront the past by deconstructing the inherited colonial state and its institutions have inevitably led to the carry-over of the disabilities of the past five centuries into the post-independence era. This failure has also led to the persistence of the loss of self-esteem among Africans and the substitution of dependence on charity for self-confidence and self-reliance. The constitution of new indigenous orders, which will renew for the longer term the underlying social relations of any given society, has sadly eluded Africa. Tragically, addressing *social conflict* has been subordinated and neglected, while *national conflict* reigns supreme. It is under the guise of national conflict, that political elites compete fiercely for power, resource control, and economic 'spoils'. This makes inevitable their neglect of social conflicts, rather than being primarily concerned with the promotion of the interest of the masses by putting in place a holistic human development strategy with the overarching goals of the eradication of poverty and socio-economic injustice.

It is sad to admit that the African state as invented by Europeans has neither been deconstructed nor reconstituted. Indeed, in some cases such as Somalia, the state has been destroyed. There is no doubt that all African countries have a historic responsibility to launch the process for deconstructing the inherited colonial state and transforming their societies. What effort has been put in place to deconstruct South Africa now that apartheid has been abolished? When will its leaders launch the process of moving from the 'democratic transition' of the first post-apartheid decade to 'democratic transformation?'[6] Or will South Africa's leaders opt for the business-as-usual approach of other African countries once they got rid of colonial rule? What are the perspectives?

THE HEAVY TOLL OF PERSISTENT SOCIO-ECONOMIC CRISES

No one now disputes that sub-Saharan African countries have suffered and are suffering heavily for their failure to launch and maintain a process of holistic human development, due to their persistent inability to confront and address the Seven Ds referred to earlier. Consequently the monocrop colonial and dualistic economy has persisted, with one, two or three primary export commodities accounting for all export earnings of most countries on the continent. Not only is the demand for most of these commodities income inelastic, they are also primarily responsible for economic and consequently political and social instability – because of their price instability and the boom-and-bust cycles that invariably accompany commodity prices and exports.

Commodity booms result in high export earnings that invariably lead to increased public expenditure because of the virtually insatiable demand for public service delivery. However, with the perennial price instability of these commodities, a bust sooner or later follows – resulting in severe damage to the economy; the reduction in, or even closure of, essential services; widespread economic depression; and the aggravation of unemployment. The boom-and-bust nature of the commodities trade accounts for the failure of foreign trade to become the prime mover in Africa's development process. The boom-and-bust cycle also exacerbates the debt crisis, resulting in debt overhang – the inability to service an external debt of US$290 billion and the need therefore to seek debt rescheduling, relief and forgiveness. Although members of the Paris Club of creditor countries have recently granted some measures of debt relief to a few heavily indebted countries, the forces promoting indebtedness are still operational and powerful.

The cumulative effect of this boom-and-bust of economic and political instability, and of the failure to deconstruct the African colonial political economy, is that Africa entered the new millennium faced with basic problems of survival. The 'revolution of rising expectations' of the 1960s has yielded to revulsion at the unfulfilled dreams once promised by a new century. Poverty, ignorance and disease have become the pathetic plight of Africa's population.

Africa's five post-independence decades can be divided into four phases – (i) the human development period of the first two post-independence decades – the 1960s and the 1970s; (ii) the neo-classical economism of the 'lost decade' of the 1980s; (iii) the restoration of democracy – even if it is fledgling, low-intensity and donor-driven – during the transition decade of the 1990s; and (iv) the rediscovery of the paradigm of holistic human development at the beginning of the new millennium.

During the colonial era, in order to ensure sustained extraction of commodities, the primary role of the colonial government was regulation; defence; the maintenance of law and order; the setting of standards; the establishment of model institutions; and the provision of grants-in-aid to private service providers. Except in white settler countries, services that were essential for human development and security – education; public health care; potable water and sanitation; basic infrastructural facilities; law and order; and tax collection – were generally left to voluntary and missionary organisations and local governments.

But with the approach of, and the dawn of, independence in the late 1950s and early 1960s, African governments prioritised service delivery. Indeed, every independent African government saw the delivery of adequate quantity and high quality of public services that were essential for human security as its primary challenge. The basic supplier of these core frontline public services was, of necessity, the state. Not only are these services essential for enhancing the productive capacity of the people – particularly as a labour force – but they are also essential for improving the competitiveness of Africa in this era of globalisation.

It was during this phase – the first two decades of independence – that Africa's development strategy emphasised human development. The 1960s and 1970s witnessed the introduction, in many African countries, of universal primary education, vastly expanded secondary and tertiary educational institutions and enrolment, and adult literacy campaigns – all very critical factors in the promotion and achievement of sustainable human development. However, the achievement of sustainable human development demands long-term commitment.

Unfortunately, during the 1980s, the decade of the narrow economism of structural adjustment programmes (SAPs), human development was severely truncated. Primary school enrolment which had expanded every year between 1960 and 1979, began to contract; public health services declined; and given the rapid annual increase in population, fewer and fewer people had access to potable water, sanitation, and agricultural extension services. It is estimated that, between 1980 and 1995, access to public services in Africa declined by 50 per cent.

The cumulative effect of this paradigm shift is that African countries currently dominate the lowest rungs of the Human Development Index (HDI) league table. Of the 36 countries with the lowest HDI rankings, 29 are in sub-Saharan Africa. The countries with low HDI are also those with the highest human and income poverty ranking, as well as the probability at birth of between a third and half of their population not surviving until the age of 40.

Another consequence of the economic policies of the 1980s was the failure to diversify African economies. Although the manufacturing sector grew rapidly in most African countries (between 10 and 20 per cent between 1960 and 1985), due to the dictates of SAPs in the 1980s, the tariff and non-tariff protection given to infant industries had to be removed. As if this was not enough, most of the manufacturing activities in Africa had become *last stage* factories overly dependent on imported inputs (raw material, and intermediate and capital goods). Africa's industrial development process thus became a major consumer of scarce foreign exchange resources. Given the external debt overhang of most countries and the consequent need to preserve hard-earned foreign exchange for servicing external debt, the de-industrialisation process became part of the SAP package, and the share of manufacturing in the GDP of many African states declined precipitously. Low capacity utilisation continues to exacerbate the state of the African manufacturing sector, as locally manufactured goods compete against imports dumped at low prices on African markets. This has inevitably led to a cessation in the diversification of the African economy and tightening of its bonds to monocrop exports. Even within the mining and agricultural sectors, there is a lack of diversification. Only about five per cent of the minerals, fuels and metals, and six per cent of agricultural commodities exported from Africa are processed before being exported. The rest are exported without any value added.

This process of de-industrialisation must be halted and reversed urgently if an end is to be put to capital wastage and decumulation. This requires avoiding devaluation; preventing regression in external balance and employment; and correcting the distortions affecting interest rates, domestic price levels, wage rates and exchange rates. Devaluation not only scares away foreign investors, but also promotes macro-economic instability, unemployment, and the aggravation of poverty. The premature imposition of the policy of liberalisation on economies that are very uncompetitive, without measures to make them competitive, has also contributed to the demise of Africa's nascent industrialisation process and led to the aggravation of massive unemployment in sub-Saharan Africa. Poverty alleviation is practically impossible in a political economy in which a 'free-for-all' regime of the importation of consumer goods exists, in which indigenous enterprises are put out of business, and in which educated and skilled people are put out of jobs.

By 1989, the balance sheet of Africa's political economy reads as follows:

- Pervasive lack of democracy due to the dawn of the era of military rule and one-party dictatorship;
- the short-, medium- and long-term adverse consequences of the macro-economic core policies of SAPs had been pro-cyclical and contractionary, contributing in large measure to Africa's economic stagnation and recession;
- lack of progress in finding a comprehensive solution to the debt burden and overhang;
- escalation of the struggle for the control of resources underlying economic power, the manipulation of ethnicity and regression to 'tribalism' – all leading to civil strife and conflict (since 1960, 80 violent changes of government have occurred in Africa, with more than 24 heads of state and government having been assassinated), and;
- the collapse of the state in several African polities because governments at every level have become besieged in their relations with their societies. Governments and the machinery of governance are set apart and alienated; and, as executor of policies and deliverers of services and public goods, governments have become ineffectual, deficient and overloaded.

In other words, Africa has failed woefully to address the menace of the Seven Ds, which over time have become worse. The UN Economic Commission for Africa (ECA) – where I served as Executive Secretary between 1975 and 1991 – developed an *African Alternative Framework to Structural Adjustment Programmes for Socio-Economic Recovery and Transformation* in 1989. The non-implementation of this, and the OAU/ECA *Lagos Plan of Action for the Development of Africa up to 2000*, of 1980, continues to haunt the continent.

THE DECADE OF DEMOCRATIC TRANSITION

At the beginning of the 1990s, the world witnessed three momentous developments:

- The collapse of the Soviet Union and communism which resulted in the end of the Cold War and the globalisation of liberal democracy;
- the end of institutionalised and legally sanctioned racism in South Africa; and
- the unleashing of the forces of globalisation through the revolution in information and communications technologies, and the universalisation of neo-classical economies of marketisation, deregulation, privatisation and the abolition of subsidies.

All three developments have jointly and severally brought profound changes to the world – at the national as well as the international levels. With the collapse of communism and the Soviet Union, the bipolar world yielded to a unipolar world dominated by the US. The built-in contradictions, inequity and inhumanity of apartheid eventually led to its paralysis and collapse in its South African citadel. And the acceleration of the process of globalisation led to unprecedented growth in the extensiveness and intensity of inter-connections on a truly global scale. This process was aided by the revolution in information and communications technologies (ICT) – particularly fax, e-mail, the Internet and electronic communications. The ICT revolution opened the way to massive computerised dealings and unregulated flows in the financial markets. But above all, the 1990s was also a decade of the globalisation of liberal democracy.

These developments were not without their paradoxes. Even with the emergence of a unipolar world, international insecurity has been exacerbated despite the end of the Cold War. In spite of the rapid advance in globalisation, fierce nationalism reared its ugly head from the Balkans to Burundi with the cohesion of states being threatened by brutal strife with ethnic, religious, social, cultural and linguistic dimensions. The collapse of communism and the Soviet Union unleashed centrifugal forces, with the result that the membership of the United Nations increased from 150 to 192 states. However, although there has been greater universality in the UN's membership, universal peace still remains unattainable. And not only has the world not yet achieved 'freedom from fear', it has also failed to secure 'freedom from want'.[7]

While these developments have had, and continue to have, a tremendous impact on the African political economy, the most immediate effect from the point of view of the balance sheet of Africa's first three post-independence decades is the devastating impact of these trends on military and one-party dictatorships in Africa. The end of communism and the Cold War gave the West a historic opportunity to globalise not only economic liberalisation and marketisation, but also political liberalism and democracy. The donor countries stimulated the wave of democracy throughout the world. And so, one by one like dominoes, African countries opted for democracy as the system of governance that would make states less dysfunctional.

The pro-democracy movement in Africa had also been spearheaded by the UN Economic Commission for Africa (ECA) which, taking the democracy bull by the horns, organised an international conference in Arusha, Tanzania, in February 1990 on the imperative of popular participation in development and transformation. That conference – whose theme was *Putting the People First* – had three sets of co-participants: governments, civil society and the private sector, with international organisations also lending additional support. The meeting featured an Ideas Market Place and Exhibition, which reminded participants of the limitless talents and ingenuity of African grassroots and small- and medium-sized enterprises. For the first time and on the basis of equality, the representatives of the public sector, the people, and the private sector, rubbed shoulders and devised the African Charter for Popular Participation in Development – or, as some delegates christened it, Africa's *Magna Carta*. This charter called for a new era of democracy; accountability; economic justice; the supremacy of the rule of law; transparency; and the empowerment of the people and the reconstruction of societies.

The African Charter of 1990 asserts that nations cannot be built without the popular support and full participation of their people; that popular participation is, in essence, the empowerment of citizens; and that the role of the people and their popular organisations is central to the realisation of popular participation in governance. The people thus have to be fully involved, committed and, indeed, seize the initiative.

By the end of the 1990s, the vast majority of African countries had succeeded in introducing 'electoral democracy' whose main components were multi-party systems based on western models, the ballot box, and periodic elections. Because of the involvement of donors in this process, it has been christened 'donor democracy'. Many external donors have provided various incentives and imposed several conditionalities and cross-conditionalities on African governments to reform. However, it is not generally appreciated that elections and multi-party systems are no more than milestones in a long road to transformational democracy. What is now in place in many parts of Africa has been described variously as low-intensity, quasi-, illiberal or, as Russian president Vladimir Putin put it, 'managed' democracy. Without doubt, virtually every country in Africa is in a state of democratic transition, though the democratic process is often fledgling and fragile.

While democracy is not new to Africa, as it is currently practised, there is a structural disconnect between the African indigenous mode of governance and the western mode of democracy that is now in vogue in many parts of Africa. This 'electoral democracy' does not reflect the actual societal behaviour of different African communities, and consequently, the system faces a crisis of ownership and legitimacy. The sustainability of this 'electoral democracy' is difficult to guarantee since it has no cultural roots and exacerbates dualism in African polities. But this is the beginning of a process in which the ultimate goal is to lay the foundation for democratic transformation based on popular participation, human rights, and the rule of law. While this will be the product of each African country's historical and cultural circumstances, this process must involve fundamental societal transformation.[8]

THE EMERGENCE OF A MAJORITY-RULED SOUTH AFRICA

It was on the eve of the UN Economic Commission for Africa's seminal international conference on popular participation in development and transformation held in Arusha in February 1990, that the announcement was made in South Africa of the release of Nelson Mandela from prison after 27 years of incarceration. Not only was there much rejoicing at our meeting, the timing of the release to coincide – more by accident than design – with the conference, was seen by the 500 participants as a good omen for the realisation of the overarching objectives of the meeting. Accordingly, a message of congratulation and solidarity was immediately sent to Nelson Mandela. His release heralded the end of apartheid and the dawn of majority rule in Africa's last racist enclave.

After a four-year negotiation process for a democratic, non-racial society and the holding of the first-ever non-racial general elections and installation of the government of national unity in May 1994, South Africa joined the ranks of the rapidly growing number of democracies in the world. During the decade of the 1990s, the number of countries claiming to be democratic rose to 140 out of a total of 191 UN members at the time. However, by the dawn of the new millennium only 80 out of the 140 countries – 57 per cent – remained democratic. Fortunately, in South Africa, democracy has been waxing strong. Three successful general elections have been held in 1994, 1999 and 2004.

Like the 52 other African countries that had become independent before institutional apartheid was transcended in 1994, South Africa, for a variety of reasons, settled for democratic transition. Despite the promise of a participatory democracy enshrined in its 1996 constitution, ANC negotiators – in the interests of peace – had to settle for formal liberal democratic procedures rather than insist on a constitution whose thrust would be the restructuring of social relations in South Africa. Under pressure from domestic interests as well as several capitalist countries – notably the US, Britain, Italy, Japan and Germany – the ANC had to give up the notion of restructuring South Africa's socio-economic inequalities and instead embrace the neoliberal marketisation orthodoxy.[9]

Globally, the linear link that the West has always insisted on making between democracy and neoliberal economics, has often been the undoing of the democratic process. Marketisation and globalisation are seen in many developing countries as forces of inequity and marginalisation. At the domestic level, marketisation has meant reduced state intervention, reduced subsidisation, and increased privatisation. Since many developing countries are convinced that proactive developmental states with built-in social and economic equity are urgently required, this linking has in practice been weakened. Nor is there evidence of such a relationship in the real world: statistical evidence provides no evidence that diminished marketisation inevitably compromises democracy. While the process of economic development will inevitably result in large-scale social transformations, which in turn will create material conditions for deepening and strengthening democracy, there is no automatic link between liberal democracy and liberal economics.

Neither the democratic revolution in America nor that in France (both of which took place in the late eighteenth century) was inspired by the pursuit of a neo-classical economic paradigm. Their overarching objectives were human and political rights as the foundation for freedom, justice, peace and human security: the guaranteeing of life, liberty and the pursuit of happiness. Britain was already an industrialised country by the time that it launched the process of democratic reform in the early nineteenth century. Aneurin Bevan, in a lecture to the Fabian Society on 'Democratic Values' in London in 1950, expressed doubts as to whether the achievements of Britain's industrial revolution would have been possible if the franchise had been universal, since a great deal of the capital aggregation that took place was partly the result of the low wages that were paid to workers. Nor has the 'Asian Miracle' of the late twentieth century been achieved through the simultaneous pursuit of a neoliberal economic paradigm and democracy. On the contrary, its emphasis has been not democracy but:

- The installation of effective systems of public administration with a view to achieving 'good governance';
- systematic intervention by governments in the development and transformation process through such multiple channels as targeted and subsidised credit, protection of domestic import substitutes, and the development of export marketing institutions;
- taking full advantage of the Asian cultural heritage of the cohesiveness of these societies and the 'herd instinct' of their investment communities; and
- putting in place policies of austerity requiring frugality in the living standards of the mass of the people (generating a high rate of domestic savings constituted the bedrock of the 'Asian Miracle').

This shows that democracy and development are not always in tandem.

THE REASSERTION OF A HUMAN DEVELOPMENT STRATEGY: SOUTH AFRICA'S EVOLVING ECONOMIC AND POLITICAL LANDSCAPE

It is significant and not accidental that barely four months after the African Charter on Popular Participation for Development was signed, the United Nations Development Programme (UNDP) published the maiden issue of its annual *Human Development Report* in June 1990. These two initiatives prompted and heralded the return to a holistic human development strategy and discourse at the international and regional levels: a 'return to roots', as it were.

The human development paradigm has put the people back at the centre of development, focusing on the population being well nourished, healthy, educated, skilled, economically alert and politically empowered, with full commitment to social equity and social discipline. This strategy also makes it incumbent upon policymakers to link development with human rights and freedom and recognises that, to establish sustainable and durable human development, political and democratic transformation is imperative.

Human freedom, of course, encompasses human security. The security of all people everywhere is paramount, and productive investment – both foreign and indigenous – is not security neutral. Where feelings of insecurity are pervasive, speculative rather than productive investment will exist. In economically predatory conditions, in states in which illiteracy and large-scale unemployment are pervasive, poverty becomes endemic, and development and transformational democracy are conspicuous by their absence.

This ECA/UNDP reassertion of the imperative to return to a holistic human development paradigm in 1990 was partially taken up in 2001 when several African governments, led by South Africa, unveiled the New Partnership for Africa's Development (NEPAD) (see Landsberg in this volume). This initiative is, in part, quite explicit in integrating conditions for sustainable development as basic requirements for success, although its economic theoretical underpinning is neoliberal and based on the 'terrible triplets' of marketisation, deregulation, and privatisation.[10]

In the domain of human security, NEPAD's three main areas of focus are:

- Democracy and good governance;
- economic and corporate governance; and
- an African Peer Review Mechanism.

These objectives together constitute the basis for bringing about democratic transformation in Africa. This attempt to tie democracy to the apron strings of neoliberalism will, however, not work. The rigorous and consistent operationalisation of neoliberal policies will sooner or later bring home the imperative of dumping their pursuit and will eventually compromise the democratic process.

Without doubt, South Africa's shift, into a neoliberal, socio-economic dispensation during the Codesa process, negated a great deal of the ANC's long-held positions of democratic advance based on popular mobilisation with a strong emphasis on self-determination, national self-reliance, the sovereignty of the people, and the economic equality of the black majority, as enshrined in the Freedom Charter of 1955.[11]

It must, however, be admitted that in spite of this paradigm shift, South Africa's first decade and a half of democratic transition succeeded in establishing and entrenching democratic institutions and practices which have ensured checks and balances within the state. The independence of the judiciary, the supremacy of the rule of law, ensuring the accountability of political institutions – the parliament and the executive branch – and the promotion and protection of the media and civil society are some of the landmark achievements of thirteen years of freedom.

Without doubt, South Africa's political landscape has been fundamentally transformed. White minority rule is gone forever. The country has been stable during this period – no civil war, no political unrest, and no protracted labour unrest. A great deal of effort and investment has gone into health services, housing, education and social development, even if the share of GDP of all these components of the social sector except social development was reduced during the first decade of independence. Overall, total social spending in South Africa decreased from 15,5 per cent to 12,7 per cent of GDP by 2004.

The South African government has, in spite of its governance constraints, provided basic services to a larger number of communities than any post-colonial government in Africa during a comparable period. The South African Social Services Agency (SASSA) had a budget for administration and grants in 2007/2008 of R66,6 billion, which is to grow to R78 billion in 2009/10.[12] However, the majority of the black population still faces income inequality and deprivation. The skewed distribution of income, resources, and economic opportunities along racial lines, which existed during the apartheid era, has persisted. South Africa has the highest Gini coefficient index (of nearly 60 per cent) in Africa. Globally, South Africa shares the highest Gini indexes with Brazil. However, countries such as Guinea, Kenya and Zimbabwe are very close. In these countries, internal marginalisation has been eroding the foundations of their societies.

There is therefore a growing body of opinion about the need to revisit the Growth, Employment and Redistribution Programme (GEAR) versus the Reconstruction and Development Programme (RDP) debate of 1994 and 1995.

Let us briefly compare the two programmes. The prime aims of the GEAR, crafted to reflect South Africa's settlement for democracy-in-transition with a neoliberal economic approach, are:

- Reduction or at least 'freezing' of government expenditure, with a three per cent ceiling on the budget deficit, which is also the ceiling for euro-currency zone countries;
- privatisation of the state and parastatal corporations and abolishing monopolies in public services;
- linking of wage increases to productivity growth;
- liberalisation of external trade and capital movements; and
- tax incentives to promote new domestic investment.

These, it was projected, would bring about an annual growth rate of between five and seven per cent; a significant increase in both domestic and foreign investments; and the creation of about 400 000 jobs a year.

The RDP was crafted by the ANC in collaboration with the Congress of South African Trade Unions (Cosatu) and the South African Communist Party (SACP), immediately after the ban on the ANC was lifted in 1990. This programme was far from being 'leftist', and more like a social democratic agenda in content and orientation. It had five specific objectives:

- Meeting basic needs;
- developing human resources through education and training;
- reconstructing the economy;
- democratising the state and society; and
- implementing the RDP through a people-driven process.

The RDP's social objectives raised no objections. But the restructuring of the economy and the central importance given to the question of workers' rights were opposed by the agents and apostles of the DMS. GEAR – which has econ-omistic objectives and which was reportedly prepared behind closed doors by a small team of economists from the South African Reserve Bank – is in total conformity with the 'Washington Consensus', and superseded the RDP. The message implicit in GEAR is that human-centred development and 'good governance' must be subject to the dictates of liberalisation and marketisation. GEAR effectively failed to deconstruct the apartheid polity and its institutions, and South Africans must still await the constitution of a new indigenous social democratic order. In other words, the adoption of GEAR meant that the dualism that has plagued South Africa persists: while the self-conscious citizens of the modern sector and the wielders of corporate power are put in a privileged position, the rural poor who constitute the vast majority of the population remain trapped in a vicious circle of poverty.

There is no doubt that by opting for GEAR, which is a South African version of a SAP – the bullet which the rest of sub-Saharan Africa has been biting since the 1980s – post-apartheid South Africa has demonstrated that it is 'just another kid on the block' (see Schoeman in this volume) and that, just as the rest of black Africa has failed to deconstruct its inherited colonial political economy, so post-apartheid South Africa, in deference to a compromise based on sufficient consensus, has not chosen the path of fundamental socio-economic transformation.

The UN's Millennium Development Goals (MDGs) of 2000 constitute the road map for achieving the UN Millennium Declaration which has attempted to mainstream human development. This plan consists of eight programmatic goals, 18 targets, and 48 indicators with deadlines for their implementation. But the MDGs are obviously not new. All developing countries – including African countries – have, for decades, been pursuing these goals and their many targets.

The main contribution that the Millennium Declaration is expected to make is to generate new political momentum to push ahead with the implementation of these goals and targets. Unfortunately, seven years after the adoption of the declaration, there is no discernible evidence of a gathering momentum, as demonstrated by the disappointing outcome of the five-year review conference during the UN General Assembly meeting in New York in September 2005.

The UNDP's *Human Development Report* of 2003 has examined the capacity of each region to achieve the MDG's various goals. Unfortunately, sub-Saharan Africa has the lowest capacity among all regions, and most African countries will not meet the MDGs. For example, it is postulated that, on the basis of current efforts, it will take sub-Saharan Africa until 2129 (instead of 2015) to achieve universal primary education; until 2147 (instead of 2015) to reduce extreme poverty by half; and until 2165 (instead of 2015) to reduce child mortality by two-thirds. These sobering data and extremely pessimistic postulations make imperative urgent actions to deconstruct and reconstitute all African polities.

The question which cannot but be posed in the context of South Africa's role within Africa is: will this forecast apply to South Africa, or will the country exhibit some form of 'exceptionalism' by achieving all the goals of the MDGs even if the rest of sub-Saharan Africa fails to do so? It is doubtful that South Africa will meet all the 18 MDG targets unless, of course, it dumps GEAR and its neo-classical economic framework. In other words, South Africa must cease to be 'just another kid on the block' by tracing its way back to the goals and ideals of the RDP and the ANC Freedom Charter, to map out the road to becoming a truly developmental state.

It is indeed reassuring that, towards the end of the first decade of the post-apartheid era, a marked disillusionment with GEAR has developed and, with this, a renewed effort to rediscover the path to building a developmental state in South Africa. As the Commission on the Theory of Development set up by the ANC's National General Council postulated in its report of 29 June to 3 July 2005, South Africa's developmental state needs to be buttressed and guided by a mass-based democratic liberation movement in a context in which the economy is still dominated by a highly developed, and largely white, capitalist class. In other words, a developmental state is one that is able to mobilise society at large and has the capacity to intervene in order to deconstruct and restructure the inherited apartheid economy.[13]

The concept of a 'people's contract' has now re-entered the South African policy lexicon on the developmental state. One cannot talk about one without the other. Under GEAR, policymaking became the preserve of government officials whose economic prescriptions were often couched as non-negotiable. The people rarely entered the equation and often did not matter. By usurping the power of the political elite and the people at large to set the policy agenda, the bureaucratic economic czars have assumed both the role of rulers and the ruled. Consequently, their policies are often introduced in isolation from the considerations of political stability or the legitimacy and authority of elected bodies.

A truly developmental state is a shared or common project between the state, the political elite and the people. The sharing of common development goals increases the chances of successfully building a coalition around a developmental agenda. Accordingly, building any successful developmental state, particularly in South Africa, will require:

- Identification of state institutions whose reform would be required to establish an effective developmental apparatus;

- reconstitution and modernisation of traditional institutions and governance structures as part of the process of improving grassroots and local government capacity to mobilise and engage the people in the transformation of South Africa into a developmental state;
- economically and technically empowering the people with the requisite capacity and skills to be in the driver's seat in the transformation process (in other words, an effective human resource development strategy is an imperative for transformation into a developmental state);
- a strong commitment by South Africa's political leaders to the transformation process, without which state coherence and autonomy will be lacking;
- a private-public sector partnership (PPP) is essential, requiring all stakeholders to be prepared to make the inevitable initial sacrifices to achieve important developmental goals; and
- a proactive policy of bridging the divide between South Africa's 'first' and 'second' economies which must encompass land and agrarian reform which accommodates the mass of the people in productive and income-generating activities (see Moyo and Hall in this volume), reducing and eventually eliminating dualism from the South African political economy.

It is in this context that South Africa's paradigm of Accelerated and Shared Growth Initiative (ASGISA) was developed by 2006, specifically in a bid to halve unemployment and poverty by 2014 in line with the UN Millennium Development Goals. ASGISA's proponents argue that the initiative is not intended to replace GEAR. Nothing could, however, be further from its real intentions, since ASGISA pins much of its hope on partnership between business, civil society and labour. The initiative's focus is on the micro-economy and it will rely on South Africa's National Treasury and the South African Reserve Bank to create the enabling environment for its success by removing or ameliorating the impact of binding constraints such as: the volatility and level of the rand; the cost, efficiency and capacity of the national logistics system; the shortage of suitably qualified labour; barriers to entry limits to competition and limited new investment opportunities; the burden on small- and medium-size businesses of a regulatory disenabling environment; and deficiencies in state organisation, capacity and leadership.

The removal of these binding constraints will be a boost to the production of public goods and services, which provide employment and reduce poverty. These include, for example: infrastructure development; educational services; acquisition of skills; public administration and management; and intervention in the informal sector or 'second economy'. Other sectors earmarked for ASGISA include: tourism, business, process outpouring, and local government.

SOUTH AFRICA AND AFRICA: WITHIN OR APART?

In concluding this review of South Africa's political economy within the broader African context, it is important to return to the workshop held in Namibia in January 1994 to assess the newly independent South Africa's role within Africa's political economy. The focus of ACDESS's Windhoek workshop was twofold.[14] We have already argued that South Africa should embark on the difficult but nevertheless fundamental task of reconstructing the inherited legacy of apartheid, or remain apart from itself.

The second area of focus was the need for South Africa to stand up against the African continent's growing international isolation, and to play a proactive role through a process of regional cooperation in building what the Windhoek seminar defined as 'Common Home Africa', an Africa where there is a free movement of the factors of production – capital, labour, entrepreneurship, and technology – as well as effective and dynamic continental institutions, to enable Africa to regain its rightful place within the comity of nations. In other words, the question in 1994 was: Will the new South Africa choose to be within or apart from Africa? It is indeed of paramount importance that South Africa defines its place in Africa positively and affirmatively.

Thirteen years after the Windhoek meeting, people may be wondering about the need for this second area of focus, but South Africa's history justifies it. Since the Union of South Africa was established in 1910, South African leaders have always seen their country as a European outpost. For nearly eight decades, the invocation of *swart gevaar* – black peril – has shaped the social and political psychology of South Africa's white ruling elite (see the introduction of this volume). Since unlike the other British colonies of New Zealand, Australia and Canada, South Africa is physically integrated into Africa, it could not remain an island onto itself. Under white minority rule, South Africa's relations with its neighbours were domineeringly hegemonic. Therefore, until the 1990s, South Africa saw itself as being apart from Africa (see Matlosa and Schoeman in this volume).

But since 1990 and, particularly, since May 1994, South Africa has left no one in doubt of its intention to remain within Africa and to play a proactive leadership role (see Adebajo and Landsberg in this volume). South Africa has moved from a role of domineering hegemony to one of multilateral partnership in its relationship with other Southern African countries (see chapters 4 and 5). South Africa has been fully and dynamically reintegrated into the Southern African region. It has been playing a positive role in the Southern African Customs Union (SACU) as well as the Southern African Development Community (SADC) – an institution initiated by western donors in 1980 to help combat apartheid that has transformed somewhat uneasily into an organisation to promote free trade. However, South Africa has not joined the Common Market for Eastern and Southern Africa (COMESA). Since post-apartheid South Africa has opted to adopt a neoliberal economic strategy, it is not surprising that it has taken practical responsibility for the regional restructuring required for a market-based, export-oriented accumulation process within Southern Africa, and indeed in the rest of Africa. Spatial Development Initiatives (SDIS) – corridors linking key nodes of accumulation which embody features of Export Processing Zones – have been created. An example is the Johannesburg-Maputo trade corridor.

With regard to Africa's bilateral trade with South Africa, progress has been quite phenomenal. Africa is now, by region, South Africa's fourth largest export market and the trend is steeply upward. The balance of trade between South Africa and the rest of the continent is also disproportionately in its favour. South Africa's total trade with Africa in 2001 (excluding the Southern African Customs Union) amounted to $856 million in imports and $3,7 billion in exports: an imbalance of nearly five to one.[15]

Unlike apartheid South Africa whose trade and economic relations were limited to Southern African countries, post-apartheid South Africa's corporate operations in Africa are continental and quite extensive (see Hudson in this volume). Indeed, South Africa is the biggest single investor in Africa; its foreign direct investment (FDI) into SADC between 1994 and 2000 alone was $5,4 billion. South Africa's projects in the pipeline are many. Developing an energy grid across Africa is South Africa's flagship venture. This would involve linking Southern Africa with the Grand Inga Dam in the Democratic Republic of the Congo (DRC) and eventually creating a trans-African electricity grid linking all five subregions of the continent. Mention must also be made of the provision of telecommunications (especially cellular telephones) by South African companies, MTN and Vodacom, in several African countries.

There are, in different African countries, mounting criticisms about the behaviour and practices of South African corporations on the continent. Complaints have been voiced in some countries that South African business executives bulldoze their way around and manifest behavioural patterns reminiscent of apartheid South Africa. The response to these criticisms is that South Africa's business executives are driven by typical corporate interest and motivation: profit, market share, and elimination of competition.

South Africa's penetration of the African economy is, however, not the monopoly of its private sector. The South African state, through entities such as the Industrial Development Corporation (IDC), is widely involved in these activities by providing both funding and risk-sharing and taking a direct stake in some of these projects. Currently, the IDC is involved in about 60 projects in 21 countries, including Egypt, Algeria, Nigeria, Senegal, Sudan, Uganda, Kenya, Tanzania, Malawi and Swaziland.

It is in the area of long- and medium-term development strategies for Africa in the twenty-first century that South Africa has been playing the most prominent role. The initiative that eventually led to the creation of NEPAD was led by South African president Thabo Mbeki, who had earlier made a ringing call for an 'African Renaissance'. However, if African governments could reduce the wastage of their domestically generated resources by just 25 per cent and plug capital leakages and capital flight by another 25 per cent, these two actions alone would result, on average, in between $30 billion and $40 billion per annum of additional capital for development and other purposes. Second, if the continent's adverse terms of trade and debt problems were seriously addressed by the donor community, resources as large as $35 billion could be released for development. Third, the expectation by some developing countries that overseas development assistance (ODA) to sub-Saharan Africa – which was merely $14,57 billion in 1998 – would be quadrupled, is highly unrealistic. This goes against the trend of dwindling ODA, which has persisted for many years. In addition, this approach fails to recognise the fundamental shift in aid necessitated by the demands of globalisation. Aid resources are now focused primarily on addressing cross-border problems of direct concern to donors rather than on financing purely national projects and programmes in developing countries. Examples of such cross-border projects are: preventing the spread of infectious diseases such as HIV/AIDS (see Ndinga-Muvumba and Mottiar in this volume), fighting organised international crime, and arresting the degradation of the national environment in order to protect the global environment.

In other words, foreign aid is now being increasingly used to provide a wide array of international public goods.

If Africa were to base its new partnership with the rich world on the imperative of the need to reverse its persistent adverse terms of trade, it would be backing a sure horse. According to the *World Bank African Development Indicators 2001*, Africa's terms of trade index dropped from 158,3 in 1980 to 96,5 in 1999 (with 1995 being the base year for the index at 100). Specifically, sub-Saharan Africa's export unit value fell from 121,8 in 1980 to 89,4 in 1999 (with 1995 being the base year); but the region's import unit value during the same period rose from 77 to 96,2. As earlier noted, Africa's export commodities are characterised by highly income-elastic demand with supply being price-elastic. The inevitable consequence of this phenomenon is the boom-and-bust cycle which has resulted in severe damage to African economies and a reduction in the provision of essential public goods in many African countries.

The reactivation of the two-gap model in Africa is also unfortunate because it was precisely the cause of the current debt trap and the exacerbation of the continent's dependency syndrome. What Africa needs is not to add to its debt burden of $290 billion, but to reduce it and eventually be relieved of it. In any case, there is an element of oversimplification of a rather complex problem by postulating that, to achieve a seven per cent growth rate per annum in Africa requires an investment of about 30 per cent of GDP. No doubt an incremental capital-output ration (ICOR) has been assumed. How has this been arrived at? Given the abysmally low level of productivity on the continent, is it new investment or increased productivity that is urgently required? How can countries that are consistently unable to implement their modest capital budget be pleading for massive investment? Where is the executive capacity to come from? Importing such capacity will only result in 'growth without development'. This approach also throws overboard the proposition that development has to be engineered and sustained by African people. Sustainable development surely has to be the organic outcome of a society's value system, perception, concerns and endeavours.

While we are still far from turning the continent into a 'common home' for all Africans and still far from getting rid of the menace of visas and cross-border prohibitions, a lot has been done by South Africa to demonstrate its own commitment to the continent. President Mbeki has constantly assured the people of Africa that the fate of democratic South Africa is inextricably bound up with what happens in the rest of the continent, and recognises that his country cannot become an island of prosperity in a sea of poverty.

The emerging resurgence of pan-Africanism and the clamour for an African Renaissance are two of the most important developments in Africa during the first decade and a half of post-apartheid South Africa. Both will, however, redound creditably on the African (including South Africa's) political economy only if necessary lessons are drawn from the experiences of the last five decades. One such lesson is that the neoliberal economic paradigm is likely to continue to delay the deconstruction and transformation of Africa's political economy.

What Africa urgently needs is not just economic growth – important as it is – but holistic human development and the democratisation of the development process. Only these factors can internalise the culture of people-centred democracy and put in motion an irreversible process of diversification of economies, both intersectorally and intrasectorally. It is through such a process that job creation will become the benchmark of progress. A people-centred focus necessitates that employment generation should constitute the benchmark of public policy and private investment. Reducing poverty by 50 per cent by 2015 – one of the key objectives of the Millennium Development Goals – can be achieved only if Africa succeeds in making productive job creation the central plank of public policy. What South Africa and the rest of Africa need is not just growth, but development and a culture of personal and social discipline. Only then will African states be on the road to becoming 'rainbow nations of God'.

2

Black economic empowerment: Myths and realities

KHEHLA SHUBANE

Despite numerous attempts at pointing out what black economic empowerment (BEE) entails, many, including organisations that are close to the ruling ANC, continue to view the policy in a narrow way and to criticise it. What appears to upset many about BEE is that it empowers only a few people, many of whom have connections to the ANC. The focus is on transactions in which black groups buy a stake in white-established companies. Other important aspects of the transaction, such as the participation of black staff in these businesses, have often been completely ignored.

Company reports on BEE – certainly those of listed companies – often go on to mention even more elements of the scorecard for depth of empowerment, such as skills development and preferential procurement, and the extent to which the company in question contributes to them. In the popular representations of BEE, these elements are often ignored, in favour of an exclusive focus on shifts of equity. But while the purchase of shares by black groups is important, it is not the overriding factor in BEE. There are other elements just as important, if not more so. Ownership of shares can only be meaningful if it is supported, among other things, by, for example, skilled managers to husband the assets of companies.

Like their white counterparts the new black shareholders understand that their wealth will grow only if there is a corps of management who can work the assets that they have purchased. Consequently no objection is ever heard from empowerment groups against the participation of black managers as shareholders in empowerment transactions. This is why virtually all recent BEE transactions include significant participation by black management. In the case of the Standard Bank/Liberty Life transaction concluded in July 2004, no less than 40 per cent of the sale of shares to empowerment groups went to black managers and staff. In a new development, one or two deals have staff and management – and no outside parties – as equity participants in BEE transactions. Only management was invited to participate in the Edcon (holding company of Edgars, a big clothing chain in South Africa) empowerment transaction.

Other than the participation of management in equity transactions, there are other elements of empowerment that are always implemented at the same time. The fact that black management participates in any transaction implies the existence of such a grouping in the company concerned. It is often forgotten that these groupings, and the increasing numbers of women in management positions, were created by BEE.

This chapter is concerned with dispelling a widely held view that BEE is coterminous with a single element of empowerment: the equity element. Several authors have focused on other interesting aspects of BEE.[1] Roger Southall, for example, has explored the effects of BEE on the type of economy South Africa is building. He has expressed concern that empowerment is likely to promote practices which might promote 'crony capitalism'. Southall has also written about the increasing inequalities embedded in South Africa's economy, which are not being reduced by the models of BEE that have been adopted.

WHY BEE?

Black economic empowerment is necessary because of a history of dispossession that was a key feature of apartheid, and other forms of white domination that preceded it. To ensure that black people were relegated to, and maintained at, the lowest rung in the racial hierarchy of apartheid society, they were stripped of many of the assets they might have had. The history of land dispossession, of limiting the number of animals that blacks could keep, of restricting their participation in the labour market to menial and low-paid occupations, and of denying them freehold rights, has been well recorded (see Moyo and Hall in this volume). While these actions started early in the history of colonial conquest, they were continued until very recently. Some black communities were removed from their land as recently as the 1980s. A key reason for implementing BEE now is to correct the dispossession that took place in the past.

To function maximally, white domination and apartheid denied blacks assets on which they could rely for their livelihood. Severe limitations were placed on business entities that were allowed in urban townships. Elaborate laws and regulations about where, what, and how trade could be conducted by black people were in place: all aimed at ensuring that black people could not build meaningful businesses. The worst of these restrictions were reserved for black African people who today constitute some 70 per cent of South Africa's population.

So far-reaching were the measures that were adopted that, by the 1970s, the deep impoverishment of black people in South Africa was almost complete. The few blacks with assets or an education were an aberration in a sea of a people bereft of these. The work of building assets among blacks and educating them was to start almost from scratch once apartheid had been removed in 1994.[2] Over a decade later, this task is still barely underway. It is these historical wrongs that BEE seeks to correct.

Though there is still a long way to go, what has been achieved in just over a decade is remarkable. It has now become possible to conduct a discussion on the black middle-class and what this class has done to increase demand within South Africa's economy. Black people now earn a comparatively high percentage of the share of income earned by highly paid people in South Africa. The numbers of black students have increased significantly at formerly white universities in the country, with blacks accounting for over 50 per cent of admissions at the universities of the Witwatersrand and Cape Town.

In the current period, BEE is necessary to deracialise the ownership of significant economic assets. Indeed there would have been little purpose in mounting a struggle that took long and resulted in huge loss of life – and then not oppose continuing apartheid within the white-dominated economy. Over 90 per cent of the individually owned shares at the Johannesburg securities exchange (JSE) continue to be owned by whites. After all, the South African economy was built in large measure by apartheid, which massively exploited black labour. The growth trajectory of the country would have been fundamentally different had it not been for apartheid specifically, and racial discrimination in general.

The black-led government after 1994 must have concluded that continuing with arrangements inherited from apartheid, in which business assets were owned by one racial group, would be a source of great political instability. BEE is thus a practical solution to a practical problem. Government must be seen to be not only concerned with inequities resulting from apartheid, but must also show that it is doing something to reverse this legacy.

Aimed at speeding the acquisition of assets by black people, BEE is founded on the basis of an assumption that this is a plan through which the economy can grow. The point is better conveyed by stating it in reverse: South Africa's economy cannot grow with the majority black population effectively locked out of certain key sectors.[3] To the extent that BEE seeks to ensure the participation of all South Africans in the entire economy, the initiative is a basis for normal-ising the country. With all its warts, BEE remains the only practical solution to a complex problem. In the relatively short time during which it has been implemented, the initiative has proved its worth.

Critics of BEE are many and varied. Some – especially among white share-holders – often argue that they worked for what they have and did not dispossess anyone. Consequently, they should, in their view, not have to assist anyone to acquire assets through any means other than those provided by the market.

BEE is also often criticised for its inability to distinguish business people from those who are said to be seeking a free ride from empowerment with no long-term intentions to invest their assets in businesses. If there were a way, the argument goes, of ensuring that assets from empowerment could be directed to black people with an inclination to business, this would be the best way of ensuring that assets are reinvested in businesses and benefit a larger number of people, rather than creating a politically connected black bourgeoisie class. This argument is based on the premise that business people are a lot more likely to put the assets they acquire to business use. According to these critics, beneficiaries of BEE with no long-term interest in business are more likely to consume the assets that they obtain.

THE FOCUS ON EQUITY

Much as talk of empowerment has dominated debates since 2004, BEE has suf-fered from a widespread refusal to focus on all the dimensions of the policy. In the public eye, BEE has been reduced to little more than the selling and buying of shares in established white companies. Perhaps this reflects the recent past when BEE was indeed nothing more than a sale of shares to black groups. At the time, it was assumed that once blacks were part of the shareholders of a company, somehow transformation would come about in a fit of political alchemy. The sale of shares to Nail and Rail, in the early days of empowerment, was not part of a broader initiative. The notion of broad-based empowerment came about much later. It was the BEE Commission, created in 2001,[4] which started people thinking about broad-based BEE.

Only when there is a sale or purchase of shares by black groups have BEE transactions been reported.[5] By itself, the employment of black executives is hardly ever reported nor seen as a BEE-related development. If this is reported at all, it is presented as the achievement of the individual concerned and not in any way connected to BEE. The significant movement of blacks into managerial position, both in the private and public sectors, is normally not linked to BEE, nor are developments on the skills development front.

Perhaps the key culprits in this collective amnesia have been certain organisations that are close to policymaking processes as well as the media. The journalists writing screaming headlines on BEE when a white company has invested in a black company have simply not been there to report on what should be viewed as a significant BEE development. When companies report on their procurement spending as part of their BEE policy, the media often simply ignores this fact.

Surprisingly, groups such as the Congress of South African Trade Unions (Cosatu),[6] the ANC,[7] as well as the South African Communist Party (SACP)[8] – which constitute the ruling tripartite alliance – have in different ways also not given much weight to BEE developments besides the equity element. This is surprising because the ANC has driven the legislation on BEE and is in an alliance with the other two organisations. Surely, it is not a huge leap of logic to assume that a policy as central as BEE would be canvassed at their joint meetings. These groups should be aware of the other elements of BEE and how important they are. This aside, Cosatu, in particular, over an extended period of time, convincingly and persuasively argued against apartheid in the work place. Surely redressing this policy must include the advancement into managerial positions of blacks? An integral part of apartheid in the work place was bunching blacks at the bottom of the employment hierarchy and whites in the upper reaches of the structure. Cosatu opposed this approach for years. But now that victory is starting to unfold, somehow the reality of black advancement as being part of this victory is not recognised by the union. Why is Cosatu not recognising this development as its own initiative when it is made part of BEE? Why does it not celebrate when these policies are embraced by an ever-increasing number of people?

Skills development – an element of the BEE scorecard, which incidentally is given the same weighting as equity participation by the government – was in no small measure spearheaded by Cosatu. Arguably, the level of awareness of the importance of skills development in South Africa owes a debt of gratitude to the work that Cosatu did in the 1980s. With skills development being integrated into BEE, it is sad that Cosatu does not recognise this as work that it pioneered. Is the acquisition of equity by black groups – a key point around which Cosatu criticises BEE – such a terrible development that the organisation must be blinded to the reality that there are other dimensions of empowerment which are worthy of praise?

Even adopting a left-wing worker perspective, it would appear counter-productive simply to focus attention on equity issues when there are so many other elements that constitute BEE. Why throw the BEE baby out with the equity bathwater by reducing a broad programme to only one element – equity – each time BEE is spoken about?

All three groups (the ANC, Cosatu and the SACP) have been critical of wealth accumulation in the hands of a few and have virtually offered no comment on the very visible advancement of the black managerial class as a BEE development. Where comment has been forthcoming, this development has often been decoupled from BEE.

Despite clear indications that policymakers did not intend to privilege equity above other elements, the fixation on equity has continued unabated. Clearly, by allocating a weighting of 20 points out of 100 to equity in the scorecard – a weighting that is equal to that given to skills development as well as preferential procurement – policymakers must surely have intended that these three elements be given the same weight. This should have led to the conclusion that these three elements are given the same level of importance. Contrary to this expectation, the other two elements hardly receive a mention in the current public debate.

ALLEGATIONS OF POLITICAL PATRONAGE DISCOUNT BLACK INITIATIVE

The wealth allegedly building up in the hands of a few black individuals has also fuelled this distorted focus on equity as if BEE was reducible to this one area. How much money is building up in the hands of these individuals is often never disclosed.[9] Instead, the focus is usually placed on the value of the transactions in which they are involved, and it is frequently assumed that the bulk of the money from BEE deals will end up in the pockets of these black businessmen. The fact that large debts – that will have to be repaid – often underpin these transactions before these individuals pocket any money is simply ignored. The impression that these individuals are rolling in money is indelibly etched in the public mind.

The net wealth of the most high-profile BEE 'tycoons', Saki Macozoma,[10] Patrice Motsepe,[11] Cyril Ramaphosa[12] and Tokyo Sexwale[13] was published in South Africa's *Sunday Times* in December 2005. According to the paper, the wealth of these individuals is nowhere near the figures often cited by groups accusing them of accumulating too much money. To be sure, these men are all rich, and but for BEE could not have been so wealthy. However, relative to their richest white counterparts, the money of these black individuals appears to be modest.

At issue though is a narrow focus on a single variable – equity transactions – in what is intended to be a broad BEE process. In the case of these high-profile black businessmen, the story is often made more graphic by the fact that they are well connected to the ANC and their wealth is therefore considered a result of patronage rather than business acumen. Somehow, the impression is created that this wealth is ill-gotten.

Enterprise on the part of some of these individuals is lost in a litany of questionable facts presented to obfuscate some interesting developments in the accumulation process. The fact that the path to wealth followed by these new black businessmen is often diverse, has been largely ignored. Some of these individuals run companies and take risks every day of their working lives. Others run investment firms in which the nature of the risk they face is different from that faced by people in operating companies.

One side of this story, which never makes the headlines, is that there is evidence suggesting real enterprise on the part of Patrice Motsepe in building his company. He took huge risks in buying what were marginal mines at the time in the Free State Gold Fields. Motsepe – helped by changing trends in the gold price that coincided with his investment – turned these mines into profitable operations in a relatively short period of time. He was not as connected to the ANC as is, say, Tokyo Sexwale, and others whose connection to the ruling party is direct and long-standing. Motsepe might well be an ANC member now, but this has never been a major part of his identity or efforts. His connections to the ANC are at best tenuous; two of his sisters are married to leading members of the ANC and these relationships have been cited to suggest he occupies the same camp as Cyril Ramaphosa, a former secretary-general of the ANC. For those who dislike Ramaphosa, this appears to be a clear case of 'guilt by association'.

Support for entrepreneurial flair – an integral part of BEE – is forgotten in an attempt to draw a picture of BEE as a single moment – a process in which political chums are rewarded for their loyalty to a political party. In this view, BEE is simply reduced to a corrupt exercise in which political patronage is a major vehicle for creating wealthy black individuals.

To sustain the view that BEE has been limited to the creation of a handful of excessively wealthy blacks, other participants in equity transactions have had to be ignored. The many other groups – in particular black employees – who are among the participants in many equity transactions, simply never get a mention. This would clearly not fit the distorted image that a handful of well-connected individuals are running away with the country's 'crown jewels'.

Unsuspecting readers of the media – and sadly in some cases, academic articles by authors such as Jeffrey Herbst[14] – (happily, only a few of these have been written so far) are led to believe that the government somehow arranges the participation for these well-connected individuals in specific transactions in which they benefit. The matter is presented in a way that gives the impression that an invisible government hand is at work to ensure that a select group of individuals are always part of any BEE transaction. This builds on the theme by now well established in certain quarters, that the dispensing of patronage is in overdrive.

The plain and simple reality is that private companies have selected groups with which they undertake empowerment transactions. No empowerment group is imposed – certainly not by government – on any company as an empowerment partner. The selection of empowerment groups to participate in any transaction is solely the business of the private sector and the private sector alone.

It may be that private companies embarking on BEE transactions think that if they select individuals with good connections to government, this will somehow improve their standing with government. This is plausible, but has not yet been convincingly proved.

Perhaps the key elements in the decisions of private companies selecting empowerment partners are the relationships maintained by individuals who have repeatedly participated in empowerment transactions. In the case of the Standard Bank transaction, there is reason to believe that a personal relationship between Cyril Ramaphosa and Saki Macozoma on the one hand, and leading executives within the bank on the other, played a key role in ensuring the inclusion of the former among participants in the equity stake. It is a matter of public record that Tokyo Sexwale had a personal relationship with ABSA (the second largest retail bank in South Africa) executive managers long before they finalised the ABSA BEE transaction. In this case too, an existing relationship rather than the political connectedness of the individuals concerned appears to have been a more significant factor.

Some analysts who reduce empowerment to equity participation accept that private sector players find their own partners and, within the constraints of the law, craft transactions that suit them. Inexplicably, this view then goes on to suggest that white business executives and shareholders generally are deliberately currying favour from government by privileging those who are politically connected. Empowerment transactions are thus about buying favours from political elites.[15] In this view, business people are, and always have been, buying influence. They bought it in the past from those who were politically powerful under apartheid and they are now buying it from different clients. The notion of business people who honestly conduct business without resorting to peddling influence is therefore a myth, in this view.

THE BLACK MIDDLE CLASS

The dominant criticism against empowerment – that it has empowered very few individuals – does not accord with reality. Cosatu[16] and the SACP go further – to charge that BEE has done nothing to reduce poverty. This may be so, though some analysts have noted the not insignificant progress that has been made in tackling poverty since 1994. However, it should be said that this has been a result of policies other than BEE. There remains a great deal of poverty in South Africa with some estimates of unemployment as high as 40 per cent, but considerable ground has been covered in reducing the burden of poverty on many people. Nevertheless, it is the black middle class that is the focus of this section of the chapter.

The existence of a large and growing black middle class in South Africa has now become a generally accepted proposition.[17] Figures vary widely from a few people to about 12 per cent of the population.[18] It is this middle class, among other factors, that has been driving increasing levels of demand, which in turn resulted in a buoyant economy by 2005.[19] Surely this higher demand cannot be solely explained by the benefits that have accrued to a handful of individuals who have benefited from BEE equity transactions.

Critics of empowerment point to the very limited number of beneficiaries of empowerment.[20] Some have argued that the culprits (those who are said to have benefited from the equity element of BEE) number less than a dozen. Some have used this fact (of very few individuals benefiting) to point to a worsening Gini coefficient among black South Africans since the advent of democracy in 1994. If consideration is also given to the fact that BEE transactions have been financed by the extensive use of debt – which has to be repaid – then it is improbable that the relatively broad-based black middle class can be explained only by the equity element of the scorecard.

Blade Nzimande, Secretary-General of the South African Communist Party, alluded to other developments at work within the BEE process, which explain the reasonably broad-based black middle class. He pointed to a group at the helm of state-owned firms.[21] These black individuals are, however, not limited to state-owned firms. They are diffused in the economy and are more numerous. They are now in many management positions. But, there are relatively few of them at the very highest levels of companies.

Another group, which hardly ever receives a mention in the BEE debate, is individuals who are running small firms. Entrepreneurship is thriving at this level. Funds that invest in these firms run very profitable operations. This again demonstrates the hollowness of the argument that empowerment is limited to equity transactions.

The size of the black middle class is a subject of dispute. Some hold that it is small and fragile while others are of the view that it is sizeable.[22] What is generally agreed is that it is large enough to have contributed significantly to sustained growth of nearly five per cent in 2006.[23] To even receive a mention as an important factor contributing to economic growth means that the black middle class must be significant.

BROAD-BASED BLACK ECONOMIC EMPOWERMENT

Even if it were to be conceded that participation in the equity element of BEE is limited, taken as a whole, 'true' empowerment is broader than many of its critics are prepared to admit. The authors of the formal BEE policy carefully ensured this. This breadth derives from the fact that there are seven elements of BEE.[24] Complying with all seven factors constitutes broad-based black economic empowerment, while complying with any one element does not officially constitute broad-based participation – even if there are large numbers of participants. Ideally, companies should comply with all seven elements. In practice, they often comply to varying degrees but do not meet all seven. A quantitative measure has been developed to measure the extent of companies' compliance with BEE guidelines, in order to be considered sufficiently 'empowered' to qualify for public sector business.

Admittedly, this measure permits transactions with very few equity participants to qualify as broad-based. If the company concerned scores well in other elements it can achieve a good overall score. It should be borne in mind, however, that other elements force the participation of the many. Employment equity would ensure that many people working within any firm benefited from empowerment. Procurement from an empowered firm would also in its own way benefit many. Skills development would ensure that skills were imparted to a larger number of black people. Investing in black-owned and controlled companies would also, in all likelihood, benefit many.

The draft of the BEE codes offer incentives for broad-based participation by awarding bonus points for firms which attract the participation of broad-based as well as new groups in ownership structures. This creates an incentive for empowering groupings such as empowerment entities that have not benefited from previous transactions. But, for a firm looking for sufficient points to qualify as an empowered firm, the number of participants in the equity element of a broadly empowered firm is immaterial. It is possible to score very well with very few equity participants.

Because of a fixation on equity participation, informally, a transaction is viewed as broad-based if there are a large number of equity beneficiaries. Even with no reference to other elements of the scorecard, many commentators conceded that the ABSA deal was broad-based. This conclusion was informed by the numbers of an impressive list of entities drawn from all over the country that participated in the shareholding of the transaction.

It is often not recognised that empowerment occurs even in firms that do not specifically intend to conclude a BEE transaction. Two, maybe, three BEE elements for some firms are obligatory as they are a subject of legislation other than BEE legislation. For example, employment equity and skills development are dealt with in pieces of legislation that are independent of BEE laws. Virtually all firms have to comply with such legislation independently of their BEE views. For firms wishing to do business with the public sector, complying with the Preferential Procurement Act is crucial to be considered for business. For such firms, this is the third piece of legislation with which they have to comply to be able to conduct business. In respect of preferential procurement, it should be noted that there is a gap between the expectation of this element's implementation, as set out in the BEE codes on the one hand, and the way it is written in the law on procurement on the other.

OTHER ELEMENTS

Besides the equity element, other elements of the scorecard and the weightings they are given are: management (10 per cent); employment equity (10 per cent); skills development (20 per cent); enterprise development (10 per cent); preferential procurement (20 per cent); and the residual element (10 per cent).[25] Each is discussed briefly in turn.

The management element of BEE aims to increase the participation of black managers at all levels of firms but especially among the very top leaders. In the short time during which this element has been in operation, the pool of management talent in South Africa has grown. Periodically, reports of poor management in some areas are heard and attributed to this element of the scorecard. Power outages in Johannesburg, for example, have been attributed to poor management resulting from promoting people without the required management experience.

This element recognises that wealth and status do not only derive from wealth built through owning assets (though that is important), but that controlling such assets is just as critical. Increasingly, modern firms are run not by those who own them, but by skilled individuals whose unique contribution is their ability to manage the firms. To the extent that ability is not the exclusive preserve of the rich, it is a good development that this element was included in the empowerment laws. Talented individuals from less wealthy backgrounds can and do lead big firms and make successful managers. Since empowerment legislation has been passed, South Africa has seen a number of individuals who would not have been considered for the positions they now occupy in leading firms in the country without BEE.

Though the emphasis has been on race, the scorecard is very explicit in encouraging firms to appoint women as well into top management positions. A few women have been appointed within private sector firms. The public sector has set an excellent example of appointing women to the higher echelons of firms, and such women have proved themselves in these positions. Thanks to this development and the inclusion of gender in BEE, South Africa now boasts numerous women in positions of power whose record of excellence speaks for itself. A by-product of this trend is a society that is starting to face up to broader gender issues in society as a whole.

Employment equity is one of the elements of the BEE scorecard that is also the subject of a separate piece of legislation.[26] Significantly, the law was driven by South Africa's Department of Labour, drawing from the extensive experiences of Cosatu. Under this law, there are separate penalties for not implementing employment equity. The inclusion of employment equity in the scorecard underscores the broad-based nature of BEE laws. All black working people face the effects of discrimination based on the history of apartheid in the workplace, and the employment equity element of BEE is designed to correct this. It does this by being very specific about the numbers of formerly subordinated groups who should be included at various levels within the workforce. As with the management element, employment equity is concerned with discrimination against a range of people rather than merely race-based discrimination. All groups that were previously excluded from benefits of employment or upward mobility in employment can seek redress using employment equity.

Skills development is another element drawn from already existing legislation.[27] Like employment equity, this initiative owes its existence to the experiences of Cosatu. It has been difficult to conduct skills training in the numbers that were initially anticipated. Some of the Sector Education and Training Authorities (SETAs) – bodies created by the Department of Labour to encourage and speed up the training of working people – are not functioning as well as was initially intended. But a start has been made and many lessons learned. A considerable amount of money has been collected and is with the various SETAS. These funds still need to be used to achieve the best results. The results so far have been encouraging, but can still be improved on.

The Preferential Procurement Policy Framework Act of 2000 is yet another law which is included in BEE as an element that has become important in driving empowerment. Arguably, many of South Africa's big firms have embraced empowerment as a result of this piece of legislation. The swiftest advance of black decision-makers has occurred within the public sector as well as state-owned enterprises. It is, in part, the presence of these individuals as decision-makers in these entities that has quickened the pace of transformation more broadly in the economy. Anecdotal evidence suggests that these managers have pressed their counterparts in the private sector to appoint black managers in leadership positions within their firms.

The fear that companies may lose business to their empowered competitors has also driven private sector firms to appoint blacks in management positions. The public sector generally spends large amounts on procurement. Firms do not want to lose business with the public sector and hence have a large incentive to comply with their procurement obligations.

To be sure, the procurement policy is not as geared to working to achieve BEE objectives as it could. Although the separate piece of legislation itself is not clear on the fact that firms must comply with BEE to be considered as suppliers to the public sector, the view is still generally held that firms wishing to supply to public sector companies should comply with BEE. But even with the current somewhat confused position, preferential procurement has achieved much progress for BEE.

Enterprise development is another element of the BEE scorecard that should have been given a 20 per cent – rather than 10 per cent – weighting. This is very important since this initiative makes entrepreneurship a part of BEE and rebuts the view that BEE is a 'get-rich-quick scheme' for blacks. The inclusion of enterprise development in BEE shows that policymakers are awake to the fact that BEE is also about blacks building enterprises, and not simply relying on handouts from existing companies.

Evidence emerging from the market suggests that there are many black people quietly at work to build their own companies. Anglo Zimele – an Anglo American Corporation (AAC) initiative aimed at helping emerging black-owned companies essentially with capital – is doing well. This company virtually takes private equity positions in emerging black-owned companies and helps these companies in other ways such as giving them long-term contracts to supply their products to AAC companies. At some stage in the growth of the black-owned company, Anglo Zimele sells its stake in the black company and the company funds its capital on its own.

Similar work is going on at the National Empowerment Fund (NEF), which invests in very small black-owned companies. The NEF's investments take a private equity form. The intention is to ensure that small companies with the potential to succeed are not denied this success by a lack of access to capital. NEF staff describe exciting developments in this area of their work. They have invested relatively small amounts in small companies that have grown to a point at which the NEF can sell their shares in these companies to invest in others. Though it is more common to hear talk of equity deals than talk about entrepreneurship, this is a part of BEE that is working and producing black entrepreneurs. Capital is invested in small emerging companies that grow and produce a return for investors.

The last formal element of BEE, with a weighting of 10 per cent, is the residual element. This is an element decided by the company undertaking an empowerment transaction. Seeing that companies are in different sectors, the residual factor seeks to give them the freedom to do what is appropriate in their sector to advance empowerment objectives. This could be to direct their social responsibility investments in ways that empower communities in which the company concerned works. Private companies have been undertaking such investments for a long time in South Africa. Once all the elements of the scorecard are presented together, it is clear that empowerment is far broader than is often admitted by its critics.

CONCLUSION

It may be that equity gives shareholders the ultimate power in any firm. After all, shareholders take the critical decisions that affect companies. If shareholders want to employ a black person in any position, they have the power to do so. Even under apartheid, shareholders could have done more to achieve a less racially divided work force.

But however important shareholding is, it is not, in the context of empowerment, capable of effecting the changes that need to be implemented within companies and South Africa's economy. Patterns of control as well as ownership of the past will be changed by a combination of ownership and control. BEE combines both dimensions to achieve the desired outcome.

If implemented fully, BEE laws have a built-in broad-based aspect to them. These essentially lie in implementing all seven elements of the scorecard. A BEE transaction with as many equity participants as possible is not, in and of itself, broad. However, it is important to note that it is not the number of participants that makes a transaction broad, but rather whether all the elements of the scorecard are properly implemented.

3

Race and reconciliation: *E pluribus unum?*

YASMIN SOOKA

In June 2004, South Africa made its final presentation to the International Football Federation (FIFA) bid committee to host the World Cup in 2010. Included in the delegation to Zurich, Switzerland, were two former presidents: Nelson Mandela and F.W. De Klerk, symbols of the 'rainbow nation'. Also present was another icon of South Africa, the former Archbishop of Cape Town, Desmond Tutu. All three were Nobel laureates. The Latin dictum *e pluribus unum* ('Out of many, comes one') seemed particularly apt for this polyglot nation.

Watching the bid committee make its presentation, I was struck by the fact that the bid team had found it necessary to strike this note of a 'rainbow' nation reconciled with each other, even at the international level. The picture of former presidents Mandela and De Klerk posing together in harmony was flashed across the globe. Not unsurprisingly, South Africa won the bid to host the football World Cup in 2010. At the same time, I could not suppress my own internal nagging voice and the total revulsion I felt that F.W. de Klerk – one of the leading apostles of apartheid before 1989 – should at any stage in South Africa's history be treated as a hero. After all, this was the man who denied in public that he knew about the atrocities that were taking place in South Africa during the apartheid period. While it is true that De Klerk began the process which led to majority rule in 1994 and while he should be acknowledged and remembered for his part in this historic achievement, he failed – at a crucial moment – to take responsibility for the violence that had taken place in South Africa. De Klerk's act gave rise to despair in the ranks of the soldiers who had carried out these brutal acts, as they felt let down by their political leadership. Colonel Eugene de Kock, the former head of the apartheid security agency, noted about De Klerk:

> ... He simply did not have the courage to declare, "Yes, we at the top level condoned what was done on our behalf by the security forces. What's more we instructed that it should be implemented."[1]

I began to wonder how this had come to pass. It was striking that, in dealing with the international community, it has become necessary for South Africa to present the face of a reconciled nation. Most people believed that it was the saintly presence of Nelson Mandela that stabilised South Africa's nascent democracy. The overwhelming sense, outside the country, is that South Africa had really achieved reconciliation; it should thus be justly rewarded for having behaved nobly thirteen years ago by deciding not to send all those who had supported apartheid and had benefited from it into exile, and for not doing to them essentially what they had done to the black majority. The outside world wondered why blacks had not responded to the opportunities for legitimate vengeance presented by liberation with the same savagery that their oppressors had previously employed while self-righteously calling it justice.

After all, the world has developed very sophisticated laws – both internationally and nationally – which demand that those who offend against the code of what is acceptable behaviour should be punished, and that only when they are punished can societies learn lessons to prevent future atrocities. These are the lessons that are meant to ensure that nations behave in a civilised way towards their citizens. Chastening for many, it is not white people who behaved so nobly in South Africa by forgoing greater vengeance but the 'black savages' whose legitimacy and 'just cause' many in the international community had refused to accept during the dark days of apartheid. Race therefore remains an intrinsic factor in the debate on reconciliation in post-apartheid South Africa.

It is useful to trace back the origins of the notion of 'reconciliation' in South Africa. The public dialogue began with the political negotiations that were launched in 1990, and the postscript to the interim constitution of 1993, the origins of which are still shrouded in deep mystery.[2] Leon Wessels, the former apartheid minister of law and order, who was part of the negotiating team of the National Party (NP) government, described his anxieties during the negotiation period: 'One question haunted me, when a new dispensation came about, how would South Africans deal with the past? Would they try to speak about and deal with it – or would they simply take the easy option and ignore it? You cannot ignore the past, but you also cannot deal with it in a spirit of emotional bullying and vengeance.'[3]

What is ironic about this statement is that it was made by a serving minister in the apartheid government who himself noted that the new African National Congress (ANC) government would not do to whites what they had done to their former black enemies. The story that is commonly told is of how the issue of amnesty was holding up the adoption of the interim constitution, when at the stroke of midnight, the ANC capitulated and accepted the notion of an amnesty.

This became the basis on which the Truth and Reconciliation Commission (TRC) was established. While many human rights scholars in the world refer to the TRC as South Africa's 'pact with the devil', it is important to contextualise the debate that framed the process. Apartheid was declared to be a 'crime against humanity' by the international community in 1973. The system was responsible for the systematic exploitation of the black majority in order to privilege and benefit a white minority. Being born white conferred the status of a superior human being allowed to access privileges, jobs, land, education and benefit from a racial economy to the exclusion of those born black.

Apartheid had also criminalised any opposition to the government of the day and made criminals of people who tried to live with any dignity or humanity. The year 1994 ushered in a period during which the transition to democracy involved a transfer of power from a white minority, which ruled illegitimately using the law and fear, to a black-led democratic constitutional state. Essentially, this was the 'two nations' that then deputy president, Thabo Mbeki, had famously and controversially referred to during a speech on reconciliation and nation-building in South Africa's parliament in May 1998: one nation consisted of a wealthy, white minority with a standard of living equal to that of Spain, while the other nation was a black population living in acute poverty with a standard of living comparable to that of Congo-Brazzaville. The transformation of South African society required that the country deal with its atrocious past. The national project that started in 1994 required a socio-economic and political transformation of society that was expected to lead to a change in attitudes, a change in political culture, and most importantly, a change in the material circumstances of the black population.

Johnny de Lange, the former chair of South Africa's parliamentary committee on Justice, describes a programme, the main content of which 'is the transformation of political, economic, social, ideological and moral aspects of the apartheid dispensation. This is achieved by building a single nation that acknowledges the diversity of its people; instilling a new sense of patriotism, healing the wounds of a shameful past; liberating black people from political and economic bondage; eradicating gender inequalities and women's oppression in particular; improving the quality of life through the eradication of poverty and the attainment of the basic needs of the majority; and creating a culture of

democracy and human rights.'⁴ De Lange thus identified the three elements of
the national political and socio-economic project which have become the cor-
nerstones of political debate in South Africa: reconciliation, reconstruction and
development. He also noted that, 'One of the ways to start the healing process
in South Africa is an honest assessment of the illness within our society, in an
attempt to give people, both perpetrators and victims, an opportunity to face
the past and its consequences and to start afresh.'⁵

The establishment of a truth commission was thus regarded as the moral
mechanism needed to build a 'new' South Africa from the ashes of a discredited
apartheid past. Of course the morality of the structure, if one is to be cynical,
was built on an immoral deal: it was a pact with the devil which took the rights
away from victims, and set an invidious precedent that is even now enshrined
in both international human rights law and international humanitarian law. The
influence of this precedent can now be seen in cases such as Liberia, Sierra Leone
and Chile where amnesties were granted for heinous human rights abuses.

But to create a secure space to transform and unify South Africa's two
societies of black and white, it was necessary to consider an amnesty. Leon
Wessels, like many others in the former apartheid regime, was relieved when
the post-amble to the Constitution was accepted, and amnesty became a real
possibility, since many whites had feared the threat of being prosecuted for
their past crimes. The post-amble reads: 'the divisions and strife of the past …
generated gross violations of human rights, the transgression of humanitarian
principles in violent conflicts and a legacy of hatred, fear, guilt and revenge.
These can now now be addressed on the basis that there is a need for understanding but not for vengeance, a need for reparation but not for retaliation, a
need for *ubuntu* but not for victimisation. In order to advance such reconciliation and reconstruction, amnesty shall be granted in respect of acts, omissions
and offences associated with political objectives and committed in the course
of the conflicts of the past.'⁶

While amnesty was a given due to the post-amble, it is clear that South
Africa's generals would not have accepted anything less from the negotiating
process. However, it is doubtful that they expected the amnesty deal that they
eventually received. We know that it was this clause that held up the signing of
the interim constitution, as South Africa's military top brass held their politicians to ransom. Apartheid's military did not want to be treated the way that
it had treated its former enemies.

What many fail to understand or appreciate is that South Africa could have had an amnesty committee that sat in secret and heard only from the perpetrators. Instead, the new black-led government decided that the amnesty process would be coupled with a process to examine the violations that victims had suffered and that their needs and concerns would also be taken into account.

Amnesties typically offend one's moral sensibilities, and yet increasingly, they have become necessary in the world of *realpolitik*. We would be foolish to pretend that South Africa would have come as far as it has today without this amnesty deal having been done. As South Africans celebrated a decade of democracy in 2004, one of the major legacies that the country has passed on to the world is the truth and reconciliation project. While there had been more than 15 other truth commissions before the South African one, none had been on the scale and magnitude of the South African commission and none had had the power to grant amnesty.

Looking back thirteen years later, it is clear South Africa had to be innovative, due to the difficulty of the circumstances in which the country found itself. Johnny de Lange noted:

> While the TRC is a product of our country's unique history and the nature of our particular transition, we share many similarities with other transitions especially in Latin America and Eastern Europe, which necessitated compromises that placed certain limitations on the final scope of our TRC.[7]

I mention seven of the most pertinent issues:

- A stalemate was reached in the balance of forces with neither side being able to claim outright victory;
- A negotiated settlement ensued – not a revolutionary over-throw, but a gradual shift from a dictatorship (a minority, illegitimate government) to democratic majority rule;
- A fragile democracy and a precarious national unity existed in 1994;
- The capacity of the outgoing regime – including the military and the security forces which commanded huge resources – to delay and derail the process or, at the least, to support and promote resistance to change, was enormous;
- A legacy of oppression and serious human rights violations existed;
- There was a determination to avoid a recurrence of human rights violations; and

- The establishment of a constitutional state marked a shift from parliamentary sovereignty to constitutional sovereignty.

A general amnesty would have allowed the military to remain largely untouched with its power base still mostly intact, and the new transitional state had to deal urgently with this issue. The gradual shift from one legal order to another meant that apartheid laws remained on the statute books. If prosecutions had taken place, they would have been detrimental to the liberation movements, criminalised under South Africa's apartheid laws. This would also have worked in favour of the security services; under then South African law, most of their members would have been protected.

In the last decade, the debate between the proponents of retributive justice and restorative justice has been intense. The realities of the peace deal brokered in South Africa have meant that, in most instances, the two mechanisms have been seen as different means to reach the same goal. In most conflict regions in the world, truth commissions and *ad hoc* tribunals have now been established.

It took a year for the legislation on the TRC to be passed after an incredible consultative process which involved many stakeholders, including civil society groups working with victims of apartheid. The Act that finally brought the TRC into being was the Promotion of National Unity and Reconciliation Act (34 of 1995).

It was clear from the outset that the intention of the new legislation was that the TRC, through its work, would promote national unity and reconciliation. The commission was frequently presented with a poisoned chalice: if it did its work effectively, of necessity, this work would cause divisions; and yet, at the same time, the TRC's work had to lay the basis for reconciliation.

The amnesty laws were challenged in the highest court of the land – the newly established Constitutional Court – by the relatives of prominent families who had fought against the apartheid system. The Biko, Mxenge and Ribeiro families, as well as the Azanian People's Organisation (AZAPO) all challenged the validity of the amnesty laws, which they contended had removed their rights to prosecution. These groups, which had all lost loved ones in the struggle against racist minority rule, sought to bring civil claims against the perpetrators of human rights abuses under apartheid.

The amnesty laws were challenged on the basis that the amnesty process would allow people who were guilty of committing crimes and gross abuses under apartheid to go unpunished. This was seen as inappropriate since apartheid was widely regarded as having been a crime against humanity, and South

Africa thus had an international obligation to punish those who had committed crimes under apartheid.

In an extraordinary judgment, the moral and political dilemmas that countries in transition face when dealing with their past were elegantly and logically presented by the late Justice Ismail Mahomed, the first black chief justice of South Africa. He argued that it was impossible to punish those who had committed such violations in the context of an internal armed conflict when it was now necessary, in the reconstruction of a new society, for former adversaries to work together. Mahomed noted that:

> The erstwhile adversaries of such a conflict inhabit the same sovereign territory. They have to live with each other and work with each other and the state concerned is best equipped to determine what measures may be the most conducive for the facilitation of such reconciliation and reconstruction.[8]

The former chief justice captured the despair and poignancy that many felt:

> This Act seeks to address this massive problem by encouraging these survivors and the dependants of the tortured and the wounded, the maimed and the dead to unburden their grief publicly, to receive the collective recognition of a new nation that they were wronged, and crucially, to help them discover what did in truth happen to their loved ones, where and under what circumstances it did happen and who was responsible ... With that incentive [of amnesty], what might unfold are objectives fundamental to the ethos of a new constitutional order.[9]

This discourse – even at the highest level in the Constitutional Court – deemed amnesty to be necessary for the rebuilding and reconciling of the nation.

Based on this discussion, many might be forgiven for thinking that all truth commissions have had reconciliation as their goal. However, before the South African commission, only the commission in Chile had been tasked with this role. Reconciliation presents a major challenge to any commission, and the South African one was no exception. In the evolution of the TRC, the most important objective was to prevent further violence and abuses of human rights. The deal which gave rise to South Africa's commission halted the violence, reduced the possibility of a military coup, and, at a political level, laid the basis for three peaceful elections (in 1994, 1999 and 2004) to take place in the country.

It is important when dealing with reconciliation that we distinguish between national or political reconciliation, and *individual* reconciliation. The strength of the South African commission was how, through its work, it was able to advance national political reconciliation. Looking back, it was an extraordinary process, since this was the first truth commission in the world to hold public hearings. The commission took its work to the people, importantly, reclaiming apartheid spaces throughout the country. As a member of the TRC, I travelled around South Africa with my colleagues visiting places that we had only known on maps. Sadly, wherever we went, the story was the same: horrific tales of torture and brutality on an unimaginable scale. Also, we saw people continuing to live in grinding poverty, at best eking out a survival.

When victims first started speaking out in South Africa, white South Africa was sceptical. Many felt that their testimonies were exaggerated and that these atrocities could not have happened. Of course, once the first amnesty hearings began, not only did white South Africa discover that they did happen, they also discovered that these events were much worse than many victims had testified. Many of us had already worked with detainees and so had a fairly informed view of what had happened under apartheid. However, even we were shocked at the depravity and horrors that had taken place, particularly after the 1980s.

It is important that we not denigrate how powerful the TRC experience has been for many perpetrators. Confronting their demons, the public exposure of their hidden lives in front of family and friends and the whole society, could not have left apartheid's henchmen unmarked or unchanged. As Priscilla Hayner, one of the foremost scholars on transitional justice, has noted:

> An official accounting and conclusion about the facts can allow opposing parties to debate and govern together without latent conflicts and bitterness over past lies. This is not to suggest that the knowledge or memory of past practices should not influence current politics but if basic points of fact continue to be the source of conflict or bitterness, political relationships may be strained. In a negotiated transition out of a civil war, these latent tensions may be of special concern, as opponents can move quickly from the battlefield to the floor of congress.[10]

The TRC process not only succeeded in formally uncovering much of the concealed and abominable past; but also helped many South Africans on personal journeys towards reconciliation with that past. It did not, of course, uncover all the gory details, but enough is now known to ensure that nobody can deny that the apartheid state was responsible for planning, ordering and perpetrating gross human rights violations against its own citizens. In addition, South Africans also learnt that their liberation movements had not always observed the tenets of international humanitarian law. This made it all the more surprising when former president F.W. de Klerk appeared before the commission, on behalf of the former state, and testified that human rights abuses were the work of a 'few bad apples' and that neither he nor his colleagues had known about these crimes. De Klerk implausibly argued that he had not known that the state had been financing death squads and that his government had not created an atmosphere in which these atrocities could flourish.

These words echoed *déjà vu*-like recently, when listening to US president George W. Bush, and his acerbic former defence secretary, Donald Rumsfeld, speak about the atrocities that had taken place in Abu Ghraib prison in Iraq after the 2003 invasion. Of course, politicians rarely commit to writing their approval of violations. Instead they create, with a nod and a wink, environments in which it is possible to commit violations, and duties and pressures that transform ordinary people into monsters.

The amnesty hearings provided an important lesson, since the men – and it was mostly men – appearing before it were quite ordinary. They would have described themselves as decent, God-fearing Christian men, and yet their actions were utterly ungodly. For many of us, the shock was that these were quite ordinary, quite pathetic men. The public uncovering of what they had done reinforced the banality of it all.

The TRC hearings had an extraordinary effect on the nation, since it involved a public shaming process for those involved. My criticism of the process was that it let white South Africans who had clearly been the main beneficiaries of apartheid, off the hook. They were allowed to disassociate themselves from these evil deeds. The foot soldiers took the blame, and those who had benefited from their deeds in preserving the monstrous system escaped to claim that they had been unaware of what had been done in their name. Mahmood Mamdani, a Ugandan scholar who was teaching at the University of Cape Town during this period, is also of the view that the TRC allowed the beneficiaries of apartheid to escape scrutiny.[11] By not also examining the effect of apartheid's policies, the TRC had allowed only the 'trigger-pullers' to bear the collective shame of the nation.

While the TRC has argued that it held hearings that examined the role of the judiciary, the security forces, the medical profession and business, in reality, the systematic nature of the social and economic aspects of apartheid were not examined in the same detail as its political and civil violations. Internally, we argued among ourselves as commissioners about whether our mandate restricted us from doing more. In retrospect and with hindsight comes greater wisdom. While the TRC became engaged with the national reconciliation project, the politics of redress were compromised by the process. The slogans that the commission adopted did not help this cause: 'Forgiveness: the Road to Reconciliation;' and 'The Truth will set you Free' were among these slogans. TRC chair Desmond Tutu became the embodiment of the 'forgiveness' project while the symbolism of Nelson Mandela holding hands with F.W. de Klerk resonated across the world: the embodiment of a remarkable nation reconciled.

As the TRC neared the end of its work, the cleavages within the nation began to show. In a poll conducted in 1998, many respondents suggested that the work of the commission had, in fact, exacerbated tensions within society. The national survey, by Market Research Africa (MRA) showed that more than two-thirds of the public believed that the revelations that had emerged from the work of the commission had made them more angry and bitter, and had led to deterioration in relations between the country's racial groups.

What was significant about the results of the survey was that public attitudes were divided along racial lines. While close to 90 per cent of those polled 'strongly disagreed or tended to disagree' that the commission would bring the races closer together, 54 per cent of blacks 'strongly agreed or tended to agree' that the races could now interact more harmoniously. Another 24 per cent remained neutral.[12] The political editor of *Business Day* at that time, Drew Forrest, concluded that: 'The inference must be that although blacks and whites agree that the commission has made people angry, they differ profoundly on whether it has advanced the cause of reconciliation.' He went on to argue that this situation 'was not irreconcilable'; and captured the crux of the debate, adding:

> They are right, as the black respondents confirm. It would be surprising if blacks were not enraged by the revelations that the government tried to develop a chemical programme to limit black fertility, or that white policemen cooked meat on a fire while incinerating the body of a murdered township youth on a fire nearby. What is striking, however is that close to 80 per cent of the MRA's black respondents do not regard such disclosures as an insuperable obstacle to better racial understanding and that half believe that 'the people in South Africa will now be able to live together more easily.'[13]

At many different individual levels, South Africans – black and white – have come together to deal with their past and have found a place in their hearts to deal with each other. However, many black South Africans are of the view that, if there had been a conscious material effort to do more than merely 'observe' on the part of beneficiaries, reconciliation among the races would have been advanced even further. The TRC must take responsibility for this; in this regard, Mahmood Mamdani is right. The commission did not demonstrate sufficiently how apartheid had been a structural *system* depriving black South Africans of education, proper living standards, and destroying the county's social and economic fabric in a way that still haunts South Africa today. Everything one sees and takes for granted, in the 'new' South Africa – the spectacular beauty of Cape Town, the skyscrapers of Johannesburg, and the lush farms of KwaZulu-Natal – came at a great cost: the exploitation of black South Africa. The wealth of white South Africa was built upon the biggest social engineering project in the world creating structures of economic power difficult to dismantle even today (see Adedeji in this volume). White South African business still largely refuses to talk about the past, refuses to acknowledge that apartheid made possible its huge profits, and that this all came at a huge cost which South Africans are still paying today. The legacy of apartheid is that the gap between the rich and the poor is still growing, and South Africa has today, along with Brazil, the highest Gini coefficient (measuring socio-economic inequality) in the world.

South Africa has secured political stability and there have been wonderful individual acts of reconciliation, but in the area of redress, the country has failed woefully. South Africa's black-led government has had to pass affirmative action laws, and developed the Black Economic Empowerment Charter to enact economic redress (see Shubane in this volume). The government was compelled to take these actions since the beneficiaries of apartheid effectively failed to come to the table at the great reconciliation feast. But the government did not help its own case. Once political peace had been achieved and the TRC had done its work, the government simply forgot about the victims of apartheid. It took five years after the TRC had handed in its initial report for the government to begin to pass reparation laws and to begin the process of paying out compensation to victims of apartheid. Many victims became embittered and felt that they had borne the brunt of the negotiated deal. Sadly, many died before reparations were paid out. Other victims have filed claims in the US under the Aliens Tort Law for reparations to be paid by international and national corporations that had benefited from apartheid. The South African government under Mbeki took the unprecedented step of entering the fray and filing papers in support of the motion brought by South African businesses that the claims should be thrown out, since the government itself was dealing with issues of reparations. The government's action, widely regarded as a major mistake, has embittered and disillusioned many.

One of the striking images from Zurich during South Africa's successful World Cup bid in 2004 was the presence of business leaders as being very much part of 'Team South Africa Inc.' White business has been embraced by the black-led government – without ever having properly acknowledged its role in the apartheid past.

It was widely believed that the disclosure of the truth in the TRC project would bring a measure of justice and closure to the victims; and that truth, justice and reparations were the necessary ingredients for reconciliation. Amnesty would be the price that South Africans paid in order to achieve reconciliation. It was also widely accepted that, for those who did not apply, prosecutions would loom large as a threat. As one of those who support a prosecution process for those who did not apply for amnesty, even I am faced with a contradiction: if F.W. de Klerk and P.W. Botha (who died in 2006) were allowed to go scot-free, is it fair to prosecute those who carried out their orders? These individuals continue to protest that they only did what they did under orders from the government of the day.

If only De Klerk had apologised to the nation, South Africans could have embraced him and, through him, those who had committed these crimes against the nation. The project of redress could have become a national one like that of reconciliation. Horacio Verbistsky, a Chilean journalist, makes this very point: '*Reconciliation* by who? After someone takes away your daughter, tortures her, disappears her, and then denies ever having done it – would you ever want to "reconcile" with those responsible? The word does not make sense here. The political discourse of reconciliation is profoundly immoral, because it denies the reality of what people have experienced. It isn't reasonable to expect people to reconcile after what happened here'.[14] Juan Mendes, the Argentinean former director of the Inter-American Institute of Human Rights, has argued that reconciliation 'was a code word for those who wanted nothing done. *Reconciliation* in Argentina was understood by victims to mean, "We are being asked to reconcile with our torturers, and they're being asked to do nothing."'[15]

CONCLUDING REFLECTIONS

I offer a few closing comments on reconciliation. First, a distinction needs to be drawn between national and political reconciliation, and individual reconciliation. National reconciliation can be achieved to a great degree by the opening of the past, uncovering what was hidden, and speaking openly of what has divided the nation. Individual reconciliation is far more complex. Forgiveness and healing are profoundly personal processes and cannot be handled by a committee or structure, but only by victims and perpetrators. Priscilla Hayner suggests that there are three questions that need to be asked in these cases:

> First, how is the past dealt with in the public sphere? In other words, do people talk about the past, is there still bitterness, and are people comfortable with discussing the past? Second, what are the relationships between past opponents? Are relationships based on the future or the past? Finally, is there one version of the past or many versions?[16]

While South Africans have began to walk down the road to reconciliation, the journey will only be complete when the 'two nations' – black and white – cease to exist; when poverty is eradicated; and when inequality diminishes. This requires a racial transformation of the economy, the racial transformation of the inequities in the land sector, and the ability to access the formal economy (see Adedeji; and Moyo and Hall in this volume). It also requires whites to acknowledge fully how they benefited from apartheid and their willingness to be part of a new nation. When the TRC report was debated in Parliament in February 1999, outgoing president, Nelson Mandela, said:

> But above all, the TRC Interim Report is a call to action. And as we put our thoughts together on the challenges ahead, we need to remind ourselves that the quest for reconciliation was the fundamental objective of the people's struggle, to set up a government based on the will of the people, and build a South Africa which indeed belongs to all. The quest for reconciliation was the spur that gave life to our difficult negotiations process and the agreements that emerged from it. The search for a nation at peace with itself is the primary motivation for our Reconstruction and Development Programme to build a better life for all. And the TRC issues a call, which we strongly endorse, for a recommitment in both public and private sectors, with renewed

vigour to the transformation of our structures and corporations through a combination of affirmative action and employment equity together with the strengthening of a culture of hard work, efficiency and honesty.[17]

Unless we heed this call, we will remain divided by race, inequality and poverty. The Cape Town-based Institute for Justice and Reconciliation (IJR), in its 2004 barometer noted: 'Thirty per cent of South Africans admit to wanting more frequent contact across racial divides ... Between April and November last year (2003) there was a ten per cent increase in the proportion of South Africans saying it is desirable to create one nation out of the groups that live in the country bringing the total portion in support to more than 80 per cent.'[18] Such views offer a glimmer of hope for South Africa's noble efforts at reconciliation.

4

South Africa in Africa: Behemoth, hegemon, partner or 'just another kid on the block'?

MAXI SCHOEMAN

In this chapter, I address the question of where – and how – South Africa fits into Africa. I examine the roles the international community and its African counterparts expect South Africa to play. These roles emerge from the expectations that other states have of South Africa, as well as from South Africa's own conception of its role and how it has acted to appropriate a role, particularly in Africa.

Such a consideration is important. A state may see its role in a certain way (conception), but this might not reflect the role others wish to allocate it or even the way it is viewed by others – perhaps a matter of beauty lying in the eye of the beholder.

On the other hand, I would argue that even if there is a difference between a state's self-image (and therefore its role conception) and the role it has been allocated by others, it is possible for the state to strive for, and attain, at least a partial position in the international hierarchy based on its conception of its own role and position.

In the conclusion, the chapter pays particular attention to the interaction between roles given (allocation) and roles taken (conception/appropriation). This should take us some way to answering the question posed in the sub-title of the chapter: is South Africa's role in Africa that of behemoth, hegemon, partner, or is it 'just another kid on the block'? The conclusion might very well be that South Africa deserves a mix of all these labels.

What is meant by each of these possible 'roles'? Of course, they are crude – hardly any country can be slotted into only one role – but they serve as useful markers for a range of characteristics, both of the country under consideration and of the ways in which member states are viewed within the international system.

Of course, one must also be careful: talking of states as if they are unitary actors is dangerous. Different sectors within a state may not share the same attitudes or goals. There may, for example, be a huge difference between government policies and business strategies and actions. These different aspects of particular states should be kept in mind when analysing South Africa's position in Africa.

A 'behemoth' or colossus can be defined as a big and powerful state (militarily and economically) that has very little sense of, or shows little care for, the effect of its actions on other states – whether in the global or the regional arena. This would describe a country that is either isolationist (the US after the First World War in 1918 is a good example) or one that pursues its own agenda aggressively without concern for the adverse effects such policies might have on its neighbours (Hitler's Germany in the 1930s springs to mind in this regard).

Contemporary American foreign policy has the characteristics of a behemoth: it is a state that does not seem to care about the impact of its policies and often prefers to go-it-alone. The attitude of the behemoth is Machiavellian: as long as it is feared, it does not seek to be admired. A behemoth prefers temporary 'coalitions of the willing' because permanent alliances require too many compromises. Yet, at the same time, this colossus believes itself to be a benign power with good intentions and therefore does not need to seek legitimacy from others. Peter Berger refers to the foreign policy approach of the George W. Bush administration as confusing the 'idea of power of arguments with arguments of power'.[1]

This chapter does not use the term 'hegemony' in the more or less pejorative sense often read into it, which in fact belongs more to the idea of 'behemoth'. In this chapter, hegemony refers to a country that plays a firm, strong, and credible leadership role, enabled not only by (in the neo-realist definition) hegemony tied to military and political power (so-called hard power measured in crude terms of 'more' or 'less'), but also on the ability to exercise unchallenged leadership.

To this conception of consensual hegemony, we may add the Gramscian notion that real power comes not so much from tangible resources as from the fact that the hegemon's ideology is acceptable to others, and forms a consensual order in its sphere of influence. The essence of hegemony is the power to persuade. A hegemon is therefore a leader that follows its own enlightened interest with positive spin-offs for others (see Adebajo in this volume).

Our third concept of 'partnership' has to do with shared goals and objectives, with equal treatment, even though not all partners may be equal in terms of the usual indices used to measure power (economic clout, military prowess, etc). This 'partnership' also involves tolerance and a commitment to the same set of values. Perhaps the most difficult aspect of 'partnership' is the fact that the word creates the impression of equality, impartiality and the absence of conflict. Partnership, at face value, implies that the partners share the same aims and objectives and pursue these in an atmosphere of mutual trust and with a view to mutual gain. This is not necessarily the case. Partners broadly share the same aims and objectives, but do not always agree on the strategies and tactics to be followed in order to realise their goals and objectives. The relationship between France, Germany and Britain in the European Union (EU) is a prime example of this. Broadly, these countries share the same objectives when it comes to European integration, but they often differ on the ways in which such objectives should be implemented. Furthermore, their very definitions of integration may differ – Paris and Berlin adopted the euro, London did not, believing that sharing the same currency does not necessarily make for better integration.

Our final concept is that of 'just another kid on the block', indicating ordinariness in the sense that South Africa can not, even had it wanted to, fulfil any of the other roles that imply at least a modicum of 'more' – more economic clout, more military might, more capability to set and influence agendas, more capacity to act on its conception/s of its interests. Being just another kid on the block means that a country will 'win some and lose some' as far as its foreign policy objectives are concerned, and that it will join with others in alliances, or use jumping-on-the-bandwagon tactics. A country adopts such an approach not because – as a partner or hegemon – it realises that such strategies would be in its own best interest, but because it has very little choice and often jostles with other states for scarce resources, be these tangible – for example development aid – or intangible – status and prestige.

The image of 'just another kid on the block' does not preclude incidences or niches in which a state may have a particularly strong market or even status (for example Switzerland), or be considered part of a fairly powerful bloc (Italy as a member of the G8 and the EU). Such states do not command interest and attention in the same way that those classified as belonging to the categories behemoth, hegemon or partner, do.

With the above categories in mind, we now turn to a discussion of South Africa in Africa – the ways in which the government engages officially with its African counterparts, and in which particular sectors within the country – such as the business community – interact with, and in, other African states. As mentioned above, there is no such thing as a state acting as a unitary actor.

Even within governments and bureaucracies, sharp differences may exist in the area of foreign policy.[2] Exploring South Africa's relations with the rest of Africa underscores this lack of 'unitary behaviour' in many instances, as will be argued below.

SOUTH AFRICA IN AFRICA: ROLE PRESCRIPTION

Adam Habib and Thakeng Selinyane have noted that, with the birth of the 'new' democratic South Africa in 1994, 'many African states explicitly voiced the expectation that South Africa would play an active role in promoting the cause of the developing world in international fora.'[3] This sentiment was echoed by Jack Spence who refers to expectations of a 'constructive and dynamic role, both regionally and globally'[4]. Spence is in fact representing the expectations of the North – that South Africa should be a responsible global citizen, a position that actually points to potentially serious problems in that the country's international role may clash with its continental and even domestic role.[5]

A far more nuanced, careful and realistic view of what South Africa's role in Africa could and should be was expressed by Adebayo Adedeji in his 1996 publication, *South Africa and Africa: Within or Apart?* The author concludes that 'inevitably, South Africa must be a major player'[6] in the process of 'establishing mutually beneficial political and socio-economic relations' in Africa. It is Adedeji's use of the word 'inevitable', and also his warning that South Africa can only play this role if it manages to fulfil a number of conditions, that merit exploration. The requirements that Adedeji saw as necessary for South Africa to take up a leadership position in Africa are:

- A strong political commitment at the highest level of leadership;
- a resistance to trying to 'straddle the two worlds of Africa and the North', in other words, choosing a total commitment to Africa through a continental policy rather than being seen to be promoting Western interests; and
- at the domestic level, a 'fundamental socio-economic transformation that transcends political empowerment'[7] (see also Adedeji in this volume).

Essentially, Adedeji argues for a mix of hegemony and partnership. He warns that if these requirements are not met, South Africa could turn either into a behemoth (seeking only its own benefit), or into just another kid on the block –

another typical post-independence African country, beset by problems of declining socio-economic conditions and internal strife.

How is South Africa playing this leadership role and what does it mean in terms of how the country is perceived by its peers on the continent? Once again, we ask: is the country a behemoth, a hegemon, a partner, or just another kid on the block?

SOUTH AFRICA IN AFRICA: ROLE CONCEPTION

South Africa did not immediately adopt a continental policy in 1994 – apart from a somewhat formalistic and diplomatically oriented position. But since its inception in 1999, the government of Thabo Mbeki has increasingly emphasised the importance of Africa as a whole, as opposed to the Nelson Mandela administration's focus on Southern Africa between 1994 and 1999. As South Africa moved away from the Reconstruction and Development Programme (RDP), which placed a heavy emphasis on Southern Africa and adopted the Growth, Employment and Redistribution policy (GEAR) – a neoliberal economic strategy – in 1996, Africa beyond Southern Africa also came into sharper focus. South Africa accepted globalisation as the probable saviour of the African continent, a perspective initially cloaked in the term African Renaissance. By 2001, this vision had been more fully developed into the New Partnership for Africa's Development (NEPAD).

This progression from the RDP to GEAR to NEPAD needs some unpacking, as it is in these developments that the tale of 'South Africa in Africa' has unfolded. But these developments took place within a context broader than Africa, as the need for peace and security on the continent became more urgent. No longer could South Africa proclaim – rather than act on – its support for peace and security, or its preference for the peaceful resolution of conflicts. The NEPAD document is uncompromising in noting that, without peace there will be no development and without development, there will be no peace on the continent. Equally, South Africa realised that in order to achieve these goals, it would have to 'dirty its hands' by becoming involved in efforts at conflict resolution, political transformation and socio-economic development on the continent. In short, South Africa had to choose a role in Africa that transcended the Southern African region and also transcended handwringing and idealistic posturing from the sidelines. South Africa's business community was already involved in the rest of the continent, expanding the country's business interests and forging ever-closer ties with African countries beyond the Southern African Development Community (SADC) region. Finally, international expectations that South Africa should take more responsibility for peacekeeping on the continent motivated the Mbeki government's growing involvement in continental affairs.

From its position of standing somewhat apart from Africa beyond the Southern African region (except rhetorically), South Africa's foreign minister, Nkosazana Dlamini-Zuma[8] could claim by 2003 that: 'South Africa has both a responsibility and an obligation to contribute to the continent's renewal in building a peaceful and prosperous continent' and that 'South Africans are playing a major role' in various initiatives on the continent. In the ANC's weekly newsletter, *ANC Today* of 18 June 2004, South Africa's role in Africa was described as follows:

> Considering South Africa's position of relative strength on the continent and in international affairs, the country has a responsibility to play a leadership role in Africa's socio-economic development agenda in terms of developing policy, correctly channelling resources, supporting implementation and directing the NEPAD process, as well as to play a role in the international arena in negotiating a new partnership paradigm and ending Africa's marginalisation in the global community.[9]

South Africa increasingly considers itself to be an important player in, and on behalf of, Africa, with engagement at various levels by a wide range of its domestic actors.

The political sphere

We will next consider the country and the role of some of its key actors in the political and economic spheres.

- South Africa led the development of NEPAD and the African Union (AU) (see Landsberg in this volume). South Africa was also the first chair of the AU in 2002/2003; the country hosts the NEPAD secretariat and the Pan African Parliament (PAP); and won a three-year seat on the AU's fifteen-member Peace and Security Council (PSC) in 2004 and a two-year seat on the UN Security Council in 2006. South Africa's involvement in continental organisations reflects its efforts to be a partner rather than a pioneering hegemon. This is an effort to exercise influence and power through multilateral institutions in which the preference is for rules-based change and progress (a position that South Africa also holds in broader international fora and one that the country obviously views as an easier position to adopt than that of a hegemon). The role of hegemon would require a much more outspoken and forthright approach that might create tensions and raise accusations of 'bullying'.

- At the level of bilateral relations, South Africa has significantly expanded the number of bilateral and joint commissions with African states, now being party to no less than thirteen such agreements. South Africa concluded several agreements in 2000 and also has a joint bilateral commission agreement with Morocco: the only African country that is not a member of the AU. The agreement with Rwanda is aimed, among other things, at establishing common positions on democracy and security. The binational commission with Nigeria aims to coordinate the political, social and economic countries of both countries (see Adebajo in this volume).

- South Africa has opened more than 40 diplomatic missions in Africa since 1994.

- As far as peacekeeping efforts are concerned, the period after 2000 has seen a dramatic increase in South Africa's involvement in peacekeeping efforts in Africa. Initially, South Africa restricted such commitments to mediation and negotiation, as in the dying days of the Mobutu Sese Seko regime in Zaire (now the Democratic Republic of Congo [DRC]). But lately, also in line with its SADC and AU responsibilities, South Africa's military has become deeply involved not only in brokering peace agreements in the DRC and Burundi, but also in peacekeeping operations in these two countries, 'giving teeth' to the agreements and closely interacting with the UN and its then secretary-general, Kofi Annan, on the transformation of the peacekeeping force in Burundi from an AU into a UN force, with South Africa providing the core force for the mission in 2004 (see Curtis in this volume).

- Closely linked to South Africa's military role in Africa is its role in disarmament, which goes well beyond the continent. South Africa voluntarily gave up its own nuclear weapons programme, joining the Nuclear Non-Proliferation Treaty (NPT) and promoting general nuclear disarmament after 1994. The country also played a significant role in the development of the international ban on anti-personnel landmines and in various initiatives to end the proliferation of small arms. South Africa has been involved in landmine clearance in Angola and Mozambique and played a big role in the Kimberley process aimed at banning the sale of 'blood diamonds'. In certain instances, though, South Africa's arms sales to a number of countries, some of them in Africa, such as Rwanda and Uganda, generated fierce criticism at home and abroad.

- South Africa also adopted what is widely considered to be the most progressive legislation on mercenarism in its 1998 Regulation of Foreign Military Assistance Act.

- Finally, one can talk of South Africa's commitment to the 'democracy through peace deal' model that served as its own vehicle for democratic transition. The inherent requirements of this model – liberal democratic principles, negotiation, respect for human rights and a neoliberal economic base – became a product that the country was keen to 'export' and promote (see Curtis in this volume). As mentioned earlier, it took some time before South Africa was willing to commit to supporting this export 'product' with active peacekeeping engagements. As Chris Landsberg has noted, South Africa has on occasion been accused of being a lackey of the West and of pursuing a western agenda on the continent.[10] This is a particularly sensitive charge for the country's post-apartheid black government.

Economic involvement

Much more contentious than South Africa's political role in Africa is its economic role – a role that in some quarters has created doubts about the country's genuine intentions towards Africa, as well as about the true nature of its domestic transformation. Examining the facts and figures, it is not difficult to understand the suspicions and doubts surrounding South Africa's role, and to wonder to what extent the country is becoming a behemoth on the continent.

South Africa's increasing economic ties with the rest of Africa are impressive. The country's trade with the rest of the continent saw a 328 per cent increase from 1993 to 2003. Foreign direct investment into the rest of Africa increased from R8 billion in 1996 to R26 billion in 2000.[11] Large South African corporations from a range of economic sectors are taking advantage of the opportunities offered by the demise of apartheid. The retail, banking, telecommunications, hotel, tourist, mining, and other infrastructure industries and sectors are increasingly moving into the continent. In some instances, such as the trans-border spatial development initiatives, this is business conducted in partnership with other countries, and often with external investment forming part of these deals (see Hudson in this volume).

The balance of South Africa's trade with the rest of Africa is hugely in South Africa's favour: R13 billion in imports from Africa in 2003, R39 billion in exports to the continent.[12] This has resulted inevitably, in tensions between South Africa and some of its trading partners who accuse the country of being the 'bully on the block'. This situation is very difficult for South Africa: the government has to promote wealth, development and socio-economic upliftment domestically, and cannot afford, at the same time, to neglect the similar aspirations of its neighbours. South Africa also has to trade with countries with very small or narrow productive bases – largely a product of Africa's uneven incorporation into the global economy.

Furthermore, the South African government encourages its business community's forays into the rest of the continent by providing support for exporters through the Department of Trade and Industry (DTI) offices in a number of countries, while the Industrial Development Corporation (IDC) provides funding for investment projects. Again, there is a down-side to these investments: much of the investment opportunities, particularly in Southern Africa, are within the infrastructure sector of countries such as Angola, devastated by a civil war for which part of the blame can be laid at the door of the 'old' apartheid South Africa. In a strange irony, South Africa therefore stands to benefit from the very damage it had done in an earlier era.

The way in which South Africa has become involved in Africa attests to what M. Webber and M. Smith refer to in their overview of foreign policy in a transformed world of 2002: not only has the nature of issues on the foreign policy agendas of countries changed dramatically over the past several decades, interests and participation have also changed, and South Africa is no exception to this trend.[13]

Two points can be made about these political and economic aspects of South Africa's involvement in Africa:

- First, these activities are consistent with the country's long-stated foreign policy ideals of promoting democracy and human rights, and contributing to international peace and security. They also contribute to the implementation of South Africa's more tangible foreign policy goals of creating wealth and security.

- Second, these activities point to an increasing involvement in, and with, Africa, moving from an initial concentration on the SADC region to embracing the whole continent.

Such policy objectives are not easily achieved, though, and a number of obstacles and challenges remain. Chief among these is the need for South Africa to engage economically in such a way as to improve the balance of trade with its African partners. In the long run, the huge imbalance in trade between South Africa and its neighbours can only contribute to tensions and conflicts and to renewed accusations of South Africa acting like a 'sub-imperial' power that has bought wholeheartedly into the 'Washington Consensus'. At this stage, South Africa is clearly hoping that the various regional economic development initiatives through NEPAD will encourage economic growth and development across the continent. Failure to achieve NEPAD's objectives – with large trade imbalances continuing to be in favour of South Africa – will doubtless result in the country being viewed as a behemoth. Simultaneous failure on the part of South Africa to achieve higher economic growth rates and a more equitable distribution of wealth domestically, could transform the country into 'just another kid on the block' in Africa (see Shubane in this volume).

There are also other trade and economic problems that South Africa is not only expected to play a role in solving, but has, in fact, committed itself to finding solutions for; or, at the very least, has agreed to act as a spokesperson for Africa and the global South in these contexts. Thus far these efforts have met with little success. Negotiations within the World Trade Organisation (WTO) regarding Northern agricultural subsidies is one such issue, as witnessed by the disappointing outcomes of the WTO meeting in Hong Kong in December 2005. Another is the failure to find a solution to Africa's debt problem of $290 billion.[14] The NEPAD document states that member countries will have to engage with existing debt relief mechanisms 'before seeking recourse through NEPAD'.

What has happened to South Africa's previous very public stance on the need for debt forgiveness for African countries? Has this principle been dropped, or relegated to the multilateral level where South Africa no longer has to take direct responsibility? Multilateralism, incidentally, apart from its obvious advantages, also holds some disadvantages, depending on one's point of departure. It is an approach ideally suited to partnership, but two things need to be said about such partnerships: first, partnership is not necessarily a positive position; rather, it describes a neutral position indicating rules of conduct based on equality.

Second, the idea of 'partnership' does not tell us what the partnership is about, yet it may serve to legitimise unpopular behaviour, and provide 'legitimate' reasons for adopting and implementing unpopular decisions. To an extent, partnership can provide an easy way out of taking difficult decisions.

Politically, there are other obstacles to South Africa playing a leadership role on the continent. The peace agreements brokered in the DRC and Burundi are fragile. Outside Africa, South Africa has unsuccessfully attempted to become involved in resolving the Middle East conflict.

In Africa, South Africa is hoping to act multilaterally, through the various mechanisms provided by the AU such as NEPAD, the Conference on Security, Stability and Cooperation in Africa (CSSDCA), the PSC, as well as in partnership with the UN.

Another obstacle to South Africa's leadership role is the patchy compliance by AU member countries with the spirit and letter of its Constitutive Act of 2000. South Africa seems to find itself between a rock and a hard place. On the one hand, it is committed to democratic governance, a norm not necessarily shared by all African leaders. On the other hand, South Africa has to contend with the principles of sovereignty and non-interference in the internal affairs of member states which have so often been abused in Africa by despotic leaders at the expense of their citizens. A foreign policy that values democratic governance need not do so at the cost of respect for national sovereignty, or vice versa. Yet, it would seem that in certain instances, this is exactly what has happened. It is not always clear which of these principles enjoy priority in South Africa's relations with its neighbours. There are examples of South African interventions in a country *despite* the principle of sovereignty, because democratic governance is at stake. The South African invasion of Lesotho in 1998 is a prime example – and the result has been what seems to be the evolution of a stable multi-party system of governance in that country (see Matlosa in this volume). Yet many analysts point to the case of Zimbabwe, where South Africa is blatantly putting the sovereignty principle above that of its commitment to the principle of democratic governance.

The difficulties surrounding Zimbabwe – South Africa's closest and biggest neighbour – are complex. Advocating intervention is easy from the sidelines, yet one cannot but make three key observations about the way in which South Africa has been dealing with this situation:

- First, it is difficult to influence a large neighbour. Zimbabwe is not Lesotho.

- Second, certain deep-seated issues have not yet been resolved in the post-liberation era, at least in Southern Africa. The future of liberation movements-turned-governments has not yet been fully addressed. Does their liberation status ensure and guarantee perpetual rule? This is an important question for former liberation movements that now find themselves transformed into governing parties, such as the ANC and Namibia's South West Africa People's Organisation (SWAPO). How deep is the commitment of these movements to the principle of democratic governance, a principle relatively easy to adopt while one is in a 'politically safe' position of overwhelming electoral superiority?
- Related to the above is the third point: leadership/hegemony can work only as long as the hegemon is a genuine leader whose rules and values are generally accepted by others. There seems to be widespread support within the SADC region in the case of Zimbabwe, for the rule and values of Robert Mugabe, rather than those values espoused by Mbeki. Hegemony is also a difficult position to attain. Traditional attributes of power such as economic and military strength are necessary but not sufficient to become a hegemon. Sufficiency would seem to lie in the acceptance of the hegemon's goals, objectives, rules and values. Clearly Zimbabwe – at least as far as its regime is concerned – is not convinced that it would benefit from toeing the South African line, given its present embattled position. Harare's conduct begs the question of whether South Africa is a hegemon or partner in this instance, or whether it is, like so many of its African counterparts, 'just another kid on the block' when it comes to Africa's older and more reactionary leaders and stronger countries.

CONCLUSION

So how are we to assess South Africa's actual role in Africa, in the light of this analysis? Is South Africa guilty of what Patrick Bond calls – with reference to Mbeki – 'talking left, while walking right'?[15] Or is its position closer to Habib and Selinyane's verdict of 'schizophrenia': a mixture of hegemonic and 'just another kid on the block' tendencies?[16] I posit that these three authors are all partly right, but that South Africa's failure to fulfil what may have been seen as an 'inevitable' leadership role in Africa has more to do with at least three factors. (Again, it is necessary to point to the fact that the various sectors involved in the country's relations in Africa – government, business, and civil society – do not form a monolithic bloc. Some sectors conform more to one 'image' of the country and others to a different 'image'.)

These three factors, which should provide a tentative answer to the question posed in the title of this chapter, are:

First, the global setting within which South Africa and other African countries have to manage their policies with each other and harmonise attempts at closer integration. Second, Adebayo Adedeji's 'advice' on the domestic setting – that leadership in Africa will fail without domestic socio-economic transformation – and third, closely related to the second point is the issue of race in South Africa – both as a direct variable impacting the country's foreign policy and as a dynamic perceived in a specific way by many of South Africa's African neighbours (see Sooka in this volume). This last point is contentious, but needs to be discussed within South Africa and with other countries across the continent.

It is clear that South Africa is striving for a hegemonic role in Africa that also includes strong elements of partnership. In some instances, South Africa does come across as 'just another kid on the block.' As far as its business community's activities on the continent are concerned, there are allegations of the role of a behemoth – rabid self-interest (that is, profit) – being pursued at the cost of mutual benefit and good neighbourliness. Here in particular, it is important for South Africa to play the role of partner, and for the government to play the role of a hegemon with a well-developed sense of its responsibilities being based on its own long-term interests of building a strong and vibrant continent. But being a hegemon is a difficult role for South Africa to play and will remain so for a long time to come. The hegemon has to be able, for example, to 'use its domestic market to stabilise the larger continental economy and it must be able to resist domestic pressures to look out only for its citizens' own interests.'[17] Given its own domestic needs and demands, playing the role of a genuine hegemon in Africa will be difficult for South Africa, at least in the more traditional sense in which hegemony refers to a political and economic role.

South Africa's role in Africa is an evolving one, indicating increased involvement at various levels. It will not be an easy role, and embedding the country into the continent as a mixture of a hegemon and a partner will require not only dedicated leadership, but also immense sensitivity, not only from the country's political leaders, but also from those in business and civil society. In order to attain and maintain credibility and legitimacy and to mobilise the resources necessary for acting both as a hegemon and a partner, the greatest challenge lies in South Africa's domestic transformation.

5

South Africa and regional security in Southern Africa

KHABELE MATLOSA

When South Africa celebrated its ten years of democracy in 2004, were its neighbours part of the celebrations or not? Had South Africa managed to become a part of the regional community or was it still developing apart from the region? Had the ANC government managed to deal with the critical questions that were raised by the renowned Nigerian political economist, Adebajo Adedeji in 1996 in an interesting, thought-provoking and seminal treatise suggestively entitled *South Africa & Africa: Within or Apart?*[1]

The critical challenge that has confronted South Africa in its regional relations since 1994 has been how it can relate to its neighbours in ways that do not suggest insensitive hegemonism, but that at the same time provide regional leadership. This chapter assesses contemporary regional security trends, highlighting the dominant role of South Africa and outlining possible trends in the next decade following South Africa's third democratic election in 2004. I emphasise the strong role of South Africa in Southern Africa's evolving security landscape based on the country's politico-economic power *vis-à-vis* its neighbours: a historical reality defined and sustained by the structural make-up of the regional political economy (see Adedeji in this volume).

The chapter begins by contextualising the political economy of Southern Africa and revisiting the nebulous notion of regional security. The discussion on regional political economy and regional security provides a conceptual entry point into the debate around South Africa's role in the region. The contemporary trends of regional security are explored by assessing South Africa's role in the Lesotho crises of 1994 and 1998, and its differences with Zimbabwe over the Southern African Development Community's (SADC) Organ for Politics, Defence and Security (OPDS). In the process, I highlight the hegemonic role of South Africa, but note that Tshwane (Pretoria) has not exercised its regional dominance through unilateral hegemonic designs, for fear of projecting itself as a sub-imperial power whose foreign policy outreach is driven more by self-interest than by regional and continental imperatives. In order to address these sensitivities, South Africa, under the leadership of both presidents Nelson Mandela (1994–1999) and Thabo Mbeki (1999–2007), has attempted painstakingly to balance its national interests with its continental objectives.

I argue that South Africa's foreign policy outreach has been much more pronounced under Mbeki's leadership, given his commitment to the philosophy and vision of an 'African Renaissance'. The Mandela administration, in contrast, was driven by a different imperative of national reconciliation. I conclude the chapter with a discussion of the possible trends that are likely to drive South Africa's regional policy in its second decade of democracy following its elections in 2004. What emerges from this chapter is an interesting trend of inconsistencies in how South African foreign policy is projected through SADC. Yet ironically, South Africa will likely attempt to project its external image largely through just such multilateral institutions such as SADC, the AU and NEPAD (see Landsberg in this volume). South Africa seems poised to play a critical role in ensuring peace and security in the region and the African continent, primarily through multilateral institutions.

During 2004, the South African foreign minister, Nkosazana Dlamani-Zuma, chaired the AU's newly-established Peace and Security Council (PSC), and South Africa hosts the 265-member Pan-African Parliament (PAP), largely footing its bill of around $100 million: a sure sign of South Africa's commitment to African unity and integration within Mbeki's vision of an African Renaissance. Even more significantly, South Africa was chair of SADC's OPDS between August 2004 and August 2005. It is within this backdrop of South Africa's historical role in regional security, especially since the demise of apartheid, that we can better understand the deeper significance of Tshwane policymakers' perception that, 'South Africa's development is dependent on increased security, democracy and economic growth and development in southern Africa and the rest of the continent'.[2]

Ignoring calls from some scholars, like Adam Habib and Nthakeng Selinyane, for South Africa to play the role of an assertive regional hegemon,[3] the country has carefully played its leadership role through partnerships, emphasising multilateral engagement with regional issues, particularly security (see Schoeman in this volume). I argue that South Africa will continue to rely primarily on multilateral diplomacy in the next decade through assessing its economic, security and governance roles in Southern Africa.

CONTEXTUAL AND CONCEPTUAL FRAME OF ANALYSIS

Integrated regional political economy

Given the degree of integration of Southern African states, one can justifiably perceive the region to constitute a single political economy, with South Africa playing a visibly pivotal role. Southern Africa, as a region, is inextricably integrated and articulated in dependency to South Africa in many respects. For example, a majority of Southern African states are economically dependent on South Africa, and this trend, which expresses itself largely through migration patterns, is much more pronounced in those countries that, together with South Africa, constitute the Southern African Customs Union (SACU): Botswana, Lesotho, Namibia and Swaziland. Given this historically and structurally entrenched economic dependence dating back to 1910, South Africa's political dominance is more pronounced in these countries, although patterns and degrees of this preponderance differ from country to country. It is in this sense that South Africa's critical role in Southern Africa's political economy can be better understood. According to the late South African scholar, Sam Nolutshungu:

> South Africa has always attached considerable importance to the rest of Africa for both economic and strategic reasons. The Union inherited from British imperialism an economic sphere of influence in southern Africa characterised by the radial articulation of different colonial territories to the South African economy, and, in large measure, the mediation of their relations with international capital through and via South Africa which became 'a centre in the periphery' with its own sub-imperial ambitions.[4]

Thus, the incontrovertible truism of regional integration in Southern Africa today is the established hegemonic power of South Africa over the rest of its neighbours. It is not surprising therefore that American scholar Robert Rotberg observed that:

> Politically, too, South Africa is the center of the region. President Nelson Mandela's charisma and statesmanship have made a major difference. As sure as his word and touch have been within South Africa, he has been even more effective and successful internationally. Given the unquestioned competence

and prestige of South Africa's leadership, and the power and prominence of the South African nation, it is no wonder that Mandela's country has emerged from nearly four decades of apartheid as the new orchestrator of Southern African policy and the strongest force within potentially the most powerful of Africa's regions.[5]

The manner in which South Africa relates to its neighbours is thus critical for sustainable regional integration in Southern Africa. Do other countries recognise South Africa as a regional hegemon? What responsibilities and obligations does South Africa promote for, and on behalf of, the region as a regional hegemon? Is South Africa a benign or malign hegemon towards its neighbours, as they strive to achieve regional integration? All these are important questions around the regional balance of power that could either make or break sustainable regional integration.[6]

It is the interdependence among Southern African states that must be exploited for greater regional integration. The economic linkages among Southern African states include formal and informal cross-border human and capital movements, infrastructural networks and shared natural resources.[7] It is worth noting that this interdependence does not usually lead to mutual economic gain among regional states and, in some instances, amounts to dependence of the relatively worse-off states on the relatively well-endowed states. Southern Africa's disarticulated, fragmented and narrow productive base exhibits the internal weakness of the regional political economy. In almost all the countries that form part of the region, the industrial sector has experienced slow growth, and the agricultural sector has either stagnated or is generally in decline. Most of these economies are driven largely by service sectors that provide a major part of these countries' GDP as detailed in the table on the facing page.[8]

Furthermore, some Southern African countries are still overly dependent on particular sectors, concentrating production on either a single mineral or agricultural export. This again suggests that the regional economy lacks sufficient diversification for trade creation through regional cooperation. Both internal and external dynamics help explain the generally unimpressive performance of the regional economy in the recent past. This is also evidenced by lack of progress in sustainable human development, as indicated by the United Nations Development Programme (UNDP) in its 2005 global human development report[9] (see Adedeji in this volume).

CHANGES IN CONTRIBUTIONS TO GDP OF KEY SECTORS IN
SADC COUNTRIES (%)

COUNTRY	AGRICULTURE		INDUSTRY (manufacturing)		SERVICES	
	1993	2003	1993	2003	1993	2003
Angola	11,6	8,2	51,2 (5,7)	60,3 (3,8)	37,2	31,5
Botswana	4,5	2,5	47,9 (4,3)	43,5 (4,4)	47,6	54,1
DRC	51,3	58,7	16,4 (6,8)	12,5 (5,3)	32,3	28,8
Lesotho	18,5	15,7	39,2 (16,6)	42,1 (18,5)	42,3	42,1
Malawi	48,9	38,4	24,1 (15,7)	14,9 (9,5)	27,0	46,7
Mauritius	11,2	6,1	33,0 (23,5)	30,6 (22,0)	55,8	63,3
Mozambique	29,5	26,1	20,7 (7,3)	31,2 (15,5)	49,8	42,8
Namibia	9,5	10,0	29,0 (14,1)	31,1 (10,9)	61,5	59,1
South Africa	4,2	3,8	35,5 (21,1)	31,0 (18,9)	60,3	65,2
Swaziland	13,2	11,3	41,5 (34,4)	47,8 (39,9)	45,2	40,8
Tanzania	48,1	45	15,6 (7,5)	16,4 (7,2)	36,3	38,6
Zambia	34,1	19,3	41,9 (27,9)	29,7 (11,3)	24,0	51,1
Zimbabwe	15,0	17,4	33,3 (23,0)	23,8 (13,0)	51,6	58,8

Source: G. Oosthuizen. 2006. *The Southern African Development Community: The organization, its policies and prospects.* Midrand: Institute for Global Dialogue, p. 262.

Yet another important feature of Southern Africa's political economy is the entrenched culture of human movements across boundaries. Migration is so entrenched in Southern Africa that, in his seminal work that classified various regions of Africa in 1981, Egyptian scholar Samir Amin characterised Southern Africa as 'Africa of the Labour Reserves.'[10] This characterisation depicts the uniqueness of the capitalist penetration in this region relative to other African regions. In Southern Africa, settler colonialism concentrated investment, extraction and production mainly in South Africa and Zimbabwe. These two countries became the principal poles of capital accumulation within the region, while neighbouring states became 'labour reserves' servicing the labour needs of the two white settler colonies. This pattern of migration – both oscillatory and permanent – involving both skilled and semi-skilled labour, still characterises the political economy of Southern Africa. Four major types of migration can be identified throughout Southern Africa. First, contract migration of semi-skilled labour mainly to South African mines; second, 'undocumented' or irregular migration of unskilled labour who informally cross borders and seek menial jobs such as street vendors, domestic workers or farmworkers; third, refugees who cross borders either to flee political persecution or because they are forcefully displaced by violent internal conflicts; and fourth, 'brain drain' involving the migration of highly-skilled professional labour that amounts, in most instances, to 'resource drain' on the part of a supply state, and 'resource gain' on the part of a recipient state.[11] Writing about migration as a challenge for the nation-state project in Southern Africa, Peter Vale and I observed in 1995 that:

> Literally, thousands of traders are ignoring borders to broaden their economic prospects. Fishermen are moving … in search of new catches, while farmers are moving to escape drought and pestilence. Others, such as the female traders who travel daily between Zimbabwe and South Africa, represent new important forms of employment in a region desperately short of jobs. It is certainly true that many new forms of cross border activity, such as smuggling of small arms and narcotics and rustling of cattle, for instance, are far less benign than the movements of peasants and professionals in search of work. It is also true that these issues are readily translated into 'security' concerns by nation-states.[12]

Interestingly, much of the flow of human movement has tended to come from the rest of the region into South Africa, and this trend has been viewed, in some policy circles in Tshwane, as a security threat requiring military and police build-up around the country's expansive, albeit porous, borders. Not only has migration into South Africa from the SADC region been perceived within South Africa itself as a threat to security, but foreign migrants – especially those from the rest of Africa – have tended to be greeted with an upsurge of sometimes brutal xenophobia. This negative perception of foreign migrants has run counter to regional integration impulses, although Thabo Mbeki's policies aimed at an African Renaissance have helped somewhat to reduce the intensity of South Africa's negative image in the rest of Africa.

SOUTH AFRICA'S REGIONAL ROLE, 1994-2006

When South Africa's black majority gained their political independence in 1994, the key question was whether or not South Africa would develop as a part of, or apart from, Southern Africa and the African continent. On the regional security front, fairly optimistic projections marked the academic discourse. In this regard, Robert Rotberg remarked that 'South Africa, once the warmonger of the region is now a potential peacemaker and peacekeeper. Its combined army, airforce and navy of 100 000 [now 55 000] is far larger, better organised, and trained than that of Zimbabwe or those of the smaller, weaker nations in the region'.[13] For his part, eminent Nigerian scholar-administrator, Adebayo Adedeji, was quick to advise, wisely, that, 'it is ... of paramount importance that South Africa defines its place in Africa positively and affirmatively. The momentum generated by the enthusiasm over the successful elections [in 1994] and the assumption of power by the liberation movement should be allowed to propel the state to the second phase. Instead of looking furtively at the rest of the world – second guessing how that world may perceive and judge its actions – South Africa should become a self-confident force, reinvigorating Africa's drive and resourcefulness and playing a leadership role in this important endeavour: putting Africa's house in order'.[14]

During the apartheid era, South Africa was, to all intents and purposes, the region's major destabilising force until the early 1990s. A regional hegemonic role since its historic election of 1994 has shifted the imperatives of *Pax Pretoriana* from being malevolent to being benign. This has occurred through Nelson Mandela's policy of nation-building and reconciliation within the country, diplomatic engagement in South Africa's 'near abroad'[15] and later, through Thabo Mbeki's much more forthright embrace of *Pax Africana*: promoting peace on the continent through regional actors.[16] Thus Mbeki's twin policy of *Pax South Africana* and *Pax Africana* has attempted – largely successfully – to coalesce South Africa's interests with the larger interests of the African continent. This is one important way to understand South Africa's leadership role in continental initiatives such as the African Union and NEPAD. It is thus not surprising that Mbeki's passion for *Pax Africana,* predicated on African Renaissance, dovetailed neatly into the Conference on Security, Stability, Development and Cooperation in Africa (CSSDCA) pioneered by Nigerian president, Olusegun Obasanjo in 1991[17] (see Adebajo in this volume). It is no surprise, therefore, that today, Africa's continental security agenda is driven primarily by the twin imperatives of NEPAD and the CSSDCA through the African Union.

Following the demise of apartheid, South Africa has begun to play an important role in regional security efforts in Southern Africa largely through SADC.
Since 1992, SADC has attempted to drive both its economic integration and
collective security projects in tandem. This, in part, rests on the belief that the
region forms a single economy even if truncated, fragmented and bifurcated.
Southern Africa still constitutes a single security and conflict complex. Article
4 of the SADC Treaty of 1992 notes the following five principles to which its
member states must adhere:

- The sovereign equality of all member states;
- solidarity, peace and security;
- human rights, democracy and the rule of law;
- equity, balance and mutual benefit; and
- the peaceful settlement of disputes.[18]

SADC'S 'ORGAN FAILURE' – THE LIMPING OPDS

As SADC states were attempting to find the appropriate framework for security cooperation after the dissolution of the Frontline States (FLS), a violent
conflict erupted in Lesotho in 1994. This conflict involved faction-fighting
within the country's armed forces, and a conflict between these forces and the
new Basutoland Congress Party (BCP) government which had been installed
in power through a general election in 1993. Lesotho's King Letsie III also
became embroiled in this conflict. Through the initiatives of the London-based
Commonwealth secretariat and the Organisation of African Unity (OAU), SADC's
members embarked on preventive diplomacy to manage the crisis after internal
efforts at conflict resolution had failed to bear fruit. SADC established a task
force on the Lesotho crisis, comprising Botswana, South Africa and Zimbabwe.
With a mandate to find a lasting solution to the conflict, the task force engaged
the disputing parties in preventive diplomacy for the larger part of 1994. Despite
these concerted diplomatic initiatives, the conflict escalated: the BCP government established a commission of inquiry on alleged political interference by
King Letsie III's father, Moshoeshoe II, and, in response, the King suspended
the constitution and dissolved the BCP government.[19]

King Letsie III then appointed a six-person Council of Ministers to form a
transitional government in a move that was deemed to be a 'royal coup'. After
holding an emergency meeting in Gaborone, Botswana, the SADC task force

intervened in this crisis and ultimately reinstated the legitimate BCP government in power through a memorandum of agreement signed on 2 September 1994. The memorandum committed the parties to promote peace, reconciliation, and the stability of the country. Much more importantly, the memorandum stated that Pretoria, Gaborone and Harare would remain the guarantors of Lesotho's democracy and stability, with the power to intervene on behalf of SADC in case of any instability that threatened the country's democracy. Following the 1998 SADC summit in Mauritius, Mozambique was added to the list of SADC countries mandated to guarantee Lesotho's fragile democracy.

This was the first time that SADC had taken such a bold and decisive action in a regional political crisis. This arrangement also signified that Lesotho's sovereignty had been eroded in the eyes not only of its own people, but – also equally importantly – in the eyes of other SADC states. For instance, Lesotho was chair of SADC's Organ for Politics, Defence and Security in 2003/04, yet much of its leadership role on regional security issues depended on South African support. This may, in part, explain why the efforts of Lesotho's prime minister, Pakalitha Mosisili, to meet the Zimbabwean government on that country's political crisis, failed. Yet the Zimbabwean president, Robert Mugabe and opposition parties, discussed these issues with the South African president, Thabo Mbeki and the South African government on a regular basis. This development was not totally surprising: Zimbabwe was one of the four guarantors of Lesotho's democracy and was not willing to allow a small, land-locked country to monitor its political situation, even while Lesotho chaired the OPDS. Of course, this situation confirms the old international relations dictum that the big and powerful nations do what they want, while the small and weak nations accept what they must.

In the recent political history of Lesotho, no incident better fits this dictum than the 1998 violent conflict and its regional political ramifications. Following its second general election since the restoration of democracy and the withdrawal of the military from state power, a number of opposition parties contested the election outcome, camped within the premises of King Letsie III's palace, and organised protests which in many instances led to violent encounters with the security forces. What seemed to be a disagreement over the election outcome progressively turned into a violent conflict, nearly escalating into civil war.

The belligerent forces in this dispute, namely the Lesotho Congress for Democracy (LCD) government and the main opposition parties, could not resolve this conflict through dialogue and constructive mechanisms of conflict resolution as neither side was prepared to shift from their positions regarding the election and its outcome. Regional actors then became directly involved in the Lesotho conflict through both diplomatic and military means. South Africa, through its Minister of Safety and Security, Sydney Mufamadi, played a major diplomatic role in mediating a settlement of the violent conflict leading to the establishment of the Interim Political Authority (IPA) that proposed a variety of constitutional and electoral reforms as part of conflict resolution efforts. Additionally, a prominent judge of the South African Constitutional Court, Justice Pius Langa, investigated the allegations of electoral fraud and irregularities surrounding the 1998 general election by some opposition parties. It is thus evident that South Africa (and not SADC) played the most prominent role in the management of the Lesotho crisis of 1998 both militarily and diplomatically. That South Africa assigned its minister of safety and security to manage Lesotho's political crisis and not the minister of foreign affairs, is a clear sign of the low position accorded to Lesotho in South Africa's diplomatic pecking order. Peter Vale, a respected scholar of South Africa's foreign policy, noted that:

> It must be said that not a little of the symbolism in the relationship between South Africa and Lesotho is located in the fact that South Africa's minister of safety and security, not foreign affairs, led the delegation that delivered the Langa Report to Lesotho's government and the country's people. If there had been a hope that it would quell the anger of the protestors, let alone, restore order, this was mistaken.[20]

Not only did South Africa get directly involved in the Lesotho conflict diplomatically, but at the invitation of the LCD government, South Africa and Botswana sent military forces to Lesotho.

There are sharply divided perceptions about the character and nature of this military expedition. But whether it is perceived as an 'invasion' or an 'intervention', the stark reality is that, following a dismal failure of local efforts by civil society and churches to contain the crisis and resolve the conflict through constructive means, South Africa and Botswana were able to rein in the belligerent forces both diplomatically and militarily, and ultimately Lesotho's near civil war was nipped in the bud. Ironically, the role of South Africa and Botswana in Lesotho's 1998 conflict was not managed through the then embattled OPDS.

It is now common knowledge that the Organ was marked by a deep-seated crisis leading to its paralysis for about six years. Some SADC member states (led by South Africa) felt that the OPDS should be fully integrated within SADC through its founding treaty and become answerable to the SADC summit. Others (led by Zimbabwe) argued for an independent structure with its own chairperson, able to respond to political and security issues without reference to SADC's broader agenda.[21]

The gulf of opinion between and among SADC members regarding the structure, mandate and leadership of the OPDS undoubtedly paralysed this important institution and generated mutual distrust and tension among SADC members. As a result, the OPDS generally failed to respond to multiple conflict situations in the region, including the protracted and costly war in Angola and sporadic political unrest in Swaziland. It was only in 1998 and 1999 that SADC was able to make a collective effort to sanction military interventions aimed at resolving intra-state conflicts in Lesotho and the DRC respectively. By 2000, the Lesotho conflict had been sufficiently resolved and the parties reconciled, while a tenuous political settlement of the DRC conflict was achieved in 2002 both through military intervention by Zimbabwe, Angola and Namibia, and the peace process largely brokered by Mbeki and Angola's Eduardo dos Santos. Clearly, the health of the OPDS as a regulatory mechanism for peace and security in the region remains extremely poor owing primarily to complications at birth.

It was not only balance of power politics that was at work here. The personality of the then leaders in Pretoria and Harare – Nelson Mandela and Robert Mugabe – also played a considerable role in the conflict over the OPDS. The key point here is that, in Southern African politics, personality matters as much (if not more) than power politics, institutions, systems and structures. Mandela's personality mattered immensely in South Africa's political change of 1994 and its aftermath, including its foreign policy outreach. 'Madiba' still has enormous stature in South African politics in the Mbeki era. In some instances, when it suits his political stance, Mbeki has found it convenient to don the aura of Mandela's charismatic personality, though Mandela exited from state power in 1999.

The same is true of Zimbabwe: Mugabe's personality is critical to understanding Zimbabwe's internal political development as well as its foreign policy projection. The personalities of both leaders have therefore had a significant bearing on the progress (or lack thereof) of SADC's efforts at regional security cooperation. The political change in South Africa in 1999, which saw Thabo Mbeki take the reins of power from Mandela, put paid to the Mandela-Mugabe tussle over the OPDS. The Pan-Africanist thrust of Mbeki's governance style endeared him to the Mugabe regime, and this was reinforced by his 'quiet diplomacy' towards Zimbabwe.[22]

When a proposal for an Association of Southern African States (ASAS) was tabled at the SADC summit in Johannesburg in August 1995, 'Zimbabwe ... apparently insisted that the permanent chairmanship of ASAS should be given to the longest serving SADC head of state (then already Mugabe), but it was Namibia's proposal that a two-yearly revolving chairmanship would be more appropriate which had won the day.'[23]

The OPDS was officially launched in Gaborone, Botswana, on 28 June 1996 and formally adopted during the SADC summit of the same year in Maseru, Lesotho. The launch of the OPDS was attended by the presidents of South Africa, Zimbabwe, Namibia, Botswana and Mozambique; the deputy prime ministers of Lesotho and Mauritius; and the foreign ministers of Tanzania, Zambia and Swaziland. Angola was not represented.

During the launch, Mugabe was confirmed as chairman of the OPDS. In his address, he argued that the establishment of the OPDS represented a firm commitment and resolve by regional leaders that Southern Africa would 'never again recede to the situation of conflict and confrontation. SADC leaders [sought] to build a new Southern Africa focused on 'peace and development, democracy and protection of human rights.'[24] The 1996 SADC summit in Maseru ostensibly endorsed the OPDS, although details were avoided as, in traditional diplomatic fashion, major differences were papered over. However, even after the Maseru summit, disagreements continued to deepen and eventually culminated in unprecedented political wrangling among SADC members during the 1997 SADC summit in Blantyre, Malawi. The clash was principally between South Africa and Zimbabwe, over whether the OPDS was subordinate to, or separate from, the SADC summit. The then president of South Africa, Nelson Mandela, who was chairing the SADC summit, threatened that, if a decision were made to establish the OPDS as a separate entity, his country would be forced to relinquish SADC's chairmanship. Due primarily to the tensions that marked deliberations at the cantankerous Blantyre summit, the meeting's final communiqué did not provide any details on the summit decisions on the OPDS. The summit downplayed the intensity of the internal conflict on the Organ through a diplomatically couched reference to the importance of the OPDS as a vehicle for strengthening democracy in the region and cooperation in defence and security matters. Evidently, the Blantyre summit did not resolve the two-summit impasse that remained at the heart of the paralysis of the OPDS.

As the tension and bitter conflict between Mandela and Mugabe continued, debate focused on the tug-of-war between the two elderly and respected statesmen over the OPDS. Only two years later, during the 1999 SADC summit in Maputo, Mozambique, was a decision taken to review the Organ. This was to be part of a review of all SADC institutions for purposes of restructuring the secretariat and its agencies. Between the 1998 and 1999 SADC summits, there were conflicting perceptions between South Africa and Zimbabwe regarding the functionality of the OPDS. While Pretoria contended that the Organ had been suspended, Harare maintained that the OPDS was alive and kicking since it continued to execute its mandate through SADC's Inter-state Security and Defence Committee. Conflicting strategies over SADC's involvement in the DRC conflict further aggravated the internal crisis within the OPDS. South Africa and some SADC member states (including Botswana, Lesotho, Swaziland and Mozambique) preferred preventive diplomacy and a negotiated settlement of the conflict, while Zimbabwe, Angola and Namibia opted for a military intervention into the DRC in 1998 in support of Laurent Kabila's government.

As this division within SADC widened, Angola, Namibia, Zimbabwe and the DRC signed a mutual defence pact in April 1999 that excluded other SADC states, despite the organisation's earlier commitment to a regional defence pact. After a long and protracted tug-of-war over the control and functions of the OPDS, steady progress has been made towards normalising the situation and giving the OPDS its appropriate position and role within SADC structures. The 1999 SADC summit in Maputo finally broke the impasse over the OPDS. In SADC summits after 1997, the tense discussions over the Organ have disappeared. Significantly, the SADC summit of 2003 held in Tanzania adopted the new SADC Mutual Defence Pact (MDP) that, among other things, aims to promote security cooperation in the following three areas:

- Joint military training and peacekeeping exercises;
- exchange of military intelligence and information, subject to constraints of national security; and
- joint research, development and production/procurement of military equipment.[25]

While it is not entirely clear how the SADC-wide mutual defence pact will relate to the mutual defence pact signed by Angola, Namibia, DRC and Zimbabwe, it is significant that the stalemate around the OPDS and the bitter dispute between Mandela and Mugabe was resolved in 1999: the year that Mandela was replaced by Thabo Mbeki as president of South Africa. It is worth noting that, whereas

Mandela was much more concerned with national reconciliation at home and diplomatic engagement with the 'near-abroad', Mbeki's approach was slightly different. Mbeki was more concerned than Mandela with economic transformation at home and promoting an 'African Renaissance' in the region and the continent. Thus, the end of the Mandela-Mugabe tussle came at an auspicious moment. It is also worth noting that the 2000 SADC summit in Windhoek, Namibia, deliberately avoided a discussion on the future of the OPDS. However, SADC's extraordinary meeting of its council of ministers held in Swaziland in 2001 made considerable progress towards resolving its OPDS 'organ failure'. In its communiqué, the meeting resolved that:

1. the OPDS must become an integral part of the SADC summit and answerable to the chair of SADC;
2. the leadership of the OPDS should rotate annually on a troika basis;
3. the 1992 SADC treaty must be amended to accommodate the restructuring of the OPDS;
4. the restructured OPDS would be a subject of discussion during the forthcoming SADC summit in Malawi in August 2001 where a revised protocol on peace and security was to be presented; and
5. Robert Mugabe would remain chair of the OPDS until the 2001 summit which would elect another chair.[26]

Undoubtedly, 2001 was a significant year for SADC's efforts at promoting security cooperation. It was during this year that a major stumbling block to collective security in the region was removed. Indeed, during the substantive SADC summit in Blantyre Malawi, in 2001, the decision relating to the restructuring of the OPDS was officially adopted. Furthermore, SADC member states signed the revised version of the Protocol on Politics, Defence and Security. According to this protocol, the OPDS is mainly responsible for managing both inter-state and intra-state conflicts; promoting political integration and security cooperation (including facilitating the signing of a multilateral mutual defence pact); devising a common foreign policy of SADC member states; promoting democratic governance; developing regional peacekeeping capacity within SADC; and ensuring observance of UN and other international conventions in relation to peace, security and conflict management initiatives. The protocol further states that the objectives of the OPDS would include:

- Promoting peace and security in the region;
- protecting people and safeguarding the development of the region against instability arising from a breakdown of law and order, intra-state conflict, inter-state conflict and aggression;
- promoting regional coordination and cooperation on matters related to security and defence and the establishment of appropriate mechanisms;
- considering enforcement action in accordance with international law as a matter of last resort where peaceful means have failed;
- considering the development of a collective security capacity and concluding a mutual defence pact to respond to external military threats; and
- developing the peacekeeping capacity of national defence forces and coordinating the participation of state parties in international and regional peacekeeping operations.

The protocol also resolved the leadership of the OPDS as follows:

- The Summit shall elect a chairperson and deputy chairperson of the OPDS on the basis of rotation among the members of the summit, except that the chairperson and deputy chairperson of the summit shall not simultaneously be the chairperson of the OPDS;
- The term of office of the chairperson and deputy chairperson of the OPDS shall be one year respectively; and
- The chairperson of the OPDS shall consult with the SADC Troika and report to the summit.[27]

PROSPECTS FOR SOUTH AFRICA'S REGIONAL ROLE, 2006–16

Since its 2004 election and the ten-year celebration of its constitution in 2006, South Africa's regional role has been enhanced. The 2004 election has not only ensured and solidified the legitimacy of the ruling ANC government at home, it has also enhanced its regional and international credibility. Increased domestic legitimacy and enhanced foreign credibility are bound to embolden South Africa in its foreign policy, especially in its immediate neighbourhood. This final section attempts to assess South Africa's likely regional relations in the next decade, and suggests that there are likely to be more continuities than discontinuities in both policy and practice. We should remain conscious of the internal and external dynamics that will shape and/or influence South Africa's regional foreign policy in its second decade of democracy.

The first projection to make in relation to South Africa's regional role over the period 2006–2016, is that the country will remain the region's dominant power, with tremendous influence on peace and security issues in the region and beyond.

South Africa's successful 2004 election will also position it strategically to encourage its neighbours towards democratic consolidation, peace and stability. The country is likely to play this regional role highly sensitively, first and foremost in response to its own interests, and to the fears and interests of its neighbours, while responding less and less to the exhortations and pressures placed on South Africa by the West. It is worth noting that the West would prefer South Africa to be a hegemonic power directing the future and destiny of Southern Africa through a more aggressive, assertive and unilateralist foreign policy outreach. This has been most pronounced in the case of Zimbabwe. Thus far, South Africa has avoided this approach. It is worth noting, though, that recently some calls have also been made for South Africa to exercise an avowedly hegemonic role in its relations with its regional neighbours. Contesting the notion of a 'pivotal state' – advocated by Garth Le Pere and Chris Landsberg – in terms of South Africa's regional role, Adam Habib and Nthakeng Selinyane, in contrast have argued that:

> South Africa's role should be that of a hegemon. Simply being a pivotal state, an important one, means a rejection of the role of leadership. This is not in the interest of South Africa; nor of other states in the region. Instability in Southern Africa, which hinders development and democracy, will be addressed only when a regional hegemon is prepared to underwrite these objectives. If that does not happen, South Africa's economic goals will remain compromised.[28]

Whatever the conceptual and policy differences between a pivotal state and a hegemonic state, the reality is that South Africa has projected its regional leadership role through multilateral partnerships and avoided heavy-handed hegemonic designs because, in large measure, of its unpleasant historical baggage (see the Introduction to this volume). We posit that this role will continue for some time to come, especially in the next decade of the country's democracy.

Second, South Africa will continue to pursue a foreign policy geared towards managing violent conflicts in the region and on the continent through both bilateral and multilateral arrangements despite the earlier failures of its controversial military intervention in Lesotho in 1998. Garth Shelton makes a sound observation in this regard:

> Despite the problems encountered in the Lesotho peace-enforcement operation, the SANDF has become increasingly involved in other similar, but less demanding missions. On 1 September 1999, the SANDF began deployments to the Democratic Republic of Congo (DRC) as part of the UN's peacekeeping operation there. This was followed in November 2001 by a smaller SANDF military observer mission to Ethiopia and Eritrea. In April 2001, a technical support force of 150 was deployed to the DRC to assist the 3 000 strong UN peacekeeping mission, followed ... by a far larger contingent. In December 2001 a four-person observer team was sent to Comoros to participate in OAU election monitoring and weapons collections. Since 2001, a fairly large SANDF contingent of almost 700 troops has been stationed in Burundi as part of a UN-endorsed mission to protect VIPs and provide military assistance to the transitional government.[29]

Of course, it is worth noting that there will always be variations in South Africa's approaches to managing regional conflicts depending on the country concerned. That is why Tshwane has responded in different ways to the political crisis in Lesotho and the equally compelling crisis situations in the DRC, Angola, Swaziland and Zimbabwe. While both Swaziland and Lesotho are small land-locked and impoverished states directly under South Africa's economic suzerainty, Zimbabwe was, until recently, a strong economy and is second only to Mozambique as South Africa's main regional trading partner. The DRC and Angola are highly resource-endowed and potentially rich economies, and neither country is dependent on the regionally dominant South African economy (on Angola and Mozambique, see Conchiglia in this volume).

Third, South Africa will continue to avoid unilateral interventionism that could give regional states the impression that it is acting like a bull in a China shop. Outside Africa, this unilateral approach has proved the main undoing of America's foreign policy towards Afghanistan and Iraq, which was predicated on a 'war on terror' which the South African government has itself criticised. Instead of opting for George W. Bush-style unilateral hegemonism, South Africa should opt for collective leadership acting largely through existing multilateral institutions such as SADC, the AU, and NEPAD. After making a concerted effort to win the hosting of the Pan-African Parliament – competing against Libya and Egypt – South Africa was mandated by the AU summit of July 2004 to become home to the 265-member Pan-African Parliament. The cost of constructing the PAP is estimated at between $14 million and $25 million and it goes without saying that South Africa 'will foot the bill'.[30]

Fourth, this multilateral approach will be pursued in line with Mbeki's African Renaissance vision. As Shelton puts it: 'South Africa's active participation in peacekeeping also clearly forms part of Mbeki's efforts to advance the African Renaissance by contributing to greater peace and stability in Africa ... President Mbeki has stressed that "without peace, stability and democracy" Africa has no chance of economic development and prosperity'.[31] In the areas of regional security and democratisation within SADC, South Africa's role over the past decade has been marked by a deliberate diplomacy of collective leadership and an overt avoidance of unilateral hegemonism in part due to the past apartheid regime's regional destabilisation. Mbeki's 'quiet diplomacy' towards Zimbabwe, which has earned him both friends and enemies at home and abroad, should be understood within this context. South Africa's regional policy over the next five years is spelled out in the ANC's election manifesto as speeding up 'economic integration in Southern Africa and strengthening democracy, peace and stability as well as economic growth and development; and in particular, devot[ing] time and resources to assist in social and economic reconstruction in Zimbabwe, Democratic Republic of Congo, Angola and Swaziland'.[32]

Fifth, we should also make a specific point regarding South Africa's relations with Lesotho, given the unique geopolitical location of the latter *vis-à-vis* the former. South Africa intervened militarily during the Lesotho conflict of 1998, while at the same time being openly critical of Zimbabwe's intervention in the DRC, launched in collaboration with Angola and Namibia in the same year.

In order to camouflage the hegemonic design of its military intervention in Lesotho, South Africa involved Botswana in the operation so that the mission could pass as a 'SADC intervention'; in much the same way that the DRC intervention was described as a 'SADC intervention' by Angola, Namibia and Zimbabwe. South Africa's interventionist political postures towards Lesotho have to be understood in the context of the latter's location in the belly of South Africa, which raises the stakes every time instability threatens political order within Lesotho. Realpolitik suggests that South Africa is always bound to consider Lesotho's insecurity as directly affecting its own security. Thus, the puzzle that still needs to be resolved is whether South Africa's 1998 military intervention in Lesotho was predicated upon Tshwane's desire for Maseru to embrace democratic governance, restoration of political stability, or safeguarding South Africa's own interests, especially around the Lesotho Highlands Water Project. Kenyan scholar Rok Ajulu aptly posited that, whereas during the apartheid era Lesotho was a hostage dependency par excellence always struggling for survival in that 'rough neighbourhood'; today, Lesotho resembles a semi-colony of the newly formulated SADC in which South Africa remains the country's prime patron.[33] Ajulu further observed that 'Lesotho has progressively become the subject of regional diplomacy as SADC power brokers attempt to subordinate it to the wider regional logic of democratisation.'[34] Thus, Lesotho is not only an important 'sphere of influence' for South Africa, but is economically an integral part of the country. But in order to avoid sensitivities linked both to the old era of destabilisation and to eschew suspicions of imperial and hegemonic ambitions, South Africa will, in future, intervene in Lesotho not on its own accord, but in collaboration with other SADC states. South Africa's relations with Lesotho will always be unique and different from those with other SADC member states, given the unique position of Lesotho as a hostage state overwhelmingly dependent on South Africa both for economic survival, as well as internal and external security.

For example, South Africa 'quietly' observed the general election in Lesotho held on 17 February 2007 with keen interest. Tshwane continues to monitor closely the ostensibly tense post-election situation in Lesotho, given that oppositions parties – especially the new All Basotho Convention, the Basotho National Party, Marematlou Freedom Party and the Alliance for Congress Parties – raised objections about the electoral process and its outcome, whch returned the incumbent government to power. In the immediate aftermath of this dispute, South Africa adopted a cautious 'quiet diplomacy' approach, covertly cajoling the parties to compromise without overtly intervening. In order to avoid criticisms of using 'big brother' tactics and unilateralism, Tshwane's future involvement in Lesotho is likely to take the route of multilateralism, especially through SADC and the AU.

Sixth, now that South Africa has undergone its third democratic election, it is able to focus its attention on how democracy evolves in the SADC region and other parts of the continent from a moral high ground. South Africa and its non-governmental organisations (NGOs) have closely monitored elections in 2004 in Malawi, Namibia, Botswana, and Mozambique. Tshwane has led SADC election observer missions during the general elections in Botswana, Namibia and Mozambique. South Africa plays this regional role in line with its broader continental role within NEPAD, especially the African Peer Review Mechanism (APRM). South Africa underwent its own self-assessment as part of the APRM process in 2006 (see Landsberg in this volume). Following the successful completion of the APRM process in Ghana and Rwanda, South Africa faced enormous pressure to complete a credible, legitimate and nationally-owned APRM process. South Africa's concern for regional democratisation is born out of the recognition that insecurity in any part of the SADC region could translate into insecurity for all other SADC member states. Thus, in terms of Tshwane's regional relations, the twin processes of security and democratisation could form the fulcrum of its future foreign policy in SADC and Africa as a whole.

One of the most important developments around democratisation in the region has been the adoption of the SADC Principles and Guidelines Governing Democratic Elections, which in accordance with the AU principles adopted in Durban in July 2002, commit member states to seven principles for democratic governance through credible and legitimate elections:

- Full participation of citizens in the political process;
- freedom of association;
- political tolerance;
- equal opportunity for all political parties to access the state media;
- equal opportunity to exercise the right to vote and be voted for;
- independence of the judiciary and impartiality of the electoral institutions; and
- voter education.[35]

During the SADC summit in Tanzania in 2003, Lesotho's prime minister, Pakalitha Mosisili, as chair of the OPDS, presented the Strategic Indicative Plan for the OPDS (SIPO) which essentially defines how SADC's security and political mandate would be operationalised with a view to achieving regional peace and institutionalising democratic governance.[36] SIPO views one of the key objectives of the OPDS to be the promotion and development of democratic institutions and practices by SADC members and the encouragement of the observance of universal human rights. In order to achieve this objective, SIPO offers the following five policies:

- Establishment of common electoral standards in the region including a code of electoral conduct (hence the adoption of the above guidelines during the Mauritius summit of August 2004);
- promotion of the principles of democracy and 'good governance';
- encouragement of political parties to accept the outcome of elections held in accordance with both the African Union and the SADC Electoral Standards;
- establishment and defining the functions of a SADC Electoral Commission; and,
- establishment of a Regional Commission for the promotion of, and respect for, human rights.[37]

South Africa faces a Herculean task in ensuring the implementation of SIPO and the adherence to the Principles and Guidelines governing democratic elections in the region. The first tests of the principles, during 2004 and 2005, have been the elections in Botswana, Namibia, Mozambique (in 2004), Zimbabwe, Tanzania, and Mauritius (in 2005).

Finally, while much progress has been made to heal the old wounds of apartheid in South Africa itself through, for example, the Truth and Reconciliation Commission (TRC) process under the able stewardship of Archbishop Desmond Tutu (see Sooka in this volume), not much healing has been done by South Africa in the 'near abroad' of the SADC region. In the recent past, various 'cleansing ceremonies' have been held in Mozambique, Lesotho and South Africa, and these are planned to continue. These initiatives do play an important role towards healing the wounds of apartheid in the region. However, some have called for reparations to be paid to those countries that suffered socio-economic, political and other costs due to the apartheid regime's destabilisation of its neighbours. According to Nigerian scholar, Adekeye Adebajo, 'South Africa should consider paying reparations to its neighbours for its past military and economic destruction.'[38] I argue, however, that it may not be possible for South Africa – given its own domestic economic problems and the demands for economic transformation within the country – to pay reparations to its neighbours. Instead, South Africa should make a deliberate effort to ensure a more equitable regional development process through SACU and SADC, as well as through building other bilateral relations with its neighbours.

CONCLUSION

This chapter has explored regional security with a view to locating South Africa's role in the post-Cold War era. I have explored South Africa's dominant role in Southern Africa's evolving security architecture and suggested that this dominance will continue in the foreseeable future. In order to understand regional security, one needs first to make sense of the broad features of the political economy of the region. It is worth noting that, to a considerable degree, the nature of the regional political economy and the manner in which regional economies relate to each other is one of the key determinants of the patterns and evolution of the security landscape in Southern Africa. This conceptual understanding helps us explore and understand contemporary trends in regional security in the post-apartheid era. It has also assisted us in projecting possible scenarios for regional security and South Africa's regional role in the next decade. The pattern of regional security initiatives in Southern Africa has been state-centric and has addressed more state than human security challenges. The key question is thus whether the SIPO adopted by SADC during its annual summit in Mauritius in August 2004 will go beyond the state-centric nature of the regional institution's security initiatives.

South Africa's regional dominance of Southern Africa is likely to continue in the foreseeable future. This situation will allow the country to play an important role in how regional security evolves, and we are likely to witness more continuity than discontinuity in respect to South Africa's regional relations over the next decade. Security in Southern Africa will be driven more and more by a projection of South Africa's regional image, through multilateral bodies such as SADC, than by unilateral hegemonism. South Africa will remain sensitive to the fears of bullying tactics from its neighbours, due to its history of apartheid destabilisation, particularly in the 1980s. South Africa is thus likely to continue to link its national interests with imperatives for regional and continental integration though SADC, NEPAD and the AU. While Tshwane may adopt a unilateral hegemonic approach to small, dependent economies such as Lesotho and Swaziland, this approach will not be employed in cases of larger and less dependent economies such as the DRC, Angola and Zimbabwe. All three countries could eventually compete with South Africa for regional economic and political dominance in Southern Africa.

In terms of the prospects for South Africa's regional role in the next decade, we proffer five conclusions. Firstly, South Africa will remain a dominant regional force with corresponding leverage on the region's evolving security architecture. Second, much of South Africa's regional leverage will be invested in promoting democratisation in the region and managing violent conflicts, through a strategy that aims to advance the country's national, strategic, and commercial interests as well as promoting regional security and stability. However, at almost all times, South Africa's national interest will reign supreme over regional concerns. Third, South Africa will exert its regional influence more and more through multilateral approaches and by deliberately avoiding the unilateral hegemonism of the apartheid era. Fourth, this foreign policy outreach – dubbed 'quiet diplomacy' – will dovetail neatly into Thabo Mbeki's African Renaissance vision, which in part triggered the transformation of the OAU into the AU. Finally, this strategy will also be consonant with Mbeki's passionate commitment to continental initiatives such as NEPAD and the APRM.

6

South Africa's economic expansion into Africa: Neo-colonialism or development?

JUDI HUDSON

South Africa's *Financial Mail* posed an interesting question in 2003:

> Will the nations of Africa be able to look back and say that the SA companies played a critical role in their recovery? Or will they be regarded as exploitative neo-colonialists?[1]

Four years later, the answer remains unclear.

Few could have predicted the speed at which South Africa has become the largest investor in the rest of Africa, eclipsing even the recent increased interest from non-African investors. This 'rush' has been described as 'one of the biggest economic phenomena of the last decade'.[2] South Africa's relative strength on the continent and the fact the country is a key political player through initiatives such as NEPAD, suggests that South Africa can play a leadership role in the promotion of peaceful democratic transitions, 'good governance' and human rights.

This situation – in which South African companies are building a presence across the continent, its politicians promote an 'African Renaissance' and president Thabo Mbeki speaks for the developing world in international fora – is somewhat different from the apartheid years when South Africa was an agent of destabilisation and consequently isolated. Once a pariah state, South Africa now 'seems poised to dominate the continent that once shunned its products and leaders'.[3] The more recent concerns are that South Africa's rapid corporate expansion has led to new relations of dependency and exploitation of workers in the African operations of these companies; in addition to unequal exchange and terms of trade that disproportionately favour South Africa. Some have felt that while 'partnership' may be South Africa's official policy, in power terms 'hegemon' may be closer to reality (see Schoeman in this volume).

As the strongest economy in Africa, South Africa's economic role on the continent is complex. To what extent has South Africa become 'big brother' in Africa? How best can the country respond to allegations of being the 'new colonisers'? Is South African capital playing a sub-imperialist role in Africa or is it a 'motor for revival'? What informs the South African perspective as its firms fan out across the continent? To what extent do South African businesses see themselves as ambassadors for South Africa as they move into the continent? Is the peacemaking role that is being played at the regional level being undercut by the mercantilism of some South African corporates? Are South African companies taking out more than they put into African countries, dominating markets to the detriment of local industries? What kinds of standards and operating procedures are these firms applying to their African operations in terms of labour, human rights or environmental quality? How can positive – rather than exploitative – outcomes of this expansion into the continent be maximised?

The right answer to these questions is that we do not yet know the full details of this remarkable phenomenon. There is little strong research-based evidence from which to draw firm conclusions; evidence is often patchy, contradictory, over reliant on anecdote and reported 'perceptions'. Nevertheless, some thirteen years into South Africa's democracy, it is important to reflect on these issues and more broadly, the economic role that South Africa has played on the African continent and the challenges and opportunities that this role presents. Enough data has been generated to draw some tentative conclusions and make some policy recommendations on this vital issue, one that will determine the future perception of South Africa's role in Africa.

SOUTH AFRICA: A PIVOTAL BUT RELATIVELY SMALL PLAYER

In just over a decade of transition from pariah to legitimate player, South Africa has asserted its presence on the continent through corporate and parastatal investments, which in turn generate trade. In so doing, South Africa has become pivotal to the flow of capital, goods and people on the continent. South African businesses have emerged as the leading investors on the continent (outside the mining and energy sectors) and are involved in a number of sectors including retail, property, construction, manufacturing, tourism, transport, telecommunications and financial services.[4] According to a 2005 study by the South African Institute of International Affairs (SAIIA) only eight of the top 100 companies listed on the Johannesburg securities exchange (JSE Limited) did not have a presence in the rest of Africa in 2005. In addition, many unlisted companies are also active in South Africa's neighbouring states.[5]

South Africa has been an active foreign investor in all of the other 13 countries of SADC, and it has been easier for South Africa to invest in countries close to it geographically, many of which it has historically traded profitably with, even during the apartheid era.[6] South Africa's economic expansion is much more limited in francophone Africa due to the continued dominance of French and Belgian companies in the *Francophonie*, as well as language barriers, different legal systems and business cultures.[7]

In 2003, Mozambique passed Zimbabwe as South Africa's largest trading partner in the region and is the recipient of major South African investments. Exports to Mozambique increased by 860 per cent from a low value of R899,5 million in 1992 to R6 419 billion in 2002. South African imports from Mozambique have grown commensurately by 900 per cent from R46,8 million in 1992 to R403 million in 2002.[8] South Africa has become the largest investor in Mozambique, representing 49 per cent of total FDI from 1997–2002, followed by Britain (30 per cent) and Mozambique's former colonial power, Portugal (11 per cent)[9] (see Conchiglia in this volume). Many Kenyans chattily refer to neighbouring Tanzania as 'little Jo'burg' because of the predominance of South African companies there. South African Airways (SAA) flights to the rest of the continent are full of South African corporate executives; since 1996, SAA has increased the number of flights to Accra, Ghana, to four times a week owing to a growth in demand from the business community.

South African Reserve Bank figures show that the country's investment in the continent grew threefold, from R8 billion in 1996 to R26 billion in 2001. Between 1994 and 2000, South African foreign direct investment (FDI) into the SADC region amounted to $5,4 billion: a total more than the combined British and American FDI in the subregion.[10] BusinessMap estimates that South African companies invested an average of $435 million a year in SADC countries between 1994 and 2003.[11] The 2004 World Investment Report estimates that South Africa's investment in the continent grew to 7 per cent of its total FDI abroad in 2002.[12]

South Africa's Shoprite Checkers' more than 72 stores in 13 African countries outside South Africa do business that accounts for 12 per cent of the group's turnover.[13] South African firms have significantly expanded their mining operations into Zimbabwe, Mozambique and Zambia, as well as light industry such as breweries and bottling plants. South African companies continue to dominate the food service industry in the SADC region, as well as the banking and finance sectors. Franchises have emerged as a convenient investment vehicle, with South Africa's Nandos and Steers enjoying a significant presence in many African countries. South African multinational corporations are also at the helm of new shopping centre investment in Africa. Particularly active in this area are Engen, Kwikserve, Woolworths, Game and Shoprite Checkers. The expansion of these major retailers – together with Pep Stores, Truworths, Metro Cash and Carry, and Massmart – across the continent has 'been mirrored by an accompanying movement of South African property developers who are building shopping centres to house these chains'.[14] Mvelaphanda Holdings – one of South Africa's most promising black-managed and black-owned investments groups – is a new entrant to the mining sector in recent years.

Importantly, South Africa's economic expansion is not just private sector-driven, but actively government-promoted, with the Industrial Development Corporation (IDC) providing funding (and risk-sharing) by investing in some 60 projects in 21 African countries. State-owned enterprises have begun to pursue a strategy more in line with the principles embodied in NEPAD, with greater emphasis placed on partnerships for infrastructural development as a basis for fostering productive forces and laying the foundation for the industrialisation of the continent. Sanusha Naidu noted that, the 'investment pattern has been the targeting of Africa's generally underdeveloped – or in some cases non-existent – infrastructure and it has proved to be a boon for South African contractors and parastatals. It is here that one finds the "big league" South African players on the continent – Eskom Enterprises and Transnet, or more specifically in regard to the latter, its rail division, Spoornet, and subsidiary Comazar.'[15] Eskom Enterprises is active in the energy field in 17 African countries in a bid to secure South Africa's electric power and sources of revenue. Eskom's largest external project is its participation in the Southern Africa Power Pool incorporating a common power grid among SADC member countries.

Trade with the rest of Africa jumped 328 per cent between 1993 and 2003.[16] John Daniel, Varusha Naidoo and Sanusha Naidoo point out that 'with each of its African partners, South Africa enjoys a surplus. For example, of South Africa's R20,3 billion trade with the member states of SADC in 1999, R17,7 billion were exports to the region. This is an imbalance of almost 7:1.'[17] Total trade with the rest of Africa in 2001, excluding the Southern African Customs Union (SACU) – consisting of Botswana, Lesotho, Namibia, Swaziland and South Africa – amounted to $856 million in imports and $3,7 billion in exports: an imbalance

of nearly 5:1.[18] The trade imbalance between South Africa and the rest of the
continent is further illuminated in the table below, comparing South Africa's
trading partners by region.

SOUTH AFRICA'S TOP REGIONAL TRADING PARTNERS:
FIGURES FOR THE FIRST QUARTER OF 2004, R BILLIONS

	TOTAL EXPORTS	TOTAL IMPORTS
European Union	20,50	26,82
East Asia	10,96	12,16
North America	7,02	6,22
Whole of Africa	7,01	1,90
Middle East	1,96	2,43

Source: Trade and Industry Policy Strategies June 2004

However, it is important to note exceptions to the above picture. While South
Africa enjoys a trade surplus with most African countries, three countries enjoy
marginal surpluses with South Africa: Egypt, Nigeria, and Tunisia.[19] And while
most trade balances remain in South Africa's favour, it is important to note the
downward trend: dropping from 5:1 in South Africa's favour in 2001 to 4:1 in
2003 and 3:1 in 2004.[20] The strengthening Rand has contributed to declining
exports to the rest of the continent.

South African corporate investment in Africa is driven by two key factors:
the South African market of 47 million consumers is too small to absorb its
products, while South African companies are generally too small to compete in
the rich world. An aggressive drive into the rest of Africa is thus perceived to
be in South Africa's own national self-interest. In addition, years of economic
sanctions and diplomatic isolation during apartheid meant that surplus capital
had been accumulated which could now be invested in African markets. The
African Institute for Corporate Citizenship (AICC) adds that the 'liberalisation of South Africa's regulatory regime for outward FDI has facilitated South
African companies' expansion into the rest of Africa. This has been assisted
by the country's signing of trade and investment agreements with African
countries and regions.'[21]

Indeed, investment opportunities on the continent climbed gradually after 1994, and took off in the past five years, helped in part by the South African government's relaxation of foreign exchange controls for businesses investing in Africa.[22]

While this growth in South Africa's trade and investment into the rest of Africa is noteworthy, it is sensible to maintain a proper perspective on this issue. A study by the International Monetary Fund (IMF) noted that, 'during 1994–2002, the average share of SA in the rest of Africa's external trade rose to three times its 1970–1993 average, but it was still only 2 per cent of the total. As a percentage of GDP, the rest of Africa's trade with SA during 1994–2002 rose to four times its 1970–1993 level, but was only equivalent to 0,5–1 per cent (of Africa's) GDP.'[23] The share of intra-African trade in South Africa's total African trade stood at 9,6 per cent in 2003, which 'though an improvement from previous years is a meagre figure'.[24] Reserve Bank figures show South African investment into Africa was R32,3 billion as at 31 December 2003, representing a relatively small proportion of total South African investment: 4,7 per cent. It is important to note that many South African firms are still investing predominantly in Europe, the US and Asia.

South Africa's increased investment in the rest of Africa is also in line with an overall investment in Africa: the continent has managed to increase its share of global FDI inflows from 1,7 per cent in 2002 to 2,6 per cent in 2003,[25] suggesting improved confidence in the region's prospects. For example, South Africa's telecommunications giants, Vodacom and MTN, have been profitably active in Africa, most notably MTN in Nigeria (see Adebajo in this volume). However, South Africa is by no means the only telecoms investor, as the table on the following page demonstrates.

It is possible that, in the same way as fishermen describe their catch as much bigger than they really are, South African expansion into the rest of Africa has looked more impressive or threatening (depending on one's perspective) than it really is, perhaps because this expansion happened as British, American, Japanese and Portuguese investors were disengaging from Africa. Many of these investors, no longer spurred by Cold War dynamics which had encouraged leaving footprints in Africa, steadily left the continent during the 1990s. Set against the backdrop of Africa's seemingly greater marginalisation in the global economy, this phenomenon increased the perception of a major expansion of South Africa's economic role on the continent. John Daniel and Jessica Lutcham captured this well in noting that:

TOP TEN FOREIGN INVESTMENTS IN AFRICAN TELECOMS
JANUARY 2001–AUGUST 2003

	TYPE OF INVEST-MENT	TARGET CO	TARGET COUNTRY	SOURCE COUNTRY	SOURCE COUNTRY	$M
FDI-Africa	Privatisation	Maroc Telecom	Morocco	Vivendi Universal		2 200
FDI-Africa	Privatisation-bidding	Nigeria telecom-munications Ltd (Nitel)	Nigeria	A Singaporean telecoms company	Singapore	1 010
FDI-Africa	New	Djezzy	Algeria	Orascom	Egypt	737
FDI-Africa	Licences	Second GSM licence	Tunisia	Orascom	Egypt	454
FDI-Africa	Expansion	MTN Nigeria	Nigeria	MTN	SA	385
FDI-Africa	Equity Stake	MobiNil	Egypt	Orange	UK	318
FDI-SADC	Privatisation	Mauritius Telecom	Mauritius	France Telecom	France	261
FDI-Africa	Intention	Econonet Wireless Nigeria (EWN)	Nigeria	Econet Wireless of Zimbabwe, along with Autopage and 2 South African companies	Zimbabwe and SA	150
FDI-SADC	Privatisation-pending	Tanzania Telecommunica-tions Company Ltd (TTCL)	Tanzania	MSI Cellular and Detecon		120
FDI-Africa	Equity stake	Orascom Telecom Tunisie	Tunisia	Wataniya Telecom	Kuwait	114

Source: BusinessMap Telecoms Database

This Western withdrawal from Africa coincided with South Africa's post-1990s 'discovery' of the African market ... What this meant is that for the best part of the decade 1994–2004 not only was South Africa the 'new kid on the block' in the African marketplace, it was also frequently the 'only show in town'.[26]

In addition, the perception of rapid South African expansion has obscured a general slowing down in recent times. South Africa's exports were just over R37 million more in 2004 than in 2003, representing a somewhat measly 0,11 per cent increase. Daniel and Lutcham noted that: 'Overall, their near decade-long dash into the African market slowed in 2004, while some sectors, like aviation, banking and road construction, actually showed a decline.'[27] For example, Shoprite Checkers opened only one store in 2004 in Africa – in Nigeria's commercial hub of Lagos. Daniel and Lutchman further argued that, 'the fact that the company in this same period opened its first outlet outside of Africa (a hyperstore in Mumbai in India) suggests that its appetite for new African outlets may have peaked'.[28] Nevertheless, Shoprite Checkers opened its first supermarket in Accra in 2007.

NOT EVERYBODY IS DELIGHTED

A certain discomfort is felt within Africa about South Africa's perceived economic dominance. Some countries, like Nigeria and Kenya, might see themselves as powerhouses within their own sub-regions and could be upset at South Africa's growth in influence. The pill is more bitter, according to Neuma Grobbelaar, for 'South African FDI is not combined with the sweetener of donor assistance that other investors are able to offer African governments, contributing to accusations of neo-colonialism'.[29]

SADC has made little progress in regional integration and trade since it was established in 1980 as an effort to reduce dependency on apartheid South Africa. Its fourteen member states still face challenges of external dependency, lack of diversification of production, and national rivalries. No longer united against a common enemy – apartheid South Africa – regional relations are now both constructive and competitive, while new tensions and differences have emerged (see Matlosa in this volume). These tensions have been sharpened, as South Africa has become a favoured 'emerging market' for institutional investors abroad,[30] with many multinationals now establishing their African head offices in South Africa.

To quote an illustrative example in the East African context, a specific worry for Kenya is that South Africa is emerging as 'a supplier of choice'[31] to Kenya's neighbours, potentially eroding Kenya's influence.

While there is the uncomfortable possibility that some countries might be tempted to distort or label what South African companies are doing for their own benefit, there may also be room for improvement in terms of how South African companies manage local sensitivities.

THE IMPACT OF SOUTH AFRICAN INVESTMENT IN AFRICA

The task of assessing South African investment in the rest of Africa and its impact is enormous, particularly given the economic, social and cultural diversity characterising the continent and the limited availability of data. In addition, this impact may also be uneven, mixed or both. In this section, general points are raised in an effort to tease out the issues and complexities involved in these issues.

While the value of South African investment into the rest of Africa is relatively small, the effect is significant. According to the United Nations Conference on Trade and Development (UNCTAD): 'In absolute terms, the amounts invested in African countries [by South Africa] may be small, but they account for a significant share of FDI for some African economies (eg. Mozambique).'[32] Small investments can make a big difference in small economies.

There is a Jekyll-and-Hyde quality to South Africa's economic expansion. Rather than pushing 'the little guys' out of business, South African companies argue that they are breaking up local monopolies and bringing prices down; creating jobs – particularly in tourism; boosting consumer choice; transferring skills and technology to local workers; 'ensuring the reindustrialisation of some economies through the acquisition and revitalisation of moribund state-owned enterprises';[33] and increasing revenue generation for African governments. To cite one example, SABMiller's 1997 merger with Accra Brewery – which had been using outdated machinery and was reportedly mired in debt – saw the South African firm acquiring a controlling interest of 69 per cent, and was instrumental in 'rehabilitating the Accra Brewery and in this way helped to turn the enterprise around' transforming it into 'one of the most viable enterprises in Ghana'.[34]

South Africa's involvement as a significant, and importantly, *fellow* investor is considered to have played a role in 'boosting investment confidence from other foreign investors who have tagged on to South African FDI'.[35] A specific benefit of South Africa's investment in the rest of Africa is the promotion of external investor confidence. While it is hard to ascertain direct causality, there has been increased investment in Africa in tandem with South Africa's increased expansion into the continent. These positive factors undeniably form part of the overall picture in attempting to assess the impact of South African investment.

However, there is a less savoury aspect which cannot be ignored. While there are few who reject the idea that FDI is important for development in Africa, there has been increasing questioning of the easy acceptance of this investment as an unqualified good. An UNCTAD report in 2005, *Rethinking the Role of Foreign Direct Investment,* questioned 'over-emphasis on FDI as a source of development finance in Africa'[36] and rejected the idea of FDI as an 'unalloyed good'.

Pointing to the potentially negative impact of FDI, Ralph Hamann of the AICC outlines the following factors: the disruption of local supply chains; disregard for labour and human rights standards; environmental damage; anti-competitive behaviour; and low levels of transparency and disclosure.[37] Interviewing workers at a Shoprite store in a Zambian shopping mall, Darlene Miller found a dissatisfied workforce, members of which were apparently 'plucked unceremoniously from their homes on very short verbal notice, and with one or two exceptions, no company help in relocating. At a meeting when the store was opened, they were promised a bright future at the new, magnificent store. Their experience turned out to be very different. They live in makeshift rooms at the back of other homes or in crude, concrete, two roomed rental dwellings.'[38] She continues: 'Cultural styles have a bearing on workplace practices. Many Southern Africans can attest to the brusque forthrightness of many urban South Africans, a kind of modernised haste with which matters are executed ... the 'straight-talk' culture of white South African management is likely to offend the cultural sensibilities of [some] Zambian [for example] workers, making them feel demeaned in their work environments.'[39]

Casualisation is another key issue, with these workers enjoying no statutory protection. Miller argues that 'workers in the region feel that, next to South African workers, they are treated as second-class citizens'.[40] This may stem in part from the strong regulatory framework in South Africa.

Research conducted by SAIIA found that: 'South African investments have limited links with local businesses because of their capital intensive nature and knowledge specificity'.[41] Local procurement is less evident than one might have hoped, and importing South African products and services may distort local markets.[42] Granted, this might be because of the absence of consistent supplies at the right quality and/or price, but this still suggests that there is room for improvement in terms of the quality of South African investment and the management of local sensitivities.

There is also the widespread complaint from neighbouring countries that South African companies are 'dumping' their goods on local markets and are advantaged by incentive schemes to entice foreign investment, schemes which exclude local businesses, and thus contribute to distorting markets further.[43]

Reg Rumney of BusinessMap argues that when a region receives a surge of external investment there is a 'fear that an "enclave economy" is created, as was the case in Angola where investment for offshore oil platforms created a circle of wealth insulated from the rest of the poverty stricken country'. He continues: 'there is a real possibility that such surges of investment may exacerbate inequality within a country, with damaging political and social consequences.'[44] The BusinessMap Foundation notes in one of its update publications that 'history and geography have combined to shape FDI flows mainly toward resource extraction, principally mining and oil, often creating enclave economies with little development benefit for African countries'.[45]

More specifically, in 2002, a UN Report to the General Assembly named some 12 South African companies in a list of firms accused of looting mineral resources in the DRC during its civil war, which erupted in 1997, as part of the world body's investigation into the role of illegal exploitation of natural resources in the Congo's conflicts. These firms included 'blue-chip' names like Anglo American, Anglovaal mining, De Beers and Iscor.[46]

Responsibility for minimising the potentially negative aspects of South African FDI into the rest of Africa cuts both ways. Some South African companies need to modify their behaviour, but responsibility must also be with each African country to provide an appropriate regulatory framework to attract, promote and retain local and international business confidence in such a way as to maximise the benefits and minimise the potential negative aspects of South Africa's corporate expansion. Governments all over the world do not want powerful foreign businesses to overwhelm their local firms and thus be left without industries whose economic interests are tied to their own economies. Historically, both the US and Germany protected their infant industries during their industrialisation processes. It is trite but true to say that a balance needs to be struck between the national interest and that of foreign vested interests.

The previously quoted UNCTAD report argues that a country may wish to limit or exclude FDI if it threatens infant industries or affects policies designed to help those firms reach the scale and technological levels needed to make them competitive. 'At other times it may be advisable to have an "open door" policy with few restrictions, and at yet other times it may even be desirable to use an array of incentives to attract FDI into preferred sectors.'[47] Thus a more nuanced understanding of FDI and the question of whether it brings about an improvement in living conditions in the host country – not merely as a goal in and of itself – is emerging. This stands in contrast to the fairly static conception of FDI in terms of economic flows into a given country per year.

It is also worth noting that limiting FDI and undertaking specific policies designed to protect local firms can encourage inefficiencies, distort the market for potential investors, deprive a country of business spending, and discourage growth of these businesses into more sophisticated firms. Problems and unintended consequences can attach to attempts to protect local industry, providing businesses with incentives not to grow beyond certain thresholds. Firms provided with special support may break up strategically as soon as this threshold is passed. Such an approach would run counter to the NEPAD initiative, which emphasises the critical importance of the private sector in the continent's economic development (see Landsberg in this volume).

THE HIGHS AND THE LOWS

According to a recent study, South African companies in Africa are earning profits two to three times higher than those earned in their home operations.[48] Reported average returns of between 30 per cent on equity in the banking sector and up to 60 per cent in other sectors illustrate how profitable doing business in Africa can be.[49] Former UN Undersecretary-General for Political Affairs, Ibrahim Gambari, has noted that: 'The rates of return on investment in Africa are possibly the highest in the world.'[50] In many African countries – Botswana, Ghana, Kenya and Nigeria in particular – the availability of educated and enterprising people has boosted business operations. With former British colonies, South Africa shares many institutional, political, economic and cultural traditions and consequently South Africans find these business environments familiar. More generally, South African companies are assumed to have greater familiarity with conditions on the continent than investors from elsewhere outside Africa.

Indeed, the rest of Africa has proved to be fertile ground for many South African investors. But the risks are high and it has not always been plain sailing for many companies. The chief executive of South African road construction company, Aveng, has been quoted as saying that the company was not 'making money out of a significant portion of our African activities'.[51] Corporate South Africa's fairly aggressive efforts at economic penetration into Kenya for example, culminated in the 'Beer Wars' in which SAB Miller eventually lost out to Kenya Breweries (45 per cent owned by Guinness). South Africa's Metro Cash and Carry in Kenya closed its doors in March 2005 after eight years of not making a profit. While Shoprite Checkers has registered a company in Kenya, strong levels of competition from established local businesses has prevented it from opening its stores there. In effect, Kenya has managed to keep the South African 'big brother' at bay. In Nigeria, SAA's acquisition of a 30 per cent stake in the new Nigerian national carrier, Eagle Airlines, was 'abruptly cancelled'[52] by the Nigerian government in favour of the British airline Virgin Atlantic.

There are a number of logistical challenges in many African countries that may act as constraints to South African investor enthusiasm. These would clearly vary from country to country. Significantly, not all businesses are affected in the same way – sectoral considerations, the size of the firm and how long it has been in operation are all important factors to bear in mind. Other constraints include: high business costs due to inadequate and patchy infrastructure; transportation and freight costs; poor airlines; unreliable electricity; currency fluctuations; poor governance and corruption; the challenge of the HIV/AIDS pandemic; red tape; high crime rates; lack of market intelligence and up-to-date data; lack of education and skills; and inefficient banking systems.

The table below gives some indication of perceptions of corruption in selected countries in sub-Saharan Africa.

CORRUPTION PERCEPTIONS INDEX 2004: SELECTED COUNTRIES IN
SUB-SAHARAN AFRICA

COUNTRY	2004 RANKING	2004 SCORE	2003 SCORE	% CHANGE
Botswana	31	6,0	5,7	5,3
South Africa	44	4,6	4,4	4,5
Ghana	64	3,6	3,3	9,1
Tanzania	90	2,8	2,5	12,0
Ethiopia	114	2,3	2,5	-8,0
Zimbabwe	114	2,3	2,3	0,0
Uganda	102	2,6	2,2	18,2
Kenya	129	2,1	1,9	10,5
Nigeria	144	1,6	1,4	14,3

Source: Transparency International

The third annual report of the World Bank and the International Finance Corporation (IFC) *Doing Business in 2006: Creating Jobs* provides a ranking of 155 countries in terms of the ease of doing business in these markets. The study considers the following factors: how easy it is to start a business; obtain licences; hire and fire workers; register properties; access credit; trade across borders; enforce contracts; close a business; how well investors are protected; and characteristics of the economy. According to this report, there are more regulatory obstacles in most African countries than elsewhere; business taxes in Africa are also higher than anywhere else. There are, of course, some bright spots. Rwanda, for example, is singled out as one of Africa's top performers in 2005 in improving the environment for business, with reforms to the courts and customs procedures as well as updating of the credit registry. Mauritius is said to be one of the most business-friendly countries in Africa.

In several African countries though, companies routinely have to purchase back-up generators, dig their own wells and repair their own roads. The cost of electricity in Kenya is reportedly four times that of South Africa.[53] According to one retailer, it is more expensive to ship goods between Beira and Maputo in Mozambique than from Hong Kong to South Africa.[54] Restricted supply of airline seats can also make it as expensive to fly from Johannesburg to Luanda as from Johannesburg to London – three times the distance; limited routes between SADC countries further means that the cost per kilometre of flying from Johannesburg to Maputo, a 'highly constrained route' on which only the national airlines of each country are allowed to fly, can be three times the cost per kilometre of flying to Windhoek, Namibia, a relatively unconstrained route.[55] Competition and capacity are restricted on many routes between SADC countries, flight frequency is low, and ticket prices high. This is largely unhelpful to increased investment and trade.

In addition to 'hardware' shortcomings of African countries which investors encounter, there are also 'software' problems. Political risk or changes in a ruling regime can mean that 'agreements are not honoured or the economic environment is altered at short notice'.[56] Blatantly anti-South African sentiment is also increasingly evident in many countries. The perceived volume of South African investment is causing resentment. In a series of interviews conducted in Kenya, South African businesspeople – both black and white – were described as 'brash, arrogant, insensitive, selfish, the Americans of the continent'.[57] South Africa could be in danger of acquiring the image of the 'ugly American' that Uncle Sam continues to have in Latin America and the Caribbean.

It has however been suggested that some South African corporates have been picking up on these perceptions, with many companies now reportedly becoming more sensitive in their behaviour. Are these sensitivities and resentments a reflection of South African corporate conduct? If so, this is fortunate since this perception falls within the power of South African corporates to change.

Three waves of investment

Quoting the *Financial Mail* of 6 May 2005, the AICC distinguishes between a 'first wave' of investments into Africa during the 1990s, dominated by the 'old economy' sectors such as mining and infrastructure, and the current 'scramble', headed by 'the more service-oriented firms in the telecommunications, IT, banking, media and advertising industries'.[58] There appears to have been a further wave in 2005 characterised by 'levelling off of the pan-sectoral nature of South Africa's involvement'[59] combined with 'an intensification of interests and activities on the continent in two niche areas. Both were resource-related – mining, on the one hand, and energy broadly defined, on the other'.[60]

South Africa is dependent for about 98 per cent of its oil needs on imports – some 75 per cent from the Middle East and 23 per cent from Africa, up from 9 per cent in 2001.[61] According to Thulani Gcabashe, chief executive of Eskom: 'If we do not take corrective measures now, South Africa will run out of excess peaking capacity and excess base load by 2010'.[62] Thus, Africa's oil, gas and hydropower resources are important in South Africa's emerging energy strategy and its long-term objective of ensuring self-sufficiency in electricity. In this context, South Africa is increasingly having to grapple with the recent interest of non-African players – notably the US and China – in Africa's energy and mineral resources sectors (most notably oil). In light of the post-9/11 security context, alternatives to Middle East oil are becoming increasingly attractive to the US.

The DRC has assumed strategic significance given Eskom Enterprise's ambitious scheme, the Grand Inga hydropower project: a three-phase activity over a time span of some 20 years. Parts one and two of the project would involve an extension and upgrade of an existing but degrading hydroelectric facility built in the Congo decades ago. Phase three would be the responsibility of Westcor, a joint venture company comprising the national utilities of five Southern Africa Power Pool member utilities: Angola, Botswana, the DRC, Namibia and South Africa. On completion in the 2020s, the Grand Inga scheme would aim to generate sufficient electricity to meet the needs of the entire continent, as well as generate revenue for members by exporting surplus power to Europe. 'Little wonder then,' argue Daniel and Lutchman, 'that the South African government has committed so much in the way of time and effort, as well as military peacekeepers, to the task of bringing political stability to the DRC and to ending the endemic conflict in particularly the eastern region (Ituri) of the country'[63] (see Curtis in this volume).

Some analysts have argued that PetroSA's agreement with the Sudanese state oil company, Sudapet, was 'almost certainly an expression of gratitude'[64] to the South African government for its role in helping to broker the peace agreement between the government of Sudan and the Sudanese People's Liberation Movement (SPLM) in January 2005.

This new wave and focus led Daniel and Lutchman to suggest in 2005 that:

> In the last five years ... South Africa – or more precisely South African companies with state support – has moved to reduce its [oil] import dependency through a process of buying into the African oil market as either a sole proprietor or in a partnership arrangement. In pursuit of this goal, South Africa has employed a combination of economic muscle, technical edge and tactical diplomacy.[65]

They continue, somewhat provocatively:

> In its scramble to acquire a share of this market, the ANC government appears to have abandoned any regard to those ethical and human rights principles which it once proclaimed would form the basis of its foreign policy. Its approach to energy is one in which the national interest is being interpreted purely on material grounds ... The ANC has in the last decade moved a long way from its condemnation of the execution in Nigeria in 1995 of the anti-oil campaigner, Ken Saro-Wiwa, to the point where it is now prepared to deal in oil and energy matters with one of Africa's most corrupt and unaccountable regimes, Angola, and in the cases of Sudan and Equatorial Guinea, with two of the most abusive regimes on Earth, let alone in Africa. When it comes to South Africa's economic relations, it now seems that anything goes – or rather if it is oil any government will do. In this regard, it seems that the South African government is not unlike the Bush administration.[66]

There is a different perspective on this engagement. Firstly, why shouldn't South Africa engage with its neighbours north of the Limpopo? South Africa's economy is inextricably linked not only to the Southern African region, but also to Africa as a whole. Thus, South Africa's engagement with the rest of the continent outlined above can be viewed in the context of its importance in the context of South Africa's global economic strategy. As the then director-general of the Department of Foreign Affairs, Jackie Selebi said in 1995, 'By actively encouraging and assisting with trade promotion in the region, we are ensuring that new employment opportunities are created in South Africa. The latter objective is also being achieved by promoting and facilitating the active involvement of the South African private sector in development and construction projects in the region.'[67] South Africa's relations with the rest of the continent are thus important in addressing South Africa's own domestic development challenges, while simultaneously seeking to address the continent's development challenges. The international prestige attached to South Africa's democratic transition has conferred a new respectability on the region's prospects and projects.[68] South Africa's success is also good for the continent. In addition, South Africa has an interest in promoting Africa 'higher up the global agenda'[69] and in mitigating or eliminating 'the impact of spillovers from the rest of the continent'.[70] Prosperity and stability in the rest of Africa is, of course, consistent with South Africa's own national interest. Investors often, somewhat unhelpfully, treat Africa as a single entity.

Whether or not African markets can in fact be significant drivers of growth in South Africa is open to question – sluggish growth and limited market size suggest otherwise. But it would appear that establishing regional linkages might be part of an overall strategy of building more effective linkages with the global economy. This is important since, as Stephen Gelb points out, 'most African states are ill-equipped to address the particular challenges posed by globalisation, making a strong case for collective action by states'.[71] (See also Adedeji in this volume.)

BusinessMap notes that there 'appears to be a dichotomy in the South African approach to the rest of the continent between the use of political power and economic power. The enthusiasm of firms and state-owned enterprises in venturing into Africa has been balanced by a cautious and some would say too hesitant – use of political power.'[72] It is also the case that some learning in terms of tactical diplomacy in the school of hard knocks has taken place. Former president Nelson Mandela's public criticism of the Nigerian military government's execution of activist Ken Saro-Wiwa in 1995, for example, failed to win much support from other countries, prompting a shift towards collective action and a multilateral approach (see Adebajo in this volume).

The set of factors outlined above suggests that South Africa's engagement with African countries such as the DRC, Burundi and Sudan may well not be disinterested peacekeeping but more informed by hard-headed self-interest, given the factors outlined above. This is not to argue that it is unwise to be vigilant, or that some necessary modifications might be called for – an aspect which is discussed in more detail below.

A CODE OF CONDUCT?

Increasing calls are being made in South Africa to regulate corporate behaviour and thus promote ethical corporate citizenship. As this chapter has argued, South Africa's new role in the international – particularly African – arena is complex. Philip Armstrong, convenor of South Africa's King Committee on Corporate Governance, noted:

> I believe that given the proliferation of South African business in Africa, that some form of integrated and substantive guidelines could be useful … Given the role of South Africa in NEPAD and its own acknowledged record of democracy and governance, we would not want to see our national reputation or stature compromised by irresponsible conduct.[73]

NEPAD, however, provides scant guidelines in terms of how business should play a responsible role and effectively partner with governments.

Is it time to put pressure on South African companies to be more transparent in their activities on the continent? What about the potential of regulation to stifle the development aspects of FDI? Is there a need to entice or compel certain businesses to act against their own perceptions of short-run profit?

It is easy to imagine howls of predictable protest emanating from businesses already feeling weighed down by 'standards fatigue' and red tape. But South African firms would be wise to reflect on these issues not so much from a moral perspective, but in terms of their own self-interest: the longer term competitiveness and success of the South African private sector on the continent could well be harmed if unhelpful activities for short-term gain are allowed to continue unchecked. Bad behaviour on the part of one South African company could muddy the water for others in their operations on the continent. Once the public gets wind of bad behaviour, this may provoke legislation that companies might find more cumbersome than exercising self-restraint. Being pressured is worse than being regulated. This should provide persuasive, prudential grounds for South African corporates voluntarily to adopt a more socially responsible attitude and/or a code of conduct with regard to broader societal concerns in the African countries in which they operate.

There are already a number of initiatives that might guide South African companies operating in Africa – namely the King II report; the UN Global Compact, and JSE Limited's social responsibility index (SRI). However, these initiatives have been criticised on the following grounds: they fail to take into account issues such as labour or human rights (in the case of the King II report); the UN Global Compact and the JSE SRI are said to be 'dominated by an international, universal set of priorities that leaves out African priorities, such as work creation',[74] and more broadly, these initiatives have all been criticised as 'lacking teeth'.

A number of key questions arise: What are the institutional mechanisms to institutionalise, promote and monitor a code of conduct? Who will compile it? Should the code of conduct incorporate social responsibility aspects? And, how can the situation be avoided where South African investors might be discriminated against in terms of a code of conduct, providing an advantage to other investors such as the Americans or Chinese? These questions suggest the need for a wider accountability mechanism which can hold all corporates to a set of behaviour or code of conduct.

In this regard, the Paris-based Organisation for Economic Cooperation and Development (OECD) Guidelines for Multinational Enterprises – part of the OECD Declaration on International Investment and Multinational Enterprises – are already widely regarded as the landmark instrument for promoting corporate responsibility. Under this mechanism, adhering governments establish a National Contact Point (NCP) – often a government office, but also increasingly collaborative structures involving labour, business and/or civil society organisations. The NCP is 'responsible for encouraging observance of the OECD guidelines and for ensuring that the guidelines are well-known and understood by the national business community and by other interested parties'.[75] Accusations that a multinational corporation has contravened the guidelines are brought to the attention either of the NCP in the host country or the NCP in the company's domicile country. The interested party must then substantiate its claim in order for it to be taken forward by the NCP. In this way, the guidelines 'provide a suitable model for the government's role in promoting corporate responsibility'.[76] The addition of specific priority areas – community reinvestment requirements, local procurement, and an emphasis on HIV/AIDS[77] could well be suitable adaptations of these guidelines to the African context.

South African businesses should be encouraged by the fact that the NCPs have played an important role in investigating allegedly irresponsible business practices by companies operating in the DRC, as noted earlier in this chapter – including some South African companies. De Beers, registered in London, was asked by Britain's NCP to respond to these allegations of contravention of the OECD guidelines for Multinational Enterprises. After all roleplayers were given an opportunity to present their evidence, a statement was issued exonerating De Beers from any contravention of the OECD guidelines. As the AICC points out:

> This experience illustrates that a transparent and formal process for querying concerns about responsible conduct can be in the company's interest, in that De Beers was spared [a potentially] damaging media campaign.[78]

ELEMENTS OF THE OECD GUIDELINES FOR MULTINATIONAL ENTERPRISES[79]

- 'The common aim of the governments adhering to the guidelines is to encourage the positive contributions that multinational enterprises can make to economic, environmental and social progress and to minimise the difficulties to which their various operations may give rise';
- Enterprises should inter alia 'contribute to economic, social and environmental progress with a view to achieving sustainable development', 'respect human rights' and 'encourage local capacity building';
- With reference to disclosure, companies are to provide 'timely, regular, reliable and relevant information … regarding their activities, structure, financial situation and performance';

- Regarding employment and industrial relations, a chapter reiterates the ILO's (International Labour Organisation) core labour standards and also asks companies to 'take adequate steps to ensure occupational health and safety' and 'to the greatest extent practicable, employ local personnel and provide training';
- Environment: A chapter requires the establishment and maintenance of an appropriate environmental management system, including information disclosure, avoidance or mitigation of environmental impacts, employee education, and continuous improvement of environmental performance;
- With reference to combating bribery, there is the requirement to enhance transparency and employee awareness and to adopt suitable management control systems;
- A chapter on consumer interests involves fair business, marketing and advertising practices, including issues such as consumer health and safety; appropriate information disclosure and consumer privacy;
- A chapter on science and technology encourages companies to 'permit the transfer and rapid diffusion of technologies and know-how' and to allow science and technology to 'address local market needs';
- A chapter on price-fixing requests companies to refrain from price-fixing and other anti-competitive measures;
- A chapter on taxation requires companies to 'act in accordance with both the letter and spirit' of tax laws and regulations.

CONCLUDING REMARKS

Fellow Africans have, in varying degrees, been dependent on European brands and products for some time. South Africa's assertive promotion of its goods has provided alternatives for African consumers. The involvement of South Africa's business sector in African economies is desirable, and may well pave the way for the private sector to play a significant role in the continent's economic development – a key plank of NEPAD.

However, South Africa's prominence has thrown up complexities and challenges associated with post-apartheid South Africa's role on the continent, the complex relationship between business and government, and the economic and political aspects of South Africa's engagement on the continent. This complexity has prompted a helpful shift in analyses of South Africa's role in Africa, from focusing on somewhat crude assessments of how much investment has flowed into individual economies each year, towards a more nuanced appreciation of the quality of investment, with the major benchmark being whether or not this brings about a broader improvement in living conditions in the host country.

These factors have put pressure on South African corporates to look beyond the factory gate in their engagement with their neighbours north of the Limpopo. Careful management of local sensitivities combined with good corporate practices are as critical in the rest of Africa, as they have proved to be in South Africa. In this regard, the OECD guidelines could provide a useful point of departure and should be embraced by South African corporates in their own self-interest, with the necessary adaptations to the African context.

A stronger emphasis on greater intra-African trade as a way of driving sustainable economic growth on the continent is a desirable path for South Africa to follow, thus countering Africa's economic marginalisation in a global context. In terms of South African investment, perhaps the real question is why South Africa does not invest more in Africa.

7

Conflict and land reform in Southern Africa: How exceptional is South Africa?

SAM MOYO AND RUTH HALL

Land reform is an inherently conflictual process. It challenges established economic and political structures and dominant cultural identities. While peaceful land reform is usually the objective of public policy, such policy must be informed by a realistic assessment of the sources of conflict and the implications of different models of land reform. In recent years, market-based land reform experiments, such as in South Africa, Zimbabwe, Brazil and elsewhere, have been more utopian than realistic in their expectations of the process, pace, and scope of market-based reforms, thus fueling rather than resolving conflict. In Southern Africa, redistributive land reforms have been adopted to transform the skewed landholding patterns structured by race.

South Africa's attempts at land reform in the first thirteen years of democracy have proved to be slow and have made little headway towards the goals of rural restructuring and poverty alleviation. Politicians and policymakers in South Africa have yet to draw relevant lessons about the limits of market-based land redistribution from other countries in the region. Instead, South Africa appears to be repeating the tendencies towards elite capture, moderate deracialisation of the land-owning class and the growth of a small black commercial farming class in place of wider agrarian reform. With respect to land tenure, South Africa is pursuing tenure reforms in the former 'homelands' that are contrary to established best practice throughout the continent, and have opened the way to the commodification and privatisation of communal resources.

Despite public commitments to democratic norms, this has also led to the privileging of control over land by traditional authorities. In both respects, South Africa appears to be bucking the experience and lessons from the rest of the region and the continent. Signs of conflict emerging both from unmet land demands and from the process of reform itself are now evident. The emergence of rural social movements giving voice to rural dissatisfaction is now a feature of

South Africa as well as several of its neighbours within SADC. Widespread land occupations in Zimbabwe – and their representation in the media – have both driven land reform up the political agenda in South Africa, and spurred more conservative responses to the expression of demands for land. In the sphere of land rights and land reform, South Africa appears to be in a state of denial rather than embracing its identity as part of the region and the continent.

To understand the process of land reform, we need to recognise that historically three models of land acquisition – namely 'state', 'market', and 'popular' – which have been pursued by different social forces, have shaped the conflict over property rights. These models are distinguishable by their approach to four elements of the land reform process: first, the selection of land; second, the method of acquisition from landowners; third, the selection of beneficiaries; and fourth, the method of transfer to beneficiaries.

The 'popular' model of land reform is the most basic of these, where landless workers and peasants – often together with the urban poor – choose and occupy land, often illegally, and seek post facto regularisation of title from the state.[1] In the state model, governments play a prominent role, either acquiring land compulsorily or purchasing it while compensating landowners.

The 'market' model of land reform has sought to displace the state from directing land reform. Market-based land reforms, contrary to their 'peaceful' designs, have been socially inflammatory, given their utopianism on landlord-landless relations. This has resulted in a slow pace, limited scope and quality in the delivery of land, and the absence of integration of resettled communities into a coherent national development project. State-based reforms, on the other hand – especially of the compulsory type – have more potential in delivering land, as well as integrating new farming communities into national development, but they lack the financial resources, given conditions of fiscal austerity in much of the continent.

From the 1980s onwards, under the influence of international finance and neoliberal economics, state-led and interventionist land reform was removed from the development agenda and replaced by a concerted market-based land policy. This policy framework has pursued the privatisation and commercialisation of land and has sought to confine land transfers to the market principle. The neoliberal policy framework has had two implications for national development: it has abandoned the project of integration of agriculture and industry on a national basis, promoting instead their integration into global markets; and second, it has aggravated economic and social insecurity, intensified migration to urban areas, and created a deepening pattern of maldevelopment.[2] With the end of the Cold War by the early 1990s and the re-emergence of organised rural movements, as well as the end of white rule in Southern Africa by 1994, land reform returned to the development agenda, but remained within the market paradigm. Land redistribution programmes increasingly combine these methods, although the market-based approach has remained dominant, given greater donor support for it.

LAND REFORM IN SOUTH AFRICA

Land dispossession and agrarian dualism

The extent of land dispossession through colonial conquest and apartheid rule distinguishes South Africa from other countries in the region, including the former settler colonies of Zimbabwe and Namibia. After an initial expansion of peasant production in the late nineteenth century in response to growing markets for agricultural produce following the discovery of gold and diamonds, successive legal and economic coercive measures forced the African peasantry from its land and into selling its labour in white-owned mines, factories and farms.[3] The subsequent creation of native reserves – or 'Bantustans' – served to entrench the agrarian dualism of highly subsidised white commercial farming areas. These communal areas were characterised by overcrowding, labour migration, and remittance economies, all of which were integral to processes of capital accumulation in 'white' South Africa.[4]

Forced removals from white-owned farms and from 'black spots' continued through the twentieth century and formed the centrepiece of rural resistance to apartheid, right up to the late 1980s, by which time most rural black South Africans were restricted to communal areas occupying approximately 13 per cent of the country's land, mostly with insecure forms of tenure under the jurisdiction of state-approved 'tribal' authorities enforcing state-approved customary law.[5] About 19 million South Africans now live in rural areas, of whom about 16 million (or one-third of all South Africans), are resident in the former homelands.[6] The rural countryside is where poverty is most deeply rooted. Thus land dispossession was both a cause of rural poverty and a concrete manifestation of political subjugation.

During the transition to democracy in the early 1990s, many South Africans expected that liberation would allow them to return to the land from which they had been dispossessed under colonialism and apartheid. But the terms on which South Africa's transition was negotiated between 1990 and 1994 constrained the parameters of how this could happen. At the Convention for a Democratic South Africa (Codesa) constitutional negotiations, the ANC agreed not to pursue a confiscatory land reform policy and to protect existing property rights. The ruling party later adopted a 'willing buyer, willing seller' approach to land reform. South Africa's final Constitution of 1996 guaranteed the protection of property rights, while also placing clear responsibility on the state to implement a three-pronged land reform policy of land restitution, land redistribution and land tenure reform.[7]

In line with its new Constitution, South Africa's land policy has three distinct components. A market-based *land redistribution* programme was created to broaden access to land among the country's black majority. This was to address the racially skewed pattern of land ownership, while laying the groundwork for broad-based development. The policy relies on the provision of state grants to enable people to purchase land. Second, a *land restitution* programme was adopted to restore land or provide alternative compensation to those dispossessed as a result of racially discriminatory laws and practices since 1913. The process of resolving these historical claims to land continues. Alongside these two initiatives to transfer land, a *tenure reform* programme was designed to secure the rights of people living under insecure arrangements on land owned by others, including the state (in the communal areas) and private landowners (on commercial farms).

As formulated in the *White Paper on South African Land Policy* of 1997, market-based land reform has been pursued on a 'willing-buyer, willing-seller' basis, and in the name of historical and social justice, as well as economic development.[8] There are inherent tensions among these rationales and objectives for land reform. Land reform aims, variously, to provide redress, restore rights, reconstitute communities and livelihoods and provide the basis for full citizenship in a context in which land dispossession was integral to conquest and disenfranchisement. Reform also seeks to address rural poverty and to establish sustainable land-based livelihoods for the rural poor, to stem rural-urban migration and to improve food security. Land reform, in this conception, has been in tension with the thrust of South Africa's macro-economic policy after 1994, particularly since the adoption of the Growth, Employment and Redistribution (GEAR) strategy in 1996 (see Adedeji in this volume). In practice, notions of historical justice have been pursued through symbolic restitution, including reliance on cash payouts to compensate the dispossessed, while the creation of a black commercial farming class engaged in small- to medium-scale production has emerged as the overriding thrust of government policy.

The dynamics of land reform in the first decade of democracy

Land reform has undergone significant shifts over the past thirteen years, emerging as a programme quite different from the visions of land and agrarian reform espoused by Southern African liberation movements and by rural grassroots movements in the early 1990s. Among the dynamics driving land reform, five themes are notable, and discussed briefly below: first, the very limited transformation in patterns of landholding; second, an impasse on the role of state interference in land markets to make land available for redistribution; third, the shift towards a limited programme of farmer settlement to deracialise the commercial farming areas; fourth, the influence of private sector interests in re-shaping who and what land reform is for; and fifth, the adoption of a transfer of title paradigm rather than reforming land rights administration in communal areas.

1) A moderate reform: Limited transformation in patterns of landholding

In the first decade of democracy, South Africa's official land reform programme made small and tentative inroads into the overall racial pattern of landholding. Between 1994 and 1999, less than one per cent of agricultural land was transferred into black ownership through this programme, and by 2005, about 3.1 million hectares had been redistributed, amounting to 3.6 per cent of all commercial farmland. This represents about a tenth of the official target of transferring 30 per cent of land to black South Africans by 2015. Studies of private market transactions in South Africa's KwaZulu-Natal province indicate that private market transactions may be transferring larger areas of land into black ownership than this state-led programme, though only to those with the means to engage independently in the land market.[9] Factors underlying this slow pace include: problems with identifying suitable land on the open market, the formation and management of land purchase groups, and onerous bureaucratic processes. Unlike Zimbabwe in the 1980s, the South African government does not proactively purchase land but rather facilitates market transactions between buyers and sellers in a hybrid that combines some of the worst elements of the market-led approach with the bureaucracy of a state-led approach. While the pace of land transfers has improved since the late 1990s, the overall impact of land reform has been extremely limited, with budgetary constraints recently emerging as the key stumbling block to change.

2) The 'willing buyer, willing seller' principle: Non-interference with land markets

Fred Hendricks and Lungisile Ntsebeza have argued that, given the historical nature of the land question, the protection of existing property rights in the 1990s amounted to confirming, and legitimising, 'colonial land theft'.[10] While fundamental land reform usually involves a massive restructuring of property relations, South Africa's Constitution preserves property rights established through colonial and apartheid land dispossession. In this sense, land reform in South Africa is premised on the legitimacy of precisely the social relations it seeks to transform.

However, the political compromise struck in 1994 is evident in the constitutional balance between protecting the status quo and an injunction towards transformation; the Constitution explicitly empowers the state to expropriate property subject to the payment of 'just and equitable' rather than market-related compensation, while specifying that property may be expropriated in the public interest, including in pursuit of 'the nation's commitment to land reform'. These powers, though, have been largely unused – for political rather than legal reasons.[11] A key reason why expropriation has not been used to expedite land reform is that government adopted a 'willing buyer, willing seller' policy to guide land reform, as advocated by the World Bank in 1993 in its proposals for rural restructuring which were developed for South Africa during the era of the country's negotiations. Reform is now characterised by an impasse arising from the intrinsic tension between responding to the demands of the black rural population and relying on 'willing sellers' to make land available on the open market. Despite an 'active' land market in which substantial areas are transacted each year, the commitment to limit state interference in land markets has meant that all areas of land reform have been made contingent on the willingness of the current owners of land to make their land available for sale, and to do so at prices that are affordable within the parameters of state funding for land reform.

3) From pro-poor to a commercial focus: Deracialising the commercial sector

In the first five years of land redistribution, state support was reserved for poor households. Because no mechanisms were available to subdivide agricultural holdings, applicants formed large groups and pooled their small Settlement/

Land Acquisition Grants (SLAG) of R16 000 (about US$2 500) per household in order to buy established commercial farms in their entirety. The result was under-utilisation of land and limited improvements in livelihoods as these new owners often lacked the capital to invest in production and received limited support after transfer of ownership. The SLAG programme was replaced in 2001 with the Land Redistribution for Agricultural Development (LRAD) programme, which differs from its predecessor in that it is not targeted towards the poor but is available to all black South Africans, and requires applicants to contribute labour, capital and/or assets. LRAD ostensibly addresses a range of needs, from 'food safety nets' to commercial farming. Grants currently range from R20 000 to R100 000 per individual, depending on the size of contributions that applicants are able to make.

LRAD has been firmly established as the flagship redistribution programme of South Africa's government, eclipsing other programmes such as those providing land for settlement and access to municipal commonage land to the poor. The hostile economic and institutional context for small-scale farming and for new entrants underlies the preference for commercial farming and for opening the programme to groups other than the poor. As officials acknowledge, in the absence of viable support systems, and under pressure to avoid 'failure', selection of beneficiaries must take into account the extent to which people will be able to resource their own development. This 'cherry-picking' approach has lent itself to the provision of larger grants to fewer people, thus assisting with a limited and gradual deracialisation of the white commercial farming areas without wider agrarian reform that entails a more profound restructuring of social relations and the legacy of spatial apartheid.

4) The private sector and land reform

The advent of land reform coincided with the private sector's interest in deracialising the commercial sector, particularly in order to secure export markets in the post-sanctions era. While the South African Agricultural Union (SAAU) – later called AgrisA – initially opposed land reform, the private sector has come to embrace a limited transformation within the market framework. In particular, it has welcomed the advent of LRAD, with its focus on commercial farming and on individual or small group operations, while continuing to object to tenure rights for farm dwellers on white-owned farms.

Agribusiness and commercial farmers have identified a niche for themselves in supporting land reform through equity sharing schemes in the high-value export sectors, particularly in deciduous fruit and wine in the Western Cape, and in outgrower and sharecropping schemes in the unbundling timber and sugar industries of KwaZulu-Natal and Mpumalanga provinces. Further imperatives for transformation are expected in the agricultural black economic empowerment charter – AgriBEE (on BEE, see Shubane in this volume).

A critical question for the future of land reform is whether this charter ultimately will set out a collective challenge to the agricultural sector, coupled with enforceable demands, to support land reform and to make land available; and whether it addresses broad-based redistribution and accumulation 'from below', rather than merely securing BEE shareholdings in agribusiness corporations. The draft charter, released in July 2004, emphasised human resource development, employment equity in the management of agricultural businesses and enterprise ownership and equity.[12] Since then, the state and agricultural industry have remained at loggerheads over the policy proposal's content. It appears that BEE will increasingly form the framework within which the state and industry will justify their interventions to transform agriculture, even eclipsing the land reform agenda. A revised version, debated at an *Indaba* (retreat) in December 2005, contained no concrete benefits of ownership for farm workers, nor did it speak to the needs of smallholders. With respect to land reform, it largely reiterated existing government targets but also introduced a new emphasis on the promotion of rental markets as a means of promoting the participation of black South Africans in the sector.

5) Land rights in communal areas

The dualism between the commercial and communal areas is evident not only in the types of agricultural production and levels of 'development', but also in the land tenure regime and systems of land rights administration. In the former 'homelands',[13] a range of informal and insecure forms of tenure persists, based on second-class permit-based rights like Permission to Occupy (PTO) certificates. These rights have been rendered even more insecure following the dismantling of state institutions in the former 'homelands' in the 1990s, which has produced a chaotic state of land administration in communal areas. This situation has not yet been addressed through land reform, but the Communal Land Rights Act (11 of 2004) proposed that, where deemed necessary by the minister of agriculture and land affairs, title to 'communal' lands be transferred to residents. The residents will hold and manage the land jointly through local committees or through traditional councils, where these exist. 'Tribal' authorities are to be partially reformed to include women and a proportion of elected representatives, in terms of the Traditional Leadership and Framework Governance Act (41 of 2003). These new structures will become known as 'traditional councils'.

The privatisation of these 'communal' lands may insulate some of the poorest areas both from state support for land rights and from municipal services, yet the retreat of the state from much-needed land administration functions in communal areas must be understood against the discredited history of this function formerly performed by colonial magistrates and native commissioners as part of a repressive apparatus of control.

Market-led land reform and macro-economic policy

South Africa's neoliberal macro-economic policy environment, in which market-led land reforms are being pursued, mitigates against wider agrarian reform and poses challenges for the future possibilities of 'success' among newly settled farmers. The principle of fiscal restraint informs budgeting for the inherently expensive exercise of purchasing land at market prices for redistribution. The funds allocated to land reform have remained below 0,5 per cent of the national budget since 1994 until 2005, when additional funds for restitution brought this to 0,9 per cent for the first time. Increased expenditure following the adoption of a new LRAD grant system in 2001 contributed to a funding bottleneck, in which, by 2004, over half a billion rands worth of projects were approved but could not be transferred due to a lack of funds. Meanwhile, the emphasis placed on maintaining confidence in land markets – and thereby investor confidence – appears to underpin the unwillingness to use the constitutional room for manoeuvre to expropriate property.

A further constraint is the limited state bureaucracy available for the implementation of a state-mediated land reform programme. South Africa's relatively small Department of Land Affairs – the state agency with primary responsibility for land reform – is a national competency and implements reform through its own provincial and district offices, while the national and (mostly downsizing) provincial departments of agriculture (a national *and* provincial competency) have major roles to play in providing 'post-transfer support' to newly settled farmers. However, a chronic lack of alignment between the policies, practices and budgets of the two departments, and the failure of the latter to commit clear resources towards land reform, have hampered the programme thus far.

Alongside land reform, agricultural reforms have seen the rolling back of state-funded agricultural support services including extension services, single channel marketing boards with pricing controls, a preferential lending and tax regime for farmers, production subsidies, and trade protection.[14] This elaborate institutional architecture of support, established by successive apartheid governments in order to subsidise the growth of a white farming sector, was largely dismantled by the end of the 1990s, and thus not available to new black farmers.

The challenges now facing South Africa's efforts at redistributive land reform have much in common with the experiences of the rest of the Southern African region. The limited political will to intervene decisively in land markets or to confront landowners' vested interests in maintaining the *status quo*, the continued influence of white capital on post-independence governments, the constrained fiscal environment, and wider economic and agricultural reforms that undermine the basis for peasant production, are by no means unique to South Africa. The timing of South Africa's transition to democracy in the early 1990s, though, entailed particular political constraints, coinciding as it did with the global disarray of progressive forces at the end of the Cold War, and the ascendancy of the 'Washington Consensus' and neoliberal prescriptions for land and agricultural reforms. Policy intellectuals and political leaders in South Africa have exaggerated the country's much-touted 'exceptionalism' and failed to locate the South African debate within the historical experience of the Southern Africa region and the rest of the continent.

LAND REFORM, THE AGRARIAN QUESTION AND NATIONAL DEVELOPMENT IN AFRICA

Land reform is a fundamental dimension of the agrarian question, and the agrarian question is a fundamental dimension of the national question. The classic agrarian question, concerned with the transition from feudal/agrarian society to capitalist/industrial society, has only been partly resolved by the course of development in the post-Second World War period.[15] While capitalist relations of production have displaced feudal-type relations virtually everywhere, not all parts of the world have become industrialised. Indeed, the international division of labour in industrial and agricultural production persists, with only partial transformation in the post-war era. However, the resolution of the national question continues to be dependent on the resolution of the agrarian question.[16]

The prevalence of semi-proletarianisation (worker-peasants) alongside the retention of large peasantries, or of 'small cultivators' as Archie Mafeje[17] calls them, means that, generally, African rural societies retain households with 'independent' landholdings, albeit at a diminishing scale and on increasingly marginalised lands. But critically, their production and land use activities and relations of production, are restricted by the quality and scale of land available, as well as by state agrarian policies and markets which extract significant surplus value from them. Land reforms in Africa have aimed to redress these land inequities and to direct land-use towards internally beneficial and articulated 'development' for the improved livelihoods of the majority.[18]

The legacy of settler colonial land expropriations, which accompanied colonial conquest, has found expression in demands for reparations. This national question is mirrored in the indigenous land struggles evident today. Land reform programmes in this situation – where compensation of current large landholders is considered almost normative – face popular expectations that former colonial masters should pay the 'victims' of current land reform expropriations, if not also the victims of colonial expropriation, who have suffered long-term loss. Demands for colonial land reparations have been made in Zimbabwe, Namibia and Kenya.

While some Latin American countries received financial support for their land reform from former colonial or imperial powers like the US – especially in the context of Cold War political hegemonic efforts – reparations for colonial land losses in Africa have not been adequately addressed. Some African governments – particularly the Zimbabwean government – allege that racism and protection by international donors of their land-owning 'kith and kin' and their capital in Africa is at the centre of the land reform dilemma and of the political controversy in that country. Current Structural Adjustment Programmes (SAPs) and poverty reduction strategies, which define lending and development assistance, are conditional on economic and governance models which undermine national capacities to redress these grievances according to the 'rule of law'. This feature emphasises the colonial and external dimensions of Africa's land reform processes, and the political controversy of market-driven land reform strategies in the context of the era of neoliberal 'globalisation'.

Most land use policies currently undervalue land, largely by allocating land and related resources to commodities with poor returns and domestic linkages. This external co-optation by neoliberal policies has generally led to the demise of African agriculture, expanded food insecurity and food import and aid dependence, resulting in the inability of agriculture to accumulate investible resources and finance itself, without resorting to external debt entrapment. The trend towards expanding land use patterns for exports has led not only to the loss of local livelihoods based on pastoralism and peasant cropping systems, but also to increased conflicts over the control of land and gradual processes of land alienation. One controversial trend emanating from SAP-based liberalisation is the conversion of farming land to exclusively wildlife and nature-based land uses, often justified as the most environmentally, socially and economically sustainable management of land and natural resources in fragile areas. Tourism and environmentalism have thus created a new land frontier in African states in which foreign and local 'stakeholders' are engaged in land struggles for the exploration and preservation of new forms of bio-diversity and methods of economic and social exploitation.[19]

Clearly, Africa has land questions whose social significance cannot be overstated. Land scarcity, denial of access to natural resources by large land-holders and the state – through laws that exclude many – as well as land privatisation, have all contributed to human distress, poverty and landlessness in Africa.

Redistributive land reforms

Redistributive land reforms are needed in Southern Africa and those parts of East and North Africa that have highly unequal land distribution alongside landlessness and shortages. In these territories, however, limited redistributive land reforms have been attempted since the late 1950s. Since the 1980s, gradualistic market-based land reforms have been initiated in Southern Africa. Land reform was only 'radicalised' recently under conflicted conditions in Zimbabwe. The pressure for redistributive land reforms should also be expected in other countries where localised and regional enclaves of land concentration have emerged, through gradual and piecemeal expropriation by the colonial and post-independence state.

Redistributive land reforms in Africa usually involve restoring land controlled by large landholders through the resettlement of displaced peasants and alienated semi-proletarians, and the enlargement of peasant land areas using repossessed contiguous land. Some of the stated objectives of land redistribution in Africa include: to decongest overpopulated areas; to expand the base of productive agriculture; to rehabilitate people displaced by war; to resettle squatters, the destitute and the landless; to promote equitable distribution of agricultural land; and to de-racialise and/or expand indigenous commercial agriculture. These goals are underpinned by the aim of addressing historical injustices of colonial land expropriation and to assert the right of access by 'indigenes'. Land redistribution has tended to be severely circumscribed by market-oriented approaches to land acquisition and the legal challenge by large landowners of land expropriation mechanisms, while negotiated voluntary transfer of land has not occurred on a significant scale. In East Africa, redistributive reforms were mainly pursued in Kenya and Ethiopia.

Land tenure reforms

Redistributive land reform in Africa should be accompanied by 'progressive' land tenure reforms to counter the general tenure insecurities and land-grabbing processes which have been ushered in and facilitated by regressive state-led land tenure reforms over the last fifty years. Current resistance to land marketisation and 'individualisation' schemes, the manipulative reform of land administration structures through the adaptation of customary tenure procedures and institutions; and new efforts to decentralise and reform land governance systems, encapsulated the type of contradictions which confront progressive land tenure reform.

But Africa's land tenure reform requirements also include institutional reforms that will defend the poor against potential land seizures, as well as accommodate those excluded (women, minorities, settlers) from increasingly scarce arable land. Such tenure reforms would also need to be able to prevent and resolve conflicts over competing claims to land rights and ensure the fair administration of land rights and land use regulations. Whether the land tenure reforms required would include the ability to 'transact' (rent and sell) and mortgage peasant lands – especially in the absence of measures to prevent land alienation and concentration – is as politically contentious as its feasibility is questionable.

The experience with land tenure reforms has perhaps been most widely documented in West and East Africa. Several countries in West Africa have pursued land registration as a first step towards creating land markets. Land tenure policy and legislative reforms have escalated in West Africa since the early 1990s, with countries such as Guinea, Mauritania, Guinea-Bissau and Burkina Faso introducing the concept of private property in response to such pressures for reform.[20] When empirical evidence questioned the relevance of privatisation in promoting security of tenure and the lack of marked differences in investment between customary tenure systems and private property rights, the land tenure policy debate shifted towards 'local rights recognition'.[21] The increased commercialisation and expropriation of land as a result of the production of export crops set in motion serious conflicts, increased land pressure, and resulted in the growth of a land market in Ghana.[22] These tenure reforms are essentially veering towards establishing land markets in the long term.

In East Africa and the Horn, post-independence land tenure reforms have ranged from individualisation and privatisation – in Kenya – to the collectivist approach to land reform – in Tanzania and Ethiopia – while Kenya, Burundi and the Comoros converted indigenous land tenure into private ownership.[23] Most countries in East Africa have provided some legal recognition to indigenous customary land tenure.[24] Tanzania, Ethiopia and Eritrea abolished private ownership and sought to replace indigenous tenure systems with alternative community-based tenure reforms. In North Africa, tenure reforms took ascendance from the 1970s, with an incomplete process of registration and certification of ownership in Tunisia and Morocco. The process of privatisation of state and collectively owned lands has also been slow, as has the emergence of land markets.

This Africa-wide trend in the 1970s and 1980s, towards individualisation and titling of customary lands, was sponsored by donors who were convinced of the superiority of private property rights.[25] When these schemes failed to gain social and political acceptance in the 1990s, the World Bank argued that, as population pressure increased, societies would spontaneously evolve new property relations and land markets, and the task of African governments would be to formalise such evolving property relations through titling.[26] However, contrary to the claim of recognising local land rights, the establishment of land titles and registers has also facilitated a new wave of land alienation and investment by domestic and foreign entrepreneurs. As elsewhere in Africa, land registration in South Africa's communal areas can be expected to increase transaction costs of land, with more resources being spent on registration and administration than on productive use of the land. This could exclude the poor and fuel disputes over inheritance, exclusion of women, and common land in villages.

The role of the African state in promoting equitable access to land through redistributive reforms has been limited. Tenure reforms have instead increased land concentration. Existing African legal frameworks and institutions for managing land allocation and land use or dispute resolution tend to protect the interests of those with disproportionately larger land rights including those property rights derived from past expropriation, rather than the interests of the victims of these inequities.

THE DYNAMICS OF LAND REFORM IN SOUTHERN AFRICA

Settler land expropriation has varied in Southern Africa. It was most extensive in South Africa, Zimbabwe and Namibia, and occurred to a lesser extent in Mozambique, Swaziland, Botswana, and Zambia. The largest scale of white settler land expropriation occurred in South Africa, where 87 per cent of the land was settled in the nineteenth century. In Zimbabwe, an estimated 3 500 white Zimbabwean farm landholders had dual British or South African citizenship. The definition of indigeneity remains contested by white minority groups who are citizens by birth or through naturalisation. These land distributional patterns had far-reaching effects on race relations and socio-demographic features such as wealth, income, and employment distribution and patterns of economic control. Except in South Africa, after independence, white settler populations tended to decrease although the proportion of land held by white minorities has not decreased proportionately. Instead, there has been a gradual increase in foreign landholdings in countries such as Mozambique, Zambia and Malawi, in the context of renewed interest by international capital in natural resources based on tourism and mining.[27]

Countries such as South Africa, Namibia and Zimbabwe are still confronted with unequal landholdings, with titled land in the hands of a small group of white commercial farmers. Skewed landholding is excessive in South Africa. Commercial land under freehold title in Namibia comprises approximately 6 300 farms measuring about 36,2 million hectares belonging to 4 128 mostly white farmers. This freehold land covers 44 per cent of available land and 70 per cent of the most productive agricultural land covering 36 million hectares. Only 2,2 million hectares of commercial farmland belongs to black farmers. By contrast, communal land comprises 138 000 households with an area of 33,5 million hectares, which is only 41 per cent of the land available.

In Zimbabwe most of the freehold land is in the hands of whites and located in the most fertile parts of the country, with the most favourable climatic conditions and water resources. Until 2000, approximately 4 500 white commercial farmers (0,03 per cent of the population) controlled 31 per cent of the country's land under freehold tenure or about 42 per cent of the country's agricultural land. In contrast, 1,2 million black Zimbabwean families subsisted on 41 per cent of the country's total area of 390 076 square kilometres. Per capita arable land ownership per household in Southern Africa has been declining due to the increase in population, while the few white and some black large-scale farmers continue to own most of the best arable land in farms that are oversized.

The criterion used to determine viable farm sizes in Southern Africa is based on a legacy of white settler notions of the 'small scale' being subsistence oriented and the 'commercial' being large-scale white farms. The fundamental class and racial basis of defining large farms was to prescribe higher levels of income targets for whites, against blacks, who were required to provide cheap labour to supplement their incomes. Large farms were also considered necessary for mechanised agriculture on the false premise that economies of scale obtain in farming. Yet blacks have historically been unable to acquire large-scale machinery through institutionalised resource allocation biases and financial discrimination. Still, many of the large farms, while productive on parts of the land, underutilise land, and conceal not only land under-utilisation but also speculative uses of land through wildlife ranching, whose social and economic benefits are widely contested.

The belief that blacks only aim to secure home consumption and residence, and that they do not require land for commercial uses, is a racist notion, since the output performance of small-holders demonstrates that, with adequate access to land, blacks have often contributed substantially to domestic and export markets. Unfortunately, racism – including in some donor circles – continues to reinforce the misplaced notion that when blacks obtain land through state support, this is only a reflection of unproductive cronyism rather than a process of de-racialisation. Since, historically, whites have obtained large-sized land through the same processes, which were aimed at commercialising farming, such notions are unfounded. These contradictions of access to land based on race, class and nationality cleavages are thus a fundamental source of conflict over demands for land in a Southern African region in which the hegemonic neoliberal ideology guiding land reform has actually promoted agrarian capitalism while paying lip service to poverty reduction.

Land distribution problems in non-settler countries occurred initially through rural differentiation processes, which increased in the 1970s and escalated in the 1990s. The maturation of an African *petit bourgeoisie* class after independence saw new land-holding concentrations among retired public servants, professionals, indigenous business people and other urban elites. These social forces emerged from earlier nationalist, political and administrative leaderships, 'traditional' elites, and new post-independence middle-class elements whose accumulation focused on agrarian exports. Such rural differentiation, alongside the growth of poor rural peasantries and semi-proletarians, which 'straddle' the rural and urban divide, explains the demand for land reform policies in favour of elites. Evidence from Malawi, Botswana, Mozambique, and Zambia also reveals that rural land inequality has grown in line with SAPs. Differential access to land and the growth of land concentration has thus emerged from 'below' as well as from 'above'.

Land distributional conflicts affecting some ethnic groups – especially minority 'indigenous' groups (such as the San/Bushmen/Basarwa in Botswana and the Herero in Namibia) – are common in some countries, especially where post-independence land expropriations by the state have facilitated or led to the reallocation of land to local elites and foreign capital. The minority Basarwa in Botswana have historically been a servile underclass exploited by dominant Tswana groups, and other so-called minority groups such as cattle-herders and labourers. Removed from the major urban centres and gaining limited government rural development and infrastructural facilities, they were moved out of the Central Kalahari Game Reserve between June 2001 and October 2002 in a manner which subverted their land rights and natural resources-based livelihoods, in order to expand the national tourist industry.

Unequal land distribution also arises from the growing tendency for land to be concessioned and sold to foreign companies through investment agreements in agriculture, tourism, forestry and urban land investments.[28] The increasing control of large swathes of land and natural resources for tourism in Mozambique, South Africa and Zambia is one source of land and other resource conflicts. Increased privatisation of state land as part of the foreign investment drive has crowded out the poor on to the least productive land. In Mozambique, although all land is constitutionally state-owned, 'privatisation' of land started in 1984 through leasing, as part of the country's SAP. This has created grounds for racial animosity, as foreigners – particularly white South Africans – dominate such investment. Confrontation over land in Zimbabwe has seen the emigration of white Zimbabweans to Malawi, Mozambique, Zambia, and even as far as Nigeria.

Cutting across unequal and discriminatory patterns and structures of land distribution, land tenure and land use, are gender inequalities. Women's access to, and control of, land is inadequate and constrained by various customary and generally patriarchal social relations. In general, the rights of women who hold land are extremely insecure, while women provide labour for farming under severely exploitative relations of production and social reproduction.

The main sources of this unequal land distribution and tenure problem are the dominance of patriarchal and customary land tenure systems and local authority structures. These perverse social relations, which also existed in different form in pre-colonial society, were contrived during colonial and contemporary times by the male-dominated central and local state power structures. Unequal gender relations in land control and use have worsened over time and deprived women of their land rights in many parts of Southern Africa, reduced the extent and quality of the land rights they hold, and failed to cater for new forms of land rights and the growing land needs of women.

Redistributive land reform in Southern Africa

Land reform experiences in Southern Africa exhibit a changing divide between radical nationalist-cum-socialist redistributive land reforms and liberal approaches. Where national liberation was decisively concluded – such as in Mozambique and Angola – the land distribution question appears to have been broadly resolved, although new sites of localised land concentration have emerged. Where liberation was only partially concluded – as in the main settler territories of Zimbabwe, Namibia and South Africa – negotiated settlements left both the 'national question' and land question relatively unresolved. In particular, the racial dimensions of the 'national question' have not been adequately addressed, as structures of wealth, income and land distribution remain intact and protected by liberal democratic constitutions and market principles.

'Radical' land reforms occurred during the nationalisation of colonial, foreign and settler landholdings in Zambia during the early 1970s, and in Mozambique and Angola from the mid-1970s. Zambia and Mozambique pursued 'socialistic' land and agrarian reforms based on developing largely state marketing systems and land settlement, as well as use reorganisation (villagisation and rural development in Tanzania, and resettlement and integrated rural development in Zambia). Mozambique pursued land nationalisation with more intensive attempts at socialistic transformation, using state and cooperative farms. Angola, which started off mired in civil war from 1975, did not pursue further significant land reform after land nationalisation. Civil war in the lusophone territories, fuelled by South African destabilisation and the relative international isolation of both countries (see Conchiglia in this volume), however, contained radical agrarian reforms and 'post-conflict' land tenure reforms which reintroduced some land concentration.

In contradistinction to this situation, more liberal strategies of land reform were adopted in the colonial 'protectorates' of Botswana, Swaziland, Lesotho, and Malawi, which predominantly faced indirect colonial rule accompanied by minor degrees of white settlerism alongside cheap migrant labour. Here land reform involved a limited degree of expropriation of settler lands, accompanied by market-related compensation with some colonial finance, as was the case in Swaziland and Botswana. The expropriated land was 'indigenised' as large farms. Limited foreign and white-dominated large-scale land ownership and estate farming co-existed alongside the emergence of state farms and resilient peasant and pastoral agrarian structures. Liberal approaches to land reform consisted mainly of limited market-led land redistribution efforts and attempts to modernise peasant agriculture within a contradictory context of imbalanced public resource allocations, focusing on the large-scale indigenised and state capitalist farming sub-sector, and agricultural export markets.

Since the 1980s, Zimbabwe and Namibia have used the liberal 'state-centred and market-based' approach to land transfers. Land was acquired by the state for redistribution on a 'willing-seller-willing-buyer' basis, meaning that land identification and supply were market-driven. Both governments identified demand for land and, where possible, matched it with private supply. These programmes were slow in redistributing land, except during the very early years of post-independence Zimbabwe. There, this approach was accompanied by extensive land occupations on abandoned white lands. The use of compulsory land acquisition by the state – with or without compensation for land and improvements – was pursued in Zambia and, since the 1990s, has been seen mainly in Zimbabwe. This approach involves direct intervention by the government in the identification and acquisition of land.

Another liberal approach to land redistribution attempted to a limited degree in both South Africa and Zimbabwe is the market-assisted land reform approach espoused by the World Bank. This effort is supposed to be led by beneficiaries with support from the state, the private sector and non-governmental organisations (NGOs) within a market framework. Very little land has, however, been redistributed through this method so far. This approach has been implemented in Malawi from 2004, using a World Bank grant, in the context of the usual macro-economic policy conditionalities. Finally, a community-led land self-provisioning strategy has been followed in Zimbabwe, mainly in the form of illegal land occupations by potential beneficiaries. This approach has tended to be either state facilitated and formalised, or repressed by the state at various points in time.[29] As a result, the 'fast-track' land reform programme allocated 5,7 million hectares to 130 438 households for smallholder farming and a further 12 556 farmers were allocated about 1,9 million hectares under the scheme for new commercial farmers as at November 2004.

The scale of market-based land reform in Zimbabwe, which by 1990 had transferred about three million hectares (or 155 white farms) to 70 000 families, while limited, was more extensive than the first decade of South Africa's redistribution of less than four per cent of the agricultural land held by large white farmers. Resettlement in Zimbabwe has involved supporting new farmers who contributed significant surpluses.

Redistribution in Namibia since independence in 1989 has been much slower, with only 815 farms out of 4 000 available for sale redistributed by 2004. According to the Namibian government, the price of land has been unacceptably high. As a result, the government has so far only been able to acquire 913 489 hectares since independence and to resettle only 37 100 beneficiaries against a waiting list of an estimated 240 000 applicants.[30] This pattern of slow redistribution has tended to be challenged by scattered land occupations and demands for land by significant actors such as war veterans, farm unions and traditional leaders. The eviction of farm workers by landlords in Namibia also sparked further demands for land reform.

The market approach to land reform was abandoned by the Zimbabwean government in 1997 when, under growing pressure from war veterans and land occupiers as well as increasing economic distress and unemployment resulting from the failure of SAP, the government set out to expropriate 1 471 farms (four million hectares), amounting to 33 per cent of white land, in one stroke. Failure to gain donor funding for this effort and the racial and electoral political realignments which resulted between 1998 and 1999, led to even greater radicalisation of Zimbabwe's land reform process, and heightened electoral and violent conflict between 2000 and 2003. Facing international isolation and resistance by large land-holders, the government of Zimbabwe expropriated 11 million hectares held by white farmers, alongside the growth of land occupation movements spearheaded by war veterans and supported by the ruling Zimbabwe African National Union–Patriotic Front (ZANU-PF) party.

In Namibia, since 2003, the government has embarked on a land expropriation exercise which is limited in scale (less than 15 farms), and is to be based on full market-level compensation. Meanwhile donors have pledged aid to land reform in Namibia in order to avoid a Zimbabwe-like situation. The outcome of this process, however, remains unclear. These experiences show the significant role of the international donor community and race relations in land reform processes in Africa.

LAND REFORM AND CONFLICT

Land conflicts today have resulted from grievances over, and struggles for, access to land and natural resources by both the poor and emerging black capitalist classes. Such grievances reflect the deep roots of social polarisation along racial and nationality lines. These have historically arisen from the discriminatory treatment of blacks on farms, in mines and in towns through a proletarianisation process based on land alienation and the mobilisation of cheap labour, as well as the persistence of racially inequitable development. The increasing radicalisation of land acquisition policies in Namibia and Zimbabwe, and the growth of the tactic of land occupations seen in the SADC region since the 1990s, are manifestations of this deeply-rooted phenomenon of common grievances over unresolved land questions, and the failure of markets and land-owners to reallocate land to a broader constituency.

Since political independence settlements – except for South Africa's – did not consider compensating victims for past losses of land, lives, livestock, wildlife resources and homes, land redistribution can be seen as a form of reparations. It is within this context that countries such as Zimbabwe view the former colonial master, Britain, as having an obligation to pay for the land that was expropriated during the colonial period. The failure of the international community to mobilise funds for land reform has fueled the perception among indigenous people that white landowners are protected by the donor community, because white land-owners are their 'kith and kin'. Thus, the land question in Southern Africa has been viewed as an internationalised form of racist privileging of white minorities in the face of demands for land redistribution by victims of past land expropriations.[31] One of the major impacts of Zimbabwe's land expropriation has been the translocation of large-scale white farmers from Zimbabwe to various countries in the region, facilitated by international finance, and by governments willing to provide them with cheap land leaseholds, subsidised operating and investment capital, and cheap labour. This has created grounds for racial animosity, as foreigners and white South Africans tend to dominate this investment, with little social integration of incoming white farmers who create 'white islands' in which commercial development outpaces surrounding indigenous populations.

In South Africa, the recent resurgence and reshaping of the land question has underscored how land reform is at once a response to, a cause of, and potentially a means of resolving, the roots of conflict. In the early 1990s, the World Bank advocated land reform to the ANC as a redistributive strategy necessary to guard against widespread rural instability and even, in the long term, possible civil war. This was within the tradition of pre-emptive land reforms promoted in south-east Asia and Latin America during the Cold War as a bulwark against more radical revolutionary movements. Since the World Bank's intervention, though, the demand for land has become more apparent through land occupations in urban and rural areas.

Land occupations in South Africa are an ongoing phenomenon, and vary between individual and collective encroachments onto public and private land, as well as overt and covert struggles.[32] Gillian Hart has demonstrated the interlinkages between struggles for land in rural and urban areas, and struggles for other livelihood resources and opportunities.[33] The illegal occupation of peri-urban land at Bredell outside Johannesburg, and Khayelitsha outside Cape Town, in the winter of 2001 by shack dwellers whose homes had been flooded, was overtly political and group-based. Sporadic conflicts over peri-urban land persist in most of South Africa's large metropolitan settlements. Meanwhile, in parts of KwaZulu-Natal in particular, the landless have encroached on white commercial farmland where they have established their homes and, in some cases, started to engage in some agricultural production of their own. Elsewhere, groups of restitution claimants have tried to force the hand of the state by occupying both private and state-owned land to which they have laid claim. These struggles for land are often interwoven with wider rural struggles for survival and for control of the countryside, evident in the levels of violence on farms, including murders of both farm workers and farm owners, the rise of farm commandos and patterns of fence-cutting and stock-theft.

FARM WORKERS

Another nexus of conflict evident in South Africa is embedded in the relationship between white landowners and black tenants and workers. Poor living and working conditions on farms, as well as physical and other abuses, disputes over the rights of labour tenants on white-owned farms, the continued eviction of farm workers and their families, and the problem of growing landlessness resulting from this movement of workers from farms, have combined to form a potent cocktail of human rights violations and conflict. The failure to secure rights for people living on farms since the advent of democracy in South Africa, and the absence of a coherent approach to providing alternative land or housing for those evicted, has fed into the growth of informal settlements where few, if any, economic opportunities exist, not only on the perimeter of rural towns but also in the heartland of commercial farming.

Labour tenants who have some farming base in South Africa amount to about 50 000, while about 960 000 full- and part-time farm workers were employed in 1996, amounting to 11 per cent of formal employees – though the number has dropped markedly since then due to job losses arising out of the twin processes of agricultural deregulation and trade liberalisation.[34] Slow land redistribution has forced most of South Africa's rural poor, including black rural landless workers, into increasing poverty and frustration over bureaucratic land reforms, as well as worsening working conditions on white commercial farms. Farm workers face evictions, which the state seems unwilling or unable to stem. A recent survey by Nkuzi Development Association revealed that evictions from South African farms have accelerated under the ANC government. Between 1993 and 2004, a total of 942 303 people were evicted from farms, compared to 737 114 in the preceding decade under apartheid. Gross human rights abuses by white farmers against labour tenants and farm workers continue. Beside the growing demands by farm workers for access to land and livelihoods, over 1 500 killings of white farmers since 1994 raise questions about the nature of land politics in South Africa.[35] The extent to which farmers as employers and landowners can punish workers by expulsion as an ultimate sanction, demolish their homes, close their access to water taps and natural resources (such as rivers), and bar them from rearing livestock, emphasises the insecure rights of farm workers.

That farm workers have been marginalised in the process of land redistribution is by no means an exclusively South African phenomenon. After the 'fast-track' land reform in Zimbabwe, farm workers amounted to only about five per cent (or 8 750) of the total land beneficiaries, although they constitute about 12 per cent of the farm population. A large number of farm workers were stranded, given that not more than 100 000 remain employed in the commercial farm sector.[36] Official discourses initially focused on repatriating such farm workers who were branded as migrants from neighbouring states despite having lived in Zimbabwe for over 60 years. Some were maintained as workers for new farmers, rather than address-ing their specific land rights. The land rights of farm workers, in terms of their access to residential land and infrastructure on large-scale commercial farming land and access to small food security plots have, for decades, been informal and incidental to their provision of labour services to landowners. While a few farm workers have been resettled, some were displaced, and many still reside on farms without secure land rights. Land reform in Southern Africa as a whole has not addressed farm workers' demands for their own agricultural land. A key unaddressed problem remains the need to reduce conflicts between white farmers and current and former farm workers, and the integration of former farm workers into farming communities by confirming their land rights.

LIVELIHOODS, MIGRATION AND SOCIAL MOVEMENTS

Rural livelihoods in South Africa, as in other developing countries, are characterised by strategies that straddle rural and urban livelihoods. These were mediated through influx control under apartheid and, from the 1990s, shaped by a complex and shifting mix of 'push' and 'pull' forces including disemployment trends in the formal urban sectors of mining and manufacturing; the prospect of improved access to health, education and other services in urban centres; the pressures of HIV/AIDS on household formation leading to low-risk livelihood strategies (see Ndinga-Muvumba and Mottiar in this volume); and increased reliance on extended family networks.[37] Together with the movement of large numbers of farm workers off commercial farms, as the trend towards job-shedding in agriculture and farm evictions gathered pace, these factors have led to new dynamics in migration and livelihoods, and have challenged notions of a linear process of proletarianisation. These larger economic processes, in articulation with political organisation and expressions of demands for land, suggest a potential for deepening conflict over land in rural South Africa.

Emerging social movements have focused on land reform, challenged existing land property laws and confronted the state to reject market-based commercialisation of agriculture and marketised land tenure.[38] It is not surprising therefore that, along with deepening poverty and proliferating rural violence over the last two decades, there have emerged both organised and spontaneous rural movements, outside the 'civil' framework, seeking to transform inherited property regimes and elitist land policymaking. Across the continent, peasants' resistance to land policy and their evasion of natural resource regulations are a major way in which the state-led land policy agenda has been challenged, even if such resistance has not been articulated in a formally coherent strategy or academic discourse.[39] Although not systematically coordinated on a national level, it appears that the common actions of peasant organisations, when multiplied, can initiate policy reversals.[40] This social interaction between the state and the rural poor represents a clear class dimension of the land question in Africa, whereby rural peasantries, sometimes in alliance with the urban poor, mobilise against the land policies of the ruling classes.[41]

In South Africa, land issues have received little attention from most political parties, though this has changed discernibly since the high-profile land occupations in Zimbabwe since 2000. As with the private sector, the question of whether South Africa will 'go the Zimbabwe route' has occupied the minds of politicians, the media and, to some extent, the general public. In this context, the emergence of social movements such as the Landless People's Movement (LPM) in 2001, and related localised movements such as the Anti-Eviction Campaign, has struck a chord. Operating independently of any political party, the LPM has organised around local land struggles by labour tenants, evicted farm workers, land restitution claimants and residents of peri-urban informal settlements. The movement has called for land reform to be accelerated; for the 'willing buyer, willing seller' principle to be discarded, and for underutilised land and land belonging to absentee landowners and abusive farmers to be expropriated. The LPM has threatened to occupy land illegally to drive home these demands. Though the size and radicalism of the group is often exaggerated, its appearance on the political landscape marked a new departure for the 'politics of land' in South Africa.

The challenge to the existing policy framework was reinforced when during 2005, the South African government responded to calls by the LPM and other land lobby groups to host a land summit. The key demand was to increase state intervention in land acquisition through expropriation, and to speed up land redistribution. To the surprise of land activists, the government announced at the summit that it was indeed considering a review of its 'willing buyer, willing seller' approach, and employing non-market methods to acquire land – through negotiated sales and expropriation of property – as well as regulated land markets through land taxes, land ceilings, subdivision of land holdings and restrictions on the ownership of land by foreigners. During 2006, the South African government initiated a review of the 'willing buyer, willing seller' policy principle and adopted a Proactive Land Acquisition Strategy (PLAS) which empowered officials to purchase land on the market that would be retained as state land, pending the identification of beneficiaries to whom it could be leased or sold. This resolved the problem of land availability, but not the problem of its affordability. To provide a planning framework to determine which land should be acquired, for what purpose and for whom, a wider reform involving area-based planning for land reform within local government integrated development plans (IDPs) was under discussion by early 2007. This was envisaged to be a means of identifying land needs and as a basis to guide state intervention to make land available in areas of acute demand – whether by acquiring land on the open market, by proactively negotiating with landowners to release land or, where this fails, by expropriating land. What has resulted, then, from South Africa's land summit in 2005 was not a wholesale turnaround of the market-based paradigm within land reform, but rather its modification. Two years after the 'willing buyer, willing seller' policy was apparently rejected, it continues to be implemented, alongside some moderate attempts to improve government planning and to make markets work better for the poor.

Despite these signals of increased state intervention, the South African government has shown itself to be more willing to use land markets than to override them. Expropriation has thus far only been considered with respect to historically-based land restitution claims. By early 2007, expropriation proceedings had been initiated in a few cases where landowners have been unwilling to sell their farms that are being claimed under restitution offered at prices the state valuers consider to be market prices. The first such expropriation of a 25 000 hectare farm in the Northern Cape took place in January 2007.

This prompted a degree of alarmist speculation in the media about the radicalisation of land reform in South Africa which, given the extensive legal safeguards and the government's cautious approach, seems misplaced. However, in the absence of a revised policy framework, expropriation remains an option of last resort only invoked in selected cases where restitution claims by those historically dispossessed have not been resolved because of the resistance of current landowners. State intervention in favour of the landless and for the purpose of general redistribution has not been evident thus far, despite widespread agreement – from government, from NGOs, from the LPM, and even from some landowners – on the need for a stronger role for the state in acquiring land and in planning development.

CONCLUDING REFLECTIONS

The land question and the nature of land reforms pursued or not pursued are a fundamental source of conflict in the largely agrarian and semi-proletarian societies of Southern Africa. These sources of conflict arise from a complex range of socio-political and economic dimensions. Most critically, the failure of neoliberal 'development' to resolve the agrarian question, suggests the continued significance of struggles of access to land, livelihoods and national development. The white settlerist basis of Southern Africa's land problem emphasises the primacy of racial conflicts in land reform, and nationalistic tendencies towards resolving national development. Neoliberal development and land reform policies have been unable to negotiate peaceful resolutions of these conflicts so far.

In this context, South Africa's land question is far from exceptional. The extent of land dispossession in South Africa may exceed that of other countries in the region and the continent. However, the country shares the phenomenon of agrarian dualism, pervasive rural-urban and cross-border labour migration, and newly emerging social movements giving voice to a new 'politics of land' within the Southern African region. Access to, and rights over, land as an issue of citizenship and identity, as well as an issue of survival and 'development', resonates within the wider Southern African region, not least due to the shared historical experience of institutionalised racism.

Struggles for radical land redistribution are a feature of the Southern African region, but are not always overt, nor are they separate from wider struggles of the poor. Struggles for land and for rural livelihoods have gained new clarity and momentum over the past decade and a half, often in response to sluggish attempts at market-based reforms, as in Namibia and South Africa. These struggles have been waged in South Africa and elsewhere in a context of neoliberal policies that have hastened the commodification of land as well as other natural resources, undermined opportunities elsewhere in the economy, favoured the emergence of indigenous elites, and constrained the state interventions necessary to bring about radical agrarian change. In this area, in particular, there is a shared challenge facing land reform in South Africa, Southern Africa and the rest of the continent.

The past thirteen years have seen a resurgence and a reshaping of the land question in ways that link South Africa even more strongly to the rest of Southern Africa. Conflicts over resources and livelihoods are clearly evident in South Africa, as they are elsewhere in the region. However, whether land issues emerge as a focus of conflict depends substantially on political organisation among rural people as well as on the broader political and economic trajectory of change in South Africa and beyond.

8

HIV/AIDS and the African Renaissance:
South Africa's Achilles heel?

ANGELA NDINGA-MUVUMBA AND SHAUNA MOTTIAR

*It is said that it is better to die than to be shamed, but it must be quickly
added that shame bears its own fruit, death bears none.*

– *Ahmadou Kourouma*, Waiting for the Wild Beasts to Vote[1]

South African president Thabo Mbeki's African Renaissance is contemporary
Africa's grand idea, much like Senegal's poet-president Léopold Senghor's
Negritude, and Ghanaian leader Kwame Nkrumah's 'Nkrumahism' and vision
of 'a United States of Africa'. Similar to his predecessors, Mbeki's vision for peace
and prosperity is rooted in the historical events of the liberation of his country.
South Africa's peaceful democratic transition confounds Afro-pessimist views
that the continent is doomed.[2] Meanwhile, Tshwane (Pretoria) has galvanised
leadership at all levels to engage more vigorously in Africa's development
and conflict management efforts, including the establishment of the African
Union (AU) in Durban, South Africa in 2002 (see Adebajo and Landsberg in
this volume). Yet, the 'Rainbow Nation' is still struggling to come to terms with
its HIV/AIDS epidemic – a crisis with long-term consequences for its political
economy and its character – and has failed to provide leadership on an issue
that is central to the long-term sustainability of Africa's states and societies.

For many years now, experts have speculated about the magnitude of Africa's
AIDS epidemic. In May 2006, UNAIDS confirmed that an estimated 25 million
Africans were living with the virus.[3] Although the continent has 10 per cent
of the world's population, it is home to 60 per cent of all HIV infections. The
scale of HIV/AIDS is amplified in South Africa. According to a national HIV
survey conducted in 2005, 5,6 million South Africans were HIV positive by
the end of 2003.[4] Between 1998 and 2003, South Africa's death registration
data showed a 40 per cent rise in the total number of adult deaths in the past
six years and among women between 20 and 49 years, an increase in deaths of

150 per cent. While this data needs to be carefully interpreted, it is difficult for many to believe that this dramatic increase in mortality is not related to rising levels of HIV prevalence.

This chapter is animated by an urgent question: does South Africa's response to HIV/AIDS match what might have been expected by Afro-optimists hoping for an African Renaissance uncompromised by the pandemic? We stress that Tshwane has launched the world's most ambitious treatment programme, and that this could play an important role in realising the African Renaissance. Still, we argue that South Africa's leadership in Africa is compromised by how it has related to its own AIDS crisis. The chapter confirms that while Mbeki has never claimed *that* HIV does not cause AIDS, the apparent intersections between issues of race, sex and AIDS denialism have influenced his government's response to HIV/AIDS. We also assess the implications of the ANC government's heavily criticised response to the pandemic. The chapter juxtaposes South Africa's response to HIV with examples of leadership on AIDS from Senegal and Uganda; and examines the HIV/AIDS response emanating from other fora such as SADC, the AU and the UN. We conclude by arguing that unless South Africa comes to terms with HIV/AIDS, its role in realising an African Renaissance will prove elusive.

CONTAINING HIV/AIDS: A QUESTION OF LEADERSHIP

A brief history of South Africa's HIV/AIDS response

The ANC-led government finally agreed in late 2003 – after a period of sharp and protracted resistance – to provide antiretroviral (ARV) therapy to HIV-positive patients in public health-care facilities. Critics continue to point out that the government's rollout of ARVs was conveniently initiated in an election year – 2004. Indeed, despite the fact that the ANC placed the HIV/AIDS crisis on its agenda even before it came to power in 1994, it failed to implement immediately an effective policy to deal with the HIV/AIDS crisis in the country on assuming power.

In 1991, the ANC's health secretariat and the apartheid government's Department of National Health and Population Development formed the National AIDS Convention of South Africa (NACOSA), which brought together political parties, trade unions, the business sector, civic associations, government departments, health workers and academics. Following the 1994 election,

President Nelson Mandela endorsed a formal strategy for NACOSA under his minister of health, Nkosazana Dlamini-Zuma. However, what followed was a disillusioning experience for many who had hoped there would be rapid implementation of a strategy that should have seen South Africa become a model for other countries.[5]

As Mandela's deputy president, Mbeki led the 1994 AIDS ministerial task team responsible for driving the government's response to establish an AIDS infrastructure. Yet, Mbeki barely mentioned HIV/AIDS in public.[6] The AIDS task team was mandated to augment the existing public health structure and to generate an HIV/AIDS plan. The government committed itself to mobilising awareness campaigns and supporting research and development for an HIV vaccine. Tragically, by 1996, it had become clear that the government's response was failing, with HIV levels having doubled from 7,6 per cent in 1994 to 14,2 per cent in 1996.[7] This failure was compounded by the government's refusal to make nevirapine available to HIV-positive pregnant women in order to prevent mother-to-child transmission. In July 2003, the government was compelled to provide MTCT treatment by a Constitutional Court ruling, after court action by the Treatment Action Campaign (TAC).

After South Africa's second democratic election in 1999 and under the helm of Mbeki as the new president, the health portfolio was given to Dr Manto Tshabalala-Msimang. In May 2000, the Department of Health initiated its HIV/AIDS/Sexually-Transmitted Diseases (STD) Strategic Plan for South Africa for 2000–2005.[8] The May 2000 plan focused on prevention and management of HIV/AIDS rather than on treatment programmes for HIV/AIDS infected people. Once again, AIDS activists – notably the Treatment Action Campaign – criticised this stance and advocated for affordable ARV treatment in public health-care facilities. Finally in August 2003, the government instructed the Department of Health to begin the immediate rollout of ARV therapy in public hospitals across South Africa. This was to be guided by an operational plan for comprehensive HIV and AIDS care.[9]

The rollout of ARV treatment actually only began in April 2004 and has been described as 'painfully slow'.[10] The Department of Health continues to emphasise that since there is no cure for HIV, a focus on prevention should remain paramount. Yet it has been widely demonstrated that a comprehensive response which includes the provision of antiretrovirals can save lives and provide hope, both of which strengthen the efficacy of prevention programmes. Thus, while the South African government justifiably sought to engage in prevention, its messages and slow rollout of ARVs ultimately seemed to privilege prevention over other components of a comprehensive response. Indeed, according to statistics put forward by the AIDS Foundation of South Africa, by early 2005 only about 30 000 patients were receiving ARV treatment in the public sector.[11] In December 2005, the health minister stated that 'about 85 000 people had been initiated on ARV treatment in the public health sector by September 2005'.[12] According to the TAC, by the end of 2005, 110 000 patients were receiving ARVs in the public sector.[13] Deena Bosch of the AIDS Law Project in Cape Town noted that the Department of Health claimed that by March 2006, 130 000 people were receiving treatment in the public sector. Bosch warned however, that these figures could be inflated, and that owing to poor monitoring and evaluation systems, they could not be independently confirmed.[14] KwaZulu-Natal – the province with the highest HIV/AIDS prevalence rate in the country – fell well short of its treatment goals as evidenced by detailed 2004 statistics. The province set a target of treating 20 000 patients by March 2005. By the end of 2004, however, it was only treating 3 247 adults and 167 children.[15] By October 2006, the South African government reported that 224 895 patients had been enrolled to receive ARVs through public health services in all districts and prisons of the country.[16] Civil society, on the other hand, reported estimated numbers of between 165 000 and 175 000 persons actually on treatment in the public sector by that date.[17]

Various reasons have been put forward to explain the slow pace of ARV rollout in South Africa. Among these are severe human resource and technical capacity shortages in clinics and hospitals across the country; gaps in communication and information sharing between national, provincial health departments and civil society organisations with regard to data collection, patient management and outcomes, treatment literacy and community awareness; a lack of clarity on the extent to which provinces are using grants allocated by the national treasury or funds from their own budgets to implement ARV treatment; and difficulties in monitoring ARV rollout, owing to a lack of information about budgetary allocations for medical counseling, testing and laboratory services.[18]

The racial politics of AIDS

Our brief history of South Africa's response to HIV/AIDS captures the government's policies, practices and results. In many ways, the above narrative is a 'public account', which frames the official discourse of South Africa's HIV/AIDS response. This is a history of clear and simple facts. Yet, a more complicated and messy narrative has simultaneously preoccupied South Africans. Issues of race, sex, dissent and denial explain the government's motivation to debate the cause of AIDS and its reluctance to provide AIDS drugs.

Colonial and apartheid medicine designed the treatment of sexually transmitted diseases among the black South African population on a racist premise: black people could not control their insatiable sexual drives.[19] Indeed, well before Mbeki made contact with AIDS dissidents who questioned mainstream HIV/AIDS science in 1999, the international medical community had made grave errors by imprecisely constructing a discourse that framed HIV as a consequence of deviant black sexuality. In the early 1980s, some North American journalists claimed that Haitians were getting AIDS because of their propensity for 'ritual sex and voodoo ceremonies'.[20] This pathologisation of 'black sexuality' is an essentialist hangover that still features in the politics of AIDS. It presumes that there is such a thing as 'a single black sexuality' while obscuring the material realities and historical legacies that racial groups face every day. The pathologisation of 'black sexuality' does not recognise that victims of poverty and social exclusion live in marginal conditions that exacerbate the conditions for disease. Indeed, this is the link between poverty and disease that Mbeki attempted to raise in his controversial address to the thirteenth International AIDS Conference, in Durban, South Africa in July 2000.[21] Nevertheless, the configuration of race and sex is a powerful force for re-enforcing negative stereotypes.

HIV/AIDS has been caught in this debate. Yet, there is a vast qualitative difference between the articulation of the real dangers of unprotected sex; the socio-economic and cultural factors which render groups such as young women more vulnerable to HIV; or the multiplier effect of dispersed sexual networks on one hand, and so-called licentious black sex on the other. There are important cultural practices, socio-economic realities, and gendered and political conditions that increase vulnerability to disease, and drive epidemics such as HIV/AIDS. Articulating these conditions should not be perceived as an attack on black South African people, but as an explanation of the forces that influence health. AIDS prevention activists and the medical community have never seriously addressed this distinction. The failure to do so has left room for defensive Afrocentric posturing among key policymakers. Allister Sparks has pointed out that Mbeki's initial vulnerability to AIDS denialism might indeed have been grounded in an innocent but complicated desire to defend the dignity and integrity of black people:

Somehow in this complex man there seems to be a deep-seated anger that ... the whole thing amounts to a calumny against African culture and sexual behaviour; that the disease is being used as a means to smear black people the way homosexuals were demonised when AIDS first appeared in the US.[22]

The now famous speech given by Mbeki at South Africa's Fort Hare University in October 2001 disputes mainstream HIV/AIDS scientific views *because* they seem to be racist: '... they proclaim that our continent is doomed to an inevitable mortal end because of our devotion to the sin of lust.'[23] The impression thus created is that Mbeki viewed the established scientific community's diagnosis of HIV/AIDS as racist, simply because it framed sex as the driving factor for the spread of HIV. As Peter Mokaba, a former ANC deputy minister who died in 2002, noted:

> The story that HIV causes AIDS is being promoted through lies, pseudo-science, violence, terrorism and deception ... We are urged to abandon science and adopt the religion of superstition that HIV exists and that it causes AIDS. We refuse to be agents for using our people as guinea pigs and have a responsibility to defeat the intended genocide and dehumanisation of the African family and society.[24]

The above statement is useful for shedding some light on the discourse of AIDS denialism. Steven Robins contends that prominent South African AIDS denialists – some of whom were close to Mbeki – saw the AIDS dialogue through the 'colour coded lens of colonial histories of discrimination and dispossession.'[25] Findings surrounding the AIDS discourse were understood as the product of historically constructed and politically driven processes embedded in colonialism, apartheid and capitalism. Various local social interpretations of HIV/AIDS frame this view. These include the view that 'whites' are out to contain 'black' population growth; the fear of 'white doctors' who inject 'black patients' with HIV when they go for tests; the conspiracy theory that the US Central Intelligence Agency and pharmaceutical companies are using the 'so-called AIDS crisis' to make money in African markets and using Africans as guinea pigs for scientific experiments; and the contention that ARV treatment is murderously toxic.

The fact that South Africa had emerged from apartheid, which produced extraordinary socio-economic inequalities and dehumanised black people, also explains why race and cultural identity became central to the AIDS discourse in the country. Perhaps because of its own reluctance to talk about race, the AIDS community largely failed to address these issues. In South Africa, the causes of HIV remained ephemeral, so that official government policies on HIV prevention co-exist with cultural and racial defensiveness. Institutions and policies that promoted safer sex and the protection of women against sexual violence – a driver of the epidemic – have increased since the end of apartheid. Yet, unsubstantiated myths about a global conspiracy to unleash HIV and to kill black South Africans still abound. Addressing racial issues will continue to be a dominant challenge in South Africa's AIDS saga.

Thabo Mbeki and the ANC: Dissent and denial

Mbeki's first key leadership role on the AIDS issue was to head the government's AIDS ministerial task team in 1994. The journey from that early intervention to the government's ARV rollout in 2004 has arguably done more damage to Mbeki's reputation than any other political issue during his tenure in office. Mbeki's is a path punctuated with fits of rage against the West; categorical rejection of dissent within the ANC; and battles with an organised movement of people living with HIV/AIDS. It is likely that Mbeki – the African intellectual – had the noblest intentions and sought an African solution to the HIV/AIDS crisis. However, Mbeki's willingness to re-open a debate about the cause of HIV and his explicit, and then implicit, ties with dissident American scientists who claimed that HIV does not cause AIDS, was also representative of the normal human first response to death and loss: denial and isolation.

The 1997 'Virodene' episode marked Mbeki's first foray into dubious science. In 1997, a group of University of Pretoria academics linked to the South African biomedical company, Cryopreservation Technologies, claimed that they had discovered an AIDS cure in the form of a new experimental drug called Virodene. The Medicines Control Council (MCC) – an independent government body – had declared the drug ineffectual and unsafe. However, then deputy president Mbeki's quest for a local solution to the AIDS problem made him susceptible to persuasion. The deputy president invited the researchers to present their findings to the government in early 1997 and pushed aggressively for Virodene's licensing and distribution.[26]

The Virodene experience shows that Mbeki's efforts to solve the AIDS problem were well-meaning: Mbeki simply wanted an expedient and effective solution to the human tragedy of HIV/AIDS in South Africa.[27] Unfortunately, another scientific review quickly established that Virodene had been tested on

11 AIDS patients without having been first tried on animals in the laboratory. Moreover, the so-called AIDS 'cure' was in fact an industrial solvent, and highly toxic. The opposition seized on the issue. The leader of the Democratic Alliance, Tony Leon, criticised Mbeki's pursuit of 'African solutions'.

Eventually, Mbeki's search for alternative solutions to the AIDS problem was enthusiastically joined by scientific dissidents, based in America. By the end of 1999, the president had been introduced to virusmyth.net – a website of the AIDS 'dissident' community – by Anthony Brink, a lawyer from Pietermaritzburg, and Mbeki had also consumed the work of American scientist David Rasnick and other AIDS denialists, who did not believe that HIV caused AIDS.[28] In April 2000, Mbeki wrote a letter to several world leaders defending further examination of alternative views on HIV/AIDS and accusing critics of intellectual censorship.[29]

The treatment paradox: The government's mixed signals

Early on, key members of Mbeki's cabinet questioned the validity of treating victims of a chronic, incurable disease and worried that the government's other objectives for economic growth, national security, and service delivery would suffer if there was too much of a focus on AIDS.[30] As John Illife noted:

> In 1994, the newly elected ANC was confronted with an epidemic that had no cure; would be expensive to treat; was fuelled by sex (and therefore fodder for racist views of black sexuality); and most importantly, would undermine the ANC's efforts to build a prosperous South Africa ... The subject of HIV/AIDS was a dangerous topic for South Africa's new black government: it was an embarrassing, disturbing, complex, and seemingly unresolvable dilemma.[31]

In 1995, the South African government took action against international pharmaceutical companies and contested the intellectual property claims of these firms that charged high prices for life-saving AIDS medicines. In an effort to accelerate the processes for compulsory licensing and parallel imports of medicines, the government proposed and secured legislation for an amendment to the country's Medicines and Related Substances Control Act. Under pressure from American pharmaceutical companies, US President Bill Clinton's administration threatened South Africa with sanctions if it implemented the legislation. When the Pharmaceutical Manufacturers' Association of South Africa took the government to court in 1998 on the issue of importing cheaper generics, a strategic and startling alliance emerged: the TAC supported the government and launched a wide-ranging global campaign to highlight the rights of poor people to treatment.[32] The alliance between the TAC, the ANC, trade unions and others, paid off, and by 2001, international pharmaceutical companies were morally and legally compelled to negotiate reduced prices with African governments. Simultaneously, the South African government was beginning to pour resources into a national AIDS prevention programme. In 2001–02, South Africa's national treasury reported that the government had spent US$33,3 million on HIV/AIDS programmes.[33]

Nevertheless, even as the cost of providing ARVs dropped, the government refused to distribute these drugs through the public healthcare system. The Mbeki administration argued that nevirapine and other ARVs were unsafe and toxic. Yet, as early as December 1999, the health minister's claim about the toxicity of ARVs had been debunked. A review of clinical trials and research had been submitted to the health minister stating that nevirapine was an effective option for treating pregnant mothers. Yet, the minister ignored the report. Meanwhile, the AIDS Advisory Council was renamed the Presidential AIDS Advisory Council. The new body produced no definitive views on the links between HIV and AIDS or the efficacy of ARVs.[34]

The end of denial? The ANC's promise of treatment

Disputes within the tripartite ruling alliance on the AIDS issue began to become costly. TAC formed a separate partnership with Cosatu and the SACP on the AIDS issue. Nelson Mandela met with the TAC leader Zachie Achmat. Some of the country's most visible black leaders, such as Desmond Tutu, Mamphele Ramphele, Pregs Govender, Olive Shisana, Kgotsile Letlape and William Makgoba – one of Africa's most eminent medical scientists and a former close associate of Mbeki – were expressing their dissent, and it became increasingly difficult for Mbeki to state categorically that views different from his opinions were part of a global conspiracy against black people.[35] These developments shifted the discourse away from race. Members of Mbeki's international investment council were also concerned that foreign investors viewed the president's opinions on HIV/AIDS as perplexing and shocking.[36] It began to appear that the government's involvement with 'dubious' science could affect the country's economic prospects.

By 2002, Mbeki had started distancing himself from the AIDS dissidents and claimed that the public perception of the government's support for the dissidents reflected a 'failure of communication on our side'.[37] In his 2006 'State of the Nation' speech to the South African parliament, Mbeki referred to HIV/AIDS only once. The president may not have revised his views, but instead chose to remain silent on the issue.[38] In fact, the issue of AIDS did not feature in the ANC's 2006 local government campaign manifesto.

Finally, the collision of multiple and contradictory race, sex and cultural narratives was profoundly evident in the rape trial of former deputy president Jacob Zuma in 2006. Zuma admitted to having had unprotected sex with a woman known to be HIV-positive. Moreover, it was reported that he claimed that taking a shower after sexual intercourse could reduce the risk of infection. South African AIDS activists were devastated: Zuma had served in leadership positions on issues of moral regeneration and HIV/AIDS prevention. The fact that a prominent ANC official could inhabit two inherently contradictory narratives on the causes of HIV transmission meant that the science of AIDS was still not being taken seriously at the highest levels.

The impact of an inadequate response

While Mbeki and the ANC debated the science behind HIV and AIDS, the virus was staking a claim on South Africa's future. In 2003, 62 per cent of young HIV-positive people had believed that they were at little or no risk of infection.[39]

During the August 2006 International AIDS Conference in Toronto, Canada, South Africa's HIV/AIDS response came under intense fire. The South African government's exhibition stall at the conference was 'dominated by woven baskets of plump lemons, wilted beetroot, African potatoes and clumps of garlic'.[40] Already, Health Minister Tshabalala-Msimang had been criticised for repeatedly promoting nutrition as an 'alternative' to AIDS treatments such as ARVs. The exhibition booth organised by the minister's office contributed to these perceptions. Indeed, only after journalists asked why no ARVs were displayed along with the vegetables (as part of a comprehensive approach to treatment), did one of Tshabalala-Msimang's staff members reportedly add his own bottles of ARV medication to the display. Unfortunately, the minister's response was to dig in her heels, stating that South Africa expected to be criticised but that it was 'important to allow people in the rural areas to make up their own minds' on whether they 'preferred alternative medicine or antiretrovirals'.[41] Certainly, this comment increased rather than decreased the perception that the South

African government was being driven by the whims of AIDS denialists.

Canadian development advocate, Stephen Lewis, the UN Special Envoy for HIV/AIDS in Africa, took the podium in Toronto, and noted that the South African government's HIV/AIDS policies were the worst on the African continent. More troubling, four years after Mbeki had withdrawn from the debate on the causal link between HIV and AIDS, Lewis accused the South African government of espousing views on HIV/AIDS that were 'more worthy of a lunatic fringe than of a concerned and compassionate state'.[42] Adding to the furore, South African journalists in Toronto reported the views of an Indian doctor, Dr Jaya Shreedar, who explained that, in India, apathetic government policymakers defended their inaction by stating that, at least their response to India's HIV/AIDS crisis was not as bad as that of the South African health minister's, and added that, 'you guys are like a worst practice example'.[43]

Toronto led to a brief but profoundly important confrontation on the issue of political leadership on HIV/AIDS in South Africa. Immediately after the AIDS conference, the South African government rejected international and national criticisms, while the TAC launched a mass action protest, with marches around the country, that eventually led to Mbeki's office in Tshwane. The TAC demanded that the South African government call a national meeting to address the HIV/AIDS crisis in the country and that Mbeki dismiss Tshabalala-Msimang.[44] The organisation complained that the minister was 'promoting pseudo-scientifc remedies' which undermined the rollout of ARVs.[45] Moreover, the South African National AIDS Council (SANAC) had only met twice in 2006 and had not drawn up a follow-up prevention plan to the HIV/AIDS/STD Strategic Plan for South Africa for 2000–05, nor implemented effectively the 2003 operational plan for comprehensive HIV and AIDS care.[46]

Initially, the South African government's response to these accusations was to argue that there had been a failure in communications.[47] However, by November 2006, the government had moved beyond focusing on public relations, and made significant changes. First, a decision was taken to shift the leadership on national HIV/AIDS issues to the office of the presidency, with deputy president, Phumzile Mlambo-Ngcuka, overseeing SANAC and forming a new high-level interdepartmental committee, which would monitor the implementation of the government's HIV/AIDS programme. The new committee held its first meeting in September 2006.[48] Second, together with Nozizwe Madlala-Routledge, the deputy minister of health, the deputy president played a key role in repairing relations with AIDS activists and civil society organisations. In October 2006, the deputy president addressed a Civil Society Congress made up of religious leaders, HIV/AIDS activists, and trade union representatives.[49]

Just before World AIDS Day on 1 December 2006, SANAC and the department of health issued a Broad Framework for an HIV/AIDS and Sexually Transmitted Infections (STI) Strategic Plan for 2007–11, which was developed in consultation with non-governmental organisations. The framework called for 'evidence-based' approaches and the involvement of people living with HIV/AIDS, which would presumably place at the centre of its strategies the medical needs of those most affected by HIV/AIDS.[50] Evidence of the shift in the government's policy was provided by the TAC's observation that 'the eight year struggle to end government HIV denialism and confusion has ended'.[51]

HIV/AIDS AND THE AFRICAN RENAISSANCE

The ideology of the African Renaissance espouses certain values such as self-respect and autonomy as central to fortifying African identities; constructing African institutions; and formulating African solutions to African problems. Mbeki first spoke of an African Renaissance in an address to South Africa's Parliament in June 1997. The Renaissance, he said, would be driven by the generations of Africans who had been victimised by oppression and war, and would usher in a new era of democratic stability and a better life for all Africans. Since 2001, South Africa has led efforts to realise the Renaissance through NEPAD, as well as by promoting African intellectualism, technology and trade, among other areas[52] (see Landsberg in this volume). Unfortunately within the context of the HIV/AIDS pandemic – the greatest human security threat to the dream of an African Renaissance – South Africa has played a marginal and ineffective role. Indeed, Africa's leadership on HIV/AIDS has emanated from smaller countries such as Senegal and Uganda; been augmented by SADC and the AU; and driven by the UN. However, these other voices will have limited success in leading efforts to control the African HIV/AIDS epidemic. Without constructive engagement from policymakers in Tshwane, HIV/AIDS will continue to decimate South Africa and undermine the peace and prosperity of Africa.

Another view of HIV/AIDS: Leadership in Senegal and Uganda

Throughout the 1980s and 1990s, most African leaders failed to mobilise concerted efforts to address the effects of HIV/AIDS. Bucking this trend, Senegal's president, Abdou Diouf, and Uganda's leader, Yoweri Museveni, addressed the challenges of AIDS decisively. The AIDS epidemics in these countries took on remarkably different trajectories. Senegal's national HIV rate was contained to less than one per cent.[53] Uganda's overall HIV prevalence rate fell from 13 per cent in the early 1990s to 4,1 per cent by 2003.[54] On a continent struggling with curbing the rise of HIV rates, the Senegalese and Ugandan experiences have remained the counter-examples in an otherwise disappointing record of governmental responses to the crisis.

Senegal was able to prevent HIV/AIDS from becoming a generalised epidemic for a number of reasons. Under the guidance of Diouf – who left office in 2000 – the government mobilised support from local communities and international donors to contain the epidemic in it earliest stages. Diouf's leadership helped to focus government action on key areas such as controlling the blood supply and mobilising religious leaders. Senegal's strong Islamic tradition has also been noted as a possible key to the government's efforts to stabilise its HIV epidemic. Male circumcision was also widespread. Simultaneously, since the 1970s, the government had instituted a programme to control sexually-transmitted infections, and its commercial sex industry was effectively regulated. These secondary factors were critical to Diouf's leadership on the AIDS issue, facilitating an effective response to the new threat that yielded success.

Museveni first became alarmed by the epidemic as early as September 1986, when large numbers of his senior military officers who had been sent to Cuba for training were diagnosed as being HIV-positive. Museveni understood that the epidemic would have serious consequences for his government's overall security, development and democratisation agenda. Moreover, he understood that the long-term response to this new type of disease would require a robust and comprehensive response from all sectors of society. As a first step, Museveni instructed all government officials – regardless of their specific portfolios – to discuss HIV/AIDS during public gatherings. In addition, the president included HIV/AIDS in his national political mobilisation campaign and spoke frankly about the use of condoms and the importance of remaining faithful to sexual partners in all of his speeches at the local council level. In his public comments on HIV/AIDS, Museveni used the local vernacular and underscored the connection between STIs and vulnerability to HIV. This approach greatly strengthened the work of organisations such as the AIDS Support Organisation (TASO), a group first started by people living with, and affected by, HIV/AIDS in Uganda.

SADC and HIV/AIDS

Perhaps one of the most strategic multilateral organisations for South Africa, the Southern African Development Community, has also developed its own comprehensive strategy to address HIV/AIDS (see Matlosa in this volume). A summit of Southern African heads of state and government was held on HIV/AIDS in Maseru, Lesotho, on 4 July 2003. The Maseru declaration issued from the summit noted the adoption of the SADC HIV/AIDS Strategic Framework and Plan of Action: 2003–07. The SADC Framework aims to review, develop, and harmonise policies and legislation relating to HIV prevention, care, support, and *treatment* within SADC.[55] There is, therefore, a move away from the perception that the HIV/AIDS crisis can simply be contained with various prevention strategies. It is now recognised that treatment for HIV-positive people is a vital aspect of dealing with the pandemic. [56]

SADC's fourteen member states declared that the Framework would be supported through the establishment of a Regional Fund. By early 2007, South Africa and Swaziland were the only countries that had pledged resources to the fund. Unfortunately, the amounts that were committed barely covered the administrative requirements of a small-scale project. South Africa pledged R1 million (approximately US$160 000), while Swaziland has promised US$30 000. Other Southern African governments such as Namibia are working to integrate HIV/AIDS into SADC's 2004 Strategic Indicative Plan of the Organ for Politics, Defence and Security. [57]

The gap between rhetoric and action in SADC is not unusual. However, it is alarming that Southern Africa continues to rely so heavily on support and leadership from external actors in its fight against AIDS. In 2004, the SADC secretariat in Gaborone, Botswana, entered into a Joint Finance Technical Co-operative Agreement (JFTCA) with four international donors for US$5,3 million, and the secretariat was hoping for an African Development Bank (ADB) loan of US$30 million. The United Kingdom's Department for International Development (DFID) and the European Union (EU) have supported the SADC HIV/AIDS unit's US$15 million programme for civil society HIV/AIDS pilot projects. Meanwhile, the unit relied heavily on consultants paid by donor funding to undertake most of its work.[58]

The AU, the Global Fund, and HIV/AIDS

Moving from the subregional to the continental level, in 2001, Africa's leaders pledged to lead the HIV/AIDS response from the front during the Abuja summit on HIV/AIDS, tuberculosis and malaria in Nigeria. The heads of state and government gathered in Abuja and issued the 'Abuja Declaration and Plan of Action'. African leaders agreed that HIV/AIDS, TB, and malaria should be the 'top priorities' of the first 25 years of a new century; committed 15 per cent of their national budgets to health; and promised to lead national AIDS commissions and urge all public and private individuals in leadership positions to make similar contributions.[59] The AU Commission in Addis Ababa, Ethiopia, designed an HIV/AIDS Strategic Plan for 2005–07.[60] While President Mbeki is a member of the AU's AIDS Watch Africa, an organisation of heads of state mandated to advance the continent's response to HIV/AIDS, his visible engagement on these issues has been negligible. Finally, the AU is considering ways to integrate HIV/AIDS into the establishment of an African Standby Force (ASF), which plans to lead African peacekeeping efforts by 2010. These steps reflect increased political will, but in terms of actual mobilisation of resources and implementation, not much has been done. South Africa is a key member of SADC's ASF brigade and has contributed about 3 000 troops to UN peacekeeping missions in Burundi and the DRC (see Curtis in this volume). With a 23 per cent HIV infection rate in the South African National Defence Force (SANDF), failure to reduce infections could have a negative impact on South Africa's leadership role in Africa's peace and security institutions.[61]

The mid-term review of the Abuja Declaration took place during a special AU summit in Abuja, Nigeria in May 2006. Thus far, only Botswana has met the 15 per cent health expenditure target. However, Gambia, Ghana, Tanzania, Uganda and Zimbabwe are making steady progress towards reaching this goal by devoting between 12 and 14,5 per cent of their national budgets to the health sector.[62] In Abuja, governments such as South Africa questioned how realistic the Abuja health targets were and argued that national legal and technical infrastructure for meeting these goals might not yet be established.[63] It is true that targets are not enough. The Abuja plan should have included more concrete indicators for measuring success.

Negotiations during the May 2006 review of the Abuja plan sought to remedy this omission. Delegates incorporated more specific targets into an African Common Position on HIV/AIDS which was submitted to the June 2006 review of the 2001 Declaration of the UN General Assembly Special Session (UNGASS) on HIV/AIDS.[64] The targets included providing access to antiretroviral therapy so that 80 per cent of those who need it have access to AIDS treatment by 2010. However, during the course of the debate, health ministers and government delegations – most notably South African health minister Tshabalala-Msimang – questioned the usefulness of setting such seemingly unrealistic targets and went as far as seeking to re-open the debate on the 15 per cent target for national health expenditures.

The lack of progress made by some African governments to reach health targets is disappointing. However, ambitious targets have helped to galvanise a response among African governments. Civil society observers in Abuja in May 2006 pointed out that continental campaigns to accelerate access to drugs have yielded important results. In 2002, the World Health Organisation (WHO) launched a campaign to work with countries to provide three million people with ARVs by 2005 (the '3 by 5' initiative). The WHO has not met this goal; however, in the first 18 months of the programme, 500 000 people were enrolled in drug regimens. At least 90 000 Zambians are estimated to be alive today because of the '3 by 5' initiative.[65]

In response to this debate, former Nigerian president Olusegun Obasanjo, announced that Africa's push for universal access to services had to be ambitious, inclusive and commensurate with the threat posed by the continent's health crises. One civil society observer noted that Obasanjo was embarrassed by Africa's reluctance to lead and direct its response effectively. Half-hearted measures would leave the fight to eliminate AIDS to external actors. Without vigorous commitments from Africans, the international community – which is easily distracted and tends to re-direct assistance precipitously – would not take Africa and its AIDS epidemic seriously.

Moving from the regional to the external level, in April 2001, African leaders proposed the establishment of a special fund to combat the three pandemics ravaging the continent: HIV/AIDS, malaria and tuberculosis. The world's governments subsequently agreed at the UN Special Session on HIV/AIDS in New York in June 2001 to establish the Global Fund to Fight HIV/AIDS, Tuberculosis, and Malaria. At its inception, African leaders urged donors to put US$10 billion into the fund. Yet, between 2002 and 2005, only US$1 billion had been disbursed. Although the Fund spends 60 per cent of its resources in Africa and two-thirds of its funding to support HIV/AIDS programmes, its impact has still been marginal.[66] Experts believe that funding does not reach grassroots communities and that rich countries have stubbornly refused to meet their funding objectives. It has also been noted that the most active supporters of the Global Fund are based outside Africa. While similar groups existed already in Latin America and Asia, Africa did not establish a 'Friends of the Global Fund' organisation until February 2007.[67] Despite the fact that the continent would benefit most from durable and predictable health financing, Africa has failed to implement a meaningful advocacy strategy for replenishing the Fund.

CONCLUDING THOUGHTS

The articulation of an African Renaissance doctrine by Thabo Mbeki resonates with the deepest desires of Africa itself. New leadership, particularly with the end of apartheid-rule in South Africa in 1994, ushered in the rhetoric of African 'ownership' and African 'solutions'. This idea, however, remains a pipe dream against the backdrop of HIV/AIDS and other problems on the continent such as endemic poverty and widespread conflict. It also, unfortunately, coincides with marked dependence on external donors.

Nevertheless, Mbeki, South Africa's second democratically elected president, remains the chief African statesman of this vision. Indeed, the South African president's views on all things 'African' have taken on strategic importance. Undeniably, Africa's destiny is tied to South Africa's fate.[68] Yet, until the end of 2006, the government's leadership on HIV/AIDS disappointed too many of its admirers and was fraught with a fundamentally ambiguous relationship with science itself. Despite the fact that Mbeki took the decision to 'remove himself' from the HIV/AIDS debate in 2002 and has indeed never directly refuted that HIV causes AIDS, the government's approach has been riddled with rhetoric that has undermined its own HIV/AIDS treatment policies. Finally, South Africa has relegated leadership on African AIDS issues to other actors and institutions.

Early in this new millennium, the state has been re-baptised as having a pivotal role to play in addressing HIV/AIDS and other non-traditional security threats. The UN High-Level Panel's December 2004 report, *A More Secure World: Our Shared Responsibility*, identified HIV/AIDS as a threat that is critical to international security and requires a strong state response.[69] Moreover, former UN Secretary-General, Kofi Annan, in his articulation of the nexus between development, human rights and security in March 2005, also stressed the urgent need for governments to take a strong lead in containing HIV/AIDS.[70] It is unlikely that the South African government – because of its own internal confusion on the issue – will lend its gravitas to mobilising more robust state responses in Africa. Eight years after the birth of the idea of an African 'century'; eleven years after Mbeki's famous 'I am an African' speech; and twenty-five years after the onset of humanity's most tragic recent outbreak of disease, South Africa has failed decisively to halt its own HIV/AIDS epidemic, and deferred the dream of an African Renaissance.[71]

9

South Africa and the making of the African Union and NEPAD: Mbeki's 'progressive African agenda'

CHRIS LANDSBERG

This chapter examines South Africa's attempts to help craft the continental 'progressive' public policy landscape since 1999. I will consider the African policies of President Thabo Mbeki, and particularly what he and his continental allies have referred to as the 'progressive'[1] 'African Agenda' or African Renaissance. When Mbeki talks of the 'progressive' African Agenda, he is referring to a wide range of measures to make democratic political systems, peace and security, and accelerated economic growth the basis of development in Africa. Thus, Mbeki's new progressive governance agenda seeks to achieve development, peace and security, democratic governance and economic growth, as well as the construction of the African Union (AU), the reform of Africa's regional economic communities (RECS), and the New Partnership for Africa's Development (NEPAD). These actors and programmes are required to promote African integration, peace, security and democratic governance. A key goal of the 'African Agenda' is to integrate Africa into the global economy on the basis of 'mutual responsibility' and 'mutual accountability'; that is to say, that both African states and external powers have important political, economic and social obligations in realising the goals of this agenda.[2]

One cannot make sense of Mbeki's African Agenda unless one has a careful understanding of how and why this agenda is being pursued, and unless one appreciates the sensitivities about South Africa's role, objectives and agenda in Africa. There are many concerns throughout the continent, in official circles, research quarters and non-governmental organisations about South Africa's 'giantism'. There is fear and resentment about South Africa behaving like, and harbouring the goals of, a domineering hegemon (see Adedeji; Hudson; Matlosa; and Schoeman in this volume). There is thus a perception that South Africa wishes to dominate its region. It is important that Tshwane (Pretoria) monitors these concerns and does not act in ways that reinforce these

196 · SOUTH AFRICA IN AFRICA

perceptions: that South Africa wishes to become a domineering Leviathan. South Africa is already concerned not to play to Western expectations that it will become 'Africa's policeman'. Mbeki, in particular, is careful about these apprehensions.

South Africa has deployed several tactics in an effort to counter perceptions that it wishes to dominate its region, such as subtly pushing for multilateral mechanisms and 'rules of the game' that all countries sign up to. Once these new rules have been established, it will become easier for South Africa to behave in its preferred way. For example, policymakers in Tshwane have pushed for multilateral conduct and mechanisms within the AU, NEPAD and the Southern African Development Community (SADC), and have avoided a unilateralist approach in these bodies.

SEARCHING FOR STRATEGIC PARTNERS

Above all else, Mbeki, his government and the ruling African National Congress (ANC) party in general believe in building strategic partnerships with key African governments. Mbeki has worked closely with allies like Joaquim Chissano and Armando Guebuza of Mozambique, Olusegun Obasanjo of Nigeria, Abdelaziz Bouteflika of Algeria, Benjamin Mkapa and Jakaya Kikwete of Tanzania, John Kufuor of Ghana, and their successors, to pursue his 'progressive' African Renaissance plan.[3] Former Mozambican president Chissano, and Obasanjo were Mbeki's closest and most strategic allies. Both leaders have lent legitimacy and credibility to Mbeki and South Africa. Tshwane has in turn often spoken through these leaders, who have collaborated with South Africa in a treacherous continental environment in which oversized egos and personal jealousies often reign supreme.

Mbeki, Obasanjo, Bouteflika and Chissano closely coordinated their African foreign policy strategies. A key strategy was to cajole Africa's RECS such as SADC, the Economic Community of West African States (ECOWAS) and the Intergovernmental Authority on Development (IGAD) to reform and streamline their work in ways that are consistent with NEPAD and the AU.[4]

In strategy terms, Mbeki and his allies have sought to persuade a majority of African governments to support their agenda by engaging in trade-off diplomacy: in exchange for Africans committing to political and economic 'good governance'; peace and security undertakings, as well as human rights commitments, the West would cancel Africa's foreign debt of $290 billion, improve the terms of global trade for Africa – including granting better access to markets for Africa's goods – and increase development assistance. This is what is meant by 'mutual accountability' and 'mutual responsibility': this trade-off would be presented to both sides as incentives.

At the heart of Mbeki's African Agenda is a search for a new relationship between Africa and the outside world, a shift from a relationship of 'patronage' towards one of partnership. One way that Mbeki and Obasanjo have calmed suspicions of a domineering leadership ambition is to tell their fellow Africans that the African agenda is all about 'international best practices' in the form of initiatives such as the African Peer Review Mechanism (APRM). It is not what South Africa or Nigeria wants; it is about Africa having to conform to 'international best practices'. It is this notion of 'international best practices' that has ironically created many problems for the African agenda.[5] South Africa and Nigeria have borrowed heavily from certain conventional, neoliberal economic and political orthodoxies that are seriously unpopular in some African quarters, and this has in turn created many legitimacy problems for NEPAD and other South African-inspired continental initiatives. It is through following such conventions that Tshwane and Abuja have developed a strong belief in foreign direct investment as the best way of developing African economies[6] (see Adebajo in this volume).

SOUTH AFRICA AND THE MAKING OF THE AFRICAN UNION

Fully aware of the centrality of the role which the continent's premier pan-African institutions would play in political and economic affairs, South Africa not surprisingly played a key role in the transition of the Organisation of African Unity (OAU) into becoming the new African Union (AU) in 2002.[7] South Africa devised strategies to take on board the plans and perspectives of other states, while countering the plans of others. The biggest fly in the ointment of South Africa's 'progressive' agenda was the Libyan leader, Muammar Qaddafi, with his 'radical' agenda. After Qaddafi's liberation from the shackles of western ostracism in 2003, the 'Brother Leader' began to focus on continental affairs as a way of reintroducing himself to African diplomacy. In September 1999, Qaddafi hosted an OAU special summit in Sirte[8] (see Jhazbay in this volume). At this meeting, the Libyan leader borrowed heavily from the Pan-African vision of Ghanaian leader, Kwame Nkrumah, and tabled a proposal for a 'United States of Africa' (USAF). Qaddafi further proposed that Sirte, Libya, should be the seat of the Congress of the USAF.[9]

While Qaddafi did not receive endorsement for his USAF proposal, he did succeed in forcing African leaders to focus attention on the issue of establishing an African Union. The Libyan leader should therefore be credited with having forced the issue and bringing urgency to the organisation for debate of the 'new Pan-Africanism'. The Sirte meeting concluded with a declaration calling for the establishment of an African Union. Mbeki, Obasanjo, and South African Minister of Foreign Affairs Nkosazana Dlamini-Zuma, resorted to deft diplomacy to shift the focus from establishing a United States of Africa to that of creating an African Union: a process of building common norms, values and principles that would ultimately persuade 53 African governments to live in closer union with each other. While Mbeki worked to secure the incorporation of key elements of his African Renaissance vision into the AU project, Obasanjo worked on trying to guarantee inclusion of elements of his 1991 concept of the Conference for Security, Stability, Development and Co-operation in Africa (CSSDCA) in these plans. The CSSDCA is a set of norms and benchmarks on accountability, transparency and principles of action in the areas of stability, security, development and cooperation. Its main argument is that the AU must articulate new values for African states to live by in order for the continent to become more peaceful, secure and prosperous.

In June 2000, another meeting in the Libyan capital of Tripoli called for a transformation from the OAU to the AU and the eventual establishment of the African Economic Community (AEC).[10] The meeting mandated the OAU to finalise the drafting of the Constitutive Act of the AU. One month later, in July 2000, the OAU summit in Lomé, Togo, approved the AU's Constitutive Act, and approved the Solemn Declaration of the Conference for Security, Stability, Development and Co-operation in Africa.

The July 2001 OAU summit in Lusaka, Zambia, mandated the transition from the OAU to the AU. Mbeki also embarked on carefully calibrated diplomacy to ensure that the Lusaka summit endorsed the South Africa-inspired New African Initiative (NAI), the merger of the Millennium Africa Recovery Programme (MAP) and Senegalese president Abdoulaye Wade's Omega Plan.[11] (Wade's key proposal was to increase infrastructure rapidly and to coordinate development at subregional rather than national level; he contrasted Omega's 'rigour' with the 'romanticism' of Mbeki's MAP.)[12] Mbeki's government expended much political, diplomatic, and economic capital to ensure that the AU was launched in South Africa. In July 2002, that ambition was realised when the last summit of the OAU gave birth to the AU. The meeting was hosted in Durban in 2002, making

South Africa the first chair of the AU. It is at the Durban summit that the OAU was formally buried and the AU born. The first year was designated as an interim year to allow the fledgling AU Commission in Addis Ababa, Ethiopia, to finalise proposals for the structure and financing of the new organisation.

South Africa worked hard to cajole Nigeria, Algeria, Senegal, Mozambique, Ghana, Tanzania and others to become key African Renaissance allies. Together, these states were instrumental in articulating a right to intervene in the affairs of member states in grave circumstances. Former South African president Nelson Mandela, and Mbeki, had long argued for a continental intervention regime and a move away from the OAU's obsession with the principle of non-interference in domestic affairs. As Mandela noted to his fellow African leaders at the summit in Ouagadougou, Burkina Faso in 1998: 'Africa has a right and a duty to intervene to root out tyranny ... We must all accept that we cannot abuse the concept of national sovereignty to deny the rest of the continent the right and duty to intervene when behind those sovereign boundaries, people are being slaughtered to protect tyranny.[13]

By 2001, Mbeki had worked with others to make this important shift, establishing a new OAU/AU interventionist regime. Today, the Constitutive Act of the Union singles out four pretexts for intervention: genocide; gross violations of human rights; instability in one country threatening broader regional instability; and – to date the most advanced doctrine of them all – unconstitutional changes of government, just the kind of progressivism Mbeki had in mind. This provision threatens to suspend governments that come to power unconstitutionally, and the unconstitutional regimes of Côte d'Ivoire and Comoros were thus excluded from participation in the OAU summit in Lomé in 2000. Article 4 of the Constitutive Act determines that member states have a right to '... request intervention by the Union in order to restore peace and security'.[14]

Almost as soon as he formally assumed the reins of power in 1999, Mbeki, together with Obasanjo, was instrumental in advocating this doctrine. Mbeki has said that this doctrine would be backed up by military force, if necessary.

A real progressive move was Mbeki and Obasanjo's strong backing of the 'red card, yellow card' (football analogy) approach to military *coups d'état*.[15] This approach advocates that putschists would first be cautioned and persuaded to return to civilian and legitimate rule. Failing this, orchestrators of coups would be slapped with punitive measures in an effort to return to civilian rule.

On Africa's new right to intervention, Mbeki has opined that the Constitutive Act gives the AU 'legislative powers to act against member states acting against

the ethos of good governance and the rule of law'.[16] For Mbeki, the new interventionism also challenges the traditional African notion of sovereignty.

Key actors like Dlamini-Zuma and South Africa's Ministry of Foreign
Affairs were active participants in the negotiations of the Constitutive Act. The
Act makes provision for the establishment of 18 new organs. Key among these
are: the Assembly of the Union; the Executive Council (that is the Council
of foreign ministers); the Pan-African Parliament (PAP); the Commission
(which has some executive power and authority of initiative); the influential
Permanent Representative Committee (or committee of African Ambassadors
based in Addis Ababa) – the PRC; the Specialised Technical Committees; the
Economic, Social and Cultural Council (ECOSOCC), involving representatives
of civil society; and the financial institutions.[17]

During the AU's first three years, to 2005, Mbeki directed much influence
at the supreme organ of the AU, the Assembly, its highest and most powerful
decision-making organ, to encourage the emerging 'continentalism'. He has
pushed the Union in the preferred, gradualist direction of South Africa and
its allies, rather than taking Qaddafi's more federalist approach. The Executive
Council in turn – responsible for coordinating and taking decisions on policies
of common interest to member states – was viewed by Dlamini-Zuma as a vital
political and diplomatic organ. Just as Mbeki has been a dominant player at
Assembly level, so South Africa's foreign minister exercised great influence in
the Council. But it was not only at the Assembly and Executive Council levels
that South Africa has played a visible and decisive policy role. South Africa
has also used the all-influential Permanent Representatives Council (PRC) to
advance its progressive agenda.

The unicameral Pan-African Parliament could become one of Africa's most
important representative bodies, involving five representatives from each African
legislature (at least one of which must be a woman). The parliament will adopt
legislation by a two-thirds majority and aims subsequently to evolve into a
parliament elected by universal suffrage. Over the past five years, South African
politicians and other actors like its former Speaker of Parliament, Frene Ginwala,
campaigned – sometimes subtly and sometimes openly – for sister African states
to vote for South Africa to host the PAP. In July 2004, these efforts bore fruit when
South Africa was selected as permanent host and seat of the PAP: a sign of how
successful the country had become at winning over the confidence of sceptical
African states in the short space of a decade. As a sign of its commitment to its
new pan-African credentials, South Africa offered to pay R600 million over a

five-year period towards maintaining the PAP; R200 million would go towards initial running costs, and R400 million was pledged for the actual construction of the parliament's building.[18] (By May 2006, however, there were reports that the PAP was experiencing financial difficulties as a result of non-paying members.) Soon after the announcement that South Africa would host the PAP, Mbeki closely linked democratic governance to security in noting that peace in Africa is priceless, and that hosting the PAP would be worth every cent.

In 2003, Mbeki, Obasanjo, Chissano and others were successful at pushing for their ally, former Malian president, Alpha Oumar Konaré, to become chair of the AU Commission. This appointment allowed Mbeki and his coalition partners to proceed with their continental renewal agenda and emphasised the need to strengthen AU actions in conflict prevention, management and resolution, with special emphasis on peace support missions in Burundi, Ethiopia/Eritrea, Sudan, the Democratic Republic of the Congo (DRC), and Liberia.[19] The new AU doctrine included moving away from strict notions of militarily-defined 'state' security to a greater emphasis on 'human' security and social justice. The AU developed modalities for resource mobilisation to enhance Africa's peace support operations capabilities.[20]

Regarding the political issues of governance, democratisation and the rule of law, Mbeki and his allies sought, through the AU, to ensure greater political participation, pluralism, transparency, accountability and freedoms for Africa's nearly one billion citizens to participate and entrench democratic governance processes.[21] The important issue of peace and security enjoyed serious attention, and Mbeki and his allies prioritised efforts to ensure peace and security on the continent through mediating an end to conflicts and the promotion of post-conflict peace building.

The AU's 15-member Peace and Security Council (PSC) is another mechanism whose establishment in March 2004 brought to the fore the diplomatic strategies and tactics of South Africa and its allies. The PSC can be regarded as the '… premier policy blueprint, the centrepiece of the work of the AU in the politico-military field'.[22] It is no secret that South Africa and Nigeria were in favour of an AU peace and security structure that would be modelled after the United Nations Security Council (UNSC).[23] South Africa and Nigeria pushed for seats as permanent members with veto power. They envisaged a system like the UN Security Council with five veto-wielding permanent members and ten rotating members without the right of veto. But the Tshwane-Abuja axis lost out on this particular score. No vetoes, nor permanent members, were allowed on the AU Council.

The majority of smaller AU members rejected these ideas, and in the end, its members agreed to settle for a compromise plan. Instead of permanent and non-permanent members, the AU settled on a scheme of five members elected for a three-year period that could be re-elected to serve for further terms; and ten members that would serve fixed two-year terms. The PSC started operating in March 2004, and South Africa and Nigeria were elected to three-year terms. Mbeki and others advocated that, as part of the efforts to operationalise the PSC, the AU should establish an African Standby Force (ASF) by 2010 as well as a Military Staff Committee. They highlighted the importance of strengthening relations between regional economic communities and the AU, so that the RECs could serve as implementing agencies for the AU.

At the July 2004 summit in Addis Ababa, the South African government noted the importance of operationalising the new AU organs. The emphasis was on prioritisation and resource mobilisation aimed at strengthening the AU's new institutions. South Africa openly encouraged member states to pay their dues, and was one of five countries singled out to pay a new scales-of-assess-ment of 8,25 per cent of the AU's annual budget of US$158 million. The other states were Egypt, Algeria, Libya, and Nigeria. By the beginning of 2006, South Africa put huge pressure on the other four African 'Great Powers' to increase their contributions from 8,25 per cent to a massive 15 per cent, thereby making up 75 per cent of the budget. South Africa was determined to make financial and other sacrifices in exchange for the enhanced prestige of being one of Africa's 'Great Powers'.

At the end of 2006, the Libya-inspired idea of an Nkrumahist United States of Africa, with a central-command army for the continent, a single currency, and, most likely, headquarters in Sirte, re-emerged on the agenda.[24] The idea was packaged in the form of the concept of 'an African Union Government' that would lead to a 'United States of Africa'.[25] The January 2007 AU Summit in Addis Ababa, Ethiopia, discussed the 'African Union Government' plans.[26] Some of the proposals on the table included the need to establish the Union Government as early as 2015. It was proposed that a draft Constitution of the African Union Government be adopted, and that measures to facilitate the free movement of persons and the rights of residence should also be considered.[27]

In Addis Ababa, Mbeki and his SADC counterparts distanced themselves from what they saw as a rushed process. Mbeki had long supported an incremental, functional approach to Union-building, with a strong emphasis on building institutions. A major challenge for the AU will be to convince all its member states of the need to pool some of their sovereignty under the organisation and its organs, including the Pan-African Parliament. Mbeki underscored this point in an address to a conference of representatives of African churches in 2001 when he said that 'the idea of sovereignty is a matter we need to look at. We [must] be able to act more forcefully together as Africans to take forward the whole idea of African unity'.[28] He added that the AU's Constitutive Act of 2000 had 'extra-territorial provisions', enabling it to intervene in countries in which the organisation was convinced that genocide or other crimes against humanity were being committed. These views reflect South Africa's role in articulating Africa's continental integration agenda: a complex and ambitious agenda, based on a functionalist and incremental approach.

THE NEW PARTNERSHIP FOR AFRICA'S DEVELOPMENT (NEPAD)

If Mbeki's South Africa played a key role in the making of the AU, it played an even more influential role in the making of NEPAD. Indeed, NEPAD embodies and epitomises South Africa's Africa strategy, to such an extent that it has caused much irritation among other African states. NEPAD was a plan driven in the main by Mbeki and, to a lesser extent, his allies. South Africa spent much time trying to convince the leaders of Nigeria, Algeria, Senegal, and Egypt to support NEPAD as a 'collective vision'. In short, Mbeki was determined to get the others to want what he wanted.

Mbeki sold the idea to these fellow leaders to support new salient African objectives, and to do so on the back of NEPAD. These aims included: reforming the delivery system for overseas development assistance and ensuring that assistance more effectively bolstered the development prospects of African countries. NEPAD was an attempt to build partnerships between African leaders and international donor governments on the basis of common commitments to upholding global standards of democracy and 'good governance'. A key consideration for Mbeki is relations with the industrialised North. He pushed for NEPAD to build in specific elements around a 'new', enhanced partnership with the rich world – so as to involve the north in underwriting the new African initiatives through debt relief, increases in levels of official development assistance; infrastructural development; and foreign direct investment. NEPAD was based on a trade-off: in exchange for African leaders holding each other accountable, the rich world would recommit themselves to Africa's development.[29]

NEPAD was preceded by the concept – led by Mbeki, Obasanjo and Bouteflika –

of a Millennium Africa Recovery Plan (MAP). MAP, too, was an attempt to craft trade-offs between Africa and the rich world, whereby Africa would make commitments in favour of peace, governance and security, and the industrialised powers would make commitments to improve levels of foreign assistance, open up their markets to African goods, help to fortify Africa's peace support operations capacities, and increase levels of trade with Africa. While MAP was being crafted, Senegalese president, Abdoulaye Wade, worked on the Omega plan,[30] and there was a real potential for a damaging francophone/anglophone split.

MAP was endorsed by the OAU as a continental development plan in July 2001 and renamed the New African Initiative.[31] The plan was eventually baptised 'NEPAD' in October 2001. For Mbeki, MAP, NAI and NEPAD were triggered by the post-Cold War realities of power imbalances between Africa and the industrialised North.[32] Through these initiatives, Mbeki and his allies reacted to western military and political disengagement from the continent.[33] They were attempting to change the negative perceptions of Africa that were particularly rampant in the western media. If the outside world was to respond positively and constructively to NEPAD, its re-engagement with the continent would help to arrest growing poverty and inequality on the continent, and assist in transforming Africa's political, economic and social landscape.[34]

Even before assuming South Africa's presidency in 1999, Mbeki had made plain his determination to tackle 'Afro-pessimism' in the rich world.[35] He wanted to change the impression among western observers, governments and investors that Africa was a 'dark continent' inhabited mainly by a hoard of kleptocratic regimes that were typically dictatorial with a strong penchant for violating human rights and democratic principles.[36]

Mbeki is determined to see NEPAD being turned into a marketing tool to turn around Africa's image abroad, and to encourage the continent to break with the culture and attitude of victimisation. The plan has sought to pursue a new and mature approach to governance and development by breaking with a perceived tendency of blaming the outside world for all of Africa's ills. NEPAD also hopes to inculcate into African politics a culture of 'taking responsibility' for Africa's own mistakes, and to push Africans to become more self-critical of political developments and bad practices on the continent.[37]

For Mbeki and other NEPAD architects, Africa and the rich world needed to be locked into a new and genuine partnership.[38] African governments had to become more democratically accountable, while the North had to recommit itself to helping to meet Africa's vast development challenges. According to

NEPAD, the best way to extract commitments from both sides was to lock them into a new pact.[39] But such a deal had to be based on a genuine partnership that would stress mutual responsibilities and mutual commitments on politics, democracy and socio-economic issues.

Through NEPAD, Mbeki and his allies promoted a dialectical relationship between politics and economics, and made an explicit link between development, peace, security, governance and democracy.[40] The logic for Mbeki and his partners is that there is a clear link between development and stability. This is why they singled out three prerequisites for socio-economic regeneration, poverty alleviation and empowerment: Peace and Security; Democracy and Political Governance; and Economic and Corporate Governance.[41]

The Governing Structure of NEPAD is composed of an Implementation Committee of Heads of State and Government; a Steering Committee; and a Secretariat. President Obasanjo was elected as Chairman of the Implementation Committee in October 2001,[42] and Bouteflika and Wade as his deputy chairmen. The Mbeki administration was determined to ensure that NEPAD would have its headquarters located in South Africa, and from the outset the NEPAD secretariat was based in Midrand, in the heart of the South African-based Development Bank of Southern Africa (DBSA). NEPAD members have worked on elaborating action plans for five sectors:[43] the Peace, Security, Democracy and Political Governance Initiatives; the Economic and Corporate Governance Initiative; Bridging the Infrastructure Gap; the Human Resource Development Initiative (especially Education and Health); and the Market Access Initiative.

The economic dimensions of NEPAD have been the most controversial, both for the orthodoxy underpinning them, and for the way they came about. Even though there is reference in NEPAD to the Lagos Plan of Action (LPA) of 1980, it is clear that the LPA has not been carefully studied and certainly not sufficiently incorporated into NEPAD (see Adedeji in this volume). The economic dimensions of NEPAD have been likened by some to the Africanisation of South Africa's macro-economic Growth, Employment and Redistribution (GEAR) policy. There has been increasing discussion about the 'post-GEAR phase;' about the fact that South Africa's economy and currency have stabilised; and about the country seeking to become a developmental state. If South Africa is altering its economic policy at home, then it is inexcusable to leave NEPAD's neoliberal underpinnings unchanged. South Africa would be expected to play a leading role in reshaping NEPAD's economic provisions to that of a developmental model.

South Africa was so determined to see NEPAD succeed, that by 2006, it was seeking to transform NEPAD into its domestic socio-economic plan. But the perception was also gaining ground throughout the continent that South Africa was so committed to NEPAD's success, that it would even allow NEPAD to become a rival to the AU. The first five years of NEPAD's existence saw the donor community generally lending greater support to NEPAD than the AU, and the AU generally feeling undermined by its supposed socio-economic plan: NEPAD. Both the AU and NEPAD had become notorious for developing all manner of duplicate, even rival plans in areas ranging from peace and security; governance; post-conflict peacebuilding; social development; and other strategies. This was waste of the highest order, and many observers held South Africa responsible. These tensions came to a head in March 2007 when Senegalese leader Abdoulaye Wade withdrew from NEPAD's implementation committee on the eve of its meeting in Algiers. Wade had constantly criticised the slow pace of NEPAD's implementation of projects.

Mbeki and his government invested much time in engaging the Group of Eight Industrialised Countries (G8) and the West to urge them to endorse NEPAD as their development guide and plan for Africa.[44] Here too, critics believe that South Africa was more committed to NEPAD enjoying western backing than ensuring that it becomes accepted as a genuine African plan.

THE AFRICAN PEER REVIEW MECHANISM

One of the most innovative programmes advocated by Mbeki and his allies was the introduction of an African Peer Review Mechanism. South Africa was instrumental in drafting a Political and Good Governance Peer Review Mechanism in February 2002[45] which stressed the importance of 'political will' to observing core values, commitments and obligations on democracy, human rights and 'good governance'. The APRM recognises the need to 'empower people and institutions of civil society' so as to ensure an active and independent civil society that can hold governments accountable to their citizens.[46] The mechanism also stresses the need to 'adhere to principles of a constitutional democracy, the rule of law and the strict separation of powers, including the protection of the independence of the judiciary'. The APRM further hopes to ensure 'the periodic democratic renewal of leadership, in line with the principle that leaders should be subjected to fixed terms in office'.[47]

Importantly for those who work in electoral administration, the Peer Review Process committed its 28 signed-up members to ensuring 'impartial, transparent and credible electoral administration and oversight systems'. It promotes a 'dedicated, honest and efficient civil service',[48] and the establishment of 'oversight institutions providing necessary surveillance and to ensure transparency and accountability by all layers of government'. The APRM strongly favours the creation and strengthening of 'institutional capacity to ensure the proper functioning of democratic institutions and instruments'.[49]

The Economic and Corporate Governance Peer Review Mechanism[50] went beyond just neoliberal economic and fiscal dictates. The mechanism recognised that 'good governance' is a prerequisite for sound economic and corporate governance, and that the capacity of the state to deliver on its promises was critical. The peer review singled out a number of areas in need of institutional reform including: bolstering the capacity of civil services; strengthening parliamentary oversight; promoting participatory decision-making; adopting effective measures to combat corruption and embezzlement; and undertaking judicial reforms. The mechanism outlined the key factors which enhance democratic governance and sound economies: transparency; accountability; an enabling environment for private sector development and growth; and institutional capacity and effectiveness.

Mbeki, Chissano and Obasanjo favoured a convergence between NEPAD and subregional integration processes including SADC and ECOWAS. They also called for these subregional bodies to be restructured to ensure that their programmes and priorities accorded with those of the AU and NEPAD.

THE SOUTH AFRICAN PEER REVIEW PROCESS

Because South Africa was such a key player in the articulation of Africa's emerging governance architecture, there were great expectations for the success of its own Peer Review process in 2005/2006.[51] Given that South Africa and other pivotal states like Nigeria, Mozambique and others have invested so much in the process, the very success and credibility of the APRM depends, to a great extent, on the review of these states. In September 2005, the Mbeki administration officially launched South Africa's year-long Peer Review Process. But the South African process started off with great animosity and tensions between the government and local civil society actors. Many South African NGOs were critical of what they regarded as the 'controlled' nature of the South African process, charging that the government, and the executive in particular, was seeking to dominate and dictate the process.[52] In the end, the government took these criticisms seriously, reaching out to as many stakeholders as possible. It also opened itself to dialogue and engagement on the process. South Africa's government commissioned four base study papers on political governance and democracy (which I authored); corporate governance; economic governance; and socio-economic development. It also convened public meetings throughout the country, and encouraged its citizens to participate actively in the process.[53] South Africa's parliament convened its own peer review process, and also stressed the importance of public participation in the review.

But while civil society has a pivotal role to play in this process, some of these groups can also be criticised for the manner in which they cast aspersions on the APRM process, labelling it an exercise in 'self-congratulation' and 'legitimisation'.[54] This conduct only served to polarise South African politics. Civil society cannot expect merely to sit in judgement over government through this process. While the APRM has accorded NGOs rights and privileges, these groups also have a major responsibility to help consolidate South Africa's APRM process and to address the enormous political, socio-economic, and development challenges confronting South Africa and the broader African community of states. Civil society actors must 'dirty their hands' and engage both the state and its citizens – especially the poor – to gauge their views on the state and health of democracy and governance 13 years into South Africa's liberation. NGOs and the broader civil society community should themselves promote a 'holistic approach to development' which 'requires systemic attention'.[55]

Nearly a decade and a half into the new order, South Africa still faces major challenges with regard to institutional transformation and in making the new state responsive to the needs of a post-apartheid society (see Moyo and Hall; Shubane; and Sooka in this volume). This is why the black-led government has stressed 'good governance': efficiency; effectiveness; clean and corruption-free government; and strengthening the capacity of the state to deliver services to its citizenry, with a focus on institutional design and processes. Equally significant in the 'new' South Africa is the importance of democratic governance – state-society relations – and the participation and representation of the public in political, policy, and governance processes. The government and non-state actors must address substantive governance and democracy challenges as well as issues of participation in public life. Unless these issues are urgently addressed, tensions between government and major pockets of civil society will increase. South Africa is in the grip of a serious policy debate: selling a new governance paradigm of developmental democracy and a developmental state. This is one of the most important debates in South Africa's post-settlement era, and all key stakeholders – including government, civil society, NGOs, labour, the private sector, political parties, and other organs of state such as the national parliament – have a major opportunity to help shape the future political and development trajectory of the country.

In November 2006, the draft report of the Adebayo Adedeji-led Panel of Eminent Persons of the African Peer Review Mechanism on South Africa was completed and subsequently leaked to the media. The report was titled 'Country Review Report: Republic of South Africa' (APRM Country Review Report No. 4, African Peer Review Mechanism, November 2006). The Eminent Persons cited the need for action on 11 major national cross-cutting issues, including: unemployment; capacity constraints and poor service delivery; poverty and inequality; land reform; violence against women; violence against children; HIV/AIDS; corruption; crime; xenophobia and racism; and managing diversity.[56] The Eminent Persons noted that South Africa should expand dialogue to strengthen democracy and service delivery; develop programmes to combat xenophobia; formulate a comprehensive strategy on refugees; and refocus on moral and social values to combat crime, especially against women.

The Eminent Persons further called for: transforming the judicial system to reflect the realities of South Africa; providing adequate legal services to poor and rural people; modernising and integrating the traditional and modern justice systems; and addressing capacity constraints in the judiciary.[57] In terms of deliberative democracy, the Eminent Persons noted that, over time, lack of delivery and consultation could pit South Africa's government against its citizens unless consultation procedures are improved along with service delivery. The Eminent Persons further noted the need to translate public policy documents into the country's local languages in order to make policy and budgetary information accessible to the masses.[58]

The Eminent Persons also called for incentives to attract qualified personnel to the public service; strategies to attract back skilled people who have left the country; a comprehensive skills development strategy; measures to step up the competence and accountability of the public service at all levels; and developing strategies on how to encourage a philanthropic culture. The panel suggested that chapter 9 institutions such as South Africa's Human Rights and Gender commissions should be reviewed to improve their efficiency, effectiveness, and public outreach. South Africa's party-list system was praised by the panel for ensuring that minority parties have representation in parliament. However, the Eminent Persons noted that ordinary South Africans remain alienated from their political representatives, which underlined the shortcomings of the adoption of unbridled proportional representation. The draft report noted that floor-crossing by MPs further erodes the already weak link between members of parliament and the electorate.[59]

The APRM panel further argued in the draft report that poor governance at local and provincial levels is possibly South Africa's most important fiscal management problem, blocking service delivery and leading to public protests.[60] The draft report noted that poor coordination among different departments and spheres of government had caused shortfalls in service delivery and decision-making.[61] Capacity shortages of skills and resources were said to be particularly acute at the local government level, with poor service delivery constituting a major source of conflict.[62]

In terms of Economic Governance and Management, the Eminent Persons noted that, while South Africa deserves credit for many aspects of its economic management, unemployment is structural and needs much more fundamental efforts to reduce. The draft report noted the risk of incipient and creeping corruption, which it felt could reverse the country's democratic gains after a long period of struggle.[63] On the Socio-Economic Governance score, the panel recommended that the government empower health workers and community development workers to be more efficient in assisting vulnerable groups and persons living with HIV/AIDS[64] (see Ndinga-Muvumba and Mottiar in this volume).

The draft report was met with serious criticisms from the South African government, which expressed reservations around the panel's assessments on whether or not South Africa could be classified as a 'developmental state'; rape statistics; xenophobia; floor crossing; cooperative governance; and integrated governance. South Africa's critical response was contained in a 54-page memorandum. During the January 2007 AU summit in Addis Ababa, the differences between the South African government and the panel of eminent persons had still not been resolved. The peer review of South Africa by its APRM colleagues could thus not take place as originally planned. Whether and how the tensions over South Africa's APRM draft report is eventually resolved is likely to have an enormous impact on a process that Tshwane was so instrumental in creating and shaping.

CONCLUSION

Since 1994, South Africa has gradually emerged as a key player in African politics, development, and diplomacy, pursuing a 'progressive' agenda in defence of development, peace and security, democratic and 'good governance', and a developmental role involving the private sector. The preferred strategy of both the Mandela and Mbeki governments was that of partnership and alliance-formation with key African states such as Nigeria, Mozambique, Algeria, Tanzania, Ghana and others. The key goal pursued by South Africa and its strategic partners was the promotion of an 'African Agenda' in pursuit of development on the basis of this progressive agenda.

A key tactic of this approach was to play the 'progressive' role of norms-builder and promoter of principles through initiatives such as the AU, NEPAD, and the APRM. South Africa has promoted progressive norms such as civil society participation; free and fair elections; the independence of the judiciary; combating corruption; term limits for public office holders; and gender empowerment. South Africa is also a keen supporter of the proposed African Charter on Democracy, Governance and Elections, drafted in 2005, and discussed at the AU summit in 2006.

It is not only in the area of politics that South Africa's influence has come to the fore. We have witnessed important elements of South Africa's conservative macro-economic policy of GEAR being incorporated into NEPAD, which was promptly dubbed by critics as 'the Africanisation of GEAR'. It is critical that South Africa take the lead in transforming NEPAD into a real developmental plan for the continent. NEPAD is closely associated with South Africa, and this makes it imperative that Tshwane takes a lead role in implementing the plan, without alienating other African countries.

A key goal of NEPAD has been to try and extract commitments from the northern industrialised powers in favour of greater levels of aid, market access, debt relief, and resources to bolster the continent's peace operations capacities. This is truly developmental, and South Africa and its strategic partners should continue to play this role. The strategy was clearly to engage the rich North on the basis that African states were becoming serious about implementing initiatives on democratisation, governance, peace and security, and creating conditions for private sector take-off.

It is now time to open up the NEPAD debate, and to involve African social actors in an independent and meaningful way. South Africa, should take the lead here. It is important to appreciate that a developmental model is a participatory paradigm that relies heavily on active civil society involvement. NEPAD's architects should open up this process as a matter of urgency and start to engage in a radical overhaul of the plan's economic dimensions. It is especially NEPAD's neoliberal economic underpinnings that are in need of revision so as to embody greater developmental dimensions, and South Africa should show leadership on this issue by opening up both the process and the debate.

Thus, this chapter has argued that in the post-1994 period, and particularly during the Mbeki presidency after 1999, South Africa has pursued a diplomacy that was activist in nature, economically conservative, and politically both pragmatic and principled. Politically, the agenda was progressive and the diplomacy ambitious, while foreign economic policy has been, in the main, conservative. I have argued that post-apartheid South Africa interpreted the world in rather static terms as a hostile capitalist system that would punish those who do not obey its unspoken rules. The creation of the AU and NEPAD will, however, be two of Mbeki's greatest legacies.

The chapter concludes here by stressing that South Africa cannot go it alone in hoping to build and consolidate a progressive movement on the continent; the country needs allies and strategic partners for that effort. South Africa should thus nurture its relations with Mozambique, Ghana, Algeria and Tanzania, and others, and in particular restore its concert relationship with Nigeria, while constantly reaching out to other African states.

10

South Africa and Nigeria in Africa: An axis of virtue?[1]

ADEKEYE ADEBAJO

In the post-September 11 'age of terror' in which we currently live, one of the most infamous and inelegant axioms that has been coined was the depiction, by US president George W. Bush, of Iran, Iraq and North Korea as forming an 'axis of evil'. Critics sneered that the real 'axis of evil' was constituted by the residents of the Oval office: Bush, his vice-president, Dick Cheney, and his defence secretary, Donald Rumsfeld. According to this view, these 'terrible triplets' of the world's sole 'hyperpower' plunged the US into an ill-conceived invasion of Iraq in March 2003 that was considered illegitimate and illegal by much of the world, lacking as it did a UN Security Council mandate.

In the African context, it is perhaps worth speculating whether a phrase that has taken on negative connotations can be inverted for more positive ends. One major issue that has generated much debate within and outside Africa is whether potential hegemons, South Africa and Nigeria, can form an 'axis of virtue' to play a leadership role in managing Africa's many conflicts through the African Union (AU), the Southern African Development Community (SADC), and the Economic Community of West African States (ECOWAS); drive economic integration and development through a New Partnership for Africa's Development (NEPAD); and promote democratic governance on a troubled continent.

General Abdulsalaam Abubakar, Nigeria's military leader between 1998 and 1999, called for South Africa and Nigeria to establish an 'axis of power to promote peace and stability on the continent'.[2] In the post-Cold War era, the reluctance of western countries to intervene militarily in African countries after debacles in Somalia and Rwanda in the 1990s led many observers to question whether South Africa and Nigeria – which was at that time leading a peacekeeping mission in Liberia under the auspices of the ECOWAS Ceasefire Monitoring Group (ECOMOG) – could fill this security vacuum. Though South Africa, accounting for about a third of Africa's economic strength, is wealthier than Nigeria, it faces even more powerful military challengers and political rivals in its own Southern African region. The apartheid-era army's destabilisation of its neighbours has left a profound distrust of South African military interventionism which remains strong today. During the 1990s, Nigeria was willing but unable to carry out swift and decisive military interventions in West Africa. South Africa was arguably more able but largely unwilling to undertake such military actions in Southern Africa. South Africa has military and economic capacity but lacks the legitimacy to play a hegemonic role. Nigeria has more legitimacy in its own subregion, but lacks the military and economic capacity to act as an effective hegemon. While South Africa and Nigeria are militarily and politically powerful relative to other regional states, they must still develop the capacity and legitimacy to influence their respective regions and they have often failed to convince other states to follow their lead on vital political, security, and economic issues. *Pax South Africana* has to contend with 'bargainers' like Zimbabwe, Angola, and Namibia, while *Pax Nigeriana* faces 'bargainers' like Côte d'Ivoire, Senegal, Liberia, and Burkina Faso. These states have the capability to increase significantly the costs for the aspiring hegemons when attempting to impose their will on their respective regions.

The concept of hegemony has, over the decades, conjured up images of domination, bullying behaviour, and arrogance on the part of Great Powers. It is true that past and present hegemons, such as Britain during the nineteenth century and the US during the twentieth century, sometimes used their power and primacy aggressively through colonialism and other forms of domination in Africa, Asia, Latin America, and the Caribbean. But hegemony need not necessarily be a negative phenomenon. The pound and the dollar stabilised the international monetary system under *Pax Britannica*[3] and *Pax Americana*[4] while, after the Second World War, the US helped Europe and Japan's economic recovery, provided its allies with a nuclear umbrella, and led the creation of the international trade system. One can in fact talk of 'constructive' hegemony in which hegemons are able not only to articulate the rules and norms for respective regions, but are also able to convince other states to follow such rules and respect and adhere to established norms. Hegemony is therefore about leadership and influence and not just bullying dominance (see Schoeman in this volume).

Some commentators have gone as far as suggesting that the future of the entire continent rests on the fate of South Africa and Nigeria. Nigeria's former foreign minister, Olu Adeniji, stated in 2000 that: 'Nigeria and South Africa have always been considered as the two countries that should propel Africa, south of the

Sahara, into the contemporary economic level ...'[5] The heads of South Africa's Institute for Global Dialogue (IGD), Garth le Pere, and the Nigerian Institute of International Affairs (NIIA), Joy Ogwu (later foreign minister between 2006 and 2007), both described South Africa and Nigeria as Africa's 'global power perch'.[6] Adebayo Adedeji, the Nigerian head of South Africa's African Peer Review Mechanism (APRM) review process noted: 'South Africa and Nigeria ... constitute Sub-Saharan Africa's two economic colossuses.'[7] Outside the continent, American foreign policy guru, Henry Kissinger, opined that: 'No state except Nigeria or South Africa is in a position to play a major role outside its immediate region ... African security issues ... should be left largely to African nations, with South Africa and Nigeria playing the principle roles.'[8] This chapter will investigate the validity of these claims and also examine in detail Africa's most strategic partnership. We will focus on three periods: first, the apartheid era from 1960 to 1993; second, the rule of Nigeria's General Sani Abacha and Nelson Mandela between 1994 and 1998; and third, the presidencies of Thabo Mbeki and Olusegun Obasanjo between 1999 and 2006.

THE PROPHET AND THE PARIAH, 1960–1993

The *annus mirabilis* of African independence in 1960 saw the birth of Nigeria amidst great hopes for a political and economic giant that was expected to take its preordained place in the African sun. Nigeria's leaders almost gave the impression that all the country had to do was simply appear on the African stage, and all other states would bow in deference at the splendour of the new African colossus that the gods had sent to fulfill their messianic mission in Africa. In the same year as Nigeria's independence, South Africa was about to be expelled from the Commonwealth for the bloody killing of 69 unarmed blacks in Sharpeville during another ugly display of its policy of legally sanctioned racism. Many felt that the apartheid state was heading towards civil war. Pretoria's foreign policy was also suffused with a missionary zeal, as apartheid's leaders talked patronisingly about their country having special responsibilities to spread western values north of the Limpopo in a macabre *mission civilisatrice*. In the three decades that followed, both African giants failed to achieve their leadership aspirations for very different reasons.[9]

In the case of Nigeria, its West African region was littered with francophone states that looked to France – the self-appointed *gendarme d'Afrique* – for protection against the potential neighbourhood bully: Nigeria. The Gallic power intervened in the region with reckless abandon, regularly landing its 'gendarmes' in Africa and effortlessly shuffling regimes around its pré carrée (backyard).[10] Nigeria's attempts at seeking greater political influence in West Africa through economic means were consistently frustrated by France, which encouraged francophone states to create rival trade blocs.[11] In its three decades of existence, the Nigerian-led ECOWAS did not even come close to its goals of establishing a common market. Threats to build a 'black bomb' to counter Pretoria's nuclear capability remained an empty boast.

South Africa, in contrast, was able effortlessly to subdue its neighbours both economically and militarily through a policy of destabilisation. Pretoria had nuclear capability, a flourishing arms industry, and some world-class manufacturers. South Africa dominated the Southern African Customs Union (SACU), establishing with Botswana, Swaziland, Lesotho and Namibia, the common market that eluded ECOWAS.[12] This was, however, a market that distributed its rewards unevenly. SACU was dominated by a South Africa which unilaterally determined how much to pay out to its neighbours and sometimes frustrated their efforts at industrialisation. Despite their attempts at lessening their dependence on Pretoria through the Southern African Development Coordination Conference (SADCC) – established in April 1980 – many of the region's Lilliputian states still traded covertly with, and depended on, the South African Gulliver.

In spite of the external constraints on Nigeria playing a hegemonic role in Africa, the country provided leadership to the anti-apartheid and decolonisation struggles. Lagos gave liberation movements financial and material backing, and established a Southern African Relief Fund (SARF) in 1976 to provide scholarships and relief materials to South African students and refugees. Nigeria's contributions to the liberation struggle were aptly recognised by its invitations to meetings of the Frontline States of Southern Africa; its long chairmanship of the UN Special Committee against Apartheid; and its hosting of a UN anti-apartheid conference in 1977. Since South Africa was diplomatically isolated and forced to bear the brunt of many of the international community's sanctions, it was denied a global stage, and it was Nigeria which spoke loudest for African concerns: Nigeria was the prophet, South Africa the pariah. To announce its status as the leading state in Africa, Nigeria hosted a lavish Festival of Arts and Culture (FESTAC) in 1977.[13] Nigeria's civilian president, Shehu Shagari, cut off support to Southern African liberation movements in 1980 ostensibly as part of austerity measures. This funding was resumed in 1983 and maintained until South Africa's transition in 1989.[14] Nigeria led an African boycott of the Commonwealth Games in Edinburgh in 1986 to protest Britain's refusal to impose sanctions on the apartheid regime. Its head of state between 1976 and 1979, General Olusegun Obasanjo, also co-chaired a Commonwealth Eminent Person's Group visit to South Africa in 1986.

After Mandela's release from jail in February 1990, he visited Nigeria within three months to express his gratitude for the country's support during the liberation struggle. He also received a reported $10 million campaign contribution for the African National Congress (ANC) from General Ibrahim Babangida.[15] In April 1992, president F.W. De Klerk led a South African business delegation to Nigeria: a clear recognition by South Africa's business community of the huge potential of Africa's largest market. The ANC was furious that Nigeria had not informed its leaders about De Klerk's visit, but Abuja brushed aside these complaints saying that it needed no such authorisation.[16] Despite this minor spat, there were great expectations that the impending installation of an ANC-led government in South Africa would usher in the birth of an alliance between Africa's two economic powerhouses.

KING BAABU AND THE AVUNCULAR SAINT, 1994–1998

These hopes were soon dashed by the unexpected souring of relations between Pretoria and Abuja. In order to understand South Africa's troubled relations with Nigeria during this second phase between 1994 and 1998, it is important first to understand the two main protagonists in this tale: General Sani Abacha and Nelson Mandela. In his 2002 play, *King Baabu*,[17] Nigerian Nobel laureate and political activist, Wole Soyinka, created one of the most grotesque and absurd figures in world drama. Baabu is a bumbling, brainless, brutish buffoon and greedily corrupt military general who exchanges his military attire for a monarchichal robe and a gown. The play is a thinly-disguised satire of Nigerian General Abacha's debauched rule between September 1993 and his death – in the company of Indian prostitutes – in June 1998. In a non-fictional account in 1996, Soyinka was equally merciless:

> Abacha is prepared to reduce Nigeria to a rubble as long as he survives to preserve over a name … Totally lacking in vision, in perspectives, he is a mole trapped in a warren of tunnels … Abacha has no *idea* of Nigeria. Beyond the reality of a fiefdom that has dutifully nursed his insatiable greed and

transformed him into a creature of enormous wealth, and now of power, Abacha has no *notion* of Nigeria ... Abacha will be satisfied only with the devastation of every aspect of Nigeria that he cannot mentally grasp, and that is virtually all of Nigeria.[18]

Abacha joined the Nigerian army at the age of 19 and established himself as an infantryman with training in Nigerian and British military institutions. He was involved in his first *coup d'état* in 1966, fought bravely to keep Nigeria united during the country's civil war between 1967 and 1970, and was instrumentally involved in two further coups in 1983 and 1985, with the second eventually propelling him to the position of chief of defence staff and *Khalifa* (king-in-waiting) to General Ibrahim Babangida.[19] He eventually took advantage of a weak, illegitimate interim government to seize full power following the annulment of elections in June 1993. The election was widely believed to have been won by Moshood Abiola, whom Abacha subsequently jailed when he tried to claim his mandate.

In power, Abacha was ruthless and reclusive, but hardly as inept as the caricature depicted by Soyinka and believed by many of Nigeria's political opposition, who greatly underestimated him. Depicting him as a semi-literate buffoon, Nigeria's civil society groups had assumed that Abacha would not last five weeks in power, let alone five years. But Abacha was a survivor who understood how to control Nigeria's powerful army and how to buy off the country's opportunistic political class. He was also able to ward off oil sanctions by the West by playing on the greed of western oil companies and governments; by employing lobbyists in the US; and by tacitly threatening a withdrawal of Nigerian peacekeepers from Liberia and Sierra Leone in the full knowledge that western countries were not keen to intervene in these countries. By the time of his death in 1998, Abacha had managed to have all five government-created political parties adopt him as their presidential candidate. At the time of his death, he was also four months away from achieving what no other military ruler in Nigeria had dared to do: metamorphosing from military dictator to civilian ruler.

Nelson Mandela is perhaps the starkest contrast that one can imagine to Abacha. An educated middle-class lawyer from a royal Xhosa family and a cosmopolitan anglophile, this 'father of the nation' who had spent 27 years as a political prisoner for his beliefs, embodied his people's aspirations for a democratic future. In a collection of poems titled 'Mandela's Earth,' Wole Soyinka wrote:

Not for you the olive branch that sprouts
Gun muzzles, barbed wire garlands, tangled thorns
To wreathe the brows of black, unwilling Christs ...
Your patience grows inhuman, Mandela.[20]

Mandela, an iconic figure and winner of the Nobel peace prize in 1993, has been widely celebrated as a political saint and one of the greatest moral figures of the twentieth century. As president, he came to symbolise his country's racial reconciliation and was the foremost prophet of *ubuntu* (the gift of discovering our shared humanity). His charisma helped South Africa's young, democratic institutions to flower, and gave the country an international stature that a former global pariah could never have dreamed of. Mandela served as a further contrast to Abacha by bowing out as president, as promised, after the end of his first term in 1999.[21]

Under Abacha's autocratic rule, by 1995, South Africa and Nigeria had traded places from the apartheid era: it was now Nigeria, and not South Africa, that was being considered for expulsion from the Commonwealth. It was Nigeria, under a repressive military regime, that was facing mounting criticism over its human rights record; it was Nigeria that was becoming increasingly isolated in international society; and it was Nigeria that was considered to be possibly heading towards civil war. Having abandoned its apartheid past, South Africa was widely acknowledged to be the most likely political and economic success story in Africa. South Africa seemed better positioned than Nigeria to become the continent's champion. While military leaders proliferated in West African countries like Nigeria, Sierra Leone, and Gambia, post-apartheid South Africa provided a democratic model for its region, with its *avant garde* government of national unity between 1994 and 1996 and its support for the spread or restoration of democracy in neighbouring Mozambique, Lesotho, and Malawi. Mandela set up a Truth and Reconciliation Commission (TRC) to look into the injustices of an undemocratic past; Abacha set up a Provisional Ruling Council (PRC) to bury its democratic future.

In the economic sphere, the difference between the two giants was, and to a large extent still remains, clear: in 2006, South Africa had a GDP of about US$193 billion, compared to Nigeria's US$53 billion. While South Africa has for years had a steel industry that feeds its arms manufacturers, Nigeria's Ajaokuta Steel Complex, which was planned since the early 1970s and soaked up US$4 billion, became a white elephant mired in corruption and inefficiency. While South

Africa's digital cellular telecommunications network is among the world's largest, Nigeria's phone system continues to be notoriously erratic. While South Africa has well-funded, world-class universities, Nigeria's ivory towers are crumbling monuments to years of neglect and government closures.

The nadir of relations between post-apartheid South Africa and Nigeria was undoubtedly reached after the brutal hanging by the Abacha regime of Nigerian activist Ken Saro-Wiwa, and eight of his fellow Ogoni campaigners, during the Commonwealth summit in Auckland, New Zealand, in November 1995.[22] Before this incident, Mandela – under pressure from Nigerian pro-democracy activists as well as western and a few African governments – had gone to Abuja to intercede with Abacha for the release of Moshood Abiola. During the visit, Mandela reportedly pleaded with Abacha that Africa's many conflicts were providing ammunition to Afro-pessimists who were arguing that blacks were incapable of ruling themselves. He appealed to Abacha's sense of his place in history.[23] In the same year, Mandela sent Archbishop Desmond Tutu and then Deputy President Mbeki, to Abuja to plead for the release of political prisoners, including Abiola and Olusegun Obasanjo, two close friends of many ANC stalwarts. During his visit, Tutu echoed Mandela's sentiments to his hosts: '... we in South Africa don't want to compete with Nigeria for the leadership of the continent, but we are jealous of the continent's reputation. The fact that the giant of Africa is in the state that it is in terms of its human rights record and the whole question of democracy, this has had an impact on all of us.'[24]

During the Commonwealth summit in Auckland, Mandela believed that he had received personal assurances from Abacha of clemency for the 'Ogoni nine'. Learning of the executions, Mandela felt deeply betrayed, having reassured his fellow Commonwealth leaders that the executions would not occur and having used his moral stature to assuage their anger against the Nigerian government.[25] A furious Mandela reacted impulsively, accusing Abacha of behaving like an 'insensitive, frightened dictator' who engaged in 'judicial murder' (echoing British premier, John Major's phrase), and warning that Abacha 'is sitting on a volcano and I am going to explode it under him'.[26] South Africa's president called on Washington and London to impose oil sanctions on Abacha, and advocated Nigeria's expulsion from the Commonwealth. On his return home, Mandela recalled his high commissioner to Nigeria, George Nene, who had been somewhat unfairly criticised by South African civil society groups for not having made contact with Nigerian opposition leaders and gaining better access to a notoriously reclusive leadership.[27] Nigeria's leaders, in fact, felt that

Nene had become too close to the opposition and had lost all leverage with the Abacha government.[28]

In December 1995, Mandela called a SADC summit to take collective action against Nigeria. In retaliation, Abacha refused to let Nigeria's footballers defend their African Cup of Nations crown in South Africa in 1996. The vituperative exchanges continued, as Nigeria's pugnacious minister of information, Walter Ofonagoro, accused Mandela of being a 'black head of a white country' who could not be trusted: a particularly hurtful and insensitive statement that hit at the most sensitive spot of a black-led government that had inherited a country in which whites still controlled the economy and key institutions. Ordinary South Africans would not easily forgive Nigeria for this personal slur on the country's saintly icon.

Mandela was about to learn the dismaying intricacies of African diplomacy. Even his iconic status failed to rally a single Southern African state to take action against Nigeria. The fuse of the volcano that 'Madiba' had threatened to explode under Abacha had spectacularly failed to ignite. Instead, it was South Africa that was being accused by many African leaders of becoming a western Trojan horse, sowing seeds of division in Africa and undermining African solidarity. UN Secretary-General Boutros Boutros-Ghali reminded Mandela of Nigeria's peacekeeping sacrifices in Liberia and Sierra Leone.[29] South Africa's diplomats soon became concerned that Pretoria would become diplomatically isolated within Africa, adversely affecting its bid for a permanent seat on the UN Security Council. ANC stalwarts also reminded Mandela of the country's debt of gratitude to Nigeria during the anti-apartheid struggle, as well as Nigeria's continued campaign contributions to the party. These voices eventually drowned out the efforts of South African trade union, business, environmental, women's and youth groups that were lobbying their government to take even stronger action against Nigeria.

The decisive intervention that changed South Africa's policy was that of Mbeki. Having served as head of the ANC office in Lagos between 1976 and 1978 during the military regime of General Olusegun Obasanjo, Mbeki understood both the country and its main players. Concerned that the situation could precipitate the disintegration of Nigeria, he devised a strategy with South Africa's high commissioner, George Nene, to engage rather than to confront the Nigerian regime. He embarked on diplomatic missions to Abuja and initiated contacts between the security agencies of both countries.[30] South Africa pulled out of the Commonwealth Action Group on Nigeria that had been set up shortly after Auckland; it refused to sanction Nigeria at the UN commission on human rights; and a country that had once welcomed Nigeria's pro-democracy groups, cancelled a major conference of these activists scheduled to take place in Johannesburg in early 1996.[31] The first Nigerian ambassador to South Africa, Alhaji Shehu Malami, presented his credentials to Mandela in August 1996.

Mbeki provided a detailed justification of South Africa's policy to his country's parliamentarians in May 1996, telling them: 'We should not humiliate ourselves by pretending that we have a strength which we do not have.'[32] Arguing that Pretoria did not have the leverage to dictate to Nigeria, Mbeki urged South Africa instead to encourage efforts to support Nigeria's transition to democratic rule. He warned South Africa not to overestimate its strength in a fit of arrogance, and noted the failure of the West, which had the power to impose oil sanctions on Nigeria, to act. Instead, Mbeki observed that Mandela had been set up for failure and ridicule by western countries who preferred to protect oil profits, investments, and Nigerian assets in their countries.[33] Western governments, steeped in the art of realpolitik, had made critical noises to assuage domestic public opinion in their countries while quietly continuing to do business with Abacha's autocratic regime. It is probably not an exaggeration to note that this single incident would shape Mbeki's future policy of 'quiet diplomacy' towards Zimbabwe.[34] Having felt that Mandela had been set up for failure on Nigeria by the West, Mbeki was determined not to suffer the same fate over Zimbabwe. Unlike Mandela's reaction to Abacha, Mbeki pointedly ignored calls by western leaders to sanction Robert Mugabe, judging that such actions would not only be ineffective but could result in a loss of leverage both within Zimbabwe and the broader African context.

General Abacha's sudden death in June 1998 greatly increased the chances of the tale of the prophet and the pariah becoming a tale of two prophets. Mbeki travelled to Abuja shortly after General Abdulsaalam Abubakar had assumed power, urging the Nigerian government to restore civil liberties and to release political prisoners. In August and September 1998, Abubakar travelled to South Africa. In yet another sign of restored cooperation between both countries, Nigeria's new military ruler invited Mandela to attend the ECOWAS summit in Abuja. The mild-mannered Abubakar oversaw a transition to democratic rule in Nigeria by May 1999, bowing out gracefully after less than a year in power. The conservative De Klerk – who had previously been a staunch defender of apartheid – had also, under severe domestic and international pressure, similarly reformed the very apartheid system over which his National Party (the NP) had presided for nearly fifty years. In the end, both Abubakar and De Klerk midwifed democratic transitions in Nigeria and South Africa.

THE PHILOSOPHER-KING AND THE SOLDIER-FARMER, 1999-2006

Thabo Mbeki[35] and Olusegun Obasanjo[36] assumed the presidencies of their respective countries in 1999. Both are very different personalities. Mbeki, a pipe-smoking, Sussex University-trained economist, writes his own speeches, and fancies himself as a philosopher-king who developed the idea of an African Renaissance and is widely celebrated as the intellectual father of NEPAD. Obasanjo, a career soldier and engineer who has written several biographies but is not considered to be an intellectual, established one of Africa's largest farms on retirement as military head of state in 1979 in his hometown of Ota. The two men had a close personal relationship, dating back to Obasanjo's tenure as Nigeria's leader between 1976 and 1979, when Mbeki served as the ANC representative in Lagos. Obasanjo also met South Africa's future leaders during his visit to the apartheid enclave as co-chairman of the Commonwealth Eminent Person's Group in 1986. As head of state in the late 1970s, he developed a close working relationship with Southern African leaders like Robert Mugabe, Sam Nujoma and Eduardo Dos Santos, at a time when Nigeria was considered a member of the Frontline States and a generous supporter of liberation movements in the region.[37] Obasanjo's first foreign trip abroad on becoming president was to attend Mbeki's inauguration in June 1999.

Both Mbeki and Obasanjo are respected internationally, but have faced enormous economic and political difficulties at home. Mbeki, though respected as a technocrat, inevitably struggled to fill the shoes of his saintly predecessor, Nelson Mandela. Obasanjo, rejected by his own Yoruba people in Nigeria's 1999 presidential election, has not totally shaken off his military image. Both have faced severe criticism at home for embarking on frequent foreign trips and for not spending more time on alleviating pressing problems of poverty, unemployment and crime at home. Mbeki has been criticised for his domestic AIDS policies (see Ndinga-Muvumba and Mottiar in this volume); Obasanjo has been castigated for not preventing massacres of civilians by his army. Both leaders have, however, worked closely at managing African conflicts through the AU, SADC and ECOWAS. They have attempted to promote norms of democratic government through the African Union whose founding charter they were instrumental in shaping (see Landsberg in this volume).

Mbeki's African Renaissance is defined as a doctrine for Africa's political, economic and social renewal and a call for political democratisation, economic growth, and the reintegration of Africa into the global economy. It calls on Africans to adapt democracy to fit their own specific conditions without compromising its fundamental principles of representation and accountability.[38] The African Renaissance has as its central goal the right of people to determine their own future. It calls for a cancellation of Africa's foreign debt of US$290 billion, an improvement in Africa's terms of trade, the expansion of development assistance, and better access to foreign markets for African goods. Mbeki pragmatically calls on African states to embrace the positive aspects of globalisation by attracting capital and investment with which to develop their economies. The African Renaissance does not, however, naively assume – as some of its critics have maintained – that this political and economic renewal is already underway in Africa. It merely seeks to set out a vision and prescribe the policy recommendations and actions that could create the conditions for the rebirth of a continent. There is, however, some truth to the criticism that the Renaissance is devoid of substantive policy content and is more promise than policy.[39] NEPAD and the AU thus represent attempts to add policy flesh to the skeletal bones of the Renaissance.[40]

Obasanjo's proposal for a Conference on Security, Stability, Development and Cooperation in Africa (CSSDCA) has now been integrated into two of the African Union's key institutions: the Economic, Social, and Cultural Council (ECOSOCC) and the Council of Elders who will help mediate disputes. The idea was first discussed at a conference in Kampala in 1991.[41] The CSSDCA's final report proposed developing a continental peacekeeping machinery; promoting conflict prevention and military self-reliance in Africa; establishing an African Peace Council of Elder Statesmen to mediate conflicts; and drastically reducing military expenditures in Africa.

THE AU, NEPAD AND PAX AFRICANA

Mbeki and Obasanjo challenged the Organisation of African Unity's (OAU) inflexible adherence to absolute sovereignty and non-interference in the internal affairs of member states.[42] At the OAU summit in Algiers, Algeria, in 1999, Mbeki and Obasanjo were among the leaders who pushed for the ostracism of regimes that engage in unconstitutional changes of government. The organisation subsequently barred the military regimes of Côte d'Ivoire and Comoros from attending its summit in Lomé, Togo, in 2000. The two leaders insisted that the OAU must recognise the right of other states to intervene in the internal affairs of its members in egregious cases of gross human rights abuses and to stem regional instability.

Both Mbeki and Obasanjo have stressed the importance of conflict resolution in Africa. Obasanjo hosted a Commonwealth meeting which discussed land reform in Zimbabwe in September 2001. He has led peacemaking efforts in Liberia, Sierra Leone, and in the Great Lakes region. Mbeki, with the help of Mandela and deputy president, Jacob Zuma, lent his country's weight and resources to peace efforts in Burundi (see Curtis in this volume). South Africa's president was particularly critical of the military regime of General Robert Guei in Côte d'Ivoire and Revolutionary United Front (RUF) rebels in Sierra Leone. He was active in negotiations to restore constitutional rule to Côte d'Ivoire as the AU mediator to the country from November 2004, and helped to convince Charles Taylor to leave for exile in Nigeria in August 2003. But Tshwane (the new name for Pretoria) and Abuja have felt the strain of peacekeeping burdens in Burundi (under the AU) and Liberia (under ECOWAS) on their fragile economies. In future, South African and Nigerian peacekeepers are likely to serve mainly under the UN as in the cases of Burundi and Liberia – in which both countries insisted, while continuing to contribute troops, that the UN take over these responsibilities from weak regional organisations – clearly demonstrate. This not only represents an attempt to legitimise such military actions, but is also a conscious effort to alleviate fears of aggressive regional hegemons pursuing their own parochial interests under the guise of keeping peace in Africa.

Both Mbeki and Obasanjo have lobbied the rich world on behalf of Africa at annual Group of Eight (G8) meetings, though the results have often been disappointing. Both have driven the NEPAD process. This plan is based on a straightforward bargain between Africa and its largely western donors: in exchange for support from external actors, African leaders have agreed to take responsibility for, and commit themselves to, democratic governance. In October 2001, sixteen African leaders met in Abuja for NEPAD's first implementation meeting. Obasanjo also hosted a meeting between NEPAD and the heads of Africa's Regional Economic Communities (RECs) in Abuja in October 2003 in an effort to encourage them to align their integration programmes with NEPAD's goals.[43] As key members of NEPAD's implementing committee, Mbeki and Obasanjo have pushed 26 of their fellow leaders to sign up to its peer review mechanism, which critics still argue lacks the 'teeth' to bite autocratic offenders (see Landsberg in this volume). During the process to transform the OAU into the AU, Mbeki and Obasanjo ensured that the organisation adopted a gradual-ist approach to unity rather than the more federalist model being championed by Libya's maverick leader, Muammar Qaddafi. They also successfully pushed for Mali's outgoing president, Alpha Konaré, to become the first chairperson of the AU commission, in order to have a strong, visionary leader that could interact easily with other heads of state.[44]

South Africa's efforts at promoting democracy and human rights have some-times been met with fierce opposition from other African countries. After some difficulties in its peacemaking role in the DRC, Angola, and Nigeria, South Africa has been forced to be more cautious when dealing with its African counterparts. SADC leaders like Robert Mugabe, Sam Nujoma, and Eduardo dos Santos feel that they preceded Mbeki in the liberation struggle and complain that the ANC-led government has not repaid the sacrifices that their countries made for the liberation of South Africa. South Africa contributed about 1 500 troops to a UN peacekeeping force in the DRC (MONUC) and expended much resources and time in leading peacemaking efforts, successfully brokering the withdrawal of Rwandan troops from the Congo in 2002 (see Curtis in this volume). In several unsuccessful attempts to break the political impasse in Zimbabwe, Mbeki worked closely with the leaders of Nigeria, Malawi, Mozambique and Namibia. South Africa's president learned from Mandela's difficult experience over Nigeria to rely on multilateral diplomacy to pursue his regional diplomatic goals.

The other African giant, Nigeria, has been more militarily active than South Africa in its own subregion, though facing similar suspicions from its neighbours. Nigeria's generals were fully committed to an activist security role in Liberia and Sierra Leone between 1990 and 1998, despite often strong public opposi-tion from Nigerians.[45] Nigeria provided the men and money that fuelled the ECOMOG locomotive. With 75 per cent of West Africa's economic strength, 50 per cent of its population, and a 94 500-strong army that dwarfs the combined total of those of its neighbours, Nigeria remains the indispensable local power in West Africa. ECOMOG was, however, unable to pacify Liberia and Sierra Leone militarily due to the ability of regional warlords to control mineral-rich parts of the countryside outside the capitals, often sheltered by dense forests. *Pax Nigeriana* was in effect 'hegemony on a shoestring': Nigeria simply lacked the military and financial means to impose its will on Liberia and Sierra Leone without appeasing local warlords and procuring external logistical assistance. Under Obasanjo's presidency, Nigeria withdrew the bulk of its troops from Sierra Leone by 2000, and subsumed the remaining 3 500 troops under a UN force (UNAMSIL). Nigeria also led an intervention into Liberia in August 2003, but insisted – as a condition for deployment – that the UN take over the force three months later and send troops from other countries. These are clear signs of the growing frustrations of regional peacekeeping and a desire to ease the financial burden on a fragile oil-dependent Nigerian economy. Obasanjo did, however, conduct mediation efforts in Sudan's Darfur region, Togo, and Côte d'Ivoire.

THE BINATIONAL COMMISSION AND STRATEGIC COORDINATION

Despite the domestic constraints of South Africa and Nigeria, the Tshwane-Abuja axis still has the most potential to drive Africa's Renaissance. As Obasanjo noted during a state banquet in Abuja in honour of Mbeki in October 2000: 'Our location, our destiny and the contemporary forces of globalisation have thrust upon us the burden of turning around the fortunes of our continent. We must not and cannot shy away from this responsibility.'[46] In October 1999, both countries had established the South Africa-Nigeria Binational Commission (BNC), thereby formalising the strong ties between them. The binational commission has five concrete objectives:[47] first, to provide a framework for joint efforts to bring Africa into the mainstream of global political, social, and economic developments; second, to provide the basis for the governments and private sectors of both countries to consult with each other to promote bilateral trade and industry; third, to improve bilateral relations in the fields of technology, education, health, culture, youth, and sports; fourth, to use both countries' human and natural resources to maximise socio-economic development through collaborative efforts; and finally, to establish the mechanisms to promote peace, stability, and socio-economic integration in Africa.[48]

Six BNC meetings were held, alternating between Nigeria and South Africa, in October 1999; April 2000; March 2001; March 2002; December 2003; and September 2004. The 2002 meeting initiated the idea of a South Africa/Nigeria Free Trade Area, while the 2003 meeting called for a Business Investment Forum between both countries. By the time of the sixth meeting, the focus was around eight working groups: trade, industry and finance; mineral and energy;

agriculture, water resources and environment; foreign affairs and cooperation; defence; immigration, justice and crime; social and technical; and public
enterprises and infrastructure. The sixth meeting was held in Durban, South
Africa, between 6 and 10 September 2004. Officials discussed how to increase
trade, with the Nigerians urging the South Africans to accelerate discussions
with their Southern African Customs Union partners (Botswana, Swaziland,
Lesotho and Namibia) in order to establish a free trade area with Nigeria;
and the Business Investment Forum was renamed the South Africa-Nigeria
Business Forum. The meeting further urged the establishment of a Special
Implementation Committee within the BNC to ensure an effective monitoring
mechanism, as well as to develop a concrete programme of action with clear
time frames. Continuity of officials was encouraged, as well as participation of
legislators and chief executives of South African provinces and Nigerian states
in future BNC sessions.[49]

The two key areas that appeared to dominate the BNC Durban meeting in
2004 were foreign affairs; and immigration and crime. Both countries discussed
the AU's new four-year strategic vision, urging the organisation to increase its
annual budget in order to be able to fulfil its goals; they pledged to incorporate
NEPAD into the work of SADC and ECOWAS; to work within both institutions to
finalise work on the African Standby Force (ASF), the Continental Early Warning
System (suggesting that SADC draw from the experiences of the ECOWAS early
warning system) and the Panel of the Wise. They committed to urging other
African states to join the APRM and to continue to fund the NEPAD and APRM
secretariats; they suggested that their permanent representatives in Addis
Ababa report on the effectiveness of the AU's 15-member Peace and Security
Council every six months; they stressed the importance of their permanent
representatives in New York working together on the UN reform process; and
they pledged to coordinate policies to strengthen Africa's position at the World
Bank, the International Monetary Fund (IMF) and the World Trade Organisation
(WTO). South African and Nigerian officials also discussed conflict issues in
Zimbabwe, Côte d'Ivoire, Sudan, Liberia, DRC, Burundi, Western Sahara, and
Sao Tome and Principe.

In the area of immigration and crime, the meeting encouraged closer collaboration between South Africa's Department of Home Affairs and Nigeria's
Ministry of Internal Affairs. The South Africans asked for the issuance of
Nigerian visas to be for more than six months, while the Nigerians complained
that multiple-entry South African visas for Nigerians often forced them to

return to Nigeria for verification with each entry. The Nigerians also raised concerns about the reported beatings of Nigerian nationals at South Africa's Lindela Detention Centre, as well as reports of the harassment of Nigerian citizens by members of the South African Police Service (SAPS). Both countries further pledged cooperation between the SAPS and the Nigerian Drug Law Enforcement Agency (NDLEA) to curb drug trafficking.[50] If it is to achieve its goals, the binational commission must foster greater involvement of South African and Nigerian civil society groups in its formal meetings. Two meetings of the Nigeria/South Africa Dialogue on Civil Society and Africa's Democratic Recovery were held in Lagos and Johannesburg in 1999. Such contacts – particularly strong during the dark days of the Abacha regime – need to be increased so that civil society activists can complement the efforts of both governments and their private sectors.

There have been some strains in relations between Tshwane and Abuja that the BNC has sought to address. Nigerian diplomats have often complained about negative press reports and xenophobic stereotypes, of Nigerians as drug traffickers and criminals, in the South African media and popular imagination.[51] They have noted that local South Africans as well as Mozambicans, Moroccans, Indians, Pakistanis, Chinese, Russians and Italians are also engaged in these activities, but the nationals of these countries in South Africa are not tarred with the same broad brush as are Nigerians. A Johannesburg radio station, 94.7 Highveld, was forced by South Africa's Broadcasting Complaints Commission to apologise, after it claimed that Nigerian president, Olusegun Obasanjo, was carrying cocaine in his bag when he came to attend Mbeki's inauguration in June 2004.[52] Some Nigerian diplomats have attributed these caricatures of their nationals by sections of South Africa's press to the generous contribution that their country made to the anti-apartheid struggle.[53] Showing clear concern about the image of Nigerians in South Africa, the Nigerian consulate in Johannesburg took out advertisements in major South African newspapers to warn South Africans not to become involved in the scams of Nigerian fraudsters peddling get-rich-quick letters.[54]

South African and Nigerian officials met before important AU and UN meetings to coordinate their policies.[55] Tunji Olagunju (who studied at Sussex with Mbeki and was Nigeria's influential high commissioner in South Africa between November 1999 and September 2005) and Patrick Dele-Cole, a former Nigerian ambassador to Brazil, were both involved in the process of drawing up the arrangements for NEPAD.[56]

The strategic alliance between Tshwane and Abuja came through clearly during the AU summit in Addis Ababa in July 2004 as both African powers – key actors on the AU Peace and Security Council – carefully coordinated their efforts on NEPAD and over the Congo conflict. Obasanjo, who was AU chairman in 2004 and 2005, appeared to be collecting international chieftaincy titles, as he added this accolade to his concurrent chairs of the Commonwealth and the NEPAD implementation committee. This pushiness has sometimes irked other African leaders.

At the AU summit in Addis Ababa in July 2004, Mbeki and Obasanjo strongly pushed for the grossly under-staffed AU commission to be given the resources to perform its duties effectively.[57]

SOUTH AFRICAN CORPORATES 'INVADE' AFRICA'S LARGEST MARKET

After 1994, South Africa's corporate community began to view Nigeria with great interest, helped by its energetic high commissioner in Abuja, the former trade unionist Bangumzi 'Sticks' Sifingo.[58] The South African telecommunications giants Mobile Telephone Network (MTN) and M-Net/SuperSport blazed the trail and listed on the Nigerian Stock Exchange. MTN spent US$340 million launching its mobile telephone network in Nigeria in August 2001,[59] with plans to spend US$1,4 billion in the country over a decade. In 2003/04, MTN Nigeria's post-tax profit of R2,36 billion surpassed MTN South Africa's R2,24 billion profit.[60] By June 2004, MTN had 1,65 million subscribers in Nigeria.[61] It was MTN's success that convinced many other South African firms that Nigeria was worth investing in. South Africa has only six big cities, compared to Nigeria's twenty seven,[62] a figure underlining the sheer size of the latter's huge market of 140 million potential consumers.

Other South African 'blue chip' companies that followed MTN included: Stanbic, Rand Merchant Bank (involved in equity funding deals), and Protea Hotels. Sasol, the world's largest producer of petrol from coal, made a $1,2 billion investment in Nigeria to export natural gas. The South African government-funded Industrial Development Corporation (IDC) invested in Nigerian oil, gas, infrastructure, tourism and telecommunications. South Africa's Spoornet worked with the Nigerian Railway Corporation to revive Nigeria's railways. Protea planned to build 15 more hotels in Nigeria between 2006 and 2008, at an estimated cost of R500 million.[63] Fast-food chains Chicken Licken and Debonairs

Pizzas established franchises in Nigeria. A Nigeria-South Africa chamber of commerce was established in 2001. By 2003, Nigeria had already become South Africa's third largest trading partner – and largest single continental importer – in Africa after Zimbabwe and Mozambique. Businessmen from South Africa and Nigeria now frequently visit each others' countries, with 55 South African firms working in Nigeria. The potential for trade between the two countries is enormous, growing from R730 million in 1998 to R4,9 billion in 2003. By 2003, South Africa was running a trade deficit with Nigeria of R215 million.

Of Nigeria's exports to South Africa in 2003, 98,3 per cent consisted of oil, though Nigeria's Union Bank and First Bank also had representative offices in South Africa. Many Nigerian professionals also work in South Africa, in fields like academia, medicine, accounting, human resources, and property.

In turn, South Africa sells Nigeria a more diverse range of goods including machinery, electrical equipment, wood, paper, foodstuff, beverages, spirits, tobacco, plastics and rubber. South African investors have, however, complained about corruption, fraud and '419' (a section of Nigeria's criminal code) scams that have damaged Nigeria's reputation internationally. South African investors have also noted other drawbacks to doing business in Nigeria: the need for private investors to supplement power, water, sewerage, telecommunications and transport, due to the country's dilapidated infrastructure; red tape and too much government involvement in the economy; lack of predictable and consistent economic policies; a low level of technical skills; the need to pay bribes; delays in getting supplies out of Nigeria's ports (also requiring the payment of bribes); and a weak judiciary that sometimes leads to the non-enforcement of contracts.[64]

Nigerians, for their part, have accused South African firms of patronising behaviour and for operating apartheid-style enclaves for their staff. They have described South Africans as 'neo-colonialist' mercantilists bent on dominating the huge Nigerian market and repatriating profits without opening the South African market to Nigerian goods. As Aminu Mohammed vividly noted in September 2003: 'Like wildfire tearing through dry forest, South Africa is rapidly entrenching itself in every facet of the Nigerian economy … South African companies loom large and are still growing.'[65] Other Nigerians have, however, praised the skill and professionalism of South African firms which they say has improved competition and standards in Nigeria. Nigerians have also been the main beneficiaries of jobs created by South African firms in their country (see Hudson in this volume).

Despite impressive growth in bilateral trade between South Africa and

Nigeria, there have also been some spectacular disappointments. SAA agreed a deal with Nigeria Airways in December 2000 to take over the latter's unused routes through New York and Lagos. The New York route was cancelled in March 2002 after losses of R54 million in six months.[66] Though SAA still flies to Nigeria, the relationship with Nigeria Airways ended within three years, after the Nigerian government (which owns the airline) insisted on obtaining a 10 per cent stake in a privatised SAA in exchange for SAA obtaining a 30 per cent share in Nigeria Airways. This was not acceptable to the South Africans and Virgin Atlantic eventually stepped in to agree a partnership deal with Nigeria Airways. Vodacom also left Nigeria in May 2004, two months after reportedly agreeing to a five-year contract with a South African-based partner, Econet Wireless International. Corruption allegations against two Vodacom executives had apparently contributed to its decision.[67]

Another instance of a spectacular Nigeria-South Africa business failure was the early death, after less than a year, of *This Day,* a Nigerian-owned newspaper launched in South Africa in October 2003 with an eventual R120 million worth of investments. A second Nigerian newspaper, *FS African Standard,* aimed at the estimated 100 000 West Africans in South Africa, also stopped publishing in March 2006 due to lack of financial support. More such setbacks could adversely affect growing bilateral trade relations.

TROUBLES IN A MARRIAGE OF NECESSITY

An important obstacle to the hegemonic ambitions of South Africa and Nigeria is the fact that the relationship between both countries relied too heavily on the personal relationship between Mbeki and Obasanjo. There have been many calls to institutionalise the bilateral relationship between Tshwane and Abuja, so that it would survive the exit of one or both leaders from the national stage. The creation of a binational commission and growing commercial ties may eventually help to overcome this problem, but this is far from certain. It is also uncertain whether Mbeki's successor will maintain the same level of commitment to this relationship specifically, and to Africa in general, as he has shown. By 2006, both Mbeki's dominance over the ANC, and Obasanjo's grip on the ruling People's Democratic Party (PDP) seemed to be loosening. Mbeki faced open challenges to his leadership after ousting his deputy, Jacob Zuma, in June 2005 (following corruption allegations), while Obasanjo lost a bid in Nigeria's parliament in May 2006 to amend the constitution to allow him to run for a third term in office. Nigeria's instability has continued, with violence triggered by the promulgation of *sharia* criminal law in a dozen states in northern Nigeria, and reports of a foiled coup attempt in 2004. Militias in Nigeria's oil-producing Niger Delta have frequently interrupted oil supplies and kidnapped oil workers in a bid to force the government to address the neglected area's socio-economic grievances.[68] Nigeria has also experienced sporadic ethnic and religious clashes which have resulted in over 10 000 deaths in eight years. As a civilian president, Obasanjo has found ruling an economically ruined Nigeria with a troublesome parliament and an avaricious political class far more difficult than ruling as a military autocrat during the oil boom of the 1970s. The deeply flawed elections in Nigeria in April 2007, which led to the ruling PDP's Umaru Yar' Adua being declared president, suggested that the country is still a long way from consolidating democratic rule.

The Tshwane-Abuja alliance is a marriage of necessity for Mbeki. Unable to assert leadership effectively in Southern Africa because of lingering suspicion from its neighbours – and further resistance from states like Angola and Zimbabwe seeing themselves as potential regional leaders – he had to venture outside his own region to find the allies and additional legitimacy needed to bolster his continental leadership ambitions. South Africa reached out to Africa's most populous state – Nigeria – and worked closely with it in diplomatic fora in pursuit of continental initiatives like NEPAD and the AU. This sometimes created tensions, with Obasanjo's professional diplomats and policy advisers privately criticising him for having too soft a spot for Mbeki and for ceding too much intellectual influence to Mbeki and South African mandarins who were less experienced in the labyrinthine intricacies of African diplomacy than Nigeria's diplomats.

There were some tensions between South Africa and Nigeria over Zimbabwe during the Commonwealth summit in Abuja in 2003. Mbeki had sought to ensure Mugabe's invitation to the summit, but Obasanjo, under pressure from Britain, Canada and Australia, did not want to disrupt the summit he was hosting by admitting the Zimbabwean president. In Abuja, Mbeki also clumsily tried to replace New Zealand's Don McKinnon as Commonwealth Secretary-General with former Sri Lankan foreign minister, Lakshma Kadrigamar, but lost by 40 votes to 11, with Nigeria voting against the South African proposal.[69]

By 2005, more serious differences between South Africa and Nigeria emerged over three issues: proposals for a reformed UN Security Council; Côte d'Ivoire; and the AU chair. Both countries had consistently expressed an interest in occupying one of two permanent African seats on an expanded UN Security Council. Though this proposal failed to find enough support within the UN

General Assembly in September 2005 (with most AU leaders having argued for Africa to insist on a veto), the acrimonious contest saw some Nigerian officials privately questioning the authenticity of South Africa as a black African state, while the South Africans maneuvered behind the scenes to undermine Nigeria, for example, by focusing attention on their greater financial muscle. Tensions were also evident in Côte d'Ivoire after the rebel *Forces Nouvelles* withdrew support from Mbeki's mediation efforts in 2005, accusing him of bias towards president Laurent Gbagbo. The rebels then urged the AU chairman, Obasanjo, to find an alternative way of resolving the impasse. At a meeting of the AU Peace and Security Council on the margins of the UN General Assembly in New York in September 2005, ECOWAS was tasked with overcoming this impasse: a clear attempt to shift the locus of peacemaking from Tshwane to Abuja.[70]

The Nigerians increasingly faulted Mbeki's role in Côte d'Ivoire as seeking to claim all the glory from any peacemaking success and – according to them – failing to report back on his efforts to Obasanjo, the AU chair who had appointed him.[71] Though, Mbeki and Obasanjo jointly visited Côte d'Ivoire in November and December 2005, it was clear to close observers that a rift had opened between both men. Yet another area of discord between Mbeki and Obasanjo opened at the AU summit in Khartoum, Sudan in January 2006, when Mbeki (supported by other African leaders) strongly opposed the suggestion that Obasanjo continue as AU chair for a third consecutive term. Obasanjo was not offered a third term, echoing his failure to secure a third term as Nigerian president. The incident apparently led to his early departure from the summit.[72]

The fact that the BNC meetings between South Africa and Nigeria in 2005 and 2006 failed to take place for the first time since its inception in 1999 was another source of concern for the state of Africa's most strategic bilateral relationship. The official explanation in 2005 – that South Africa's new deputy president, Phumzile Mlambo-Ngcuka needed time to settle in her job – did not convince. There were also reports that she was uncomfortable with security in the proposed location of the meeting in Nigeria's Cross Rivers state. Other complicating factors included the tensions between Obasanjo and his vice-president Atiku Abubakar over the presidential succession, and a feeling that the South Africans were uncomfortable with Obasanjo's bid for a third presidential term.[73] Lingering suspicions remained – even as a new Nigerian ambassador, Olugbenga Ashiru, replaced the trusted Olagunju by October 2005 – that the failure to fulfil the important commitment of holding a BNC was a further sign of the frosty relationship between Mbeki and Obasanjo.

CONCLUDING THOUGHTS

In concluding this chapter, it is important to assess the prospects for the future leadership role of South Africa and Nigeria in Africa. South Africa has embarked on 'cultural diplomacy' in helping to finance the restoration of one of the world's oldest libraries in Mali's famous city of Timbuktu and in championing the idea of an African Renaissance. This concept could be translated into a pan-African cultural event – a South African FESTAC – that could at once establish South Africa's leadership role on the continent and help its culturally schizophrenic country to embrace an African identity and learn more about the African culture that apartheid's leaders long denied to the majority of its population. Today, only South Africa – the wealthiest and most industrialised country on the continent – could afford to host a lavish festival on the scale of Nigeria's FESTAC in 1977.

It is, however, worth noting, that the idea of South Africa and Nigeria as continental leaders is far from universally accepted. The strategic alliance between both countries is seen by some as little more than a new breed of African imperialism. South Africa's bid for the Olympic games in 2004 failed, in part, due to a lack of African support. Nigeria failed to gain African support for its successful UN Security Council bids in 1977 and 1993, after breaking the rotation rules of the Africa Group. In the recent debates about permanent seats for South Africa and Nigeria on the AU's 15-member Peace and Security Council in 2003–04, other states refused to accept any special permanent status or vetoes for both countries, and instead created five three-year renewable seats to complement the ten biannual rotational seats.[74] South Africa and Nigeria will have to reassure other African states that their intentions are noble. Both countries must consult with other countries and ensure that their actions are not seen as attempts to dominate the continent in pursuit of their own parochial interests. Only by taking measures to alleviate such concerns can South Africa and Nigeria become the beacons of democracy and engines of economic growth to which their leaders clearly aspire.

11

South Africa and its lusophone neighbours: Angola and Mozambique

AUGUSTA CONCHIGLIA

South Africa's repositioning in the continent during the past thirteen years has, undoubtedly, been spectacular. Both from a political and an economic point of view, the former pariah state has become one of the main engines of institutional transformation in Africa. South Africa has contributed to changing Africa's image, while putting the continent's development back on the international political agenda.

However, this process has not been linear. Tempted to use its own political experience as a blueprint for others, South Africa has sometimes provoked irritation among its African partners. This has been particularly true in the case of Angola. In contrast, Tshwane's (Pretoria's) relations with Mozambique – the other lusophone country in Southern Africa – have been mutually profitable, sustained by strategic economic and political interests – resulting, however, in increasing South African economic domination.

South Africa's patterns of relations with the two former Portuguese colonies of Southern Africa – Angola and Mozambique – are poles apart. The influence that South Africa has historically exerted in Mozambique has no parallel in Angola. South Africa and Portugal entered into a convention, as far back as 1928, to regulate labour, transport and commercial relations between Pretoria and the then colony of Mozambique. South African interests in Angola have long been limited to the diamond mines of Lunda province, in the northeast of the country. The Portuguese also jealously protected their richest colony from external – specifically Anglo-Saxon – influence.

It was natural that after the end of apartheid in 1994, South Africa would become interested in its Mozambican neighbour, since the two have historically been linked by important strategic interests, particularly in the energy sector. The investments that followed solidified old links and helped to establish a strategic alliance between the two countries. In contrast, the continuation of the war in Angola, and suspicions around South Africa's real intentions, having been accused by the government in Luanda of supporting UNITA (the Union for the Total Independence of Angola) after the breakdown of the 1994 Lusaka agreement, have constituted a major hindrance to South African economic expansion into Angola.

At a regional level, a subtle but effective axis has developed over the last thirteen years between Maputo and Tshwane, supported by other South African allies such as Botswana and Tanzania. This has changed the balance of forces within the Southern African Development Community (SADC) (see Matlosa in this volume). This axis has also strengthened South Africa's hand in regional diplomacy. Previously, South Africa and its allies were unable to block a controversial SADC stand on the 'second' war in DRC in 1998. Angola and Zimbabwe, supported by Namibia, obtained a mandate from SADC for a military intervention in the Congo, on the side of then president Laurent-Désiré Kabila, on the grounds that he was threatened by foreign aggression from Rwanda and Uganda (see Curtis in this volume).

The new balance of forces in SADC allowed South Africa to put its mark on the reform process of the regional organisation and, above all, assume its current prominent role in SADC's leadership. In this tangle of alliances, Mozambique's closeness to South Africa has been at the root of a certain cooling of relations between Maputo and Luanda – which had traditionally always been very close – although this has been overtaken by recent developments.

SOUTH AFRICA AND ANGOLA: A HISTORY OF TENSIONS

Years have passed since the height of the former racist South African regime's aggression towards its Portuguese-speaking neighbours. However, the destabilisation efforts pursued by Pretoria during the apartheid years left the economies of Angola and Mozambique – South Africa's main targets – in total disarray. The agricultural production of both countries declined dramatically during this period, negatively affecting the lives of the majority of ordinary people to this day. A report by the London-based Commonwealth Secretariat issued in 1989 estimated that the Frontline states' loss of earnings caused by the destabilisation war waged by the apartheid regime was US$45 billion over ten years. The researcher and writer Joe Hanlon estimated that, between 1975 and 1988, the damage caused by South Africa's destabilisation in the region reached US$90 billion.[1]

In Angola, where armed conflict persisted long after South Africa's final with-drawal, reaching its apogee at the end of the 1990s, a deep social and economic crisis – which was exacerbated by government mismanagement – was extended for another decade after peace had broken out in Mozambique. Angolan memo-ries of the dramatic years immediately after independence remain, above all, coloured by the South African army's repeated incursions into Angolan territory and the apartheid regime's support for UNITA. Jonas Savimbi's rebel group's military strength owed much to South Africa's continuous efforts to train and supply its forces over a period of nearly a decade. It is therefore hardly surpris-ing that, after 1994, Angolan leaders began complaining that the ruling African National Congress (ANC) was not doing enough to reward Luanda for its support in their struggle against apartheid. At the same time, the much-awaited South African investments in Angola failed to arrive. Given South Africa's relative economic superiority, Angola, like many states in the region, initially expected the post-apartheid regime to assume the role of a donor country and a develop-ment cooperation partner, providing aid and investment capital.[2] These hopes were quickly dashed, at least in the initial years.

Paradoxically, the first contract signed with a South African firm after Angola's first general election in 1992 involved a group of individuals who had fought alongside UNITA rebels and later regrouped into a new security firm known as Executive Outcomes (EO). Ill-prepared to face what turned out to be the most massive UNITA military offensive since the beginning of the war, the Angolan government – whose army had complied with its 1991 Bicesse peace accord obligations by demobilising its troops[3] – turned to the veterans of South African units that had spearheaded the military destabilisation of their country: the former 32nd Battalion (mainly Angolans), the Parachute Brigade and the Namibia-based *Koevoet*.[4]

As UNITA was waging the offensive launched after it rejected its electoral defeat in 1992, the Heritage Oil and Gas group introduced EO to the increasingly desperate government in Luanda, which quickly recognised the firm's capabili-ties and signed a US$40 million one-year contract with the military security group in September 1993.[5] EO personnel, hired as advisers and instructors, also protected economic sites that had been recaptured, such as the diamond areas of Cafunfo and the oil installation at Soyo.

The Lusaka peace agreement between Luanda and UNITA rebels, signed in November 1994, called for the repatriation of all 'foreign mercenaries' from Angola.[6] Although EO represented a new brand of mercenaries who were loyal to recognised governments – instead of trying to overthrow them – the company's activities in Angola and elsewhere in Africa like Sierra Leone were a clear source of embarrassment for the new democratic government in South Africa. This eventually forced the organisation to dissolve.

The emergence of majority rule in South Africa in 1994 failed to bring any immediate bilateral political understanding with the government in Angola. Worse, the issue of UNITA's alleged continuing connections in South Africa gradually became a source of increasing tension. After the Lusaka peace accord of 1994, UNITA received several clandestine arms shipments through South Africa (as the UN Fowler report of 2000[7] later detailed). Angolan leaders became increasingly convinced that South Africa lacked the will to stop these transfers.

This political crisis came to a head in early 1999 after a failed attempt by then deputy president, Thabo Mbeki, to put the Angolan peace process back on track by inviting Savimbi for talks in South Africa. At the time, UNITA's 'militarist wing' – as it was called to distinguish it from the UNITA cadres sitting in the Government of National Unity and Reconciliation (GURN) – was continuously using delaying tactics to stall compliance with its main obligations: the disarmament and demobilisation of all its combatants. This became a source of major concern both within the Angolan government and for the UN mission in Angola.

By July 1997, it had become clear that UNITA's military capacity remained intact, and Savimbi sent troops to fight alongside Mobutu Sese Seko's army in a bid to stop Laurent Kabila's march on Kinshasa. This episode forced the UN, which had stated several months earlier that the disarmament of UNITA had been 'totally achieved', to launch a second phase of disarmament and demobilisation of 'residual troops' in 1998.

During 1995, the UN mission in Angola had repeatedly reported a worrying increase of air traffic to UNITA's main strongholds. After the death of Blondin Beye, the UN Secretary-General's Special Representative in Angola, in a plane crash on a trip from Côte d'Ivoire in June 1998, and the launching in Luanda, three months later, of 'UNITA Renovada' which excluded Savimbi from its ranks on the grounds of his 'warmongering attitude', the Angolan government halted all dialogue with Savimbi. At the SADC summit in Maputo in 1998, Luanda managed to secure a declaration denouncing Savimbi as a 'war criminal'.

However, by the end of 1998, Angolan president José Eduardo dos Santos, unwilling to be perceived as responsible for the burial of the Lusaka agreement, accepted Mbeki's proposal to make a further attempt to rescue the peace process. Thus, in January 1999, Savimbi left the Angolan 'bush' for South Africa for the first time in three years. However, the manner in which the local Angolan press reported the event – it referred to the 'new South African mediation in the Angolan conflict' – and the apparently warm reception granted Savimbi by then president Nelson Mandela in his eastern Cape ancestral village – generated the strongest tensions between Luanda and Tshwane since the end of apartheid rule.

The Angolan government immediately declared that the only valid and authorised mediation should be carried out by the UN, and rejected any 'South African interference' in the Angolan crisis, all the more since Luanda believed that South Africa had offered Savimbi an opportunity to renegotiate the Lusaka peace accords. The ruling Popular Movement for the Liberation of Angola (MPLA) further claimed that the UNITA leader had squandered all opportunities for dialogue since 1992 by systematically refusing to join the democratic process.

The MPLA government argued that the Lusaka agreements had been brought to fruition with the only valid interlocutor: the legal UNITA wing in Luanda which was participating in the GURN and sitting in parliament as required by the Lusaka protocol. As for UNITA's 'residual' rebellion, this was definitively outlawed by Luanda. It seemed the MPLA government was ready to return to the battlefield.

But many western and South African analysts felt that seeking a military victory would be a tragic mistake, with dire implications for the future of Angola. These pundits argued that the UNITA rebellion was firmly rooted in Angolan society, with all its ethnic and cultural contradictions.

The MPLA leadership dismissed this view, arguing that foreign observers, particularly South African, often failed to see that the UNITA rebellion was merely a strongly centralised military force and not a political party that was able to interact with society and interpret the people's aspirations, as subsequently recognised by several of UNITA's own leading members.[8] This does not, of course, mean that the Angolan government had been working to distinguish itself from UNITA in the eyes of Angolans by creating a better socio-economic and political environment, so as to isolate the military rebellion and therefore accelerate the end of the conflict. Much more could have been done by Luanda in this respect. But it had become clear that Savimbi was not open to compromise, and that he would fight until the bitter end.

Angola's leaders charged that Tshwane was rigidly promoting its own 'model' of achieving a peaceful solution through negotiation and compromise (see Curtis in this volume). Luanda perceived this attitude to be paternalistic, particularly given its own previous – and vain – acceptance of dialogue with the rebellion, which had led to the Lusaka accord in 1994. Nelson Mandela seemed to have grasped the Angolan government's bitterness when he told the South African parliament in February 1999 that: 'We do ask ourselves whether the time has not come to draw basic lessons from the Angolan experience; to pose the question whether the United Nations' approach has been what is required of a situation in which one party rejects the results of a free and fair election.'[9]

Mandela's official visit to Angola in April 1998, four years after he came to power, improved bilateral relations between Tshwane and Luanda. Angolan critics had interpreted the long delay in organising Mandela's visit as a calculated insult to an ally that had sacrificed so much for South Africans during their liberation struggle. But Mandela was able to dissipate much ill feeling and misunderstanding by his generous tribute to the 'heroic solidarity' of Angola, expressed in a speech to the Angolan parliament.

However, the *rapprochement* did not last long. During the last years of the Angolan war, rumours persisted, often amplified by western officials, that South Africa's relations with UNITA went as far as complicity with the rebellion. Senior government officials were reported to have approved South African military and logistical assistance to Savimbi. And South Africa was also thought to have deliberately ignored diamond conglomerate De Beers' purchases of diamonds mined by UNITA, in spite of a 1993 UN embargo. At the time, De Beers reportedly regularly bought up any rough diamonds that appeared on the market.[10] Accused of indirectly helping to fund the Angolan rebel army, which financed itself by selling large quantities of diamonds, De Beers ended a spat with the Luanda government by stating that it would stop purchasing Angolan diamonds on the free market. In 2001, De Beers was also excluded by the Angolan government from the official diamond market – despite the agreement it had signed with the national company Endiama, as part of a local producing consortium – and opted to leave the country.[11]

In the end, official Angola's deep distrust of South Africa turned into outright hostility. Some of the country's highest authorities began to allude publicly to South Africa's alleged complicity in the war waged by UNITA. Demonstrating the government's growing irritation, Angola's deputy foreign minister Jorge Chicoty told the South African newspaper *Business Day* in September 1999 that international sanctions should be placed on South Africa for its failure to clamp down on UNITA's diamond smuggling.[12] Despite these comments, South Africa had actually stepped up efforts to halt UNITA's business dealings in the country, although pro-UNITA lobbies proved to be strong and deep-rooted in certain sectors of South Africa's administration.

Meanwhile, Angola's successful military engagements in Congo-Brazzaville in 1997 and in the DRC in 1997–98, strengthened the feeling among its ruling elite that the country had acquired the status of a regional power. Sub-Saharan Africa's second-largest oil producer (after Nigeria)[13] – and the only oil-producer in the continent's southern cone – had indeed bared its military 'teeth'. This was recognised both by the French – whose interests in Congo-Brazzaville had been preserved – and by the Americans – who, after a formal condemnation of Angolan interference in the region, changed their approach and henceforth considered Angola to be 'a decisive element in the Great Lakes conflict'.[14] Luanda's rivalry with Tshwane, from this point, took on a new dimension: that of regional competition. Leading figures in Luanda did not shrink from boasting about Angola's 'superiority' – referring notably to its potential in the energy sector – without bothering to compare the two countries' economic performance or the value of their exports.

'Many Angolans, full of bravado, had a totally unrealistic view of South Africa. I was told many times by Angolan officials that South Africans were deeply concerned about their rivalry with Angola,' says Gerry Bender, American scholar and specialist on Angola and Portuguese colonialism. 'One very high official told me that he was sure that the South African leaders lost sleep at night worrying about the Angolan rivalry. Any Angolan who spends ten minutes in Johannesburg or Cape Town knows that no South African loses sleep at night worrying about Angola!'[15]

South Africa did not publicly acknowledge the existence of this conflict. Relations between the two leading parties and former allies – the ANC and the MPLA – appeared cordial when the two sides met during regional consultations. But, in private, official South Africa was actually worrying about the unnecessary tension, and seized on every opportunity that might facilitate a reconciliation with Luanda.

From 2000, a series of contacts between the two countries' armed forces chiefs of staff – initiated by Angola's General Joao de Matos – paved the way for fruitful exchanges, including the first-ever visit by South African officers to the theatres of Angola's armed conflict, which allowed them a more realistic view of the situation. This resulted in the establishment, in February 2001, of a bilateral defence committee, which held its first session several months later.[16]

Having proved to be a major player in the region, Angola wished to be at the forefront of the DRC's peace negotiations. Angola's close relations with Joseph Kabila (son and successor of Laurent Kabila, who was assassinated in 2001) and the normalisation of relations achieved with the Ugandan leader, Yoweri Museveni, allowed Luanda to mediate a peace agreement among the two regional leaders. However, this did not remove Rwanda's reticence towards cooperating with Angola in its various attempts to reach a final understanding among the belligerents in the Congo. Rwanda's Paul Kagame preferred to deal with his South African counterpart, Mbeki. South Africa took over the mediation in the DRC without involving Angola in the process, an approach that further annoyed Luanda.

These developments did not prevent the easing of political tensions between Tshwane and Luanda following the death of Savimbi in February 2002, and the rapid end to the Angolan conflict.

The upheavals in Angola since Savimbi's death have been of critical importance to South Africa's plans for achieving stability in Southern Africa. In December 2002, French researcher, Yvan Crouzel, noted that 'although South Africa's capacity for influencing Angola is extremely limited, it is counting on a diplomatic *rapprochement* between the two countries. With this in mind, the South African government is now working on a plan for the reconstruction of Angola.'[17]

The two countries are gradually moving towards a de facto normalisation of relations, as illustrated by former deputy president Jacob Zuma's official visit to Angola in August 2004. Although the visit was mainly focused on improving economic cooperation, it allowed a lengthy exchange of views with President Dos Santos. The Angolan prime minister in turn visited South Africa in February 2005.[18]

Despite political tensions, South African business with Angola has been expanding at a brisk pace. South African exports – which were about US$97 million in 1995 – had reached US$460 million by 1998. And by 2002, South Africa was the third largest exporter to Angola, slightly behind Portugal and the US, accounting for 12 per cent of Angola's total imports.[19] These figures will be further boosted by the gradual regularisation of significant informal trade: Angolan traders shuttling between the two countries carrying goods in their personal luggage. In addition, private South African enterprises have, in recent years, carried out major construction contracts in Angola worth in excess of

US$450 million. Thousands of Angolan students are also attending secondary schools and universities in South Africa: a relatively new phenomenon that might expand even further with the planned granting of scholarships and other facilities by the South African government, as announced during Zuma's 2004 visit. The impact of these South African-educated cadres on Angolan life – economic and cultural – could have a positive and profound effect on future relations between both countries.

An increasing number of Angolan officials privately admit that economic relations with South Africa will eventually have to improve, since South African companies and conglomerates are the only ones with a comparative advantage in terms of proximity and costs, compared with Angola's traditional European partners such as Portugal. However, in Angolan business circles, the suspicion that South African entrepreneurs might prove to be exploitative or dominant is still widespread (see Hudson in this volume).

At the beginning of 2004, while everything pointed to a rapid expansion of contracts with South African partners, China stepped into the Angolan market: a development that has somewhat changed the outlook for South African firms. The Chinese, eager to diversify and expand their sources of oil supply, granted Angola a US$2 billion oil-backed loan on concessional terms in March 2004, intended essentially to finance infrastructure projects. A further US$2,5 billion loan was being negotiated with China for 2006–7. This appears to have dealt a serious blow – at least temporarily – to the hopes of South African companies for further rapid expansion of business into Angola.

Indeed, the South African business sector has long been eager to raise its level of investment and trade with Angola: considered the country with the richest economic potential in the region. The South Africa/Angola Chamber of Commerce (SA-ACC), launched in 2003, has been strongly advocating increased South African investments in Angola, which, it emphasises, are far below investment levels in Mozambique. SA-ACC manager Nadia Topalova, noted in July 2004 that: 'South Africa has the resources, and is in a geographically advantageous location to be a strategic investor in Angola's economy.'[20] As an example, southern Angola, which is easily accessible by road, is traditionally attractive to South African farmers who have had a small community in Huila province since the First World War of 1914–1918.

However, according to Topalova, there is a dichotomy between the positive approach of the South African business sector – and that of the South African government: 'While historical enmity between our two governments exists, it should be put aside for the greater good of establishing a flourishing economic environment within the SADC.[21]

Topalova is one of the few people in South Africa to have acknowledged these tensions, although the reference to the 'historical enmity' between both countries might not be accurate if we discount the existence of any real continuity between the apartheid regime and a democratic South Africa. Besides, whatever the reticence of the South African government, Angola's economic environment has generally not been attractive to foreign investors, with the exception of the oil sector. The country still suffers from serious macro-economic instability, characterised by high inflation and an overvalued currency. Furthermore, the government has chronically under-invested in the social sector.[22] The main causes of Angola's macro-economic instability are the large fiscal deficit and vast unrecorded expenditure reportedly running into billions of dollars. Because of Angola's poor record of economic management and corruption, relations with the IMF have been strained.[23]

Although improvements have been reported in continuing negotiations with the IMF, the four years of dispute with De Beers has not helped to create a more conducive investment climate in Angola. The establishment, in 2001, of the Angolan Selling Corporation (Ascorp) with an exclusive monopoly on the sale of Angolan diamonds abroad, excluded De Beers from the Angolan market.[24] The ASCorp monopoly, which has mainly benefited the Russian-Israeli diamond trader, Lev Leviev, was later revised and the Angolan market reopened to other competitors.

De Beers made a significant come-back to Angola in May 2005 with the signing of a contract for a joint venture with Endiama known as ENDEB, for prospecting kimberlitic deposits in Lunda North. This region is well known by the South African company which started operating there as far back as 1970, in association with the Portuguese parastatal Diamang.

Angolan diamond production is expected to increase to 10 million carats by 2006/7, from six million carats in 2003. The country is expected to become one of the world's top three diamond producers within this period. Angola's official diamond market was estimated at US$1 billion a year in 2005, in addition to an estimated US$500 million that is smuggled out of the country each year.[25]

Until recently, what was perceived as the strained personal relations between the two countries' leaders – Mbeki and Dos Santos – has often been considered to be the cause of the prolonged tension in the bilateral relationship. In May 2004, the Angolan weekly *Agora* wrote:

The repeated and conspicuous absence of President José Eduardo dos Santos from events attended by Mbeki has led to the perception that the two men are not on the same wavelength and perhaps do not even have personal relations. South Africa is the single most influential country in SADC and the sole power in the region. In recent years, it has channelled important investments into Angola despite the rather aloof relations between the heads of state. What is more, now that he is entering his second term in office, it has become painfully clear that Mbeki has never paid an official visit to Angola, just as José Eduardo dos Santos has never officially visited South Africa. Diplomatic sources in both countries have repeatedly given the assurance that nothing abnormal is happening in relations between Luanda and Pretoria but political observers are in no doubt that if the two heads of state were to move a little bit closer to each other they would certainly increase strategic cohesion within SADC.[26]

Lopo do Nascimento, a prominent Angolan political figure – a former MPLA Secretary-General and a former prime minister – noted a few years ago, at the peak of the bilateral crisis between Tshwane and Luanda, that 'there is no real antagonism between our countries' current or future interests, neither political, economic, or in terms of security'. However, Do Nascimento observed that:

> there has been a communication failure and no common political debate. SADC has never managed to create the same kind of forum for common analysis and political discussion of regional issues as we were all used to during the time of the Frontline States. When the liberation movements came to power, it should have been possible for us to demand more of ourselves in a common endeavour to forge a real new unity and to look for common solutions to the new challenges. I think Angola and South Africa could have played the same sort of role as motors of the community of Southern Africa, as France and Germany did in forging the European Union. But we have to recognise now that the search for balance between our respective interests, and the dissipation of misunderstandings, will only be possible with a commitment to transparency and to respect for the others' opinion.[27]

As far as the African scene is concerned, Angola seems to be seeking greater integration into regional and continental institutions, as demonstrated by initiatives such as its entry, in July 2004, into the African Peer Review Mechanism of NEPAD (see Landsberg in this volume). There is also an increasing awareness in

Angola, both in some sectors of the governing elite and outside, of the strategic importance of Luanda building an economic and political pole in the region with South Africa: the 'other' regional power.

SOUTH AFRICA AND MOZAMBIQUE: A STRATEGIC ALLIANCE

Mozambique is widely considered to be one of the few UN peacekeeping success stories. Since the end of its civil war in 1992, and with the help of the donor community, the country has greatly increased its capacity for macro-economic policy-making, facilitating impressive reforms in all economic sectors. There has been considerable progress towards establishing an enabling environment for the smooth conduct of business and, as a consequence, substantial foreign capital has been attracted to the country. The privatisation of firms in tourism, industry and the banking sector has attracted foreign direct investment (FDI) in the initial period up to 1996. Since then, FDI has been mainly directed towards the exploitation of natural resources, and large-scale capital-intensive projects have been initiated. In this context, South Africa has played a largely positive role and found its Mozambican neighbour to be a good partner, despite its structural weaknesses.

Since the advent of democracy in South Africa in 1994 and the outbreak of peace in Mozambique, the two countries have strengthened their relations in all fields, especially in the area of economic cooperation and investment. In 2002, Mozambique overtook Zimbabwe as South Africa's largest continental trading partner in a year when at least 27 per cent of Mozambique's imports were coming from South Africa. In 2004, Mozambique accounted for 13 per cent of overall South African exports to Africa.

South Africa is Mozambique's leading investor, well ahead of Britain and Portugal. South African capital has contributed to accelerating the country's industrialisation. The economy – once dominated by agriculture and the service sector – has changed significantly since 1997. By 2002, industry represented 34,3 per cent of Mozambique's GDP.[28] South African investment in Mozambique (although the capital involved might not have been purely South African, since some of the investors were transnational firms) has been consistent, reaching a total of US$4,6 billion between 1994 and 2001. Other major ventures have been negotiated since then, including Vodacom's US$567 million investment programme.[29] The two governments have also signed a memorandum of understanding to facilitate the construction of a US$1,3 billion hydroelectric dam in the Zambezi valley.

These new initiatives have been concentrated in the Maputo Corridor, which forms a direct link between the port of Maputo and South Africa's industrial heartland of Gauteng. Conceived by the governments of South Africa and Mozambique and financed by privately led initiatives, the Maputo corridor has started to generate spin-offs, notably through the activation of the Mozal aluminium smelter, outside Maputo, by the end of 2000.

Mozal forecasted investments totalling US$2,3 billion: the biggest single investment project in Mozambique since its independence from Portugal in 1975. Owned by an international consortium led by the London-based BHP-Billiton (47 per cent) and South Africa's Industrial Development Corporation (24 per cent), Mozal, which has completed the extension of its production capacity, is one of the largest aluminium plants in the world. The company buys its aluminium ore in Australia and sells the final product – its aluminium bars – on the international market.

Efficient coordination between South Africa and Mozambique and their private sectors allowed the first phase of the aluminium smelter to be completed ahead of schedule in a mere 31 months at a cost that was US$130 million less than the budgeted US$1,3 billion. The second phase – budgeted at US$992 million – was also completed in a shorter period of time than projected – 26 months – and came in at US$195 million under budget. These achievements are seen as a resounding success for Mozambique, less than ten years after the end of its protracted and highly destructive civil war.

However, Mozal is a free-zone factory and has not had a direct impact on Mozambique's GDP. Contrary to initial expectations, Mozal has failed to give the expected boost to the local business community. The linkages established so far with Mozambican entrepreneurs and businessmen have been relatively few. Yet, on the scale of beneficial impact, Mozal, as well as another successful mega-project, owned by Sasol, has provided a notable opportunity for skills training of some of Mozambique's workforce, as well as the transfer of technology.[30] This is particularly significant in a country with widespread poverty and an extremely low level of education. However, these positive effects are limited in the national geographic space: 92 per cent of Mozambique's foreign and national investments have been located in Maputo province.[31]

The Sasol gas production plant in Temane might have a greater impact on the local economy than Mozal. Sasol's investment in Mozambique is, in fact, expected to provide a further spin-off in future in the form of gas supplies to spur internal industrial growth. The Sasol plant – a joint venture between Sasol and the governments of Mozambique and South Africa – is already another success story. To begin with, the US$1,2 billion project was finished ahead of schedule and within budget. US$700 million was spent on the installations in Mozambique, while the construction of the 865 kilometre pipeline from Temane to Secunda in South Africa, cost another US$400 million.[32] South African political-cal economist and deputy trade minister, Rob Davies, considers the Sasol project a good example of economic integration in Southern Africa.

These mega-projects have also led to a reduction of Mozambique's huge trade deficit. The country's total exports were just short of US$1 billion in 2004, led by the aluminium produced by Mozal. However, beyond the remarkable increase in investment and domestic consumption, Mozambique's external position remains vulnerable. In 2002, the country's foreign trade deficit amounted to 46 per cent of its GDP. Imports should edge down over the next decade, as capital investment declines with the completion of these major projects, which have accounted for roughly one-third of imports in recent years. However, Mozambique's expected first-ever budget surplus for 2005[33] was not achieved.

One of the most intangible but important effects of South African investments in Mozambique has been to bolster the confidence of other foreign investors. In 2002, private investment in Mozambique exceeded public investment as a result of additional FDI inflows. However, the country still depends on foreign aid, which accounted for 48 per cent of its 2004 national budget.

Maputo's very close relations with Tshwane are driven by trade and investments, as well as by linkages in migration, transport, tourism and culture. There is, at the same time, a high level of political coordination. Besides the Joint Permanent Commission for Cooperation – established in July 1994 – a heads of state Economic Bilateral Forum was created in 1997, with the aim of overseeing strategic projects between the two countries.[34] These meetings are held quarterly and are attended by ministers and officials of relevant ministries from both countries.

However, the existence of these official structures was of little help in efforts to resolve the long-running contract dispute between the South African electricity utility, Eskom, and the Mozambican electricity producer, Hidroelectrica de Cahora Bassa (HCB). It took five years of difficult negotiations to reach an agreement. Eskom, which is HCB's largest client – accounting for nearly half of the company's total output of 2 075 megawatts – has finally agreed to increase the amount that it pays for power from the Cahora Bassa dam on the Zambezi river.[35]

This dispute involved attempts by the Portuguese government – which was holding an 82 per cent stake in HCB – to secure a higher price from Eskom, in order to reduce its US$2,3 billion claim on the dam company. These debts were largely accumulated during the period after independence in 1975, when HCB was a non-performing asset, having ceased exports after the company's power lines were destroyed during the country's civil war.

Only in late 1998 were the powerlines fully repaired and exports of electricity resumed. As HCB's main client,[36] Eskom was in a position of strength and sought to maintain the terms of the agreement reached before independence based on unrealistically low prices. South Africa's historical responsibility in fuelling the Mozambican war during the period that HCB lines were a military target, was apparently shrugged off as irrelevant in the course of the negotiations. This phase of talks eventually ended after the South African government agreed to exert some pressure on Eskom. It should be further noted that the Mozambican national electricity utility – Electricidade de Moçambique, EDM – was at the time supplying southern Mozambique with power bought from Eskom at a much higher price than the price at which South Africa was buying electricity from HCB.

In November 2005, after long negotiations with Portugal, a memorandum of understanding on the future of Cahora Bassa was finally signed in Lisbon, securing Mozambican control over the Cahora Bassa dam. This agreement was regarded by Mozambican president, Armando Guebuza, as amounting to 'a second independence' for his country. The current shareholding structure, in which the government of Portugal holds 82 per cent and Mozambique 18 per cent, is to be reversed. Mozambique will have to pay US$950 million to Portugal (but not the US$2,3 billion initially demanded). Mozambique has been given a maximum of 18 months to pay the total amount. In the final stage of the deal, Mozambique will hold an 85 per cent stake in HCB, and might sell a third of its shares to Eskom. In this case, consistent with the agreement's provisions, the Mozambican authorities will request Lisbon to follow the same approach by selling a third of its shares to a third party at market rate. Eskom's participation in the HCB will certainly be important to enabling Mozambique to pay off its debt to Portugal in such a short time.

Mozambique's economy is strongly dependent on South Africa's. This may ultimately lead to renewed political tensions. However, given the present excellent relations between the two governments, this is currently a remote possibility.

South Africa's links with Mozambique show that economic integration in Southern Africa can move at a faster pace than initially expected. However, this integration is being driven less by new institutions of cooperation – such as SADC – than by the relaunching of the traditional South African pattern of expansion.[37] This entails an effort to ensure control of natural resources which are scarce in South Africa – above all energy and water – and the expansion abroad of South Africa's mining conglomerates and corporations enjoying technological superiority and substantial financial reserves.

In Robert Davies' opinion, SADC has, since 1992, privileged trade cooperation to the detriment of integration and economic development, and should reorient its priorities. While it can be argued that the current regional dynamic of integration results mainly from the activities of South African parastatals, some observers have contended that this 'integration by capital' has become a reality. According to French researcher, Jean Coussy, this is 'the most advanced form of quick and spectacular integration. It is what brings to the Southern Africa integration process its dynamism, its polarised and asymmetric structure and its rapid effects on regional growth.'[38]

Beside the free movement of capital, there has been a comforting episode of 'human integration' between South Africa and Mozambique. After the collapse of apartheid in 1994, a series of South African laws and bilateral agreements with Mozambique have helped many Mozambican migrants and refugees to settle permanently in their host country. By the mid-1990s, only a small percentage of the 320 000 Mozambicans who lived in South Africa in 1992, had returned to Mozambique.[39] Despite massive retrenchment in the South African mining industry which had employed an estimated 50 000 Mozambicans in 1994, a majority of Mozambican workers and refugees have apparently succeeded in making their living in South Africa and obtained permanent residence permits.[40]

In January 2003, Tshwane and Maputo signed a labour migration agreement aimed at protecting the rights of the 72 000 legal migrant workers – including 60 000 miners and 12 000 farm workers – and preventing illegal migration. Melita Sunjic of the office of the UN High Commissioner for Refugees (UNHCR) in South Africa, regarded the integration of Mozambicans into South African society as exceptional, but also as evidence that an important flow of refugees can be accommodated without major upheavals. The murder in September 1998 of a Mozambican immigrant along with two Senegalese – all thrown from a train by a xenophobic mob of South Africans – however, highlighted the less optimistic side of this development.

CONCLUDING REFLECTIONS

Globally, the friendly nature of the relations between South Africa and Mozambique, as well as the level of South African economic interests in that country have no parallel with the Angolan-South African case, despite the diplomatic initiatives undertaken by both Tshwane and Luanda in 2004. The expected South African economic expansion to Angola has not occurred, partly because of the new role of China which is pursuing a policy of financing Angola's reconstruction through huge concessional loans secured by oil supplies. The reluctance still shown by Angola's leaders to improving diplomatic relations with South Africa is also responsible for the current standoff. Business relations between South Africa and Angola are, however, gradually increasing and involve entrepreneurs from both countries who are close to their respective governments.

But Angola, which is poised to become a major world oil producer, will not attain its desired status of 'regional power' in isolation, unless it begins interacting with the richest economy and most populated country in Southern Africa. There is a growing awareness in Angola that the country's policy towards South Africa needs to be reviewed. The Mozambican case is generally seen in Angola as a positive example of the potential of economic cooperation with South Africa. There are, however, concerns about the dangers of economic dependence on South Africa.

Improved relations between Tshwane and Luanda are probably only possible after new leaderships emerge from the next elections in both countries.

As for Mozambique's unbalanced relations with South Africa, one might conclude by quoting Neuma Grobbelaar's contention that, 'every continent needs an America' (see endnote 8 to chapter 6). It would nevertheless be unfortunate if the South African government ends up by aligning itself too closely with its business sector, the natural ambition of which – as everywhere else – is to be dominant. A democratic black-led South African government will have to moderate and regulate its country's economic expansion into the rest of Africa. Otherwise, South Africa risks depriving its ambitious political design – the African Renaissance and NEPAD (see Landsberg in this volume) – of its moral content.

12

South Africa: 'Exporting peace' to the Great Lakes region?

DEVON CURTIS

In December 2006, an important milestone was reached in the peace process in the Democratic Republic of the Congo (DRC) when Joseph Kabila was sworn in as the first democratically elected president of the country in over forty years. In August 2005, Burundi observed a similar achievement in its peace process when Pierre Nkurunziza became president of Burundi following a series of local, provincial and national elections. The elections marked the end of transitional periods that were intended to usher in peaceful democratic governance in Burundi and the DRC after years of violent conflict in both countries.[1]

The elections in Burundi, along with the establishment of permanent institutions of governance and a new constitution, were acclaimed across Africa and the world. In South Africa, reactions to the elections in Burundi were overwhelmingly positive. Newspaper headlines announced: 'South Africa hails new era of democracy in Burundi',[2] and 'Hope for Burundi',[3] while a statement from the office of South African president Thabo Mbeki 'celebrated Burundi's victory' and claimed that 'their peace is our peace'.[4] Given South Africa's prominent role in the Burundian peace process, the elections appeared to offer evidence that South African encouragement and assistance in Burundi had achieved desirable outcomes. Other regional actors like Tanzania, Uganda and Rwanda had also played important roles in Burundi, but South Africa's involvement was notable due to its facilitation of various agreements, as well as its promotion of a particular kind of transitional model in Burundi. Key elements of the South African 'model' promoted and replicated in Burundi included: negotiations and dialogue with all belligerents; the establishment of a transitional national unity government; the creation of a new integrated army; and plans for a truth and reconciliation commission (see Sooka in this volume).

South Africa adopted a similar approach in the peace process in the Democratic Republic of the Congo. While different interests and issues are at stake in the DRC, South Africans and their partners supported a process of extensive dialogue with different belligerents and stakeholders leading to a negotiated settlement that included a broad-based power-sharing transitional government, the establishment of a new national army, and democratic elections. South African reaction to the elections in the DRC was positive, but cautious, possibly due to the violence that occurred in the DRC between the first and second rounds of voting in 2006. One headline optimistically declared: 'A brave new day for Congo' and went on to say that it 'is partly through South Africa's efforts, both human and financial, that the Congolese will today go to the polls to elect their own leaders'.[5] Another South African newspaper noted that: 'Congo is at the crossroads of history',[6] but two months later, cautioned that: 'Post-election violence is possible',[7] thus showing an awareness of the fragility of the transition.

The peace processes in the two countries therefore broadly reflect a South African 'approach' to transitions. This approach assumes that inclusive dialogue and broad-based national unity governments can lead to peace since differences are negotiable. It also assumes that constitutional development can contribute to ending violence. Indeed, many aspects of the two peace processes have been encouraging. Since the signing of the Arusha Agreement for Peace and Reconciliation in Burundi in 2000 and the Pretoria and Sun City Accords for the DRC in 2002–2003, there have been some hopeful changes in both countries. Nonetheless, despite the optimism surrounding the elections and the establishment of new governments in Burundi and the DRC, the experiences of both countries have exposed the limitations of a South African peace process 'model'. Specifically, the context of conflict in Burundi and the Congo, and the patterns of authority in the two countries are different from each other, as well as vastly different from the South African case. The promotion of a South African-style transition in two environments that are so dissimilar from South Africa's has led to several unexpected outcomes, which are contributing to tensions and difficulties in the post-election period.

This chapter discusses the appeal of the South African approach to transitions, while describing the shortcomings and limits of this method in the context of the conflicts in Africa's Great Lakes region. The chapter makes three broad arguments. First, there is a temptation, among policymakers everywhere, to make generalisations in a bid to reproduce 'successful' models. 'Democracy promotion' across Africa is a key South African foreign policy objective, and South African officials tend to view appropriate conflict resolution techniques and processes of democratic consolidation in terms of their own domestic experience. Second, this model of conflict resolution and democratic consolidation has faced critical challenges in the Great Lakes. These challenges are related to the political economy of conflict in this region, patterns of authority and the nature of the state in Burundi and the Congo, as well as the regional dynamics of the conflicts. Third, this chapter argues that despite the limitations in the 'export' of the South African model to both countries, some aspects of the transitional strategies have had positive effects in Burundi and the DRC. Most notably, comprehensive negotiations on a wide range of issues and sustained commitment from external peacebuilders have been constructive. It is too early to declare a decisive end to violence in Burundi and even less so in the DRC, but important, hopeful changes have occurred in both countries.

THE SOUTH AFRICAN 'MODEL'

Conflict has been a recurrent feature of colonial and post-colonial politics in the Great Lakes region. In Burundi, the latest violence was sparked by the assassination of its first democratically-elected president, Melchior Ndadaye, in 1993. In the DRC, conflict resumed in 1998 after Rwanda and Uganda invaded eastern Congo in an attempt to remove Laurent Kabila (their erstwhile ally) from power.[8] By the end of 1998, there were peace negotiations in both the DRC and Burundi. In the DRC, this led to the signing of the Lusaka (Zambia) Ceasefire Agreement in July 1999 and subsequent negotiations between Congolese political groups on political and military arrangements. In Burundi, multiparty negotiations actively began in June 1998 in Arusha, Tanzania, and the incomplete Arusha Peace and Reconciliation Agreement was signed in August 2000. Negotiations with several Burundian armed groups continued throughout the subsequent transitional period.

The UN and other international actors have been involved in the peace processes in Burundi and the DRC, but the extent of their involvement was limited, providing space for regional actors and South Africa to take leading roles in peacemaking efforts. Western powers encouraged African efforts to take responsibility for brokering peace agreements and resolving both crises. Under the general rubric of 'African solutions to African problems', the UN, the US and the EU supported South Africa's role in the Great Lakes,[9] with the UN even opening an office in South Africa to deal with the DRC.

South Africa played an important role in the negotiations in the DRC and

Burundi, particularly in the latter stages of both processes. In the Burundian case, South Africa was especially active after Nelson Mandela became facilitator of the process at the end of 1999 following the death of the previous facilitator, former Tanzanian leader Julius Nyerere. Tshwane (Pretoria) also led subsequent rounds of ceasefire negotiations on Burundi, and led an African Union peacekeeping mission in 2003. In the DRC, South Africa played a central role in the Pretoria and Sun City negotiations in 2002–3. The country has also been a significant contributor to the United Nations Organisation Mission in the Democratic Republic of the Congo (MONUC) peacekeeping force.[10] In both the Burundian and the DRC peace processes, South Africa's influence was felt not only through its role as intermediary, facilitator and guarantor, but also through the implicit and explicit promotion of certain ideas about appropriate constitutional structures and processes.

Supporting peace and democracy across Africa is a key South African foreign policy goal, as Chris Landsberg has noted.[11] The South African government seeks to advance development and economic growth across Africa, and feels that this cannot occur without peace and security.[12] South Africa's foreign policy therefore makes an explicit link between peace and security, development, governance and growth.[13] Since 1997, these goals have been expressed through the concept of an African Renaissance. Ian Taylor and Paul Williams point to the neoliberal ideology that lies at the heart of Mbeki's notion of an African Renaissance, but the operationalisation of the Renaissance concept also includes the desire to establish and maintain systems of 'good governance', often through the promotion of negotiated transitions to democracy and the rule of law.[14] Kristina Bentley and Roger Southall see South Africa's efforts to promote peace in Burundi as part of its strategy within the much larger 'central African jigsaw'. They argue that it is in the 'moral and material interests' of the South African people to become engaged in peace efforts across Africa, and that these efforts are closely related to Mbeki's promotion of the New Partnership for Africa's Development (NEPAD) to reverse Africa's marginalisation within the global economy[15] (see Landsberg in this volume). Due to its size and natural mineral wealth, the DRC is a strategic state for the success of NEPAD.[16]

Promoting South Africa's national interests and values as well as the African Renaissance is listed as the core mission of South Africa's Department of Foreign Affairs. In the Department's 2005–2008 Strategic Plan, the mission is described in the following way: 'Our vision is of an African continent that is prosperous, peaceful, democratic, non-racial, non-sexist, and united and which contributes to a world that is just and equitable.'[17] The *White Paper on South African Participation in Peace Missions* adopted by the South African Parliament in October 1999 also recognised that the country's response to conflicts must 'include a focus on effective governance, robust democracies and ongoing economic and social development'.[18] To achieve its goals and vision, South Africa sometimes offers and promotes its expertise and 'good offices' in conflict mediation and facilitation. Ending conflicts through negotiated transitions to constitutional democracy is therefore an important South African objective for the rest of the continent.

The establishment and consolidation of liberal democracy across Africa serves South Africa's interests, but is also driven by Tshwane's perception of its own liberation struggle and transition. South Africa believes that non-violent forms of conflict resolution are the most appropriate methods of achieving durable peace and stability in civil wars, and the country has been engaged in mediation and facilitation not only in Burundi and the DRC, but also in the Comoros, Côte d'Ivoire, Liberia and Sudan.[19] Influenced by its own experience with a negotiated transition, the typical strategy for South Africa is to promote democracy by mediating between all belligerent factions. The goal is to get everyone around the same table to compromise and agree on inclusive transitional political arrangements as part of a peace agreement. Usually, the agreement consists of the establishment of the following principles: a broad-based national unity government involving the warring parties; confidence-building measures and the reform of security forces; provisions to address justice issues; and a procedure and timetable for the drafting of a new permanent constitution and the holding of democratic elections. The idea behind this approach is the belief that immediate public electoral contestation can be counterproductive in countries emerging from violent conflict, whereas elite power-sharing pacts can buy time and allow liberal norms to take hold. As elites grow accustomed to working together, more integrative liberal forms of democracy can be enshrined in a permanent constitution.[20]

However, several authors have shown why this approach may be problematic. For example, Christopher Clapham criticises the model for its assumption that participants in the political process share a common value framework within which differences are negotiable. He sees a dissonance between the civic values underlying attempts at mediation, and the actual conflict in many areas of Africa.[21] Jack Spence similarly argues that these techniques of conflict resolution reflect a liberal and rational ethos that does not correspond to all conflict environments.[22]

258 · SOUTH AFRICA IN AFRICA

Other authors claim that conflict resolution and democracy promotion programmes do not necessarily lead to the desired liberal democracy. There may
be a tension between the compromise agreements between armed belligerents
(including some of the worst abusers of human rights) to stop the fighting, and
the institutions that are required for longer-term peaceful development.[23] On a
global level, Steven Levitsky and Lucan Way have shown how efforts to promote
democracy and human rights have reshaped opportunities and constraints facing elites, without necessarily leading to liberal democracy. Rather, 'competitive
authoritarianism' and other hybrid regimes are becoming common.[24] Similarly,
Thomas Carothers points out that it is mistaken to assume that transitional countries will move towards democracy in a set sequence of stages. He disputes the
notion that countries can democratise according to external blueprints despite
their underlying conditions and prior institutional legacies.[25]

There are also questions about South Africa's economic interests underlying
its peacemaking involvement. Some, like Claude Kabemba, have examined the
view that South Africa's diplomatic involvement cannot be separated from its
economic interests, for instance its concern to secure access to minerals in the
DRC for South African corporations. This South African 'imperialistic' concern
will have implications in terms of the possibilities for post-transition longer-term
development in the Great Lakes region[26] (see also Hudson in this volume).

The 'model' promoted by South Africa and others in Burundi and the DRC
has encountered some of the problems highlighted by these authors. There are
several differences in the substance and form of the peace processes in the DRC
and Burundi as well as the problems that each country has faced. Both cases,
have, however, involved elements of an emerging 'South African approach' to
peacemaking.

Having set out my understanding of the South African 'model' of peacemaking, I next turn my attention to the case study of Burundi.

THE ARUSHA PROCESS FOR BURUNDI

At the outset, South Africa played only a secondary role in Burundi's negotiations. Efforts to resolve the crisis were centred on a regional initiative, with
Tanzania's former president, Julius Nyerere, as facilitator. Nyerere and other
leaders in the region believed that it was necessary to take a strong stance
against the military *coup d'état* in Burundi in July 1996. The coup was staged
by the Tutsi former military head of state, Pierre Buyoya, who had overthrown

a Hutu president, Sylvestre Ntibantunganya. The leaders of the Great Lakes region imposed economic sanctions on Burundi, and set three conditions to be met before their removal: restoring the National Assembly; reinstating political parties; and restarting unconditional peace negotiations with all Burundian parties.[27] However, it took another two years before Buyoya's government agreed to multi-party negotiations chaired by Nyerere, which became known as the Arusha process.[28]

When the Arusha negotiations finally began in June 1998, the issues under negotiation were comprehensive. Five committees were established to deal with five specific themes: 1) the nature of the Burundian conflict; 2) democracy and 'good governance'; 3) peace and security; 4) reconstruction and development; and 5) implementation and regional guarantees.[29] Although the South African government was not directly involved with the Burundian process at this stage, two South African officials played prominent roles. Nicholas 'Fink' Haysom, a South African lawyer who had been a legal adviser to Nelson Mandela and the African National Congress (ANC) during South Africa's transition, was the chairperson of the powerful second committee on democracy and 'good governance'. This committee was responsible for drafting a power-sharing agreement and principles for a future Burundian constitution. Andrew Masondo, a South African general who had been one of those in charge of integrating the South African National Defence Force (SANDF) after 1994, was the vice-chairperson of the third committee on peace and security, which was tasked with negotiating a cease-fire and an agreement on security sector reform.

The Arusha negotiations continued over the next two years. They progressed with difficulty, and were marked by changing demands and positions, new alliances, fragmentation of Burundi's political parties, and efforts to manipulate the facilitation team. The armed conflict continued throughout this period, and the two main rebel groups involved in the conflict – the Palipehutu-FNL (*Parti pour la libération du peuple Hutu* – *Forces Nationales de Libération*) and the CNDD-FDD (*Conseil National pour la Défense de la Démocratie* – *Forces de Défense pour la Démocratie*) – did not participate in the Arusha talks.[30]

South African involvement increased when Nelson Mandela took over the facilitation of the Arusha process after Nyerere's death in October 1999. Mandela wanted to conclude the negotiations quickly, and he took a more heavy-handed approach towards the Burundian participants than Tanzania's patient and methodical *Mwalimu* ('teacher'). Characteristically direct, Mandela openly criticised Burundi's leaders. In his first speech to the country's delegates, he said: 'Why do you allow yourselves to be regarded as leaders without talent, leaders without a vision? ... The fact that women, children and the aged are being slaughtered every day is an indictment against all of you.'[31]

Mandela and his facilitation team exerted significant pressure on the Burundian parties to come to an agreement. During the Arusha negotiation sessions in February and March 2000, Fink Haysom presented a working document that included a three-year transitional power-sharing government. Mandela then submitted a draft agreement to the delegates. The Arusha Peace and Reconciliation Agreement for Burundi was signed on 28 August 2000 in the presence of visiting US president Bill Clinton and other regional leaders.

This strong external pressure succeeded in delivering an agreement that outlined specific constitutional principles and transitional arrangements. However, it was a limited agreement with insufficient political support from various Burundian parties. The accord could therefore bring about neither comprehensive peace nor reconciliation. Several Tutsi parties had signed the Arusha Agreement with formal reservations on fundamental points. Two major armed factions that had not participated in the negotiations, the Palipehutu-FNL and the CNDD-FDD, did not sign the accord and continued their military struggle. Even among those politicians and parties that had signed the agreement, it was hard to distinguish between those who were strongly committed to the Arusha constitutional principles, and those who had signed due to external pressure or personal ambitions, or both. Many individual leaders may have had mixed motives. They were willing to sign onto Arusha as long as it gave them attractive political offices and satisfied personal ambitions, but many also kept open the option of further military conflict if their interests were not served through Arusha. As such, critics of the Arusha process say that it was akin to office-trading among elites, often among the very hardliners that had provoked the conflict in the first place.

Among other provisions, the agreement specified a transitional period of 36 months. Transitional political positions were divided between the Group of Seven (G7) predominantly Hutu parties and the Group of Ten (G10) predominantly Tutsi parties.[32] Burundi's politicians, however, could not agree on who should be the president during the transitional period. One year after the signing of Arusha, Mandela broke the deadlock by announcing that Pierre Buyoya would remain president for the first 18 months of the transition, while a member of FRODEBU (*Front pour la Démocratie au Burundi*) would be vice-president. In the second 18 months of the transition, a FRODEBU member would be president and an UPRONA (*Union pour le Progrès National*) member would be vice-president. To secure the establishment of the transitional institutions, Mandela persuaded the South African government to provide a 700-member protection force for Burundian politicians returning from exile to take up positions in the transitional government. In October 2001, Burundi's National Assembly adopted a transitional constitution by acclamation, and the transitional government was inaugurated on 1 November 2001.

By the end of 2001, Burundi was in a somewhat paradoxical position of having a peace agreement and formal interim constitutional structures, but continued conflict. Negotiations for a cease-fire with the rebels were conducted on and off throughout the transitional period, with active mediation roles played by South Africa's then deputy president, Jacob Zuma – as the main facilitator – and the Regional Initiative on Burundi, chaired by Ugandan president Yoweri Museveni. In October 2002, cease-fire agreements were signed with two smaller wings of Burundi's rebel groups, and some of their leaders entered the government.[33] After much pressure from South Africa and the region, Buyoya stepped down as president on 30 April 2003, and Domitien Ndayizeye of FRODEBU took his place. In June 2003, the South African protection force was expanded to about 1 500 peacekeepers and incorporated into the first-ever African Union peacekeeping mission: the AU Mission in Burundi (AMIB). Ethiopia and Mozambique also deployed troops to the force. In November 2003, South African mediators succeeded in reaching an agreement between the government in Bujumbura and the largest active rebel faction, the CNDD-FDD Nkurunziza wing.[34] Under South African pressure to make up for the financial and logistical shortcomings of the AU force, a UN peacekeeping mission, ONUB, was deployed in June 2004 to take over from the AU.

Despite continued low-intensity fighting in Burundi, significant progress was made in the political sphere in 2004. Pressure from Jacob Zuma and the leaders of South Africa (Mbeki), Rwanda (Paul Kagame) and Uganda (Yoweri Museveni), led to the signing of a further power-sharing agreement, the Pretoria agreement in August 2004, which outlined post-transition structures and principles of governance. This accord was adopted as a draft constitution by the transitional government. There were, however, serious disagreements over the text of the constitution, which resulted in delays in holding the constitutional referendum mandated by the Arusha Agreement. A significant group of mainly Tutsi parties including UPRONA opposed the Pretoria agreement and draft constitution, arguing that the power-sharing formula did not take ethnic-based political parties into account. The constitution guaranteed Tutsi participation by specifying that the government would contain 60 per cent Hutu and 40 per cent Tutsi, but it did not specify which parties these parliamentarians and politicians should come from.[35] UPRONA and the mainly Tutsi parties feared that 'token' Tutsi aligned with traditionally Hutu parties could take up the Tutsi seats in Parliament and in the government, rather than Tutsi belonging to traditionally 'Tutsi' parties. Zuma, backed by regional leaders, rejected these claims by Tutsi parties and insisted on the implementation of the agreement.

The referendum was finally held on 28 February 2005, and Burundians across the country voted overwhelmingly in favour of the new constitution. Communal (local) elections were held in June 2005 and legislative elections took place in July 2005. The former rebel party, the CNDD-FDD, was the clear victor in both elections, winning 55 per cent of the communal seats and 58 per cent of the vote in the National Assembly elections.[36] On 19 August 2005, the National Assembly and Senate elected the new president of Burundi: Pierre Nkuruniza, leader of the CNDD-FDD. He was sworn in as president on 26 August 2005.[37]

THE INTER-CONGOLESE DIALOGUE AND THE PEACE PROCESS IN THE DRC

In the Democratic Republic of the Congo, international and regional facilitators put forward a broadly similar transitional model, but the trajectory of the negotiations in the Congo was not the same as the process in neighbouring Burundi. The large number of external countries involved in fighting in the DRC (Rwanda, Uganda, Zimbabwe, Angola, Namibia and Chad), the enormous economic stakes, the weakness of the Congolese state and the vastness of the territory, all combined to lead to very different dynamics in the DRC.

South Africa had always been interested in pursuing a negotiated settlement in the Congo. In 1996, when Laurent Kabila and his rebel movement (the *Alliance des forces démocratique pour la libération du Congo-Zaïre*, AFDL) were fighting their way to Kinshasa, Nelson Mandela had unsuccessfully tried to broker a deal between the then president Mobutu Sese Seko and Laurent Kabila. During the second rebellion in 1998 backed by Rwanda and Uganda against then president Laurent Kabila, South Africa again tried to intervene diplomatically to push for a new government that was 'broadly based with representatives of all political persuasions in that country.'[38] Several countries within the 14-member Southern African Development Community (SADC), of which the DRC is a member, did not agree with the South African emphasis on diplomatic negotiations rather than military force as a way of settling the dispute. While South Africa – supported by Botswana, Swaziland, Lesotho, and Mozambique – pushed for a diplomatic solution, Zimbabwe, Namibia and Angola deployed troops to Kinshasa to help prevent the regime of Laurent Kabila from being overthrown[39] (see Matlosa in this volume).

Negotiations finally led to the signing of the Lusaka agreement in July 1999 by the governments of the DRC, Rwanda, Uganda, Namibia, Zimbabwe and Angola. The main Congolese armed rebel groups signed the accord a month later.[40] Lusaka was a cease-fire agreement calling for the withdrawal of foreign forces from the DRC, disarmament and repatriation, and the deployment of a UN peacekeeping force. The accord also called for 'Inter-Congolese political negotiations which should lead to a new political dispensation in the Democratic Republic of Congo'.[41] The agreement further provided a timetable for the Inter-Congolese negotiations, and specified that they should include the Congolese government, the armed groups, the unarmed opposition (political parties), and civil society, all with equal status. The inclusive nature of the proposed participants was an innovative feature of the process.[42] In December 1999, Sir Ketumile Masire, the former president of Botswana, was mandated by the Organisation of African Unity to facilitate the process.

It took nearly two years for the cease-fire outlined in the Lusaka agreement to be implemented and for the Inter-Congolese negotiations to begin. Laurent Kabila refused to work with Ketumile Masire, citing his lack of French and understanding of the issues at stake. An opportunity to breathe new life into the peace process occurred when Laurent Kabila was assassinated by one of his bodyguards in January 2001 and his son, Joseph Kabila, became president. Joseph Kabila recognised Masire as facilitator for the Inter-Congolese Dialogue and promised better cooperation with the UN mission in the Congo.[43]

The Inter-Congolese dialogue finally began in Addis Ababa, Ethiopia, in October 2001, following preparatory meetings in Gaborone, Botswana, in August. Progress was slow, in part because less than a third of the designated Congolese delegates arrived in Ethiopia due to technical and financial problems. It was then decided that the Inter-Congolese dialogue had to be even more inclusive, and should involve groups such as the Mai-Mai militias, religious orders and traditional chiefs. Informal consultations, chaired by the UN between November 2001 and February 2002, succeeded in narrowing the differences among the various Congolese parties.

South Africa became increasingly involved in the process in 2002, when the Inter-Congolese dialogue resumed in the country's Sun City resort from February to April 2002. By then, there were 360 delegates for eight components and entities: the government; the RCD (*Rassemblement Congolais pour la Démocratie*); the MLC (*Mouvement pour la Libération du Congo*); the RCD-N (*Rassemblement Congolais pour la Démocratie – National*); the RCD-ML (*Rassemblement Congolais pour la Démocratie – Mouvement de Libération*); the Mai-Mai; the unarmed political opposition; and civil society representatives. The delegates split into five technical commissions dealing with: political and legal issues; security and defence; social, cultural and humanitarian affairs; economy and finance; and peace and reconciliation.

The Inter-Congolese dialogue suffered from internal and external problems. There was a lack of agreement among the parties on several important power-sharing points, and some individuals were profiting through continued conflict and insecurity in the DRC and thus had little interest in reaching an agreement. In contrast to Mandela's firm approach to the Burundian negotiations, the facilitator for the DRC dialogue, Ketumile Masire, perceived his role to be minimalist and had difficulty mediating between the belligerents and their foreign allies.[44] South Africa, however, wanted the dialogue to succeed. Mbeki managed to put the negotiations back on track through his personal intervention in Sun City, and encouraged more international pressure. As the host country, South Africa had strongly committed itself to the Inter-Congolese dialogue, and failure would have hurt Tshwane's reputation as a successful peacemaker.[45] Nonetheless, many Congolese questioned the neutrality of the South African government, which was seen to be overly supportive of Rwanda and the RCD-Goma faction. The rivalry between South Africa, Angola and Zimbabwe for lucrative contracts in the DRC (most notably mining contracts), also reportedly contributed to difficulties and delays in the Inter-Congolese negotiations.[46]

No comprehensive agreement was reached at the Inter-Congolese dialogue in Sun City. However, the Kabila administration and the MLC delegation concluded a bilateral deal between themselves, which several smaller parties also signed. Then, in Pretoria in July 2002, South Africa brokered an agreement between the governments of the DRC and Rwanda, whereby Rwanda would withdraw its forces from the Congo, in return for the disarmament of Rwandan Hutu rebels. A separate agreement was signed between the DRC and Uganda in Luanda in September 2002, brokered by the Angolan government. By the end of 2002, most of the Angolan, Zimbabwean, Ugandan, Rwandan, and Burundian troops had withdrawn from the DRC, in a process also facilitated by US pressure, particularly on Rwanda.

There was also progress in the political sphere. Following months of consultations, shuttle diplomacy and negotiations assisted by the UN Special Envoy, Moustapha Niasse, and the government of South Africa, the Congolese parties signed an all-inclusive peace agreement in Pretoria in December 2002. Drawing on the South African experience, then deputy president of South Africa, Jacob Zuma, told the Congolese: 'persistent pressure got the ANC to the negotiating table … and kept both sides there through the convoluted CODESA process'.[47] Further negotiations between the parties under joint UN/South African auspices led to agreement on the text of a transitional constitution and a memorandum on military and security issues, signed at Sun City in April 2003 with facilitator Masire.[48] The Pretoria agreement provided for a transitional government with president Joseph Kabila (PPRD),[49] and four vice-presidents from different groups and factions: Jean-Pierre Bemba (MLC), Abdoulaye Yerodia Ndombasi (PPRD), Azarias Ruberwa (RCD-G), and Z'Ahidi Ngoma (civilian opposition). Ministerial portfolios were divided proportionally between the armed groups, the unarmed opposition, civil society, and the Mai-Mai.[50] The transitional government was sworn in on 30 June 2003. In May 2005, the transitional National Assembly adopted a draft new constitution with a text agreed on by representatives of the warring parties. This constitution was approved in a referendum in December 2005; in which over 80 per cent of the votes cast were in favour.[51] By then, South Africa had deployed over 1 000 troops to the DRC under the 16 700 member UN peacekeeping mission, and was also involved in efforts to create a new Congolese army.[52] As well as contributing to the UN peacekeeping mission, the South African military was also involved in efforts to screen and train the new Congolese army.[53]

After a series of delays due to financial, technical and political problems, the first democratic elections in more than forty years were held in the DRC on 30 July 2006. Foreign observers included a South African electoral observer mission. In the first round, none of the presidential contenders won an absolute majority. President Joseph Kabila, who won 44 per cent of the votes, and Vice-President Jean-Pierre Bemba, who won 20 per cent of the votes, faced each other again in the second round of elections three months later. Tensions in the interim period were high, and there were a number of violent clashes between supporters of the two candidates in Kinshasa which were repeated in March 2007. The second round of elections was held in conjunction with provincial elections on 29 October 2006, and Kabila won 58 per cent of the vote. Although Bemba initially challenged the results, he later conceded defeat, and Kabila was sworn in as president about one month later.

IMPLEMENTATION CHALLENGES AND POST-ELECTION VULNERABILITIES

The two peace processes in Burundi and the DRC have culminated in democratic elections and the establishment of new governments under new constitutions. They could therefore appear to be successful South African 'exports'. Nonetheless, this view would be both flawed and premature, since elections do not necessarily mark the end of peace processes. The two countries are still extremely fragile and peace is by no means guaranteed. In Burundi, the new government has increasingly resorted to autocratic tactics. A number of prominent opposition politicians were arrested and tensions have increased since elections in 2005. The ceasefire agreement with one remaining rebel movement, the FNL, had, by March 2007, not been implemented. In the DRC, state institutions are very weak, violence remains pervasive in the eastern part of the country, and the security environment in other parts of the country is volatile.

Arguably, neither country would have progressed this far in their peace processes were it not for South Africa's role. Without Mandela's facilitation efforts, which led to deployment of a South African protection force for politicians returning from exile, and South African troops forming a backbone for the African Union peacekeeping mission in Burundi, it is likely that the Burundian peace process would have collapsed. Similarly, without Mbeki's pressure to resolve outstanding issues during Congo's negotiations, it is likely that the Congolese peace process would have developed quite differently.

Yet both peace processes evolved in environments that were tremendously different from South Africa's own negotiated transition, and the troubled implementation of the two agreements reflect these differences. It is still too early to assess whether or not the processes in Burundi and the DRC will lead to durable post-election peace, but several factors made the implementation of the peace agreements difficult and will continue to affect post-election politics negatively. These challenges can be traced to the political economy of conflict, patterns of authority in the two countries, and the regional dimensions of these conflicts.

The importance of understanding the economic stakes in the two Great Lakes conflicts cannot be overemphasised. Even after the Arusha and Pretoria agreements were signed, there were powerful people and interests within and outside both countries that benefited from continued conflict and insecurity. For some, war was preferable to peace, particularly if their prosperity and interests were threatened by the prospect of democratic elections. As Filip Reyntjens explained in the case of the DRC: 'local, national and regional state and non-state actors indeed act rationally, engaged as they are in cost-benefit analyses, whose outcome often shows that war, instability and state decay are more attractive than peace, stability and state reconstruction.'[54]

Reflecting pervasive war economies and patterns of authority, the violence in the DRC and Burundi was often not conducted on behalf of clearly defined political groupings with explicit grievances and objectives. Instead, rebel movements, political parties and groupings split and merged according to strategic interests and the opportunistic calculations of individual leaders. While there were legitimate grievances in both countries, these were not clearly represented by a cohesive opposition or rebel leadership. As a result, instead of negotiations leading to the all-encompassing new political dispensations that South Africa and others had envisaged, the talks in Burundi and the DRC were more akin to office-trading and bargaining between unrepresentative leaders, warlords, and ambitious politicians. Power-sharing became a tool to placate opportunistic and sometimes dangerous leaders, rather than a tool to ensure wider participation. External economic interests and networks further aggravated the process and ensured the continuation of previous patterns of enrichment at the expense of the majority of the population.

In Burundi, facilitators were frustrated by party factionalism and the search for private gain. The main rebel groups split several times over the course of pre- and post-Arusha negotiations. It was, of course, impossible to accommodate everyone in the transitional structures, as there were a limited number of offices, positions and postings. The Arusha process distributed offices among parties down to the level of diplomatic postings and provincial administrators, but it was not possible to convince everyone that they stood to gain more from peace than from violence. Transitional institutions were established while conflict was ongoing, but there were consequences to this. First, additional power-sharing positions needed to be found to entice the leaders of the rebel movements to enter these transitional institutions. This had the unintended consequence of rewarding those who stayed outside the process. It also provided an incentive to leaders to continue fighting until a better offer came their way. Negotiations with the CNDD-FDD (Nkurunziza wing) in 2002 and 2003 eventually brought the movement into the transitional government, but the attractive power-sharing provisions accorded to the CNDD-FDD were a source of serious concern for other parties and groups that had signed the original Arusha agreement. Second, continued negotiations with rebel groups throughout the transitional period ensured that certain issues were kept off the agenda. It was difficult to implement parts of the Arusha Accord, such as economic and social reform as well as the provisions on justice, and truth and reconciliation, while there was continued fighting and uncertainty.

These developments have had several effects. Burundians were largely disconnected from the Arusha peace process. They voted overwhelmingly in favour of the new constitution in the 2005 referendum at the end of the transitional period,[55] but they also registered their displeasure with the transitional politicians in the elections. The elections were a devastating defeat for FRODEBU, which along with UPRONA, had been the main political partner in the transition.[56] The CNDD-FDD, which was not associated with the transitional institutions due to its late arrival in the process, capitalised on widespread feelings of disenchantment with 'establishment' politicians among the population.

The new government, however, has not made a significant break with the past in terms of the way in which it exercises its authority. Since the elections in 2005, there have been several worrying signs of a tendency towards authoritarian-style rule. During the tortuous Arusha process, UPRONA and FRODEBU grew accustomed to dialogue and debate, but CNDD-FDD members did not participate in these sustained discussions. Already, FRODEBU and UPRONA have expressed concern over the CNDD-FDD government's lack of compliance with the constitutional requirements regarding party representation in government as well as insufficient participation of non-government parties in state institutions.[57] In July 2006, several prominent opposition members were arrested. Some were released six months later, while others remained imprisoned under charges that they were planning a coup.[58]

The last rebel movement, the FNL, signed a cease-fire agreement in September 2006, which had still not been implemented six months later. The regional dimensions of the Burundian conflict were apparent through reports of collaboration between the FNL, the Congolese, and foreign armed groups, as well as cross-border movements of arms and combatants.[59]

Similarly in the DRC, despite the efforts of the South Africans and their partners, economic agendas, structures of authority, and regional dynamics have affected transitional and post-election processes. Despite the numerous ceasefire agreements in the DRC, violence has not ceased. Fighting in the eastern part of the country continued throughout the transitional period and showed no signs of abating in the post-election period. Militias controlled large areas of eastern Congo, while Rwandan and Ugandan-backed rebels continued to operate in the DRC. Some parties and factions are fighting to preserve the financial networks that they had established since the first Congo war of 1996.[60]

Foreign countries have continued to benefit from the Congo's economic resources. A UN report on the illegal exploitation of mineral resources in the DRC of October 2002 fingered many foreign actors, including South Africans, who were involved in illegal commercial activities in the DRC during the wars of 1996 and 1998.[61] Rwanda has repeatedly sent troops to eastern Congo to pursue the Hutu extremist *Forces Démocratiques pour la Libération du Rwanda* (FDLR), but also to control and manage lucrative commercial dealings. The FDLR has an estimated 8 000–10 000 troops in the DRC and can still launch cross-border raids into Rwanda.[62] Uganda has also been accused of assisting rebel groups in the Congo's Ituri province, as well as of looting the country's resources. The UN estimated in May 2006 that there were between 8 000 and 9 000 foreign combatants in the DRC, about 5 000 in North Kivu and 3 000–3 500 in South Kivu.[63] Security threats, opportunities for economic plundering and porous borders are keys to understanding the regional dynamics of the Congolese conflict. Foreign, armed groups are engaged in a variety of licit and illicit economic activities in the DRC, and splits in these movements often have socio-economic dimensions.[64] Investigations by MONUC have shown a close link between the illegal exploitation of natural resources and violence.[65]

The weakness of the Congolese state and the existence of competing structures of local authority mean that armed groups – particularly in the eastern part of the country – continue to manipulate and abuse civilians, despite the elections. In the western part of the DRC, tensions have increased with the holding of elections. In many areas in the western and central parts of the country, presidential candidate, Jean-Pierre Bemba, received over 70 per cent of the vote. The situation in many parts of the country thus remained very tense in March 2007. Furthermore, corruption is rampant. During the transitional period, some individuals deliberately tried to keep the transitional institutions weak, corrupt and factionalised. The International Crisis Group quotes one parliamentarian as saying: 'they tried to get during the transition what they could not get during the negotiations in South Africa.'[66] Corruption shows no signs of abating in the post-election period.

South Africa and its partners had hoped that by giving the main Congolese powerbrokers a stake in governance, they would be persuaded to stop fighting and learn to work together in preparation for elections. It was also hoped that by including civil society and unarmed opposition groups in the negotiations, the interests of ordinary Congolese would be represented. These efforts have largely failed,[67] and as usual, the bulk of the Congolese population have been the main losers. The power-holders in the DRC have continued to pursue their clientilistic and predatory behaviour, following previous patterns. There has been little effort to rebuild state capacity or to finance social services. Rather, Congolese political and military leaders continue to follow well-established patterns, which include a reliance on aid, outside assistance, foreign investment, and resource extraction to compensate for their lack of domestic support. Political advancement is still often achieved through corruption and intimidation.[68] Little attention has been paid to justice issues, and the judicial system has not been able to address human rights abuses or corruption effectively. Courts also remain weak and highly politicised.

CONCLUDING REFLECTIONS: THE SOUTH AFRICAN APPROACH TO PEACE

Kristina Bentley and Roger Southall express a widely held South African view when they say that: 'Africa and the whole world look to South Africa as the key model for resolving intractable conflicts after the experience of the transition from apartheid to democracy.'[69] Indeed, the Arusha process for Burundi and the Inter-Congolese dialogue were loosely based on the principles that had guided the South African transition. South Africa's policy of promoting liberal internationalism through facilitation and multilateral engagement was therefore put to the test in both countries. Burundi, in particular, became a showpiece for the African Renaissance, as well as for Mandela's power as a mediator and South Africa's new role as peacemaker. If South Africa could not succeed in Burundi, how could it succeed in tougher cases such as the DRC? Once it had committed itself, South Africa's desire for success goes a long way in explaining the considerable energy and resources the country has expended on the peace processes in the Great Lakes.

Both Nyerere and Mandela had viewed the conflict in Burundi through the same lens as the apartheid struggle in South Africa, where an 'ethnic' dominant minority ruled over a disenfranchised majority.[70] Other comparisons between

South Africa and Burundi are put forward by Bentley and Southall, some of which are also relevant to the DRC. These include: the need to create a common citizenship by overcoming race and ethnicity as tools of division; reconciling history; dealing with amnesty and justice; addressing military dominance and minority rule; and redressing material inequities.[71]

The efforts of South Africa and other peacebuilders in the Great Lakes region were largely commendable. It is understandable to try to reproduce a successful model, and the vision promoted in the DRC and Burundi was attractive. In Burundi, Arusha was the first attempt in that country's history to address all facets of a protracted conflict openly, including divergent views on the nation's history; justice issues; economic and social issues; military reform; and, of course, power-sharing. The ideals enshrined in the Inter-Congolese dialogue went even further. This nationwide dialogue, which included civil society members and unarmed groups, was intended to set the foundations for a new political order based on consent and inclusive participation. The goal was to achieve political legitimacy, 'good governance' and an end to violence. Democratic elections would be an important part of this larger process.

Ultimately, however, both processes degenerated into a distribution of political and military 'spoils', primarily among belligerents. Reaching these agreements over political and military offices took precedence over addressing issues of justice, 'good governance' and socio-economic equality. Furthermore, these agreements have been unable to bring a decisive end to the violence that they were intended to quell.

This chapter has therefore uncovered some limitations on the viability of 'exporting' the South African model to other countries, despite its normative appeal.

First, I have shown that the nature of conflict in apartheid South Africa was fundamentally different from the conflicts in Burundi and the DRC. It is one thing to fight for a specific grievance or injustice with clear demands and a reasonably cohesive leadership, and quite another to fight for elusive and changing goals, personal privileges and wealth. In Burundi, there were clear grievances related to the historic exclusion of Hutus from structures of political, military and economic power.[72] Yet the scramble for political offices, the shifting alliances and allegiances, and the continued conflict demonstrated that disputes were not solely about ethnic grievances and socio-economic and political imbalances. Likewise, in the DRC, rebel groups had no clear, consistent grievance or coherent political manifesto. The South African peacebuilding lens does not sufficiently capture the political economy dimensions of conflict in the Great Lakes, and the myriad of reasons why individuals and factions have been fighting. New governments have been established in both Burundi and the Congo, but the continued challenges they face are not surprising, given the context from which they have emerged.

There is a real dilemma about what to do with 'spoilers' who violate ceasefires and continue to fight during political transitions. Should they be accommodated and enticed back to the negotiating table, or should they be marginalised and dealt with by the law or by force? At worst, the desire for inclusivity in the peace processes in the Great Lakes may have rewarded violent behaviour. Politicians were able to 'shoot their way to the negotiating table'.[73] Some politicians in both countries correctly calculated that continued fighting could bring them a better office. This is a dangerous signal to send, both in terms of the message it gives to those who were willing to compromise earlier and to non-violent opposition figures, as well as the message this may give to rebel groups in other countries who are developing their own strategies.

Second, a South African 'model' of peacebuilding assumes a coherent state with particular kinds of political authority. In the DRC, patron-client ties and years of predation have meant that informal systems and structures of authority have become firmly rooted. The Congolese state is weak, but this does not mean that sources of power and authority are nonexistent. On the contrary, the weakness of the state has enabled different sorts of powerful licit and illicit local-global networks of authority to gain a strong base in the DRC. Superimposing formal 'rules' and constitutional structures on an environment with deeply entrenched informal structures, has led to parallel, and sometimes conflicting, political structures. Tensions between formal and informal political arrangements in the DRC mirror the tensions between formal and informal economic structures and security arrangements in the country. Elections have not been able to resolve the problem of political authority in the DRC, as the continued conflict in the east and increased tensions in Kinshasa in 2007 have shown. In Burundi, the state is more coherent than in neighbouring DRC, but this is a state with a strong legacy of autocratic rule. The challenge in Burundi is to address the slide towards authoritarianism, and to convince the population that there are socio-economic dividends to be derived from peace.

Third, this chapter has shown that regional dynamics in the Great Lakes region are of paramount importance. An internal transitional power-sharing process is clearly insufficient when the sponsors of violent local groups are external patrons. When the economic interests of some external actors are served by conflict, there is an additional problem. Even in Burundi, military and rebel networks overlap permeable borders, with bases and arms provided by neighbours. It is inherently difficult to build peace in a dangerous neighbourhood, and it is encouraging to note that the UN recognises that the establishment of mechanisms for regional cooperation is a prerequisite for stability in the entire Great Lakes region.[74]

The human costs of the tragedies in the Great Lakes region cannot be overstated: over 3,5 million deaths have been reported in the DRC and Burundi since 1993. The critical question stemming from this conflict-ridden region is how to build peace in a context in which some key actors do not want peace; when some local and foreign interests benefit from continued conflict; and where informal structures of authority are pervasive. This is not to say, however, that peacebuilding efforts in the Great Lakes region have been in vain. South Africa's efforts, along with its regional and international partners, have contributed to a large number of important changes in the two countries. In Burundi today, competition is centred primarily among different groups of Hutu, rather than between Hutu and Tutsi groups, partly as a result of ethnic constitutional requirements and the electoral law. Furthermore, gender provisions in the Arusha agreement as well as in subsequent legislation mean that Burundian women now have a real opportunity to participate in the political institutions of their country. In the DRC, there are considerable risks but even in the face of enormous challenges, the peace process has had some notable successes. While much difficult work remains to be done, it is hoped that small successes can lead to larger changes that will make peace meaningful for the wider populations in the volatile Great Lakes region.

13

South Africa's relations with North Africa and the Horn: Bridging a continent[1]

IQBAL JHAZBHAY

We have managed to arrive at and further enhance a shared political understanding of Africa and her place in the world. Through our meetings (Algeria-South Africa) we have expanded this relationship to cover a range of economic, social, scientific and cultural sectors that can build our countries and our people. As we meet here in Pretoria and as indeed when we met last year in Algiers, I believe we are 'feeding the future with its ripeness' and making of Africa all that is beautiful, true and new. In the creation of enabling conditions for African innovation, African splendour, African ownership, African interconnectedness in all possible ways, we are indeed taking this united road of many lanes, many languages, to recovery and sustained development.

– Thabo Mbeki[2]

There are few countries outside our immediate region of Southern and Eastern Africa that we have visited as often since our release from jail as the Great Socialist People's Libyan Arab Jamahyria. Our frequent visits reflect our affection for the esteemed Brother Leader and the people of this great country. We shall never forget Libya's material and moral support of our own struggle against racist apartheid rule. It remains in our memories and spurs us on to help lighten the plight of our Libyan brothers and sisters.

– Nelson Mandela[3]

In the last decade, the people of Somaliland have been involved in a tremendous effort for reconciliation, demobilisation, rebuilding, repatriation and democratisation without outside help. It is encouraging that this unique African experience is now attracting a growing interest from South Africa, largely from civil society groups. Given South Africa's economic power and

technical know-how, plus Somaliland's untapped oil and mineral resources,
it is only right and logical to expect South Africa's government and busi-
nesses to enhance their level of engagement with Somaliland.

– *Somaliland Times*[4]

In 1986, Kenyan scholar Ali Mazrui called for a metaphorical bridge across
the Red Sea that would finally re-integrate Africa with Arabia, several million
years after a natural cataclysm had torn off the Arabian peninsula from the rest
of Africa. He noted that, just as in the view of continental Pan-Africanists the
Sahara desert is a sea of communication linking states below the Sahara with
their neighbours above the desert, so the Red Sea could become a similar bridge.
The Suez Canal, built between 1859 and 1869 by the Frenchman Ferdinand de
Lesseps, had been designed to facilitate European trade with the rest of the
world rather than increase contact between Africa and Arabia.

Mazrui also noted that Ethiopia had been a haven for early Muslims fleeing
persecution by pagan Mecca, and that Emperor Haile Selassie had officially
located Ethiopia as being part of the Middle East rather than Africa until
the 1950s. Just as Selassie had re-Africanised Ethiopia with the hosting of the
Organisation of African Unity (oau) in 1963, Egypt's Gamel Abdel Nasser
had from the 1950s also re-Africanised Egypt, with his pan-African foreign
policy.[5] Echoes of these re-Africanisation policies can be found today in the
pan-African foreign policies of two North African leaders: Algeria's Abdelaziz
Bouteflika and Libya's Muammar Qaddafi. Following the spirit of Mazrui's
call for re-Africanising states that also have other strong regional identities,
this chapter seeks to examine how an activist, developmental South African
foreign policy can build bridges between North Africa and the Horn, and the
rest of the continent.

Cecil John Rhodes, perhaps the greatest imperial figure in Africa, dreamed
of building a railway from the Cape to Cairo. It was a romantic and revolutionary concept, running against the colonial tide. For building infrastructure to
connect African countries was not on the priority list of colonial governments
once they had grabbed their pieces of real estate in the scramble for Africa,
which reached its apogee in the late nineteenth century. The infrastructural
investment of imperial governments went into building road and rail links
from the original resource pools to the coast – the quicker to get the spoils to
metropolitan markets. Years later, with Africa now free,[6] the concept of building

a bridge between the North and the Southern parts of the continent remains an ideal and, many would argue, still a distant pipedream. In this post-colonial era, when the British Empire has receded into history, the North-South bridge is something that is today being more enthusiastically pursued by the Maghreb countries, notably Algeria.

Building relations between democratic South Africa and North Africa has required a great deal of work to make up for the lack of contact in previous decades. The Sahara desert has proved to be a major barrier – rather than a bridge – to understanding and building friendship. In the apartheid era, South Africa had more in common with Europe and North America than it did with the northern or eastern parts of its own continent (see the Introduction to this volume). Today, all the North African countries – Algeria, Egypt, Libya, Morocco and Tunisia – have embassies in South Africa – including a mission established recently in South Africa by Western Sahara's Saharan Arab Democratic Republic (SADR). Tshwane (Pretoria) also has embassies in each of these five North African countries, as well as a trade office in Cairo. The African National Congress-led (ANC) government has drawn on its historical liberation experience in building its relations with these North African countries.[7] Nelson Mandela, for example, had been greatly influenced by the Algerian independence movement during a trip across Africa in 1961.

For administrative purposes, the colonial powers divided Africa into North and sub-Saharan Africa. Regrettably, international organisations like the World Bank, the International Monetary Fund (IMF), some UN agencies, and western foreign offices continue to entrench this division. African countries themselves tend to make the same distinction, prolonging the end of what should be a non-existent continental division. The proximity of North African countries to Europe has naturally led to them developing close ties with that continent, particularly with the Mediterranean countries.

An examination of South Africa's post-apartheid relations with North Africa is best divided into the two eras of Nelson Mandela (1994–99) and Thabo Mbeki (1999–2007). I will examine the bilateral and multilateral relations that democratic South Africa has developed with the North African region. Specifically, the chapter will consider how relations with Algeria and Tunisia have grown into a strategic partnership, and how ties with Egypt, Libya and Morocco have required courage, forbearance and tact of the highest order. I then briefly assess South Africa's relations with the Horn of Africa focusing specific attention on Sudan, Eritrea, Ethiopia, Djibouti, Somalia and Somaliland.

NORTH AFRICA: THE MANDELA ERA

Nelson Mandela led South Africa's move into the African continent after he became president in April 1994. The approach was cautious and deliberately sensitive to any fears of arrogance or triumphalism. Mandela was very aware of the debt that South Africa owed North African countries for their contribution to its own liberation struggle.[8] His choice of a low-key but well-connected foreign minister in Alfred Nzo epitomised a desire to engage Africa with humility and deference. The South African president was aware that every continental and regional organisation such as the Organisation of African Unity (OAU) and the Southern African Development Community (SADC) would not undergo changes simply by having South Africa join it (see Landsberg and Matlosa in this volume).

South Africa's relations with Libya best illustrate Mandela's combination of pragmatism and idealism.[9] These ties were strongly criticised from within South Africa and earned the undisguised disapproval of the US and other western governments such as Britain which were at the forefront of tightening UN sanctions – imposed in 1992 – against Libyan leader Muammar Qaddafi, a man whose country featured high on their list of so-called terrorist states. Mandela showed a penchant for irritating Washington by remaining loyal to his friends, many of whom, like Qaddafi and Cuba's Fidel Castro, were *persona non grata* in the US but had supported the ANC's liberation struggle. Chief among these was Qaddafi. Clearly, both Mandela and Mbeki have evolved distinct styles in dealing with the highly idiosyncratic approach of Libya's 'Brother Leader' to African and international relations.

Mandela's stubborn individualism paid off handsomely when, in cooperation with Saudi Arabia, he was able to use his 'good offices' to break the diplomatic logjam over the Lockerbie affair, involving two Libyan nationals charged with the 1988 bombing of an American airliner over Scotland that killed 270 people. Mandela appointed Jakes Gerwel, the head of his office, to negotiate with Qaddafi over several months. Gerwel was assisted by Saudi Arabia's ambassador to Washington at the time, Prince Bandar bin Sultan Abdul Aziz, in spite of the fact that by getting involved in this matter, Riyadh was risking its close relations with Washington and London.

In January 1999, the South African-Saudi team eventually persuaded Qaddafi to hand over the two men – Abdul Basset Al-Megrahi and Lamin Khalifa Fahima – for trial before Scottish judges at The Hague. The deal agreed on and implemented was that the UN sanctions imposed on Libya in 1992 would be suspended as soon as the suspects were delivered to The Hague, and these sanctions would be completely lifted within 90 days. Any imprisonment of the Libyans would be in a specially segregated section of a jail in Scotland, with special consideration being given to their religious and cultural needs.[10]

Mandela's emphasis on human rights led him to keep Algeria's military-dominated regime at arm's length after the annulment of elections there in 1992 that Islamist parties appeared to be on the verge of winning. South Africa's president was, however, less critical of serious human rights excesses in Morocco, Egypt and Tunisia, developing ties with these three countries. In this respect, Mandela made state visits and private visits to Cairo, Tunis and Rabat. Of particular note was Mandela's state visit to Egypt in 1997, where he conferred on Egyptian leader, Hosni Mubarak, the 'Order of Good Hope' and himself received the 'Collar of the Nile'.[11] Mbeki also visited Cairo in 2000 to attend the Africa-EU summit, in spite of the frosty diplomatic ties between Cairo and Tshwane, discussed below in greater detail.

NORTH AFRICA: MBEKI'S DIPLOMACY OF BUILDING AND MANAGING LINKS

Mbeki, who took over South Africa's presidency from Mandela in 1999, has a more confident approach to North Africa. Mbeki's yardstick for developing relations involved a more pragmatic measure of mutual economic benefit than Mandela had applied. Nevertheless, Mbeki decided that, on this basis, the countries of North Africa warranted close and consistent attention from South Africa. Even before the September 11, 2001 terrorist attacks on Washington and New York raised sympathy for Algeria's struggle against the scourge, Mbeki had identified the emerging oil-rich country as a strategic partner.[12] In 2001, Mbeki noted during a state banquet in Tshwane for the visiting Algerian leader, Abdelaziz Bouteflika, that:

> Clearly, despite the physical distance imposed upon us (South Africa-Algeria) by geography, the relationship between our two countries is an intimate one, going back many decades to the struggle of the African peoples for national liberation and freedom from colonial rule. In particular, we must thank President Bouteflika, at the time as the President of the [UN] General Assembly, for the important role he played in the decision to isolate the racist government of South Africa.[13]

South Africa's relations with Tripoli have been altogether more complicated, with an apparent rivalry between Mbeki and Qaddafi for the soul of the new African Union (see Landsberg in this volume). The most useful analogy here to describe the different approaches of Mbeki and Mandela would be that of 'good cop, bad cop', with Mandela softening Qaddafi and leading him back into the international fold, while Mbeki told the 'brother leader' some home truths about the consequences for Africa of his rhetorical outbursts and unpredictable behaviour.[14]

With Cairo, Mbeki's team has questioned the commitment of the country to African ideals. The South African president has been irritated by Mubarak first insisting on being named a key player in the Mbeki-inspired African socio-economic plan, NEPAD, but then not attending meetings of the body's steering committee.

Algeria and Morocco

During the South African liberation struggle, Algeria played host to Nelson Mandela and gave refuge and training to many cadres such as Mzwewu Henry Ntsele and Johannes Moopeloa from the ANC and the Pan Africanist Congress (PAC) respectively.[15] The military regime of Lamine Zeroual cashed in on this revolutionary link, with the faded picture of the fugitive Mandela and his Algerian guerrilla hosts becoming an iconic symbol in Algeria's liberation mythology. Algeria was an outspoken opponent of apartheid, playing an active role in the UN Special Committee Against Apartheid and as president of the General Assembly in the 1970s. That function was performed by Algerian leader Abdelaziz Bouteflika, then Algeria's foreign minister who, in 1974, presided over the suspension of apartheid South Africa from the General Assembly. Bouteflika's erstwhile South African counterpart, Pik Botha, recalls that, despite the acrimony and heat of debate over this unprecedented action, Bouteflika never treated him with anything but the greatest courtesy and civility.[16] Bouteflika was in the founding 'troika' of African leaders – along with Mbeki and Nigeria's Olusegun Obasanjo – of the NEPAD steering committee.

Morocco, by contrast, developed military and other ties with South Africa's apartheid regime. Arms bought from South Africa were used in Morocco's bid to crush the Polisario Front in the Western Sahara, a territory that Rabat has occupied since 1975 in defiance of the international community.

Given the history of South Africa and Algeria, it is no surprise that post-apartheid relations with the country have been conducted at presidential level. In fact, the relationship between Tshwane and Algiers has been developed to a strategic level that makes Algeria among South Africa's closest friends on the continent and certainly the most important partner in North Africa. An excellent chemistry and deep bond has existed between Mbeki and Bouteflika. South Africa has shared its experiences to help Algeria with internal political reconciliation, gender issues, multiculturalism and economic development, also offering Algeria assistance in its bid to accede to the WTO.

The level of diplomatic representatives sent to Algiers by South Africa further demonstrates the importance of this bilateral relationship. The South African Ambassador to Algeria in 2007, Sipho Moloi, was, prior to this appointment, responsible for the Middle East focus in Mbeki's Presidential Advisory Unit.

The presidential commission meetings between South Africa and Algeria have involved cabinet teams of unprecedented size relative to South Africa's dealings with other countries on the continent. However, at this stage, the level of bilateral business and investment does not yet match the level of political ties between Tshwane and Algiers. Political ties appear to be motivated more by long-term bilateral and multilateral strategic goals than by hard cash. Every effort is being made, however, to remedy this situation, with South African businesses being encouraged to build stronger economic relations with Algeria.

Early ties with Algeria demonstrated South Africa's naiveté in dealing with the phenomenon of 'Islamism'. Persuaded that he was dealing with a victim of Algerian repression, Mandela received the leader of what Algiers considered a terrorist organisation, the *Group Islamique Armée* (GIA).[17] Algeria responded by recalling its ambassador, Saeed Ketouni, to South Africa for consultation. This gaffe necessitated sending South Africa's deputy foreign minister, Aziz Pahad, as a special envoy to Algiers, carrying Mandela's apology for the incident. The September 11 attack on the World Trade Centre and Pentagon have earned Algeria a greater level of understanding for what it argues is the need for a tough approach in its fight against terrorism. Algeria, which has lost more than 100 000 people to violence since 1992, has become the seat of the African Union's research centre for combating terrorism. Currently, South Africa has developed a positive alliance with Algeria on various bilateral and multilateral issues.

Morocco and the Western Sahara question

Morocco has expended much effort in trying to ensure that South Africa did not join other African countries in recognising the Polisario Front's government-in-exile: the Saharan Arab Democratic Republic.[18]

In 1994, King Hassan II, with the help of Egyptian UN Secretary-General, Boutros Boutros-Ghali, managed to convince Mandela to delay his written promise to recognise the SADR. At the time of the Moroccan invasion of Western Sahara in 1975, beginning with the 'Green March' of 300 000 flag-waving Moroccans, the Polisario Front had developed strong fraternal ties at the UN with the ANC, Namibia's South West Africa People's Organisation (SWAPO) and the Revolutionary Front for an Independent East Timor (Fretelin). To counter this solidarity, Hassan had to draw heavily on his influence with Boutros Boutros-Gali, former French president, François Mitterrand, and the late Palestinian leader, Yasser Arafat. Five years later, Hassan's successor, Mohamed V, took similarly drastic action, applying intense diplomatic pressure at a time when Mbeki, who described the Western Sahara as Africa's last colonial problem, was on the brink of recognising the SADR.

Former UN Secretary-General Kofi Annan, French president Jacques Chirac and the US administration of Bill Clinton were all called upon by Rabat to press Mbeki to stay his hand on SADR recognition. Mandela also intervened by asking Mbeki to delay the decision until after he had travelled to the kingdom to express his condolences on the death of Hassan – more than a year after the regent's death in 1999.[19]

Early in 2004, the South African government sent a delegation to Western Sahara to assess possible direct health and social development support. In September that year, South Africa in a move long overdue – some ten years after Mandela's written promise to the Western Sahara leadership – announced that Tshwane would formally recognise the SADR. Morocco immediately recalled its ambassador Abdullateef Nacif for consultation and expressed displeasure at South Africa's position. Mbeki, making reference to the issue at the opening session of the AU Pan African Parliament in Midrand, South Africa, on 16 September 2004, just prior to the recognition announcement, said: 'It is a matter of great shame and regret to all of us that ... the issue of self-determination for the people of Western Sahara remains unresolved.'[20]

South Africa's position falls squarely within the SADC consensus on this issue, with the exception of Swaziland. South African diplomats have also argued that the lack of a resolution of the Western Sahara question among Maghreb states has impeded the development of the Arab Maghreb Union (AMU) and, also the goals of the African Union towards continental integration.[21] The AMU – one of the five sub-regional pillars of continental integration and of an African Standby Force (ASF) to be established by 2010 – has been largely moribund, and by 2006, its members had not met in over a decade.

The tension in bilateral relations between South Africa and Morocco was revealed on the two occasions that the countries vied for the right to host the football World Cup. In the contest for the 2006 competition, Rabat shunned the African call to allow Tshwane to make the bid for the continent in the final round. However, in the race for the 2010 bid – where an African winner was guaranteed by the International Football Federation (FIFA) – Morocco took the gloves off. Its state-controlled media made repeated, vituperative attacks on the social structure of South Africa, trying to promote a message that crime and the high incidence of HIV/AIDS made South Africa too dangerous a venue for the world's most prestigious sporting contest. By March 2007, Rabat conducted its diplomatic ties with Tshwane at the *chargé d'affaires* level without a full ambassador.

Libya: The diplomacy of accommodation

South Africa was ahead of the curve in its dealings with Libya. Long before the West had resumed political and economic relations with Tripoli, South Africa was questioning the wisdom of vilifying and isolating Qaddafi. Indeed, it could be argued that South Africa played a key role in Qaddafi's 'rehabilitation'. With UN sanctions still in force, Mandela visited Tripoli and Sirte to negotiate the Lockerbie deal in 1999.[22] He repeatedly defended his close relationship with Qaddafi, saying that neither the US nor any other power had the right to choose South Africa's friends for it.

However, this political relationship has not translated into significant economic ties. A South African business delegation, led by then minerals and energy affairs minister, Penuell Maduna, visited Sirte in 1999. It found that European business had moved quickly into Libya, even before the lifting of UN sanctions, to grab the most important projects in a country effectively rebuilding itself after nearly a decade of isolation. Qaddafi has shown himself to be extremely pragmatic in his business dealings, prioritising the bottom line over political ties.

As earlier noted, relations between Mbeki and Qaddafi have been characterised by a struggle for the soul of the African Union. Qaddafi is widely
acknowledged to have been the father of the process of transforming the OAU
into the AU, which was agreed at a special summit in Sirte in 1999. Qaddafi
then tried to have the inaugural summit of the new body moved to Libya from
South Africa in 2002. When he was unsuccessful, the Libyan leader upstaged
Mbeki whenever possible during this landmark occasion in Durban. One such
tactic was persistently to make impractical proposals for the new organisation,
including a single army, parliament and bank. Although these ideas were not
accepted by other leaders, Qaddafi's notions have been tolerated by African
leaders, including Mbeki, as have his spontaneous outbursts on AU platforms
against his perceived enemies.

Increasingly, South Africa and many other states are trying to shift Tripoli
away from what they see as its counterproductive 'chequebook' diplomacy,
through which it has bought political support from other African states by
paying their debts to the OAU.[23] As inaugural chair of the AU in 2002, Mbeki
attempted to accommodate Qaddafi by agreeing to another special summit in
Sirte to discuss the latter's elaborate plans for the organisation. In fact, much
of the energy generated between Tshwane and Tripoli has been expended on
managing a difficult relationship. But Qaddafi would later show less of an appetite
for Africa. He missed the AU summit in Addis Ababa in 2004, condescendingly
noting that he had put the African train on its tracks and seen it move down the
line. African leaders no longer needed his guidance, he said, but he nevertheless
left his lofty plans for the organisation on the agenda.

Both South Africa and Libya have common goals for strengthening African
unity and integration. Tshwane's approach differs from Tripoli's in that it is
process-driven with a different emphasis on method and a realistic timeframe
for African integration.

Tunisia: Human rights and poverty alleviation

Relations between South Africa and Tunisia got off to a good start, with Mandela
attending his first OAU summit in Tunis in 1994. Tunisian strongman Ben Ali
made a state visit to South Africa in 1995 and addressed the country's Parliament.
These ties, however, remain more symbolic than substantive.[24] Ben Ali literally
ordered Tunisian businesses to establish ties with their South African counterparts. The response from the South Africans was disappointing.

A bi-national commission has been established between Tshwane and Tunis, which had met three times by 2006. Tunisia's human rights failings notwithstanding, South Africa has expressed admiration for Ben Ali's poverty alleviation programmes and societal building projects. In spite of allegations of Tunisia being an oppressive state, South Africa also understands that this small country, sandwiched precariously between robust Libya and troubled Algeria, is forced to take extraordinary measures to guard against militancy and radicalism across its borders. As host to more than four million European tourists annually, Tunisia has had to safeguard its security. Having police on virtually all trains and buses might normally be considered the sign of a police state. In Tunisia's case, this may indicate an over-cautious administration protecting its most lucrative source of income.

During Mbeki's official state visit to Tunis in 1995 as deputy president, he volunteered South Africa to host the second Afro-Arab Trade fair, a project supported by the African Union. In a similar vein in 2003, the Malian chair of the AU Commission, Alpha Konaré, called for 'closer links between African and Arab markets to create a larger economic space within the framework of South-South cooperation'.[25]

Mbeki's October 2004 state visit to Tunisia as president helped to build on the ANC's historic friendship with Tunis. The late ANC president, Oliver Tambo – Mbeki's mentor – had been issued a Tunisian passport when denied one by apartheid South Africa. The focus of ties between the two countries has been on poverty alleviation, health and cultural cooperation. Tshwane and Tunis also have similar interests in peacekeeping initiatives in the Democratic Republic of the Congo (DRC) and Burundi, where Tunisian and South African soldiers have been stationed (see Curtis in this volume). Tunisia's poverty alleviation efforts of establishing a national solidarity fund and fulfilling the UN Millennium Development Goals of halving poverty by 2015 received attention in Mbeki's 2007 State of the Nation address.[26] Both South Africa and Tunisia have agreed that a 'Joint Military Committee' should meet alternately in Tunisia and South Africa, every 24 months.[27]

Egypt: Working with the regional giant

South Africa's relations with Egypt are among the most complex and competitive it has in Africa. Egypt's status as an African country has been questioned at the highest level by many African presidents.[28] Mubarak did not attend an

OAU or AU summit for a decade (with the exception of the Abuja meeting in 2005 when Egypt was seeking an African seat in a restructured UN Security Council), after an attempt was made to assassinate him in Addis Ababa in 1995 while attending an OAU summit. But Mubarak insisted on being part of the enlarged NEPAD Steering Committee and of the NEPAD implementation group, even though he did not attend most of their meetings.

However, Mubarak has attended summits of the Group of Eight industrialised countries (G8) as part of specially invited African delegations. Significantly, the Egyptian leader was not part of the African team at the 2004 G8 meeting on Sea Island in the US. Mubarak, who has been in power for over a quarter of a century, has not taken kindly to American pressure for democratisation.

Egyptian representatives on the continent have reacted angrily to South African suggestions that they are Africans only when it suits them, such as in their bid for the 2010 football World Cup. Cairo argued that its support for the majority of South Africans during the anti-apartheid struggle was beyond reproach, and took umbrage at its African credentials being questioned. Indeed, many South African cadres, such as the late Joseph Nduli, commissar of the ANC's armed wing, Umkhonto we Sizwe (MK), were based in Cairo during their years in exile. South Africa's first defence minister after 1994, the late Joe Modise, also set up ANC military bases in Egypt.[29]

Much of the difficulty in this bilateral relationship arises from Egypt's resentment at the multilateral role that South Africa has assumed, overshadowing Cairo as the continent's leader.[30] Egypt and South Africa share similar views on the Palestinian question and other contentious international issues, such as nuclear disarmament. But both countries remain rivals for the role of African leader in international matters. If and when the reform of the UN Security Council produces a permanent African seat, Egypt would expect to get it ahead of South Africa and vice-versa. Egypt mounted a late bid against South Africa to host the Pan-African Parliament in 2004, despite the fact that it was common knowledge that South Africa had been specifically requested, by several of its African colleagues at the African Union's 2002 Durban summit, to host the parliament. Predictably, the Addis Ababa summit in 2004 agreed to site the parliament in South Africa, despite Egypt's determination to show that it was a key player on decisions about continental issues. In the end, Cairo withdrew from the contest at the last minute.

The fact that Mubarak was seriously considering making a long-awaited state visit to South Africa in 2004 indicated that Cairo does want to build better relations with Tshwane, which can only be for the benefit of the continent. This suggests that Egypt may be re-examining its foreign policy goals towards South Africa within the changing global context. Currently, the relationship has moved beyond Egypt's losses of hosting the Pan-African Parliament and the 2010 World Cup to a greater emphasis on cooperation. Regular official exchanges now include a bi-national commission between Tshwane and Cairo meeting regularly at senior level.

SOUTH AFRICA AND THE HORN OF AFRICA

Moving from North Africa to the Horn of Africa: in Sudan's troubled western region of Darfur and in southern Somalia, the region currently contains what the popular media respectively labels 'the worst humanitarian crisis', the most ungovernable country and one of the most difficult political conundrums on the planet. The politics of whether the Darfur crisis is genocide, civil war, or both, remains fiercely contested.[31]

Those, like South Africa, that recognise the need to engage and assist this region have come to realise the need to adopt an inclusive and comprehensive approach, particularly in Africa's second most populous country Ethiopia, and Africa's largest country geographically, Sudan. Any attempt to address an isolated problem in a single country invariably leads to a crisis breaking out in another – all too often unravelling what was achieved in the first place. In its nine-page strategy document to encourage peace and stability on the Horn of Africa published in October 2006, the EU warned that if left unaddressed, problems in the Horn could easily flare into the rest of Africa, igniting further violence in the Middle East and possibly even spreading to Europe. The EU proposes introducing a budget envelope of €3 billion to reward countries in the Horn making headway on the 'good governance' benchmarks of respect for democratic values, human rights and the rule of law.[32]

It is ironic that even as this significant 2006 initiative was being announced by one of the region's most generous and sympathetic sources of humanitarian and development aid, at least two of the countries in this region were locking horns with representatives of the international community. The Ethiopian government expelled two EU diplomats ostensibly for trying to smuggle criminals into Kenya. Brussels maintained that the two – Italian and Swedish nationals – were in the company of an Ethiopian woman human rights lawyer who had been working for the European Commission in probing the crackdown by the government in Addis Ababa on opposition politicians and journalists. This followed the disputed outcome of the country's general election in 2005. At about the same time as these expulsions, the Sudanese government in Khartoum declared UN special representative Jan Pronk *persona non grata*, accusing him of waging war on the country's armed forces and asking that he leave the country. In fact, Pronk was being punished for pressuring the Sudanese government into accepting a 20 000 strong UN peacekeeping force in Darfur to replace the over-stretched and cash-strapped African Union force of 7 000, to which South Africa contributed.

South Africa does not have the resources to make a financial contribution of the magnitude of the EU's towards alleviating the crisis in the Horn of Africa. But as a country-by-country examination of its dealings with countries in the region will show, Tshwane does have the moral weight and the trust of fellow African governments that could enable it to exert some influence and play a supporting role, even if it has thus far avoided any direct intervention in this region. Increasingly, countries of the region, including the governments of Southern Sudan, Somaliland, Somalia, Ethiopia, and Eritrea have called for greater levels of South African engagement at the political, economic and educational levels.[33]

South Africa's general approach to conflict and instability on the continent is to lead by example, offer guidance, advice and support whenever asked, but to leave interventions to regional neighbours and in this case to the regional organisation: the Intergovernmental Authority on Development (IGAD). Thus South Africa's mediation effort in Côte d'Ivoire, for example, was undertaken at the specific behest of the African Union after the efforts by countries of the Economic Community of West African States (ECOWAS) had ground to a halt.

Sudan

At the second African Union summit in Maputo in 2003, South Africa was asked, but refused to get involved in efforts to broker a peace deal between the Khartoum government and the Sudan People's Liberation Movement/Army led by John Garang. Tshwane, however, agreed to chair the AU's Ministerial Committee on Post-Conflict Reconstruction in Sudan.[34]

After 1994, then president Nelson Mandela had met Sudanese president Omar al-Bashir and John Garang several times, urging them to seek a negotiated solution to Africa's longest-running civil war. From 1999, Mbeki maintained contact with both sides. He understood well the need to promote peace and reconstruction in Africa's largest country, if his vision of an African Renaissance was to take root and become a reality. Nevertheless, Mbeki declined the request to become directly involved as a mediator in Sudan.

As earlier noted, South Africa agreed to chair the AU committee for the reconstruction of Sudan. In this capacity, Tshwane was kept informed about progress in negotiations and the success of the mediation efforts by IGAD. South Africa waited for the peace accord between the government and the SPLM/A to be signed before building on its bilateral relations with Khartoum. Mbeki made his first visit to the Sudanese capital on the eve of the signing of what has become known as the Naivasha Agreement in January 2005.[35] Since then, relations have progressed to the stage where South Africa was opening a consulate in the southern capital of Juba by March 2007 and the government of Southern Sudan was planning to open an office in Tshwane.

Members of the South African army and the South African Police Service (SAPS) are among the 7 000-strong African Union Mission in Darfur, a region where the Sudanese government is widely accused of fomenting massacres. The University of South Africa (Unisa) and the South African government are involved in assisting the Sudanese government in a capacity-building programme, hosting public servants from Khartoum and Juba on courses in South Africa.[36]

Eritrea

A small South African contingent is part of the UN force of 3 800 peacekeepers monitoring the 1 000 kilometre buffer zone between Eritrea and Ethiopia since the end of the two-and-a-half year war between these two countries in 2000. These troops have provided expertise, where required, on border demarcation, an issue central to the dispute still bedevilling relations between these two countries. South Africa is one of the signatories of the peace deal between Addis Ababa and Asmara in 2000, and encouraged Algeria to facilitate the peace process between the two neighbours.

After opening an embassy in Asmara, South Africa is using its influence and resources to support Eritrea's tenuous truce with Ethiopia. Attempts at developing business relations with Eritrea have, however, not progressed well, with several South African businesses complaining that Eritrea is not a business-friendly environment.

Ethiopia

Nowhere else in Africa is South Africa's determination to 'walk the talk' on its vision for an African Renaissance more evident than in Ethiopia. This is hardly surprising since the country's capital, Addis Ababa, hosts the headquarters of the African Union. Hotel records in Ethiopia reveal that South Africa sends more delegations to African Union meetings than any other member state. Construction is also underway in Addis Ababa of South Africa's largest embassy in Africa.

Relations are being built on the bilateral commission between Tshwane and Addis Ababa which meets regularly at director-general level. This commission focuses mainly on encouraging economic interaction between both countries. Mbeki and Ethiopian leader Meles Zenawi are both members of the Progressive Governance Forum, with Meles serving as one of the eminent persons on British premier Tony Blair's Commission for Africa in 2005, along with South African finance minister, Trevor Manuel. Meles'[37] reputation was, however, badly damaged following a crackdown on opposition politicians and journalists protesting the disputed outcome of elections in 2005. Under Meles' administration, Ethiopia has been at war with Eritrea over border disputes, Ethiopian troops are in southern Somalia and is reliant on US support. Armed uprisings in Ethiopia's Oromo and Somali regions continue.

Under increasing international and domestic pressure, Meles has been driven closer to South Africa as the pivotal continental power and the country most willing to provide capacity-building assistance at the public sector level. In January 2007, South Africa proposed Meles as chair of the NEPAD heads of state implementation committee. In the same year, the University of South Africa also opened a regional campus, at the request of the Ethiopian government, to assist the University's involvement in capacity-building efforts in order to meet the country's increasing need for graduates to lead its educational development initiatives. Business links between the two countries have progressed steadily, along with Ethiopian Airlines' successful and regular direct flights between Addis Ababa and Johannesburg.

Djibouti

South Africa plans to open an embassy in Djibouti where both the US and France maintain a military presence – in a country that enjoys relative stability. Djibouti has an honorary consular official in South Africa represented by a

Johannesburg businessman. Its mercurial president, Ismael Omar Guelleh, is a difficult man with whom to do business, although bilateral economic relations are increasing between Tshwane and Djibouti. Guelleh has had to do some fence-mending with the South African government, having publicly called for Libya to host the inaugural summit of the African Union after it had been decided that Durban should be the venue for the event in 2002.

Somalia

Moving from Djibouti to Somalia; South Africa has supported the regional IGAD initiative on Somalia that includes recognising the transitional government of Abdulahi Yusuf, just as it did the previous transitional administration, which did not have an ability to govern to match the international status accorded it. The Yusuf government has been given even more muscular international backing, but has largely been unable to translate this into bringing the country out of the 16 years of anarchy it was plunged into following the fall of US-backed dictator, Siad Barre, in 1991.

South Africa has maintained close contact with the Kenyan and Ethiopian governments, which are the strongest supporters of the transitional government. Through these countries and its own intelligence gathering, Tshwane has followed issues in Somalia. But South Africa has been more cautious in its dealings with the current transitional government than it was with its predecessor. Mbeki has also resisted calls from IGAD to become more directly and formally involved in the negotiation process.

South Africa is considering capacity-building and training opportunities in South Africa for the transitional government's police and army. A South African national and leading diplomat, Welile Nhlapo, represented the UN in the International Contact Group meetings on Somalia. But developments in early 2007, following an Ethiopian military intervention that helped the transitional government capture Mogadishu from Islamists with US assistance, have made South Africa cautious about becoming embroiled in furthering American and other interests in stabilising Mogadishu.[38]

Somaliland

Finally, I conclude this survey of South Africa's role in the Horn with the case of Somaliland. Both Ethiopia and Kenya have urged South Africa either to bite the diplomatic bullet and become the first country to recognise the democratically elected government in Mogadishu, or at least to increase its engagement with the breakaway Somaliland administration in the north of the country.

Officially, South Africa has acknowledged that the Somaliland issue is not one of secession – which is anathema to the African Union – but rather a special case.[39] Somaliland is a former British colony that was granted independence in its own right. Subsequently it formed a union with the former Italian colony of Somalia and, according to its officials, chose to quit this union after the attacks launched on it by Siad Barre. There is a precedent for this move in Africa: Eritrea's independence from Ethiopia in 1993.

South Africa maintains, however, that diplomatic recognition of Somaliland must be led by the AU. Tshwane has taken a clear position of backing the 2005 African Union report stipulating that Somaliland is a special case that should not be punished for going back to its British colonial boundaries.[40] South Africa is among the African countries lobbying for this AU report to be translated into concrete action, tacitly leading to membership of the organisation. Tshwane regards the political and economic progress made in Somaliland as highly significant in the wider context of peace in Somalia. South Africa is also at pains to ensure that any progress made on the Somalia issue should not undermine the democratic progress and stability achieved by Somaliland.

Former Somaliland president Mohammed Egal died in a South African hospital in 2001.[41] His successor Dahir Riyale Kahin made a working visit to South Africa in February 2006, and officials from South Africa have been regular visitors to Hargeisa.

CONCLUDING REFLECTIONS: PROMOTING BILATERAL AND MULTILATERAL DEVELOPMENT

Politically and administratively, the South African government has built a road linking Tshwane to North and Horn of African capitals. Mbeki and his foreign affairs officials have invested much political capital in developing South Africa's critical links with North Africa and the Horn as part of its larger strategic goal 'to participate in the titanic and protracted struggle to achieve Africa's renewal'.[42] It is now up to South Africa's business and non-governmental (NGO) community to make use of the highway to build greater contact with two important regions of the Red Sea, Mediterranean basin and the Gulf linked to the Middle East and Africa.

There are huge opportunities, particularly in Algeria, Libya, Sudan and Ethiopia which have yet to be taken up. Thus far, only South Africa's more adventurous mining houses and larger corporations in the petro-chemical and construction fields have even considered doing business in many of these countries (see Hudson in this volume).

There are logistical problems for people wanting to travel between the North and South of the continent. Direct air links between Johannesburg and Casablanca and Johannesburg and Algiers have not proved viable. This has necessitated travel via Europe or other parts of Africa, which can be costly and inconvenient. The Johannesburg-Cairo air link has survived and remains a cumbersome stopover to other North African capitals. The Ethiopian Airline link with Addis Ababa has proved more successful. However, notwithstanding these problems, unless contact between North Africa, the Horn of Africa, and the rest of the continent increases, the danger exists that North Africa especially, will be drawn ever more into the European orbit. This is already happening at an accelerated rate with special market access arrangements being negotiated between the European Union and the countries of the Mediterranean basin.

In moments of candour, leaders of North Africa and Sudan confess to a certain political identity crisis. Are they African, Arab, or Mediterranean? Properly engaged by South Africa in its capacity as the emerging continental power, these leaders will be left in no doubt as to their core identity: African.[43]

Notes and references

INTRODUCTION

1   Adebayo Adedeji (ed). 1996. *South Africa and Africa: Within or Apart?* London: Zed Books.

2   For some recent studies on South Africa's post-apartheid foreign policy, see: Chris Alden and Garth Le Pere. 2003. 'South Africa's Post-Apartheid Foreign Policy – From Reconciliation to Revival?' *Adelphi Paper* 362. London: Institute for Strategic Studies. Also: James Barber. 2004. *Mandela's World: The International Dimension of South Africa's Political Revolution, 1990–99.* Cape Town: David Philip. Also: Walter Carlsnaes and Philip Nel (eds). 2006. *In Full Flight: South African Foreign Policy after Apartheid.* Midrand, South Africa: Institute For Global Dialogue. Also: Chris Landsberg. 2004. *The Quiet Diplomacy of Liberation: International Politics and South Africa's Transition.* Johannesburg: Jacana. Also: Elizabeth Sidiropoulos (ed). 2004. *South Africa's Foreign Policy 1994–2004: Apartheid Past, Renaissance Future.* Johannesburg: The South African Institute of International Affairs. And: Roger Southall (ed). 2006. *South Africa's Role in Conflict Resolution and Peacemaking in Africa: Conference Proceedings.* Cape Town: Human Sciences Research Council.

3   Adedeji (ed). 1996 above. *South African in Africa: Within or Apart?* London: Zed Books, p. 9.

4   Quoted in: James Barber and John Barrett. 1990. *South Africa's Foreign Policy.* Cambridge: Cambridge University Press, p. 6.

5   Quoted in: Peter Vale and Sipho Maseko. 2002. 'The African Renaissance'. In: Sean Jacobs and Richard Calland (eds). *Thabo Mbeki's World: The Politics and Ideology of the South African President.* Pietermaritzburg: University of KwaZulu-Natal Press, p. 122.

6   'South Africa in Africa: The Post-Apartheid Decade'. 2004. Cape Town: Centre for Conflict Resolution; Johannesburg: Centre for Policy Studies; Nigeria: ACDESS. Seminar report. Cape Town, 29 July–1 August. http://ccrweb.ccr.uct.ac.za.

7   'Budget Speech by Dr Zola Skweyiya, Minister of Social Development, to the National Assembly, Cape Town', 28 March 2007, available at http://www.sassa.gov.za/news/speeches/2007/20070328_1.asp.

8   Ben Turok. 'The Debate about Reconstruction and Development in South Africa'. In: Adedeji. 1996 above. *South Africa in Africa,* pp. 141–163.

9   South Africa's administrative capital city, until recently named Pretoria (after a 19th century Afrikaner leader), was renamed Tshwane in May 2005. Pretoria continues to be the name of the central business district.

10 Adekeye Adebajo and Chris Landsberg. 2003. 'South Africa and Nigeria as Regional

Hegemons'. In: Mwesiga Baregu and Chris Landsberg (eds). *From Cape to Congo: Southern Africa's Evolving Security Challenges*. Boulder and London: Lynne Rienner Publishers, pp. 171–203.

11   Adekeye Adebajo. 2005. 'The Pied Piper of Pretoria'. *Global Dialogue*.

12   African National Congress. 1994. 'Developing a Strategic Perspective on South Africa's Foreign Policy'. ANC Discussion Document. Johannesburg: Shell House, p. 60.

13   Chris Landsberg. 2000. 'Promoting Democracy: The Mandela-Mbeki doctrine'. *Journal of Democracy*, July.

14   This is a theme that has run through most of Mbeki's speeches on the African Renaissance and African affairs since 1999. See also http://www.anc.org.za/ancdocs/history/mbeki.

15   Thabo Mbeki. 1995. 'A National Strategic vision for South Africa'. Address to the Development Planning Summit, hosted by the Intergovernmental Forum. Pretoria, 27 November, pp. 2–4. Also: Thabo Mbeki. 1997. 'Africa: the Time has Come'. Address to the Corporate Council on Africa's Attracting Capital to Africa summit. Chantilly, Virginia, 19–22 April, pp. 2–4.

16   Mbeki. 1995 and 1997 above. 'A National Strategic vision' & 'Africa: the Time has Come'.

17   Thabo Mbeki. 1998. 'The African Renaissance Statement'. South African Broadcasting Corporation (SABC). Johannesburg, Gallagher Estate. 13 August, p. 4.

18   Mbeki. 1998 above. 'The African Renaissance Statement'.

19   'Peacemaking in Southern Africa: The Role and Potential of the Southern African Development Community (SADC)'. 2002. Task Force Meeting. International Peace Academy and Johannesburg: The Centre for Africa's International Relations: October.

20   Chris Landsberg. 2002. 'Building a Regional Society in Southern Africa: The Institutional Governance Dimension.' *Policy: Issues and Actors* 1(15). Centre for Policy Studies, November.

21   'NEPAD: African Initiative, New Partnership?' 2002. International Peace Academy Workshop Report. New York, 16 July.

22   NEPAD Secretariat. 2002. 'NEPAD at Work'. Summary of NEPAD Action Plans. Midrand, July.

23   NEPAD. 2002. 'NEPAD workshop on Indicators, Benchmarks and Processes for the African Peer Review Mechanism (APRM)'. Cape Town, 7–8 October.

24   Kevin Humphrey. 1996. 'Interview with the Deputy Minister of Foreign Affairs'. *Towards Democracy* (1st Quarter), p. 7.

25   Claude Kabemba and Chris Landsberg. 1998. 'South African Diplomacy: Ten Lessons from Africa'. *Policy Brief* 2. Johannesburg: Centre for Policy Studies.

26   Kabemba and Landsberg. 1998 above. 'South African Diplomacy', p. 3.

27   Briefing by Deputy Minister of Foreign Affairs, Aziz Pahad. 2003. GCIS Parliamentary Briefings, Cape Town, 10 September.

28   Pahad briefing. 2003 above.

29   Pahad briefing. 2003 above.

30   The rollout of antiretroviral treatment in the public sector had reached 245 670 people by March 2007, according to the government: 'Speech by the Acting Minister

of Health, Jeff Radebe, at the National Consultative Conference on HIV and AIDS', 14 March 2007, http://www.info.gov.za/speeches/2007/07031514451001.htm. But Nathan Geffen of the Treatment Action Campaign (personal correspondence, 12 April 2007) said monitoring and evaluation of the rollout was not good enough for there to be any certainty about this figure.

CHAPTER 1. SOUTH AFRICA AND AFRICA'S POLITICAL ECONOMY: LOOKING INSIDE FROM THE OUTSIDE

1   The subtitle has been inspired by Manfred Max-Neff's 1992 classic, *From the Outside Looking In: Experiences in Barefoot Economics*. London: Zed Books.

2   Adebayo Adedeji. 1994. *Africa Within the World: Beyond Depression and Dependence*. London: ACCDES and Zed Books, p. 3.

3   Mbaya Kankwenda. 2004. 'Forty Years of Development Illusions: Revisiting Development Policies and Practices in Africa'. In: Bade Onimode and others. *African Development and Governance Strategies in the 21st Century: Looking Back to Move Forward. Essays in Honour of Adebayo Adedeji at Seventy*. London and New York: Zed Books, pp. 3–19.

4   Adebayo Adedeji and Jeggan Colley Senghor, (eds). 1989. *Towards a Dynamic African Economy: Selected Speeches and Lectures 1975–1989*. London and Totowa: N.J.F Cass, pp. 15–38.

5   Adebayo Adedeji. 1994 above. *Africa Within the World*.

6   D.R. Howarth. 1998. 'Paradigms Gained? A Critique of Theories and Explanations of Democratic Transitions in South Africa'. In: D.R. Howarth and Aletta J. Norval (eds). *South Africa in Transition: New Theoretical Perspectives*. London: Macmillan.

7   *In Larger Freedom: Towards Development, Security and Human Rights For All*, Report of the UN Secretary-General Kofi Annan. Follow-up to the outcome of the Millennium Summit, 21 March 2005. A/59/2005.

8   Amos Sawyer. 2004. 'Governance and Democratisation'. In: Adekeye Adebajo and Ismail Rashid (eds). *Building Peace in a Troubled Region: West Africa's Security Challenges*. Boulder and London: Lynne Rienner Publishers.

9   See, for example, Christopher Landsberg. 2004. *The Quiet Diplomacy of Liberation: International Politics and South Africa's Transition*. Johannesburg: Jacana Media.

10 Adebajo Adedeji. 2004. 'ECOWAS, a Retrospective Journey'. In: Adebajo and Rashid (eds). *Building Peace in a Troubled Region*, pp. 21–29; see also Adebayo Adedeji. 2002. 'From the Lagos Plan of Action to the New Partnership for Africa's Development and from the Final Act of Lagos to the Constitutive Act: Whither Africa?' In: Peter Anyang' Nyong'o, Asghedech Ghirmazion, Davinder Lamba (eds). *New Partnership for Africa's Development, NEPAD: A New Path?* Nairobi: Heinrich Böll Foundation.

11 Freedom Charter. 1955. African National Congress website: http://www.anc.org.za/anc-docs/history/charter.html.

12 'Budget Speech by Dr Zola Skweyiya, Minister of Social Development, to the National Assembly, Cape Town', 28 March 2007, available at http://www.sassa.gov.za/news/speeches/2007/20070328_1.asp.

13 Omano Edigheji (ed). 2005. 'Trajectories For South Africa: Reflections on the ANC's 2nd

National General Council's Discussion Documents'. *Issues and Actors* 18(2). Johannesburg: Centre For Policy Studies, June.

14 Adebayo Adedeji (ed). 1996. *South Africa in Africa: Within or Apart?* London and Ijebu-Ode, Nigeria: Zed Books and ACDESS.

15 See, for example: John Daniel, Varusha Naidoo and Sanusha Naidu. 2003. 'Post-Apartheid South Africa's Corporate Expansion into Africa'. *Africa Business Journal* 15, August–November.

CHAPTER 2. BLACK ECONOMIC EMPOWERMENT: MYTHS AND REALITIES

1 Roger Southall. 2005. 'Black Empowerment and Corporate Capital'. In: John Daniel, Roger Southall and Jessica Lutchman (eds). *State of the Nation: South Africa 2004–2005.* Cape Town: HSRC Press; Roger Southall. 2004. 'The ANC and Black Capitalism in South Africa'. *Review of African Political Economy* 100(31), June; and Roger Southall. 2006. 'Black Empowerment and Present Limits to a more Democratic Capitalism in South Africa'. In: S. Buhlungu, R. Southall, and J. Lutchman (eds). *State of the Nation: South Africa 2005–2006.* Cape Town: HSRC Press.

2 For accounts of dispossession in South Africa see: G. Mbeki. 1984. *South Africa: The Peasants' Revolt.* London: Idaf; Colin Bundy. 1988. *The Rise And Fall of the South African Peasantry.* Second edition. Johannesburg: David Philip; and P. Delius. 1996. *A Lion Amongst The Cattle: Reconstruction and Resistance in The Northern Transvaal.* Johannesburg: Ravan Press.

3 Department of Trade and Industry. 'South Africa's Economic Transformation: A Strategy for Broad Based BEE'. http://www.dti.gov.za/bee/complete.pdf (accessed March 2007), pp. 13–14.

4 Black Economic Empowerment Commission. 2001. *Report of the Black Economic Empowerment Commission.* Johannesburg: Skotaville Press.

5 See, for example, *Business Day,* 8 November 2005, reporting on the Sun International empowerment transaction.

6 IRIN. 2004. 'South Africa: Anger over Enrichment of Black Elite'. http://www.IRINnews.org (accessed 11 November 2004).

7 Kgalema Motlanthe. 2005. 'Speech to the Black Management Forum', October.

8 Blade Nzimande. 2005. 'Black Economic Empowerment in South Africa: Towards a Lecture'. Paper delivered at the Centre for International Political Studies, University of Pretoria, 4 May. See especially point 4.3 on p. 2.

9 A list of 'The Wealthiest' in South Africa was published by the *Sunday Times* 21 December 2005. It gives an idea of the wealth of both blacks and whites in South Africa. The amounts shown represent listed assets owned by those named. Many are worth more money than is shown.

10 *Sunday Times,* 21 December 2005. The total value of Saki Macozoma's investments are estimated at R73,55 million, based on a stake of 0,45 per cent of Liberty Group.

11 *Sunday Times* above. The total value of Patrice Motsepe's investments are estimated at R2,85 billion, based on a 42,92 per cent shareholding in African Rainbow Minerals.

12 Cyril Ramaphosa's name does not appear in the list presumably because his assets are not listed. He is often mentioned among very wealthy black individuals in South Africa.

13   *Sunday Times*. 2005 above. The total value of investment is put at R260,92 million from stakes in Mvelaphanda Resources and Northam Platinum.

14   Jeffrey Herbst. 2005. 'Mbeki's South Africa'. *Foreign Affairs*, November/December, pp. 100–103.

15   Moeletsi Mbeki. 2005. 'Underdevelopment in Sub-Saharan Africa: the Role of the Private Sector and Political Elites'. *Foreign Policy Briefing*, 85 (15), April, p. 9.

16   Sunday Times.co.za. 7 May 2005.

17   L. Schlemmer. 2005. 'Lost In Transformation'. CDE *Focus* 8. September, p. 1. This paper focuses on the black African, rather than black (including mixed race and Indian), middle class. The author also challenges the notion of a huge growth of the black middle class.

18   Roger Southall. 2004. 'Political Change and the Black Middle Class in Democratic South Africa'. *The Canadian Journal of African Studies* 3 (38).

19   C. Bisseker. 2005. 'The Black Middle Class: Pump Up The Volume'. *Financial Mail*, 16 December.

20   Herbst, 'Mbeki's South Africa', p. 100.

21   Blade Nzimande, Speech delivered at the Black Management Forum conference, October 2005.

22   Schlemmer, 2005 above. Also Southall, 2004 above.

23   'The Long Journey of a Young Democracy'. *The Economist* 8518(382), 3–9 March 2007, p. 24.

24   These are set out in the 'Codes of Good Practice for Broad-Based Black Economic Empowerment'. SA DTI 2005. http://www.dti.gov.za/bee/CODESOFGOODPRACTICE2005.htm (accessed March 2007).

25   'The Codes of Good Practice'. 2005 above.

26   Employment Equity Act (55 of 1998).

27   Skills Development Act (97 of 1998).

CHAPTER 3. RACE AND RECONCILIATION: *E PLURIBUS UNUM*?

1   Eugene de Kock and J. Gordin. 1998. *A Long Night's Damage: Working for the Apartheid State*. Johannesburg: Contra Press, p. 277.

2   Post-amble in Interim Constitution. South African Interim Constitution Act (200 of 1993).

3   Leon Wessels. 2001. 'The End of an Era: The Liberation and Confession of an Afrikaner'. In: *The Post-Apartheid Constitutions: Perspectives on South Africa's Basic Law*. Johannesburg: Witwatersrand University Press.

4   Johnny De Lange. 2000. 'The Historical Context, Legal Origins and Philosophical Foundation of the South African Truth and Reconciliation Commission'. In: Charles Villa-Vincencio and W. Verwoerd (eds). *Looking Back, Reaching Forward: Reflections on the Truth and Reconciliation Commission of South Africa*. Cape Town: University of Cape Town Press, p. 17.

5   De Lange. 2000 above, p. 17.

6   Post-amble in Interim Constitution. 1993 above.

7   De Lange. 2000 above, p. 17.

8   The Azanian Peoples Organisation (AZAPO) and others vs The President of the Republic of South Africa CCT 17/96 (paragraph 31).

9   AZAPO vs The President. 1996 above (paragraph 170).

10   Priscilla B. Hayner. 2001. *Confronting State Terror and Atrocities*. New York and London: Routledge, p. 155.

11   Mahmood Mamdani. 1997. 'From Justice to Reconciliation. Making Sense of the African Experience'. Discussion Paper 8. Uppsala: Nordic Africa Institute.

12   Drew Forrest. 1998. 'Body has served National Reconciliation'. *Business Day*, 3 August.

13   Forrest. 1998 above.

14   Quoted in: Hayner. 2001 above. *Confronting State Terror and Atrocities*, p. 160.

15   Quoted in: Hayner. 2001 above. *Confronting State Terror and Atrocities*, p. 160.

16   Quoted in: Hayner. 2001 above. *Confronting State Terror and Atrocities*, p. 161.

17   Hansard. 1998. 'Debate on Reconciliation and Nation Building'. Cape Town: National Assembly, 29 May, http://www.info.gov/speeches/1999/99225_trc-ma99_10201.htm.

18   *South African Reconciliation Barometer* 5. Cape Town: Institute for Justice and Reconciliation, p. 4.

CHAPTER 4. SOUTH AFRICA IN AFRICA: BEHEMOTH, HEGEMON, PARTNER OR 'JUST ANOTHER KID ON THE BLOCK'?

1   P. Berger. 2004. 'Foreign Policy for a Democratic President'. *Foreign Affairs*. May/June, pp. 49–51.

2   See, for example: M. Webber and M. Smith. 2002. *Foreign Policy in a Transformed World*. Harlow: Pearson Education Ltd, p. 56.

3   A. Habib and N. Selinyane. 2004. 'South Africa's foreign policy and a realistic vision of an African century'. In: E. Sidiropoulos (ed). *South Africa's Foreign Policy 1994–2004: Apartheid Past, Renaissance Future*. Johannesburg: South African Institute of International Affairs, p. 49.

4   J. Spence. 2004. 'South Africa's Foreign Policy: Vision and Reality'. In: E. Sidiropoulos. 2004. *South Africa's Foreign Policy*, p. 36.

5   See, for example: Patrick Bond. 2003. *South Africa and Global Apartheid: Continental and International Policies and Politics*, (Uppsala: Nordiska Afrikainstutet) Discussion Paper 25.

6   Adebayo Adedeji (ed). 1996. *South Africa and Africa: Within or Apart?* London: Zed Books, pp. 4–27.

7   Adebayo Adedeji (ed). 1996 above.

8   Nkosazana Dlamini-Zuma. 2003. 'South Africa and Africa in the World'. Address by the Minister of Foreign Affairs, London, 25 October, http://www.info.gov.za.

9   *ANC Today*. 18 June 2004. Adapted from a parliamentary media briefing by the Department of Foreign Affairs, 24 May.

10   Chris Landsberg. 2000. 'Promoting Democracy: the Mandela-Mbeki Doctrine'. *Journal of Democracy* 11. 3 July, p. 107.

11   *South African Yearbook of International Affairs 2002/03.* Johannesburg: South African Institute of International Affairs, pp. 398–399.

12   John Daniel and Jessica Lutchman. 'South Africa in Africa: Scrambling for Energy' in S. Buhlungu, J. Daniel, R. Southall and J. Lutchman (eds). 2006. *State of the Nation: South Africa 2005–2006.* Pretoria: Human Sciences Research Council, p. 488.

13   M. Webber and M. Smith. 2002. *Foreign Policy in a Transformed World.* Harlow: Pearson Education Ltd, p. 45.

14   Patrick Bond. 2003 above, p. 5.

15   Patrick Bond. 2004. *Talk Left, Walk Right: South Africa's Frustrated Global Reforms.* Scotsville, South Africa: University of KwaZulu-Natal Press.

16   Note that: 'The bifurcated character of the country's foreign policy is shown by its ability to play a leadership [i.e. a hegemonic role] and persuade other states to subscribe to its vision on the one hand, and its tendency to be persuaded by pragmatic factors to act as only one among the many in regional engagement.' See: A. Habib and N. Selinyane, 2004 above, p. 55.

17   J. Grieco, and G.J. Ikenberry. 2003. *State Power and World Markets: The International Political Economy.* New York: WW Norton and Co, p. 112.

CHAPTER 5. SOUTH AFRICA AND REGIONAL SECURITY IN SOUTHERN AFRICA

1   Adebayo Adedeji (ed). 1996. *South Africa & Africa: Within or Apart?* London: Zed Books.

2   Government of South Africa. 2003. 'Towards a Ten Year Review?' Mimeo. October, p. 112.

3   Adam Habib and Nthakeng Selinyane. 'South Africa's Foreign Policy and a Realistic Vision of an African Century'. In: E. Sidiropoulos (ed). 2004. *South Africa's Foreign Policy 1994–2004: Apartheid Past, Renaissance Future.* Johannesburg: South African Institute for International Affairs.

4   Sam Nolutshungu. *The South African State and Africa.* In: Bernard Magubane and Ibbo Mandaza (eds). 1988. *Wither South Africa?* Trenton: Africa World Press.

5   Robert Rotberg. 1995. 'Centripetal Forces: Regional Convergence in Southern Africa', *Harvard International Review* 27(4).

6   Mwesiga Baregu and Chris Landsberg (eds). 2003. *From Cape to Congo: Southern Africa's Evolving Security Challenges.* Boulder: Lynne Rienner Publishers; a comparative analysis for West Africa is found in Adekeye Adebajo and Ismail Rashid (eds). 2004. *West Africa's Security Challenges: Building Peace in a Troubled Region.* Boulder: Lynne Rienner Publishers.

7   Khabele Matlosa (ed). 2001. *Migration and Development in Southern Africa: Policy Reflections.* Harare: SAPES Books. See also Peter Vale and Khabele Matlosa. 1995. 'Beyond the Nation-State: Rebuilding Southern Africa from Below'. *Harvard International Review* 27(4).

8   UNDP. 2005. Human Development Report: *International Cooperation at a Crossroad: Aid, Trade and Security.* Oxford: Oxford University Press.

9   UNDP. 2005 above. *International Cooperation.*

10 Samir Amin. 1981. 'Underdevelopment and Dependence in Black Africa – Origins and Contemporary Forms'. In: D. Cohen, and J. Daniel (eds). 1981. *Political Economy of Africa: Selected Readings*. London: Longman.

11 Khabele Matlosa (ed). 2001. *Migration and Development in Southern Africa*.

12 Peter Vale and Khabele Matlosa. 1995. 'Beyond the Nation-State: Rebuilding Southern Africa from Below', *Harvard International Review* 27(4).

13 Robert Rotberg. 1995. 'Centripetal Forces: Regional Convergence in Southern Africa'. *Harvard International Review* 27(4).

14 Adedeji. 1996 above. *South Africa and Africa*, p. 13.

15 Nelson Mandela. 1995. 'Building Together: A Plan for National Reconstruction'. *Harvard International Review* 27(4).

16 On the concept of *Pax Africana*, see Ali Mazrui. 1967. *Towards a Pax Africana*. Chicago: University of Chicago Press.

17 Olusegun Obasanjo. 1996. 'A Balance Sheet of the African Region and the Cold War'. In: Edmond Keller and Donald Rothchild (eds). *Africa in the New International Order: Rethinking State Sovereignty and Regional Security*. Boulder: Lynne Rienner Publishers.

18 SADC. 1992. Treaty Establishing the Southern African Development Community. Gaborone: SADC Secretariat; Also: Garth Le Pere and Elling Tjonneland. 2005. 'Which Way SADC? Advancing Cooperation and Integration in Southern Africa'. *Occasional Paper* 50, October. Johannesburg: Institute for Global Dialogue.

19 Khabele Matlosa. 2001. 'Dilemmas of security in Southern Africa: the case of Lesotho'. In: N. Poku. 2001. *Security and Development in Southern Africa*. London: Praeger. Also: Khabele Matlosa. 2001. 'Dilemmas of Security in Southern Africa: Problems and Prospects for Security Cooperation' in Eddie Maloka (ed). *A United States of Africa*. Pretoria: Africa Institute of South Africa.

20 Peter Vale. 2003. *Security and Politics in South Africa: The Regional Dimension*. Boulder: Lynne Reinner Publishers.

21 Francis Makoa. 2004. 'Conflict Resolution in Southern Africa: Trading Democracy for Regional Peace'. In: Alfred Nhema (ed). *The Quest for Peace in Africa: Transformations, Democracy and Public Policy*. Addis Ababa: OSSREA Books.

22 Christopher Landsberg. 2004. *The Quiet Diplomacy of Liberation: International Politics and South Africa's Transition*. Johannesburg: Jacana.

23 Jakkie Cilliers and Richard Cornwell. 1999. 'Mercenaries and the Privatisation of Security in Africa', *African Security Review* 8 (2).

24 SADC summit brochure. Maseru, Lesotho, 24 August 1996

25 Hussein Solomon. 2004. 'State vs Human Security: Reflections on the SADC Organ on Politics, Defence and Security Cooperation'. In: Hussein Solomon (ed). *Towards a Common Defence and Security Policy in the Southern African Development Community*. Pretoria: Africa Institute of South Africa. Also: Gina van Schalkwyk. 2005. 'Friend or Foe: Civil Society Organisations and Peace and Security in SADC'. In: Anna Hammerstad (ed). *People, States and Regions: Building a Collaborative Security Regime in Southern Africa*. Johannesburg: South African Institute of International Affairs.

26 Jakkie Cilliers. 1999. 'Building Security in Southern Africa: An update on the Evolving Architecture'. Pretoria: Institute for Security Studies Monograph Series 43.

27 SADC. 2001. 'The Protocol on Politics, Defense and Security'. Gaborone, Botswana, p. 4.

28 Habib and Selinyane. 2004. 'South Africa's Foreign Policy and a Realistic Vision of an African Century'.

29 Garth Shelton. 2004. 'The South African National Defence Force (SANDF) and President Mbeki's Peace and Security Agenda: New roles and mission'. Institute for Global Dialogue Occasional Paper 42, March.

30 *This Day*, 8 July 2004.

31 Quoted in Shelton, 2004. 'The SANDF and President Mbeki's Peace and Security Agenda'. pp. 37, 41.

32 ANC. 2004. 'A People's Contract to Create Work and Fight Poverty'. Election Manifesto (mimeo).

33 Rok Ajulu. 2002. 'Survival in a Rough Neighbourhood: Lesotho's Foreign Policy in the era of Globalisation'. In: K. Adar. and R. Ajulu (eds). *Globalisation and Emerging Trends in African States' Foreign Policy-Making Process*. Hampshire: Ashgate.

34 Ajulu. 2005 above, p. 66.

35 SADC. 2004. 'SADC Principles and Guidelines Governing Democratic Elections'. Gaborone: SADC Secretariat (mimeo).

36 SADC. 2004. 'Strategic Indicative Plan for the Organ (SIPO)'. Gaborone: SADC Secretariat (mimeo).

37 SADC. 2004 above, p. 6.

38 Adekeye Adebajo. 2004. 'South Africa: Messiah or Mercantalist?' *This Day*, 5 May.

CHAPTER 6. SOUTH AFRICA'S ECONOMIC EXPANSION INTO AFRICA: NEO-COLONIALISM OR DEVELOPMENT?

1 'SA tops Africa's investors' list'. *Financial Mail,* 7 February 2003.

2 Quoted in D. Christianson. 2004. 'South Africans doing business in Africa: The new imperialists'. *Enterprise,* December, p. 78.

3 *New York Times,* 17 February 2002.

4 N. Grobbelaar. 2005. 'Investing in Africa: SA's influence a mixed blessing'. *Business Day,* 1 June.

5 N. Grobbelaar. 2005 above. 'Investing in Africa'.

6 R. Rumney and M. Pingo. 2004. 'Mapping South Africa's trade and investment'. Presentation at the Human Sciences Research Council, May.

7 D. Games. 2004. 'The experience of South African firms doing business in Africa: A preliminary survey and analysis'. *South African Institute of International Affairs Report* 1, p. 20.

8 Neuma Grobbelaar. 2004. 'Every continent needs an America: The experience of South African firms doing business in Mozambique'. *South African Institute of International Affairs, Business in Africa Report* 2, p. 27.

9   N. Grobbelaar. 2004 above. 'Every continent needs an America', p. 30.

10 *Financial Mail,* 7 February 2003.

11 Quoted in E. Stoddard. 2005. 'SA's economic growth shows way for the rest of Africa'. *Business Day,* 11 May.

12 N. Grobbelaar. 2005 above. 'Investing in Africa'.

13 Quoted in D. Christianson. 2004. 'South Africans doing business in Africa: The new imperialists'. *Enterprise,* December, p. 78.

14 S. Naidu. 2005. 'The South Africans have arrived: Post-apartheid South Africa's economic expansion into Africa'. Presentation to the first cross-party forum hosted by the Netherlands Institute of Multiparty Democracy and the Centre for Policy Studies, Cape Town, 21 May.

15 S. Naidu. 2005 above. 'The South Africans have arrived'.

16 Quoted in Centre for Policy Studies et al. 2004. 'South Africa in Africa: The post-apartheid decade'. Seminar report, Stellenbosch, 29 July–1 August, November, p. 22.

17 J. Daniel, V. Naido and S. Naidu. 2003. 'The South Africans have arrived: Post-apartheid corporate expansion into Africa'. In: J. Daniel, A. Habib and R. Southall. *State of the nation: South Africa 2003–2004.* Pretoria: Human Sciences Research Council, p. 376.

18 *Business Day,* 17 April 2002. Quoted in J. Daniel, V. Naido and S. Naidu. 2003 above, p. 376.

19 N. Grobbelaar. 2003. 'NEPAD must guide business in Africa'. *Business Day,* 17 October.

20 J. Daniel and J. Lutchman. 2005. 'South Africa in Africa: Scrambling for energy'. In: S. Buhlungu, J. Daniel, J. Lutchman and R. Southall, eds. *State of the nation: South Africa 2005–2006.* Pretoria: Human Sciences Research Council, p. 487.

21 African Institute of Corporate Citizenship. 'Promoting South African companies' corporate responsibility in Africa'. Workshop proceedings, Sunnyside Park Hotel, Parktown, 27 May 2005, p. 9.

22 'South African business sees opportunities up north'. *Business Day,* 9 July 2004.

23 Quoted in E. Stoddard. 2005. 'SA's economic growth shows way for the rest of Africa' in *Business Day,* 11 May.

24 Quoted in BusinessMap Foundation. 2005. '*What Zimbabwe's continuing crisis means for South Africa.* BusinessMap Foundation, 24 June.

25 World Investment Report 2004 data quoted in N. Grobbelaar. 2005. 'Investing in Africa: SA's influence a mixed blessing'. *Business Day,* 1 June.

26 J. Daniel and J. Lutchman. 2005 above. 'Scrambling for energy', p. 492

27 J. Daniel and J. Lutchman. 2005 above. 'Scrambling for energy', p. 485.

28 J. Daniel and J. Lutchman. 2005 above. 'Scrambling for energy', p. 486.

29 N. Grobbelaar. 2005 above. 'Investing in Africa'.

30 S. Gelb. 2002. *South Africa, Africa and the New Partnership for Africa's Development.* The Edge Institute, September, p. 23.

31 United Nations. 2005. *Investment Policy Review: Kenya.* Unedited advance copy, p. 20.

32 UNCTAD. *World Investment Report 2004: The shift towards services.* New York and Geneva:

United Nations. Quoted in: African Institute of Corporate Citizenship. 2004 workshop proceedings above, p. 6.

33 N. Grobbelaar. 2005 above.

34 H. Besada. 2005. 'Glimpse of hope in West Africa: The experience of South African firms doing business in Ghana'. South African Institute of International Affairs Report 4, p. 51.

35 N. Grobbelaar. and K. Tsotetsi. 2005. *Africa's first welfare state: The experience of South African firms doing business in Botswana.* South African Institute of International Affairs, Report 5, 2005, p. x.

36 *Who needs FDI?* BusinessMap Foundation, Update, Ref No. 2005/005, p. 1.

37 Quoted in African Institute of Corporate Citizenship. 2004 workshop proceedings above, p. 2.

38 D. Miller. 2003. 'Malling or mauling Africa'. *SA Labour Bulletin,* 27 February.

39 D. Miller. 2003 above. 'Malling or mauling Africa'.

40 D. Miller. 2003 above. 'Malling or mauling Africa'.

41 N. Grobbelaar. 2005 above. 'Investing in Africa'.

42 African Institute of Corporate Citizenship. 2004 workshop proceedings above, p. 13.

43 N. Grobbelaar. 'Investing in Africa' in *Business Day,* 1 June 2005.

44 R. Rumney and M. Pingo. 2004. *Mapping South Africa's trade and investment.* Presentation at the Human Sciences Research Council, May.

45 BusinessMap Foundation. *Who needs FDI?* Update 2005/005, p. 1.

46 'Final Report of the UN Panel of Experts on the Illegal Exploitation of Natural Resources and Other Forms of Wealth of the Democractic Republic of the Congo'. S/2002/1146, 16 October 2002.

47 Quoted in BusinessMap Foundation. *Who needs FDI?* Update 2005/005, p. 1.

48 Quoted in 'SA companies work up profits in Africa'. *Business Day,* 11 November 2004.

49 N. Grobbelaar. 2003. 'NEPAD must guide business in Africa'. *Business Day,* 17 October.

50 Quoted in African Institute of Corporate Citizenship. 2004 workshop proceedings above, p. 9.

51 *Financial Mail* quoted in J. Daniel and J. Lutchman. 2005. 'South Africa in Africa: Scrambling for energy'. In: S. Buhlungu, J. Daniel, J. Lutchman and R. Southall, eds. *State of the Nation: South Africa 2005–2006.* Pretoria: Human Sciences Research Council, p. 486.

52 J. Daniel and J. Lutchman. 2005 above. 'Scrambling for energy', p. 485.

53 See, for example, this report: The World Bank, Kenya Institute for Public Policy Research and Analysis (KIPPRA) and Centre for the Study of African Economies (Oxford University). 2004. 'Enhancing the Competitiveness of Kenya's Manufacturing Sector: The Role of the Investment Climate', November.

54 D. Games. 2004. 'The experience of South African firms doing business in Africa: A preliminary survey and analysis'. *South African Institute of International Affairs Report* 1, p. 50.

55 A. Richman and C. Lyle. 2005. 'The economic benefits of liberalising regional air transport – A review of global experience: Headline Report'. Commark Trust, November, p. 3.

56 D. Games. 2004. 'The experience of South African firms doing business in Africa: A preliminary survey and analysis'. *South African Institute of International Affairs Report* 1, p. 33.

57 J. Hudson. 'East Africa's hub: The experience of South African firms doing business in Kenya'. *South African Institute of International Affairs*, forthcoming.

58 African Institute of Corporate Citizenship. 2004 workshop proceedings above, p. 11.

59 J. Daniel and J. Lutchman. 2005 above. 'Scrambling for energy', p. 485.

60 J. Daniel and J. Lutchman. 2005 above. 'Scrambling for energy', p. 489.

61 J. Daniel and J. Lutchman. 2005 above. 'Scrambling for energy', p. 501.

62 Quoted in J. Daniel and J. Lutchman. 2005 above. 'Scrambling for energy', p. 484.

63 J. Daniel and J. Lutchman. 2005 above. 'Scrambling for energy', p. 500.

64 J. Daniel and J. Lutchman. 2005 above. 'Scrambling for energy', p. 502.

65 J. Daniel and J. Lutchman. 2005 above. 'Scrambling for energy', p. 501.

66 J. Daniel and J. Lutchman. 2005 above. 'Scrambling for energy', p. 507.

67 L.H. Evans. 1995. Quoted in S. Gelb. 2002. 'South Africa, African and the New Partnership for Africa's development'. The Edge Institute, September, p. 13.

68 D. Miller. 2004. 'South African multinational corporations, Nepad and competing regional claims on post-apartheid South Africa'. *African Sociological Review* 8 (1), p. 176.

69 S. Gelb. 2002 above. *South Africa and [NEPAD]*, p. 25.

70 S. Gelb. 2002 above. *South Africa and [NEPAD]*, p. 36.

71 S. Gelb. 2002 above. *South Africa and [NEPAD]*, p. 3.

72 J. Daniel, A. Habib and R. Southall. 2002. *State of the nation, 2003–2004*. Pretoria: Human Sciences Research Council. Quoted in: *Foreign direct investment in services in Africa*. BusinessMap Foundation, 22 October, p. 14.

73 Quoted in: African Institute of Corporate Citizenship. 2004 workshop proceedings above, p. 1.

74 African Institute of Corporate Citizenship. 2004 workshop proceedings above, p. 25.

75 OECD quoted in: African Institute of Corporate Citizenship. 2004 workshop proceedings above, p. 28.

76 African Institute of Corporate Citizenship. 2004 workshop proceedings above, p. 28.

77 African Institute of Corporate Citizenship. 2004 workshop proceedings above, p. 27.

78 African Institute of Corporate Citizenship. 2004 workshop proceedings above, p. 29.

79 Quoted in: African Institute of Corporate Citizenship. 2004 workshop proceedings above, p. 29.

CHAPTER 7. CONFLICT AND LAND REFORM IN SOUTHERN AFRICA: HOW EXCEPTIONAL IS SOUTH AFRICA?

1 Sam Moyo. 'The Political Economy of Land Acquisition in Zimbabwe, 1990–1999'. *Journal of Southern African Studies* 26(1), pp. 5–28.

2 Sam Moyo and Paris Yeros. 2004. 'Land Occupations and Land Reform in Zimbabwe: Towards the National Democratic Revolution'. In: Sam Moyo and Paris Yeros (eds). 2004.

Reclaiming the Land: The Resurgence of Rural Movements in Africa, Asia and Latin America. London: Zed Books.

3   Colin Bundy. 1979. *The Rise and Fall of the South African Peasantry.* London: Heineman.

4   Harold Wolpe. 1972. 'Capitalism and cheap labour-power in South Africa: From segregation to apartheid'. *Economy and Society* 1(4).

5   Lungisile Ntsebeza. 2000. 'Traditional Authorities, Local Government and Land Rights'. In: Ben Cousins (ed). *At the Crossroads: Land and Agrarian Reform in South Africa into the 21st Century.* Cape Town/Johannesburg: UWC/National Land Committee, pp. 280–305.

6   Statistics South Africa. 2003. *Census 2001.* Pretoria: Government Printers.

7   Republic of South Africa. *Constitution of Republic of South Africa Act 108 of 1996.* Pretoria: Government Printers.

8   Department of Land Affairs. 1997. *White Paper on South African Land Policy.* Pretoria: Government Printers.

9   M. Lyne and M. Darroch. 2003. 'Land Redistribution in South Africa: Past Performance and Future Policy'. In: Lieb Niewoudt and Jan Groenewald (eds). *The Challenge of Change: Agriculture, Land and the South African Economy.* Pietermaritzburg: University of KwaZulu-Natal Press, pp. 65–86.

10   Fred Hendricks and Lungisile Ntsebeza. 2000. 'The Paradox of South Africa's Land Reform Policy: Failed Decolonisation?' *SARIPS Annual Colloquium.*

11   Expropriation has been used in respect of only two restitution claims and once within the redistribution programme.

12   Department of Agriculture. 2004. 'AgriBEE: Broad-based Black Economic Empowerment Framework for Agriculture'. Policy document. Pretoria: National Department of Agriculture.

13   The former 'homelands' were the self-governing territories of Lebowa, Gazankulu, KaNgwane, KwaNdebele, KwaZulu, QwaQwa and the nominally 'independent states' of Transkei, Bophutatswana, Venda and Ciskei.

14   N. Vink and J. Kirsten. 2003. 'Agriculture in the National Economy 2003'. In Lieb Niewoudt and Jan Groenewald (eds). 2003. *The Challenge of Change: Agriculture, Land and the South African Economy.* Pietermaritzburg: University of KwaZulu-Natal Press, pp. 3–20.

15   Moyo and Yeros. 2004 above. 'Land Occupations and Land Reform in Zimbabwe'.

16   Moyo and Yeros. 2004 above. 'Land Occupations and Land Reform in Zimbabwe'.

17   Archie Mafeje, 'The Agrarian Question in Southern Africa and Accumulation from Below', *SAPEM*, vol. 10:5, 1997.

18   Sam Moyo. 2004. *The Land Question in Africa: Research Perspectives and Questions.* Dakar: CODESRIA Green Book.

19   Sam Moyo. 2000. *Land Reform Under Structural Adjustment in Zimbabwe; Land Use Change in Mashonaland Provinces.* Sweden: Nordiska Afrikainstitutet.

20   P.L. Delville and others. 2002. *Negotiating Access to Land in West Africa: A Synthesis of Findings from Research on Derived Rights Land.* London: International Institute for Environment and Development.

21 P.L. Delville and others. 2002 above.

22 K. Amanor. 2003. 'Land and Sustainable Development in West Africa'. Working Paper. Harare.

23 Sam Moyo. 2003. 'Land, Food Security and Sustainable Development in Africa'. Paper prepared for the United Nations Economic Commission for Africa (UNECA), Sustainable Development Division, Ethiopia.

24 J.W. Bruce. 1996. *Country Profiles of Land Tenure*. Madison: African Land Tenure Centre, University of Wisconsin, p. 60.

25 T.J. Basset. 1993. 'Introduction: The land question and agricultural transformation in Sub-Saharan Africa'. In: T. J. Bassett and D.E. Crummey (eds). *Land in African Agrarian Systems*. Madision: The University of Wisconsin Press. Also see J.P. Platteau. 1996. 'The Evolutionary Theory of Land Rights as Applied to sub-Saharan Africa: A Critical Assessment'. *Development and Change* 27(1), pp. 29–86.

26 Sam Moyo. 20003 above. 'Land, Food Security and Sustainable Development in Africa'.

27 Sam Moyo. 2003. 'The Politics of Land Distribution and Race Relations in Southern Africa'. In: *Racism and Public Policy*. London: Palgrave Press.

28 Moyo. 2004 above. *The Land Question in Africa*.

29 J. Alexander. 2003. 'Squatters, Veterans and the State in Zimbabwe'. In: Amanda Hammar, Brian Raftopoulos and Stig Jensen (eds). 2003. *Zimbabwe's Unfinished Business: Rethinking Land, State and Nation in the Context of Crisis*. Harare: Weaver Press.

30 F. Tsheehama (Namibia's Permanent Secretary for Lands). 2005. 'Land reform in Namibia: Implementation and challenges'. Presentation at Land Summit, Johannesburg 28 July to 1 August.

31 Moyo. 2004 above. *The Land Question in Africa*.

32 Lala Steyn. 2002. 'Land Occupations in South Africa'. Unpublished report to Africa Groups of Sweden, June.

33 Gillian Hart. 2003. *Disabling Globalisation: Places of Power in Post-Apartheid South Africa*. Berkeley: University of California Press.

34 Republic of South Africa. 2001. 'Determination of Employment Conditions in South African Agriculture'. Report by the Department of Labour. Government Gazette No. 22648. Also see Regulation Gazette 7159(Vol. 435). 13 September 2001.

35 Murders of farm owners and their families have been well documented. No known sources exist to document the murders of farm workers and their families, though anecdotal evidence and localised surveys reveal very high levels of violence affecting farm workers, inflicted both by farm owners and farm commandos, and by other farm workers.

36 G. Magaramombe. 2003. 'Resource Base and Farm Production: Farm Labour Relations, Use and Needs'. Mimeo. Harare: African Institute for Agrarian Studies (AIAS). Also see W. Chambati and S. Moyo. 2003. 'Land Reform and the Political Economy of Agricultural Labour'. Mimeo. Harare: African Institute for Agrarian Studies.

37 Simon Bekker. 2003. 'Migration from rural sending areas in South Africa and its importance for planning and service delivery'. Paper presented to the ninth International Winelands Conference, Stellenbosch. 10–12 September. Also see C. Cross and others. 1999.

'An Unstable Balance: Migration, Small Farming, Infrastructure, and Livelihoods in the Coastal Provinces'. Unpublished Report. Midrand: Development Bank of Southern Africa.

38 Moyo. 2004 above. *The Land Question in Africa.*

39 Sam Moyo. 1995. *The Land Question in Zimbabwe*. Harare: SAPES Books.

40 Moyo, 'The Politics of Land Distribution and Race Relations in Southern Africa.'

41 P. Yeros. 2000. 'The Political Economy of Civilisation: Peasant-workers in Zimbabwe and the Neo-colonial World'. PhD Thesis. University of London.

CHAPTER 8. HIV/AIDS AND THE AFRICAN RENAISSANCE: SOUTH AFRICA'S ACHILLES HEEL?

1 Ahmadou Kourouma. 2004. *Waiting for the Wild Beasts to Vote*. London: Vintage Books.

2 See Peter Vale and Sipho Maseko. 2002. 'Thabo Mbeki, South Africa, and The Idea of An African Renaissance'. In: Sean Jacobs and Richard Calland (eds). *Thabo Mbeki's World*. Pietermaritzburg: University of KwaZulu-Natal Press, pp. 121–144.

3 See the Joint United Nations Programme on HIV/AIDS (UNAIDS). 2006. *Report On the Global AIDS Epidemic*. UNAIDS/06.20E, May, and UNAIDS/WHO. 2006. *AIDS Epidemic Update*. UNAIDS/06.29E, December, p. 20.

4 Department of Health. 2005. 'National HIV and Syphilis Antenatal Sero-Prevalence Survey South Africa 2004'. Pretoria: Department of Health.

5 Hans Marais. 2000. 'To the Edge'. *AIDS Review*. Pretoria: University of Pretoria, Centre for the Study of AIDS.

6 William Mervin Gumede. 2005. *Thabo Mbeki and the Battle for the Soul of the ANC*. Cape Town: Zebra Press, p. 173. Also: Samantha Power. 2003. 'The AIDS Rebel'. *The New Yorker*, May. http://www.pbs.org/pov/pov2003/stateof denial/special_rebel.html, accessed 31 May 2006.

7 Virginia van der Vliet. 2004. 'South Africa Divided Against AIDS: A Crisis of Leadership'. In: Kyle Dean Kauffman and David L. Lindauer (eds). 2004. *AIDS and South Africa: The Social Expression of a Pandemic*. New York: Macmillan.

8 Department of Health. 2000. 'HIV/AIDS/STD Strategic Plan for South Africa 2000–2005'. Pretoria: Department of Health.

9 Operational Plan for Comprehensive HIV and AIDS Care, Management and Treatment for South Africa, Department of Health, South Africa, 2003.

10 Ian Hodson. 2006. 'Dazed and Confused: The Reality of AIDS Treatment in South Africa'. 11 January. http://www.opendemocracy.net, accessed 30 May 2006.

11 See the AIDS Foundation of South Africa statistics. www.aids.org.za, accessed 30 May 2006.

12 Department of Health. 2005. 'Speech by Health Minister Dr Manto Tshabalala-Msimang World AIDS Day National Event'. Durban, South Africa, 1 December. http://www.doh.gov.za/docs/sp/2005/sp1201.html, accessed 31 May 2006.

13 TAC. 2006. 'Resolutions of National Executive Committee Meeting'. Cape Town, 20–21 June. http://www.tac.org.za, accessed 30 May.

14 Telephonic interview with Deena Bosch, 30 May 2006.

15 See Lloyd Gedye, Cheri-Ann James and Motlatsi Lebea. 2004. 'Putting the Government's HIV/AIDS Plan to the Test'. *The Mail & Guardian,* 30 November.

16 Social Cluster, South African government. 2007. 'Government's Programme of Action – 2007'. February. http://www.info.gov.za/aboutgovt/poa/report/social.htm, accessed 22 February 2007.

17 Estimate based on government figures and reported by the International Treatment Preparedness Coalition (ITPC), as reported in 'ARV targets fall short'. 2006. Health-e News, 6 December. http://iafrica.com/aidswise/news/511247.htm, accessed 13 March 2007.

18 Nhanhla Ndlovu and Rabelani Daswa. 2006. 'Monitoring AIDS Treatment Roll-out in South Africa: Lessons From the Joint Civil Society Monitoring Forum'. *Budget Brief* 161. Cape Town: IDASA, 13 April.

19 See Mandisa Mbali. 2004. 'HIV/AIDS Policy-Making in Post-Apartheid South Africa'. In: John Daniel, Adam Habib and Roger Southall (eds). *The State of the Nation 2003–2004.* Cape Town: The Human Sciences Research Council (HSRC), p. 321.

20 Alex Irwin, Joyce Millen, and Dorothy Fallows. 2003. *Global AIDS: Myths and Facts.* Cambridge, Massachusetts: South End Press, p. 19.

21 Richard E. Chaisson. 2000. 'The World AIDS Conference in Durban, South Africa – Science, Politics, and Health'. *The Hopkins HIV Report.* Baltimore, Maryland: John Hopkins AIDS Service, September.

22 Allister Sparks. 2003. *Beyond the Miracle: Inside the New South Africa.* Jeppestown: Jonathan Bull Publishers, p. 293.

23 William Mervin Gumede. 2005 above. *Thabo Mbeki,* p. 163.

24 Peter Mokaba (former ANC chief electoral officer). Cited in J. Gitay. 2002. 'Rhetoric, Politics, Science, Medicine: The South African HIV/AIDS Controversy'. Unpublished paper. University of Cape Town: Centre for African Studies, 18 September.

25 Steven Robins. 2004. 'Long Live Zackie, Long Live AIDS Activism, Science and Citizenship after Apartheid'. *Journal of Southern African Studies* 3(30), September.

26 William Mervin Gumede. 2005 above. *Thabo Mbeki.*

27 Allister Sparks. 2003 above. *Beyond the Miracle,* p. 285.

28 Allister Sparks. 2003 above. *Beyond the Miracle,* p. 286.

29 Tom Lodge. 2003. *Politics in South Africa: From Mandela to Mbeki.* Bloomington: Indiana University Press, p. 258; and BBC World Service. 2000. 'Mbeki's Letter to World Leaders'. 20 April. http://news.bbc.co.uk/2/hi/africa/720448.stm, accessed 12 March 2007.

30 William Mervin Gumede. 2005 above. *Thabo Mbeki,* p. 152.

31 John Iliffe. 2006. *The African AIDS Epidemic.* Cape Town: Double Storey Press/Oxford: James Currey, p. 66–67.

32 Samantha Power. 2003 above. 'The AIDS Rebel'. *The New Yorker.*

33 H. Gayle Martin. October 2003. Comparative Analysis of the Financing of HIV/AIDS programmes in Botswana, Lesotho, Moçambique, South Africa, Swaziland and Zimbabwe. Prepared for the Social Aspects of HIV/AIDS and Health Research Programme of the

Human Sciences Research Council (HSRC). Readable at http://www.hsrcpublishers.ac.za/download.asp?id=1924, accessed 30 March 2007.

34 William Mervin Gumede. 2005 above. *Thabo Mbeki*, p. 161.

35 Edwin Cameron. 2005. *Witness to AIDS*. Cape Town: Tafelberg, p 107. Also: Lodge. 2003 above. *Politics in South Africa*, p. 259.

36 William Mervin Gumede. 2005 above. *Thabo Mbeki*, p. 171.

37 See *The Cape Times*, 25 April 2002. Cited in: Steven Robins. 2004 above. 'Long Live, Zackie', p. 661, footnote 20.

38 Thabo Mbeki. 2006. *State of the Nation Address of the President of South Africa, Thabo Mbeki: Joint Sitting of Parliament*. Cape Town, 3 February.

39 John Iliffe. 2006 above. *The African AIDS Epidemic*, p. 44.

40 Anso Thom. 2006. 'Beetroot Battle at World AIDS Conference'. Health-E News, 21 August. http://www.health-e.org.za, accessed 22 February 2007.

41 Thom. 2006 above. 'Beetroot Battle at World AIDS Conference'.

42 IRIN. 2006. 'South Africa: Government Pressured to Review HIV/AIDS Communication Strategy'. *HIV/AIDS News Service, PLUSNEWS*. Johannesburg, 25 August.

43 Thom. 2006 above. 'Beetroot Battle at World AIDS Conference'.

44 TAC. 2006. 'Memorandum To President Mbeki and All Members of Parliament.' Cape Town, South Africa, 18 September. Also: Nathan Geffen. 2006. 'How the Health Minister Hurts SA'. *Business Day*, 19 September. Also: TAC. 2006. 'Why We Need a New Health Minister'. *Equal Treatment*. Cape Town: TAC, November 2006. Also: IRIN. 2006 above. 'South Africa: Government Pressured'.

45 Geffen. 2006 above. 'How the Health Minister Hurts SA'.

46 IRIN. 2006 above. 'South Africa: Government Pressured'. Also: TAC. 2006 above. 'Memorandum to President Mbeki and All Members of Parliament'.

47 IRIN. 2006 above. 'South Africa: Government Pressured'.

48 'South Africa's New HIV/AIDS Strategy to Be Announced In December; Might Expand Treatment, Address Health Worker Shortage, Official Says'. 2006. *Medical News Today, 8 November, http://www.medicalnewstoday.com/medicalnews.php?newsid=55993, accessed 22 February 2007.*

49 TAC. 2007. 'Government Leadership on HIV/AIDS Irrevocably Defeats Denialism! Implement a New Credible Plan with Clear Targets!' http://www.tac.org.za/AIDS DenialismIsDead.html, accessed 22 February 2007. Also: 'South Africa's New HIV/AIDS Strategy'. 2006 above. *Medical News Today.*

50 Department of Health. 2006. 'Broad Framework for an HIV and AIDS and STI Strategic Plan for 2007–11'. Pretoria: Department of Health, November, p. 5.

51 TAC. 2007 above. 'Government Leadership on HIV/AIDS Irrevocably Defeats Denialism!'

52 Lodge. 2003 above. *Politics in South Africa*, pp. 227–31.

53 UNAIDS/WHO. 2006. *AIDS Epidemic Update*, December, UNAIDS/06.29E, p. 20.

54 UNAIDS/WHO. 2004. *AIDS Epidemic Update*, December, UNAIDS/04.45E, p. 25.

55 SADC. 'HIV/AIDS Framework and Programme of Action, 2003–2007: Managing the HIV and AIDS Pandemic'. Gaborone, Botswana: SADC, p. 18.

56 See '2003 SADC Heads of State and Government Summit on HIV/AIDS,' and the 'SADC Declaration on HIV/AIDS'. Maseru, Lesotho, 4 July 2004. http://www.sadc.int, accessed 31 May 2006.

57 Centre for Conflict Resolution (CCR) and the University of Namibia (UNAM). 2006. 'HIV/AIDS and Southern Africa's Militaries'. Windhoek, Namibia, 9–10 February 2006. http://ccrweb.ccr.uct.ac.za, accessed 22 February 2007.

58 CCR/UNAM. 2006 above. 'HIV/AIDS and Southern Africa's Militaries'.

59 African Union. 2001. 'Abuja Declaration on HIV/AIDS, Tuberculosis and Other Related Infectious Diseases'. Abuja, Nigeria, 24–27 April, OAU/SPS/Abuja/3.

60 AU. 2005. *The AU Commission HIV/AIDS Strategic Plan 2005–2007*. Also: *AIDS Watch Africa (AWA) Strategic Plan*, Sirte, Libya, 28 June–2 July, EX.CL/194.

61 South African Military Health Services (SAMHS). 2005–06. *Masibambisane*. http://www.mhs.mil.za/masi/index.htm, accessed 23 June 2006. Also: SAMHS. 2005. 'The Comprehensive Plan for the Holistic Management of HIV and AIDS'. Tshwane (Pretoria), 5 March, p. 1.

62 AU. 2005. 'Progress Report on the Implementation of the Plan of Action of the Abuja Declaration for Malaria, HIV/AIDS and Tuberculosis'. Gaborone, Botswana, 10–14 October.

63 Angela Ndinga-Muvumba attended the mid-term review of the Abuja Plan of Action in Nigeria in May 2006.

64 AU. 'Africa's Common Position to the High Level Meeting of the UN General Assembly Session on AIDS'. June 2006. Also: AU. 2006. 'Report on the Outcome of the Special Summit on HIV/AIDS, Tuberculosis and Malaria' (ATM), 1–2 July 2006, Banjul, Gambia, 1–2 July, Assembly/AU/5 (VII).

65 Angela Ndinga-Muvumba. 2006. 'No Half Measures in the Fight for the Health of Africa'. *The Cape Times*, 22 May.

66 Angela Ndinga-Muvumba. 2005. 'Too Late to Make HIV/AIDS History'. *South African Labour Bulletin* 4(29), August/September.

67 'Africa: Rwanda's President to Host Gowon and Others'. 2007. *The Daily Champion*, Lagos, Nigeria, 8 February. http://allafrica.com/stories/200702080640.html, accessed 22 February 2007.

68 Calland and Jacobs (eds). 2004 above. *Thabo Mbeki's World*, pp. 257–276.

69 UN High-Level Panel on Threats, Challenges and Change. 2004. *A More Secure World: Our Shared Responsibility*. Report of the Secretary-General. December, A/59/565.

70 UN. 2005. *In Larger Freedom: Towards Development, Security, and Human Rights for All: Report of the Secretary-General*. A/59/2005, 21 March.

71 CCR. 2005. *Building an African Union for the 21st Century: Relations with the RECS, NEPAD and Civil Society*. Cape Town, South Africa, pp. 23–24. http://ccrweb.ccr.uct.ac.za, accessed 21 February 2006.

CHAPTER 9. SOUTH AFRICA AND THE MAKING OF THE AFRICAN UNION
AND NEPAD: MBEKI'S 'PROGRESSIVE AFRICAN AGENDA'

1 For an elucidation of 'progressivism', see: Frederick Bartol and Susan Rose-Ackerman. 1995. In: *The Encyclopedia of Democracy* 3. Washington D.C.: Congressional Quarterly Inc, pp. 1002–1007.

2   For an elucidation of the 'African Agenda', see: Chris Landsberg. 2004. 'The Fifth Wave of Pan-Africanism'. In Adekeye Adebajo and Ismail Rashid (eds). *West Africa's Security Challenges: Building Peace in a Troubled Region*. Boulder and London: Lynne Rienner Publishers.

3   Adekeye Adebajo and Christopher Landsberg. 2003. 'South Africa and Nigeria as Regional Hegemons'. In: Mwesiga Baregu and Christopher Landsberg (eds). *From Cape to Congo: Southern Africa's Emerging Security Challenges*. Boulder and London: Lynne Rienner Publishers, p. 179.

4   Adebajo and Landsberg. 2003 above. 'South Africa and Nigeria as Regional Hegemons'.

5   Chris Landsberg. 2002. 'From African Renaissance to NEPAD … and Back to the Renaissance'. *Journal of African Elections* 2(1). September, p. 91.

6   Landsberg. 2002 above. 'From African Renaissance to NEPAD … and Back to the Renaissance'.

7   Chris Landsberg and Shaun Mackay. 2003. 'The African Union: Political will and commitment needed for new doctrine'. *Synopsis* 1(7). Johannesburg: Centre for Policy Studies, April.

8   African Union. 2004. 'Vision of the African Union and Mission of the African Union'. Draft, March.

9   Kwame Nkrumah. 1963. *Africa must unite*. London and New York: Heinemann.

10 African Union. 2004 above. 'Vision of the African Union and Mission of the African Union'.

11 OAU. 2001. 'A New African Initiative: Merger of the Millennium Partnership for Africa Recovery Programme and Omega Plan'. OAU Summit. Lusaka, July.

12 For a brief description by Wade of his Omega Plan, see: AllAfrica.com. 2001. 'Africa: President Wade Says Joint Plan for African Development Under Study'. http://allafrica.com/stories/200106280650.html. Posted 28 June 2001, accessed 15 March 2003. For Wade's further comments, see: 'Africa, an Outcast or a Partner? An Interview [with Abdoulaye Wade] by Charles Zorgbibe'. Undated, post 2002. http://www.african-geopolitics.org/show.aspx?ArticleId=3147, accessed 15 March 2007.

13 Mandela quoted in: Eboe Hutchful. 2000. 'Understanding the African Security Crisis'. In: Abdel-Fatau Musah and J. Kayode Fayemi. *Mercenaries: An African Security Dilemma*. London: Pluto Press, p. 218.

14 Quoted in Landsberg and Mackay. 2003 above. 'Political will needed for new doctrine', p. 4.

15 Adekeye Adebajo and Chris Landsberg. 2001. 'The Heirs of Nkrumah: Africa's New Interventionists'. *Pugwash Occasional Papers* 1(2). January, p. 75.

16 K. Mamaila. 2001. 'Mbeki maps out Africa's fresh beginning'. *The Star*, 20 July.

17 Chris Landsberg and Shaun Mackay. 2003. 'Is the AU the OAU without the O?'. *South African Labour Bulletin* 4(27), August. See also: Centre for Conflict Resolution. 2005. 'Building an African Union for the 21st Century: Relations with RECS, NEPAD and Civil Society'. Seminar Report. Cape Town, 20–22 August. http://ccrweb.ccr.uct.ac.za.

18 SAFM. 2004. Radio interview with Ambassador Jesse Duarte, South African Foreign Ministry official, 12 July.

19 Chris Landsberg and Shaun Mackay. 2003. 'The African Union: Political will and commitment needed for new doctrine'. *Synopsis* 1(7). Johannesburg: Centre for Policy Studies.

20 Landsberg and Mackay. 2003 above. 'The African Union: Political will and commitment'.

21 Chris Landsberg. 2003. 'Building Sustainable Peace requires Democratic Governance'. *Synopsis* 1(7). Johannesburg: Centre for Policy Studies, April.

22 Musifiky Mwanasali, 2004 above. 'Emerging Security Architecture in Africa', pp. 12–13.

23 Musifiky Mwanasali. 2004 above. 'Emerging Security Architecture in Africa'.

24 For a discussion of this idea, see Christopher Landsberg. 2004. 'The Fifth Wave of Pan-Africanism'. In Adekeye Adebajo and Ismail Rashid (eds.) *West Africa's Security Challenges*. London and Boulder: Lynne Rienner Publishers, p. 137.

25 African Union. 2006. 'Study on An African Union Government: Towards the Establishment of the United States of Africa'. Addis Ababa, November.

26 African Union. 2006 above. 'Study on An African Union Government'.

27 African Union. 2006 above. 'Study on An African Union Government'.

28 Quoted in K. Mamaila. 2001. 'Mbeki MAPs out Africa's fresh beginning', *The Star*, 20 July.

29 For critiques of NEPAD, see: Patrick Bond (ed). 2002. 'Fannon's Warning: A Civil Society Reader on the New Partnership for Africa's Development'. Trenton, New Jersey: AIDC. Also: Libhongo Ntlokonkulu. 2003. 'NEPAD demonstrates Continent's Fragmentation'. *Synopsis* 1(7). Johannesburg: Centre for Policy Studies.

30 OAU. 2001. 'The OMEGA Plan'. Senegal, Dakar, February.

31 OAU. 2001 above. 'A New African Initiative'.

32 Landsberg. 2002 above. 'From African Renaissance to NEPAD…and Back to the Renaissance', p. 91.

33 See Candice Moore. 2003. 'Democratic Governance and Peace: Two Sides of the same Coin?' *Policy Brief* 27. Johannesburg: Centre for Policy Studies, April.

34 Moore. 2003 above. 'Democratic Governance and Peace'.

35 Landsberg. 2002 above. 'From African Renaissance to NEPAD … and Back to the Renaissance', p. 91.

36 Landsberg. 2002 above. 'From African Renaissance to NEPAD … and Back to the Renaissance', p. 91.

37 Moore. 2003 above. 'Democratic Governance and Peace'.

38 John G. Nyuot Yoh. 2002. 'NEPAD and AU: Problems and Prospects'. *Global Dialogue* 7.2, July.

39 Khabele Matlosa. 2004. 'New Regionalist Impulses: Implications of the New Partnership for Africa's Development (NEPAD) for Regional Co-operation in Southern Africa'. *Policy: Issues and Actors* 5(17). Johannesburg: Centre for Policy Studies, February, p. 19.

40 Moore. 2003 above. 'Democratic Governance and Peace', p. 6.

41 NEPAD Secretariat. 2005. *What is NEPAD?* Midrand, South Africa.

42 NEPAD Secretariat. 2005 above.

43 Shadrack Gutto and Chris Landsberg. 2006. 'New Partnership for Africa's Development'. Qatar: Doha. First Seminar, 5 February.

44 See for example: Chris Landsberg. 2005. 'Africa's G8 wishlist'. *SA Labour Bulletin* 4(9). August/September, pp. 7–9.

45 NEPAD. 2002. 'NEPAD: Democracy and Political Governance Initiative'. Draft document. Pretoria, February.

46 NEPAD. 2002 above. 'NEPAD: Democracy and Political Governance Initiative'.

47 NEPAD. 2002 above. 'NEPAD: Democracy and Political Governance Initiative'.

48 NEPAD. 2002 above. 'NEPAD: Democracy and Political Governance Initiative'.

49 NEPAD. 2002 above. 'NEPAD: Democracy and Political Governance Initiative'.

50 Economic Commission for Africa. 2002. 'Draft Codes and Standards for Economic and Corporate Governance in Africa: Summary of Key Issues and Declaration of Principles'. Ethiopia: Addis Ababa, March.

51 Chris Landsberg. 2006. 'A Developmental Democracy? Democracy and Political Governance'. Discussion paper prepared for Phase One of the South African APRM process. Johannesburg, January, p. 2.

52 Landsberg. 2006 above. 'A Developmental Democracy? Democracy and Political Governance'.

53 Landsberg. 2006 above. 'A Developmental Democracy? Democracy and Political Governance', p. 3.

54 Such aspersions came from individuals like Ross Herbert from the South African Institute of International Affairs.

55 Landsberg. 2006 above. 'A Developmental Democracy? Democracy and Political Governance', p. 2.

56 African Peer Review Mechanism. 2006. 'Country Review Report: Republic of South Africa'. APRM Country Review Report 4. November, p. 17.

57 African Peer Review Mechanism. 2006 above, pp. 90–91.

58 African Peer Review Mechanism. 2006 above.

59 African Peer Review Mechanism. 2006 above, p. 77.

60 African Peer Review Mechanism. 2006 above, p. 74.

61 African Peer Review Mechanism. 2006 above.

62 African Peer Review Mechanism. 2006 above.

63 African Peer Review Mechanism. 2006 above, p. 23.

64 African Peer Review Mechanism. 2006 above, p. 22.

CHAPTER 10. SOUTH AFRICA AND NIGERIA IN AFRICA: AN AXIS OF VIRTUE?

1 This chapter builds on Adekeye Adebajo and Chris Landsberg. 2003. 'South Africa and Nigeria as Regional Hegemons', in: Mwesiga Baregu and Chris Landsberg (eds) *From Cape to Congo: Southern Africa's Evolving Security Challenges*. Boulder and London: Lynne Rienner Publishers, pp. 171–203. The author would like to thank Dianna Games for extremely useful comments on an earlier version of this chapter.

2 Quoted in: Solomon O. Akinboye. 2005. 'From Confrontation to Strategic Partnership: Nigeria's Relations with South Africa, 1960–2000', in: U. Joy Ogwu (ed). *New Horizons*

for Nigeria in World Affairs. Lagos: Nigerian Institute for International Affairs, p. 217.

3   See, for example: Paul Kennedy. 1987. *The Rise and Fall of the Great Powers*. New York: Vintage, pp. 151–158. Also: Ali Mazrui. 1990. 'Hegemony: From Semites to Anglo-Saxons', in: *Cultural Forces in World Politics*. New Hampshire and Nairobi: Heinemann; London: James Currey, pp. 29–64. Also: James Morris. 1968. *Pax Britannica: The Climax of an Empire*. San Diego, New York and London: Harvest and Harcort Brace.

4   See, for example: Charles Kindleberger. 1977. *America in the World Economy*. New York: Foreign Policy Association. Also: Joseph Nye Jr. 1990. *Bound to Lead: The Changing Nature of American Power*. New York: Basic Books.

5   Olu Adeniji. 2000. 'The Emergence of South Africa into the Global Economy and its Consequences for Nigeria and Africa'. In: *Essays on Nigerian Foreign Policy, Governance and International Security*. Ibadan: Dokun Publishing House, p. 79.

6   Garth le Pere. 1999. 'South Africa and Nigeria: A Strategic Partnership'. *Global Dialogue* 3(4). December, p. 9. Also: Joy Ogwu. 1999. 'South Africa and Nigeria's Relations with the World'. Paper presented at the Second Nigeria/South Africa Dialogue Conference, 26–27 August. Johannesburg, South Africa. See also: Ali A. Mazrui. 2006. *A Tale of Two Africas: Nigeria and South Africa as Contrasting Visions*. London: Adonis and Abbey Publishers.

7   Adebayo Adedeji. 1999. 'Democratic Transformation in South Africa and Nigeria: Prospects for a Strategic Partnership'. Keynote address at the Second Nigeria/South Africa Dialogue Conference, 26–27 August. Johannesburg, South Africa, p. 5.

8   Henry Kissinger. 2001. *Does America Need a Foreign Policy? Toward a Diplomacy for the 21st Century*. New York: Simon and Shuster, pp. 208–9.

9   Adekeye Adebajo. 1995. 'Tale of Two Giants'. *Newswatch*, 11 September 1995, pp. 9–10. Also: Adekeye Adebajo and Chris Landsberg. 1996. 'Trading Places: Nigeria and South Africa'. *Indicator* 3(13). Winter, pp. 64–68.

10   See, for example: John Chipman. 1989. *French Power in Africa*. Oxford: Basil Blackwell. Also: Guy Martin. 1995. 'Francophone Africa in the Context of Franco-African Relations'. In: John Harbeson and Donald Rothchild (eds). *Africa in World Politics: Post-Cold War Challenges,* Second Edition. Colorado and Oxford: Westview Press, pp. 163–188. Also: Kaye Whiteman and Douglas Yates. 2004. 'France, Britain, and the US'. In: Adekeye Adebajo and Ismail Rashid (eds). 2004. *West Africa's Security Challenges: Building Peace in A Troubled Region*. Boulder and London: Lynne Rienner Publishers, pp. 349–379.

11   See, for example: Adebayo Adedeji. 2004. 'ECOWAS: A Retrospective Journey'. And: S.K.B. Asante. 'The Travails of Integration'. In Adebajo and Rashid (eds). 2004 above. *West Africa's Security Challenges*.

12   See, for example: James Barber and John Barratt. 1988. *South Africa's Foreign Policy 1948–88: The Search for Status and Security*. Johannesburg and Cambridge: Southern Book Publishers and Cambridge University Press. Also: Deon Geldenhuys. 1994. *The Diplomacy of Isolation: South African foreign policy making*. Johannesburg: Macmillan. Also: Sam Nolutshungu. 1975. *South Africa in Africa: A Study in Ideology and Foreign Policy*. Manchester, England: Manchester University Press.

13   See, for example: Andrew Apter. 2005. *The Pan-African Nation: Oil and the Spectacle of Culture in Nigeria*. Chicago: University of Chicago Press.

14 Akinboye. 2005 above. 'From Confrontation to Strategic Partnership', p. 215.

15 James Barber. 2004. *Mandela's World: The International Dimension of South Africa's Political Revolution, 1990–99*. Cape Town: David Philip, p. 110.

16 Barber. 2004 above. *Mandela's World*, p. 64.

17 Wole Soyinka. 2002. *King Baabu*. London: Methuen.

18 Wole Soyinka. 1996. *The Open Sore of A Continent: A Personal Narrative of the Nigerian Crisis*. Oxford and New York: Oxford University Press, pp. 14–15.

19 See Ifeanyi Ezeugo. 1998. *Abacha: Another Evil Genius?* Lagos: El-Rophekah International. Also: Chuks Illoegbunam. 1998. 'A Stubborn Dictator'. *The Guardian* (London), 9 June 1998, p. 16. Also: Eghosa E. Osaghae. 1998. *Nigeria since Independence: Crippled Giant*. Bloomington and Indianapolis: Indiana University Press, pp. 273–310.

20 Wole Soyinka. 2001. *Selected Poems*. London: Methuen, p. 197.

21 See: Kader Asmal, David Chidester and Wilmot James (eds). 2004. *South Africa's Nobel Laureates: Peace, Literature and Science*. Johannesburg and Cape Town: Jonathan Bull, pp. 74–100. Also: Tom Lodge. 2006. *Mandela: A Critical Life*. Oxford, New York and Cape Town: Oxford University Press. Also: Nelson Mandela. 1994. *Long Walk to Freedom*. New York: Little Brown and co. Also: Anthony Sampson. 1999. *Mandela: The Authorised Biography*. London: HarperCollins.

22 See Adewale 'Segun Banjo. Undated. 'South Africa's Policy Toward Nigeria: 1994–2004'. Unpublished paper. Also: Barber. 2004 above. *Mandela's World*, pp. 108–110. Also: Paul-Henri Bischoff and Roger Southall. 1999. 'The Early Foreign Policy of the Democratic South Africa', in: Stephen Wright (ed). *African Foreign Policies*. Colorado and Oxford: Westview Press, pp. 172–173. Also: Maxi van Aardt. 1996. 'A Foreign Policy to Die For: South Africa's Response to the Nigerian Crisis'. *Africa Insight* 2(26), pp. 107–117.

23 Banjo. Undated, above. 'South Africa's Policy Toward Nigeria,' p. 8.

24 Quoted in: Banjo. Undated, above. 'South Africa's Policy Toward Nigeria', p. 10.

25 Emeka Anyaoku. 2004. *The Inside Story of the Modern Commonwealth*. London and Ibadan: Evans Brothers, p. 162.

26 Quoted in: Banjo. Undated, above. 'South Africa's Policy Toward Nigeria,' p. 14.

27 Cited in van Aardt, 'A Foreign Policy to Die For', p. 112.

28 Confidential interview.

29 Banjo. Undated, above. 'South Africa's Policy Toward Nigeria', p. 15.

30 Personal Interview with Ambassador George Nene, Former High Commissioner of South Africa to Nigeria. Pretoria, 22 July 2004.

31 Osaghae. 1998 above. *Nigeria since Independence*, p. 309.

32 Quoted in: Barber. 2004 above. *Mandela's World*, p. 110.

33 Barber. 2004 above. *Mandela's World*, p. 110.

34 See, for example, Chris Alden and Garth Le Pere. 2003. *South Africa's Post-Apartheid Foreign Policy – From Reconciliation to Revival?* Adelphi Paper 362. London: Institute for Strategic Studies. Also: Chris Landsberg. 2004. *The Quiet Diplomacy of Liberation: International Politics and South Africa's Transition*. Johannesburg: Jacana. Also: Lloyd Sachikonye. 2005. 'South Africa's Quiet Diplomacy: The Case of Zimbabwe'. In: John

Daniel, Roger Southall and Jessica Lutchman (eds). *State of the Nation: South Africa 2004–2005*. Cape Town, South Africa: Human Sciences Research Council Press, pp. 569–585.

35 See: Adrian Hadland and Jovial Rantao. 1999. *The Life and Times of Thabo Mbeki*. Rivonia: Zebra Press. Also: William Mervin Gumede. 2005. *Thabo Mbeki and the Battle for the Soul of the ANC*. Cape Town: Zebra Press. Also: Sean Jacobs and Richard Calland (eds). 2002. *Thabo Mbeki's World: The Politics and Ideology of the South African President*. Pietermaritzburg: University of KwaZulu-Natal Press. Also: Lucy Mathebe. 2001. *Bound by Tradition: The World of Thabo Mbeki*. Tshwane: UNISA Press. Also: Mukanda Mulemfo. 2000. *Thabo Mbeki and the African Renaissance*. Pretoria: Actua Press. Also: Thabo Mbeki. 1998. *The Time has Come: Selected Speeches*. Cape Town and Johannesburg: Tafelberg Publishers and Mafube Publishing. Also: Thabo Mbeki. 2001. *Mahube: The Dawning of the Dawn, Speeches, Lectures and Tributes*. Braamfontein, South Africa: Skotaville Media.

36 See: Reuben Abati. 2001. 'Obasanjo: A Psychoanalysis'. Lagos. *The Guardian*, 8 July, p. 57. Also: Olusegun Obasanjo. 1980. *My Command*. London, Ibadan and Nairobi: Heinemann. Also: Olusegun Obasanjo. 1990. *Not My Will*. Ibadan: University Press. Also: Olusegun Obasanjo. 1999. *This Animal Called Man*. Abeokuta, Nigeria: Africa Leadership Forum Publications, 1999. Also: Onukaba Adinoyi Ojo. *Olusegun Obasanjo: In the Eyes of Time*. Lagos and New York: Africana Legacy Press, 1997.

37 See Obasanjo. 1990 above. *Not my Will*. pp. 123–148.

38 Thabo Mbeki. 1999. 'Prologue'. In: Malegapuru William Makgoba (ed). *African Renaissance*. Cape Town: Mafube and Tafelberg, p. xv.

39 See the insightful article by Peter Vale and Sipho Maseko. 'Thabo Mbeki, South Africa, and the Idea of an African Renaissance'. In: Jacobs and Calland (eds). 2002 above. *Thabo Mbeki's World*, pp. 121–142.

40 I thank Chris Landsberg for this important observation. See also: Chris Landsberg. 2002. 'From African Renaissance to NEPAD ... and Back to the Renaissance'. *Journal of African Elections* 1(2), pp. 87–98.

41 See: Olusegun Obasanjo and Felix Mosha (eds). 1993. *Africa: Rise to Challenge*. New York: Africa Leadership Forum. Also: I. William Zartman. 1996. 'African Regional Security and Changing Patterns of Relations', in: Edmond J. Keller and Donald Rothchild (eds). *Africa in the New International Order*. Boulder and London: Lynne Rienner Publishers, pp. 62–65.

42 Adekeye Adebajo and Chris Landsberg. 2000. 'The Heirs of Nkrumah: Africa's New Interventionists'. *Pugwash Occasional Paper* 1(2). January, pp. 65–90.

43 See Progress Report of the chair, Olusegun Obasanjo, to the third Ordinary Session of the Assembly of Heads of State and Government of the African Union. 6–8 July 2004, Addis Ababa, Ethiopia, NEPAD/HSGIC/07-2004/Doc 4, pp. 4–5.

44 Personal interview with Ambassador Welile Nhlapo, Head of South Africa's Presidential Support Unit. Tshwane, 22 July 2004.

45 See, for example: Adekeye Adebajo. 2000. 'Nigeria: Africa's New Gendarme?' *Security Dialogue* 2(31). June, pp. 185–199. Also: Stephen Wright and Julius Emeka Okolo. 'Nigeria: Aspirations of Regional Power', in Wright (ed). 1999 above. *African Foreign Policies*, pp. 118–132.

46 Olusegun Obasanjo. 2001. 'Nigeria-South Africa: Bond Across the Continent'. In: Ad'Obe

Obe (ed). *A New Dawn: A Collection of Speeches of President Olusegun Obasanjo* 2. Ibadan: Spectrum Books, p. 137.

47   Department of Foreign Affairs of South Africa. 1999. *South Africa and Nigeria Bi-National Commission Communiqué*. Pretoria, 6 October.

48   Department of Foreign Affairs of South Africa. 1999. *South Africa and Nigeria Bi-National Commission Communiqué*.

49   Agreed Minutes of the 6th Session of the Binational Commission between the Republic of South Africa and the Federal Republic of Nigeria held in Durban, South Africa from 6–10 September 2004.

50   Agreed Minutes of the Binational Commission, 2004 above.

51   Confidential interview.

52   I am indebted to Dianna Games (2004) for: 'The Oil Giant Reforms: The Experience of South African Firms Doing Business in Nigeria'. *Business in Africa Report* 3. Johannesburg: The South African Institute of International Affairs.

53   Confidential interviews.

54   Adeniji. 2000 above. *Essays on Nigerian Foreign Policy*, p. 84.

55   Personal interview with Gert du Preez, South African Foreign Ministry. Tshwane, 22 July 2004.

56   Personal interview with Ambassador Tunji Olagunju, High Commissioner of Nigeria to South Africa. Tshwane, 22 July 2004.

57   The author attended the AU summit in Addis Ababa in July 2004.

58   See the interview with Bangumzi Sifingo, South Africa's High Commissioner to Nigeria. *Traders* 13, February–May 2003 pp. 18–19.

59   See: James Lamont. 2001. 'Mobile phone network opens in Nigeria'. *Financial Times*, 10 August, p. 7.

60   Games. 2004 above. 'An Oil Giant Reforms', p. 57.

61   John Daniel, Jessica Lutchman and Sanusha Naidu. 2005. 'South Africa and Nigeria: Two Unequal Centres in A Periphery'. In: John Daniel, Roger Southall and Jessica Lutchman (eds). *State of the nation: South Africa 2004–2005*. Cape Town: HSRC Press, pp. 559–560.

62   Games. 2004 above. 'An Oil Giant Reforms', p. 66.

63   William M. Gumede, Vincent Nwanma and Patrick Smith. 2006. 'South Africa/Nigeria: The Giants Tussle for Influence'. *The Africa Report* 3, July, p. 16.

64   Games. 2004 above. 'An Oil Giant Reforms', p. 67–83.

65   Quoted in Daniel, Lutchman and Naidu. 2005 above. 'South Africa and Nigeria,' p. 544.

66   Games. 2004 above. 'An Oil Giant Reforms', p. 58.

67   Daniel, Lutchman and Naidu. 2005 above. 'South Africa and Nigeria,' p. 561.

68   See: Apter. 2005 above. *The Pan-African Nation*. Also: Eboe Hutchful and Kwesi Aning. 'The Political Economy of Conflict', in: Adebajo and Rashid (eds). 2004 above. *West Africa's Security Challenges*. Also: Karl Maier. 2000. *This House Has Fallen: Midnight in Nigeria*. New York: Public Affairs. Also: Ali Mazrui. 2003. 'Shari'ahcracy and Federal

Models in the Era of Globalisation: Nigeria in Comparative Perspective', in: Alamin Mazrui and Willy Mutunga (eds). *Governance and Leadership: Debating the African Condition, Mazrui and His Critics* 2. Trenton and Asmara: Africa World Press, pp. 261–276. Also: John N. Paden. 2005. *Muslim Civic Cultures and Conflict Resolution: The Challenges of Democratic Federalism in Nigeria.* Washington D.C.: Brookings Institution.

69 Patrick Bond. 2004. *Talk Left, Walk Right: South Africa's Frustrated Global Reforms.* Scottsville: University of KwaZulu-Natal Press, pp. 112–113.

70 This information on Côte d'Ivoire has drawn upon the Fifth and Sixth Progress Report of the UN Secretary-General on the UN Operations in Côte d'Ivoire. 17 June 2005, S/2005/398; and 26 September 2005, S/2005/604, respectively.

71 Confidential interview.

72 Confidential interview.

73 Confidential interview.

74 Musifiky Mwanasali. 2004. 'Emerging Security Architecture in Africa'. *Policy: Issues and Actors* 4(7). Johannesburg: Centre for Policy Studies. February, p. 14.

CHAPTER 11. SOUTH AFRICA AND ITS LUSOPHONE NEIGHBOURS: ANGOLA AND MOZAMBIQUE

1 Action for Southern Africa and World Development. 1998. 'Paying for apartheid twice: The Cost of Apartheid Debt for the People of Southern Africa'. London.

2 Richard Gibb. 1998. 'Southern Africa in Transition: Prospects and Problems Facing Regional Integration'. *The Journal of Modern African Studies,* June.

3 At the time of the election, the first nucleus of the new Angolan army was made up of 3 000 men from both the government and UNITA.

4 Herbert Howe. 1998. 'Private Security Forces and African Stability: The Case of Executive Outcomes'. *The Journal of Modern African Studies,* June.

5 Howe. 1998 above. 'Private Security Forces and African Stability'.

6 A few leading EO figures have been rewarded by the Angolan government with (minor) diamond-mining concessions.

7 Final Report of the UN Panel of Experts on Violation of Security Council sanctions against UNITA directed by Ambassador Robert Fowler, 10 March 2000.

8 Jorge Valentim, a UNITA leader and Savimbi's class-mate since secondary school in Lubango, told the author in 2000 that, 'although Savimbi was a charismatic leader, he led UNITA in a despotic way. He did not hesitate to eliminate physically his potential rivals within the organisation and he established a power based on terror and obscurantism. His relations with the population were of mere exploitation or opportunism.'

9 Quoted in: *Angola Peace Monitor* 6(5), 26 February 1999. London: Actsa.

10 *The Economist.* 2004. 'The Cartel isn't forever', 17 July.

11 In this respect, a legal judgment was expected in 2004 at the London Court of International Arbitration over a US$50 million loan granted by De Beers to Endiama in 1991, which was then worth around US$100 million, including interest cumulated after the breakdown of the agreement. A privately negotiated solution was reached in 2005.

12 *Business Day*. 1999. Johannesburg, 28 September.

13 Angola's oil production is expected to reach two million barrels a day by 2010.

14 Unofficial statement made in early 1999 by State Department and Pentagon officials to the Angolan army chief of staff, General Joao de Matos, during his first visit to Washington. Matos' interview with the author.

15 Interview with the author.

16 A similar delay occurred between the setting up of the two countries' bilateral commission in 2000, and its first meeting in late 2002.

17 Yvan Crouzel. 2002. Afrique du Sud: moteur d'une nouvelle donne continentale? Politique Africaine, Paris, December (my translation).

18 On this occasion, three agreements were signed, in the fields of: social protection and re-integration; reciprocal promotion and protection of investments; and defence cooperation.

19 In 2004, South African exports to Angola were stabilised at US$480 million and imports at US$230 million.

20 'SA-Angola chamber accuses SA government of lack of interest'. *Engineering News*, 14 June 2004.

21 'SA-Angola chamber accuses SA government of lack of interest'. *Engineering News*, 14 June 2004.

22 The Angolan economist, Vicente Pinto de Andrade, pointed out that the Angolan allocations for education between 1997 and 2001 amounted to 4.7 per cent of the state budget, compared to an average of 16.7 per cent in the other 13 SADC countries. The Angolan government budgeted 3.3 per cent of its spending for health care, while the other SADC countries allocated 7.2 per cent for the same purpose.

23 Economist Intelligence Unit (EIU). 2004. Quarterly report on Angola, April.

24 By the time the government won Angola's war in 2002, thereby gaining control of all the country's diamond mines, the contracts it had struck with Mr Leviev (that is, those lost by De Beers) were worth US$850 million a year: a sum greater even than that lost by De Beers in Russia. See *The Economist*, 2004 above. 'The Cartel isn't for ever.'

25 Hadas Manor. 2005. 'Diamonds aren't forever'. Rishon Lziyyon Globes, 2 May (Internet English version).

26 'Why is President Dos Santos running away from Mbeki?' 2004. Agora (Angola), 15 May.

27 Interview with the author.

28 Economist Intelligence Unit (EIU). 2004. Country report, January.

29 Vodacom Mozambique was established in 2003.

30 Noemia Grobbelaar. 2004. *Every Continent Needs an America*. Johannesburg: South African Institute of International Affairs.

31 Grobbelaar. 2004 above. *Every Continent Needs an America*.

32 The first gas was delivered on 19 February 2004.

33 EIU. 2004 above. Country report, January.

34 More than 20 economic agreements, including protocols and memoranda of understanding, have been signed at the highest level by the two neighbouring states since 1994.

35 Prior to this agreement, Eskom had been paying 0.05 cents (US) per kilowatt hour. An initial increase to 0.1 cents/kwh, increases again to 0.16 cents/kwh in 2007.

36 HCB's only other customer, the Zimbabwe Electricity Supply Authority, contracted to receive 500 megawatts of power.

37 Jean Coussy. 1999. 'Idéologies et Pratiques d'intégration régionale'. In: Dominique Darbon (ed). *L'Après Mandela*. Paris: Karthala (my translation).

38 Coussy. 1999 above. 'Idéologies et Pratiques d'intégration régionale' (my translation).

39 Tara Polzer. 2004. 'Researching on Forced Migration'. Quoted in: 'Les Mozambicains en Afrique du Sud'. 2004. Amadoo.com, 23 June.

40 Most of these Mozambicans are established in the former 'Bantustan' areas of Gazankulu and Lebowa. See: Polzer. 2004 above. 'Researching on Forced Migration'.

CHAPTER 12. SOUTH AFRICA: 'EXPORTING PEACE' TO THE GREAT LAKES REGION?

1 This chapter builds on an earlier paper that was published in: Carlo Fusaro and Veronica Federico (eds). 2006. *Constitutionalism and Democratic Transitions: Lessons from South Africa*. Florence: University of Florence Press.

2 *The Star*. 2005. Johannesburg, South Africa. August 25.

3 *Business Day*. 2005. South Africa. July 11.

4 Quoted in: *The Star*. 2005. Johannesburg, South Africa. August 25.

5 *Sunday Times*. 2006. South Africa, July 30, p. 34.

6 *Business Day*. 2006. South Africa, August 2, p. 10.

7 *Business Day*. 2007. South Africa, October 27, p. 15.

8 For accounts of the background to the conflicts in the region, see: Jean-Pierre Chrétien. 2003. *Great Lakes of Africa: Two Thousand Years of History*. New York: Zone Books. Also: René Lemarchand. 1994. *Burundi: Ethnic Conflict and Genocide*. Cambridge: Cambridge University Press. Also: René Lemarchand. 1970. *Rwanda and Burundi*. New York: Praeger Books. Also: Collette Braeckman. 1992. *Dinosaure: le Zaïre de Mobutu*. Paris: Fayard. On the more recent causes and consequences of conflict in the region, see: John F. Clark (ed). 2002. *The African Stakes in the Congo War*. New York: Palgrave MacMillan. See also: Gérard Prunier. 2004. *From Genocide to Continental War: The Congolese Conflict and the Crisis of Contemporary Africa*. London: Hurst and Co. Also: Filip Reyntjens. 1999. 'The Second Congo War: More than a Remake'. *African Affairs* 98, pp. 241–250.

9 Kristina Bentley and Roger Southall. 2005. *An African Peace Process: Mandela, South Africa and Burundi*. Cape Town: HSRC Press, pp. 11.

10 By March 2007, South Africa was still contributing 1 056 military personnel to MONUC, out of a total MONUC force of 16 475. http://www.monuc.org/contributions.

11 Chris Landsberg. 2006. 'South Africa'. In: Gilbert Khadiagala (ed). *Security Dynamics in Africa's Great Lakes Region*. Boulder and London: Lynne Rienner Publishers, pp. 121–140. Also: Chris Landsberg. 2000. 'Promoting Democracy: The Mandela–Mbeki Doctrine'. *Journal of Democracy* 3(11), July.

12 For a review of South African foreign policy, see: Chris Alden and Garth le Pere. 2003. 'South Africa's Post-Apartheid Foreign Policy: From Reconciliation to Revival?' *Adelphi*

Paper 362. London: Oxford University Press and IISS, December. See also: Adam Habib and Nthakeng Selinyane. 2004. 'South Africa's Foreign Policy and a Realistic Vision of an African Century', in: Elizabeth Sidiropoulos (ed). *South Africa's Foreign Policy 1994–2004: Apartheid Past, Renaissance Future.* Johannesburg: South African Institute of International Affairs.

13 Chris Landsberg. 2006 above. 'South Africa'.

14 Ian Taylor and Paul Williams. 2001. 'South African Foreign Policy and the Great Lakes Crisis: African Renaissance Meets Vagabonde Politique?' *African Affairs* 100, p. 268.

15 Bentley and Southall. 2005 above. *An African Peace Process*; pp. 2–3, 12.

16 Claude Kabemba. 2007. 'South Africa in the DRC: renaissance or neo-imperialism?' In: Sakhela Buhlungu, John Daniel, Roger Southall and Jessica Lutchman (eds). *State of the Nation, South Africa 2007.* Cape Town: HSRC Press, p. 533.

17 South Africa Department of Foreign Affairs, Strategic Plan 2005–2008, p. 18.

18 Government of South Africa. 1999. 'White Paper on South African Participation in Peace Missions'. October, p. 5.

19 Laurie Nathan. 2005. 'Consistencies and Inconsistencies in South African Foreign Policy'. *International Affairs* 81(2), pp. 362–364.

20 This is a similar justification to the use of political pacts in transitions to democracy, discussed extensively in the democratisation literature in the late 1980s. This literature was initially based primarily on the Iberian, Southern European and Latin American transitions from authoritarian to democratic rule. See, for example: Guillermo O'Donnell and Philippe Schmitter. 1986. *Transitions from Authoritarian Rule: Tentative Conclusions about Uncertain Democracies.* Washington D.C.: John Hopkins University Press.

21 Christopher Clapham. 1998. 'Rwanda: The Perils of Peacemaking'. *Journal of Peace Research* 2(35).

22 Jack Spence. 'South Africa's Foreign Policy: Vision and Reality', in Sidiropoulos (ed). 2004 above. *South Africa's Foreign Policy 1994–2004*: pp. 46–47.

23 Donald Rothchild. 2002. 'Settlement Terms and Postagreement Stability'. In: Stephen Stedman, Donald Rothchild and Elizabeth Cousens (eds). *Ending Civil Wars: The Implementation of Peace Agreements.* Boulder and London: Lynne Rienner Publishers.

24 Steven Levitsky and Lucan A. Way. 2002. 'The Rise of Competitive Authoritarianism'. *Journal of Democracy* 2(13), p. 63.

25 Thomas Carothers. 2002. 'The End of the Transition Paradigm'. *Journal of Democracy* 1(13), pp. 6–9.

26 For a discussion of this argument, see: Claude Kabemba. 2007 above. 'South Africa in the DRC: Renaissance or Neo-Imperialism?'

27 Joint Communiqué of the Second Arusha Regional Summit on Burundi. Arusha, Tanzania, August 31, 1996.

28 There were nineteen Burundian delegations in the Arusha negotiations. These delegations were the Government and the different Burundian political parties, including parties that represented some (though not all) the armed movements.

29 Each Burundian delegation sent one or two members to each committee. The committee chairs and vice-chairs were chosen by Nyerere. The chairpersons were Armando

Guebuza of Mozambique, Fink Haysom of South Africa, Reverend Matteo Zuppi of Italy, and Georg Lenk of Austria. Nelson Mandela became the chair of the Fifth Committee on Implementation and Guarantees, but this committee was established later in the negotiations process.

30 For a discussion of this period, see: Bentley and Southall. 2005 above. *An African Peace Process,* chapters 7–8.

31 Mandela quoted in: Ian Fisher. 2000. 'Warring sides in Burundi get a scolding from Mandela'. *New York Times,* January 17, p. A4.

32 For more information on the transitional arrangements, see: Devon Curtis. 2007. 'Transitional Governance in Burundi and the Democratic Republic of Congo'. In: Karen Guttieri and Jessica Piombo (eds). *Interim Governments: Institutional Bridges to Peace and Democracy?* Washington: United States Institute of Peace.

33 These smaller wings, the CNDD-FDD (Ndayikengurukiye wing) and the Palipehutu-FNL (Mugabarabona wing), signed under strong South African pressure. The Nkurunziza wing of the CNDD-FDD and the Rwasa wing of Palipehutu-FNL continued to fight.

34 The Global Ceasefire Agreement was an agreement that finalised earlier political and security power-sharing agreements signed in Pretoria on October 8, 2003 and November 2, 2003. The CNDD-FDD was given four ministerial positions, 15 seats in the transitional national assembly, and 40 per cent of the officer positions in the new defence force (Burundi National Defence Force).

35 The constitution also guarantees that 30 per cent of parliamentarians must be women.

36 For a detailed discussion and analysis of these elections, see: Filip Reyntjens. 2006. 'Burundi: A Peaceful Transition after a Decade of War?' *African Affairs* 105, pp. 117–135.

37 One smaller rebel movement, the FNL (*Forces nationales de libération*), continued to fight after the elections. A cease-fire agreement was signed in September 2006 but this has not been implemented.

38 Chris Landsberg. 2000 above. 'Promoting Democracy'.

39 These countries also accused South Africa of double standards, since South Africa was selling arms to Rwanda and Uganda, who had intervened in the DRC on the side of the rebels. South Africa eventually reversed its decision to sell arms to Rwanda and Uganda and continued to say that the problem in the DRC could not be solved militarily but had to be resolved through negotiations. See: Stefaan Smis and Wamu Oyatambwe, 'Complex Political Emergencies, the International Community and the Congo Conflict', *Review of African Political Economy* 93/94, 2002, p. 417. There is also an argument that South Africa's reluctance to intervene militarily in favour of Laurent Kabila was driven by economic interests, since Kabila had not wanted to grant mineral concessions to two South African companies. For a discussion, see: Claude Kabemba. 2007 above. 'South Africa in the DRC: renaissance or neo-imperialism?', p. 537.

40 The MLC signed on August 1, 1999 and 50 people representing both factions of the RCD signed on August 31, 1999.

41 Lusaka Cease-fire Agreement Chapter 5 (5.1).

42 The inter-Congolese negotiations were therefore even more inclusive than the Burundian Arusha negotiations, since the participants at Arusha were limited to political parties.

43 Quett Ketumile Joni Masire and Stephen R. Lewis, Jr (ed). 2006. *Very brave or very foolish? Memoirs of an African democrat.* Gaborone, Botswana: Macmillan, pp. 308–316.

44 International Crisis Group. 2002. 'Storm Clouds over Sun City: The Urgent Need to Recast the Congolese Peace Process', 14 May.

45 For a discussion of South Africa's motives, see: Emeric Rogier. 2004. 'The Inter-Congolese Dialogue: A Critical Overview'. In: Mark Malan and Joao Gomes Porto (eds). *Challenges of Peace Implementation: The UN Mission in the Democratic Republic of Congo.* Pretoria: Institute for Security Studies.

46 Initially, there was also some rivalry between South Africa and Zambia over who should lead the DRC process. See Filip Reyntjens. 2001. 'The Democratic Republic of Congo: From Kabila to Kabila'. *African Affairs* 100, p. 315.

47 *Mail & Guardian*, 27 June 2003. Quoted in: Adam Habib and Nthakeng Selinyane. 2004 above. 'South Africa's Foreign Policy and a Realistic Vision of an African Century', p. 57.

48 The Sun City Agreement was a political compromise between the main armed groups in the DRC, the *Forces Armées Congolaise* (FAC – the former government army), the *Mouvement du Libération du Congo* (MLC, led by Jean-Pierre Bemba), the *Rassemblement Congolais pour la Démocratie–Goma* (RCD-G, led by Azarias Ruberwa), the *Rassemblement Congolais pour la Démocratie–Mouvement de Liberation* (RCD-ML, led by Nbusa Nyamwisi), the *Rassemblement Congolais pour la Démocratie–National* (RCD-N, led by Roger Lumbala), and *Mai-Mai* militias. These groups converted themselves into political parties that agreed to share power in Kinshasa, along with representatives from civil society and the political opposition.

49 Kabila's party is the *Partie du Peuple pour la Réconstruction et la Démocratie* (PPRD).

50 The transitional parliament consists of a national assembly with 500 members and a senate of 120 members.

51 Under the constitution, the current 10 provinces will be divided into 26. The DRC will be a decentralised but unitary state, where the provinces will manage 40 per cent of the country's resources.

52 See Adekeye Adebajo. 'The United Nations'. In: Khadiagala (ed.). 2006 above. *Security Dynamics in Africa's Great Lakes Region*, pp. 141–161. Also: Thomas Mandrup Jørgensen. 2007. '"You Do Need a Stick to Be Able to Use It Gently": The South African Armed Forces in the Democratic Republic of Congo'. In: Lars Buur, Lars, Steffen Jensen and Finn Stepputat (eds). *The Security-Development Nexus.* Uppsala, Sweden: Nordic Africa Institute and Cape Town: HSRC, pp. 37–62.

53 For a discussion, see: Thomas Mandrup Jørgensen. 2007. '"You Do Need a Stick to Be Able to Use It Gently": The South African Armed Forces in the Democratic Republic of Congo'. In: Lars Buur, Lars, Steffen Jensen and Finn Stepputat (eds). *The Security-Development Nexus.* Uppsala, Sweden: Nordic Africa Institute and Cape Town: HSRC. Jorgensen argues that compared to the success of South African diplomatic efforts, the South African National Defence Force (SANDF) was unable to live up their high expectations. The SANDF faced operational limitations, such as problems with standards of training and equipment.

54   Filip Reyntjens. 2001 above. 'The Democratic Republic of Congo: From Kabila to Kabila'. *African Affairs* 100.

55   In the February 2005 referendum, 92 per cent of Burundians voters were in favour of the new Constitution, Voter turnout was over 90 per cent.

56   In the legislative elections, the CNDD-FDD won 58,23 per cent of the vote, FRODEBU won 22,33 per cent, UPRONA 7,3 per cent.

57   Sixth Report of the Secretary-General on the United Nations Operation in Burundi, 21 March 2006, S/2006/163, par. 11.

58   International Crisis Group. 2006. 'Burundi: Democracy and Peace at Risk'. *Africa Report* 120, November.

59   Sixth Report of the Secretary-General on the United Nations Operation in Burundi, 21 March 2006, S/2006/163, par. 35.

60   The mineral reserves at stake in the DRC are impressive. Despite prolonged instability, at their peak in December 2000, revenues from the export of coltan were over US$1 million a month. That year, the RCD also exported gold and diamonds worth $30 million. See: Denis Tull. 2003. 'A Reconfiguration of Political Order? The State of the State in North Kivu (DR Congo)'. *African Affairs* 102, p. 435.

61   'United Nations Final Report of the Panel of Experts on the Illegal Exploitation of Natural Resources and Other Forms of Wealth in the Democratic Republic of Congo', 16 October 2002.

62   In March 2005, following negotiations with the DRC Government under the auspices of the Community of Sant'Egidio in Rome, the FDLR announced that the movement was willing to cease military action against Rwanda and return home. However the Rwandan government expressed doubts. See: International Crisis Group. 2005. 'The Congo: Solving the FDLR Problem Once and for All', 12 May.

63   Report of the Secretary-General pursuant to paragraphs 10 and 14 of Security Council Resolution 1649, 22 May 2006, S/2006/310.

64   Report of the Secretary-General pursuant to paragraphs 10 and 14 of Security Council Resolution 1649, 22 May 2006, S/2006/310: par. 36.

65   It cites, for instance, frequent violence related to the illegal exploitation of diamonds in Mbuji-Mayi, and human rights violations linked to illegal tin mining in Walikale, North Kivu. Twentieth report of the Secretary-General on the United Nations Organisation Mission in the Democratic Republic of the Congo, 28 December 2005, S/2005/832: par. 49.

66   International Crisis Group. 2006. 'Congo's Elections: Making or Breaking the Peace'. Africa Report 108, 27 April, p. 2.

67   Henri Boshoff and Martin Rupiya. 2003. 'Delegates, Dialogue and Desperadoes. The ICD and the DRC Peace Process'. *African Security Review* 3(12). Also: Emeric Rogier. 2004 above. 'The Inter-Congolese Dialogue: A Critical Overview'. In: Malan and Porto (eds). *Challenges of Peace Implementation*, p. 32.

68   International Crisis Group. 2006. 'Congo's Elections: Making or Breaking the Peace'. *Africa Report* 108, 27 April, pp. 22.

69   Bentley and Southall. 2005 above. *An African Peace Process*, p. 163.

70 See discussion in: Jean-Pierre Chrétien and Melchior Mukuri (eds). 2002. *Burundi: La fracture identitaire*. Paris: Karthala, p. 126.

71 Bentley and Southall. 2005 above. *An African Peace Process*, chapter 14.

72 Though as Ahmedou Ould-Abdallah, former Special Representative of the UN Secretary-General to Burundi points out, many of the people fighting in Burundi had grown up in the same communes and attended the same schools. See: Ahmedou Ould-Abdallah. 2000. *Burundi on the Brink, 1993–95*. Washington D.C.: United States Institute of Peace Press.

73 Emeric Rogier. 2004 above. 'The Inter-Congolese Dialogue: A Critical Overview', p. 39.

74 Twentieth report of the Secretary-General on the United Nations Organisation Mission in the Democratic Republic of the Congo, 28 December 2005, S/2005/832, para. 11–12.

CHAPTER 13. SOUTH AFRICA'S RELATIONS WITH NORTH AFRICA AND THE HORN: BRIDGING A CONTINENT

1 This chapter builds on an earlier version of a paper on North Africa which appeared in the *South African Journal of International Affairs* 2(11), 2004, pp. 155–168.

2 Cited in the speech made by President Thabo Mbeki: 'Remarks at the Closing Ceremony of the Second Session of the South Africa-Algeria Binational Commission', Pretoria, 19 October 2001.

3 Address to the Congress of the People, Libya, Tripoli, 19 March 1999. See: http://www.anc.org.za/ancdocs/history/mandela/1999/nm0319.html.

4 Yusuf Gabobe. 'South Africa's Democracy and Its Implications for Somaliland'. Editorial in the Somaliland Times, April 26–May 2, 2003, http://somalilandtimes.net/2003/118/11819.shtml, accessed 6 April 2007.

5 Ali A. Mazrui. 1986. *The Africans: A Triple Heritage*. London: BBC Publications, pp. 11–39.

6 The exception is the struggle of the peoples of Western Sahara and Somaliland. For an incisive analysis on why there is a reduced urgency to find a solution to the Morocco-Western Sahara conflict, see: Adekeye Adebajo. 2002. 'Selling out the Sahara? The Tragic Tale of a UN Referendum'. *Occasional Paper Series*. Institute for African Development, Cornell University, March 2002. On Somaliland's struggle to free itself from the clutches of Somalia's militia leaders, see: M. Schoiswohl. 2004. *Status and (Human Rights) Obligations of Non-Recognised De Facto Regimes in International Law : The Case of 'Somaliland'. The Resurrection of Somaliland Against All International 'Odds': State Collapse, Secession, Non-Recognition and Human Right*. Leiden: Martinus Nijhoff Publishers.

7 The ANC had offices in Algiers, Cairo, Tripoli and Tunisia and a representative in Casablanca. Today, most of its cadres hold diplomatic positions in the South African foreign service in Qatar, Islamabad and other countries. For further details, see: S. Thomas. 1996. *The Diplomacy of Liberation: the Foreign Relations of the African National Congress since 1960*. London: Tauris Academic Studies.

8 'First International Conference in Solidarity with Peoples under Racial Discrimination', held in Tripoli, Libya, 23–27 November 1985, organised by the Socialist People's Libyan Arab Jamahiriya in cooperation with the Guild of Lawyers and the Regional Office of

326 · SOUTH AFRICA IN AFRICA

the Organisation of African Lawyers, http://www.anc.org.za/ancdocs/history/solidarity/ conferences/confs.html. See also the letter dated 25 March 1960 from the mission of Libya in New York to the President of the UN Security Council requesting consideration of the situation in South Africa, at http://www.anc.org.za/un/undocs.html.

9   For further details on this approach, see: I. Jhazbhay. 1997. 'Mandela visit to Libya shows the world that SA is nobody's lapdog'. *Sunday Independent*, 25 October. See also the ANC statement issued on Mandela's visit to Libya, 18 October 1997, at http://www.anc.org.za/ ancdocs/pr/1997/pr1018.html.

10 See Mandela's speech, 'Speech at a Banquet Hosted by Colonel Qaddafi, Tripoli', Libya, 22 October 1997.

11 Notes for a 'Speech on Being Awarded the Collar of the Nile by President Hosni Mubarak of Egypt', Cairo, 21 October 1997, at http://www.anc.org.za/ancdocs/history/mandela/1997/ sp1021.html. See also Mbeki's statement at the Africa-EU Summit, Cairo, 4 April 2000, at http://www.anc.org.za/ancdocs/history/mbeki/2000/tm0404.html.

12 See Mbeki's speech: 'Vote of Thanks at the Closing Session of the 35th Ordinary Session of The OAU Assembly of Head of State and Government', Algeria, 14 July 1999, at http:// www.anc.org.za/ancdocs/history/mbeki/1999/tm0714.html. Also: 'Address at the Opening Session of The South Africa-Algeria Binational Commission', Algiers, 22 September 2000, at http://www.anc.org.za/ancdocs/history/mbeki/2000/tm0922.html.

13 Cited in the speech made by Mbeki at the state banquet for President Bouteflika, Pretoria, 16 October 2001, at http://www.anc.org.za/ancdocs/history/mbeki/2001/tm1016.html.

14 This emerges from numerous discussions with South African foreign affairs officials and discussions with key South African policy makers.

15 See the ANC website archive which documents ANC relations with Algeria, at http://www. anc.org.za/ancdocs/pr/1980s/pr881208.html. Also: 'Brief Profiles of the Men and Women Receiving Their Isitwalandwe Medals on the Occasion of the 80th Anniversary of the ANC in Bloemfontein', 8 January, 1992, http://www.anc.org.za/ancdocs/history/awards/ isitwala_10.html and http://www.anc.org.za/ancdocs/pr/2001/pr1126c.html. Also: Oliver Tambo's statement: 'Algeria Honours Chief Luthuli'. *South Africa Freedom News*. Dar es Salaam, November 30, 1964, http://www.anc.org.za/ancdocs/pr/1960s/pr641130.html. See, more specifically, the role of Bouteflika described in: 'Ruling by the President of the General Assembly, Mr. Abdelaziz Bouteflika (Algeria), concerning the credentials of the delegation of South Africa'. Paper presented by the Chairman of the Special Committee against Apartheid, Edwin Ogebe Ogbu (Nigeria), to the Extraordinary Session of the Council of Ministers of the Organisation of African Unity, held in Dar es Salaam, Tanzania, April 1975, http://www.anc.org.za/un/undocs2a.html.

16 Information gleaned from journalist J.J. Cornish's account of an interview with Pik Botha. Personal correspondence with J.J. Cornish, 10 January 2004.

17 South Africa's small but vocal Muslim population of about two per cent has voiced concerns about Algeria's troubled transition to democracy. But the issue has neither topped the agenda of the Muslim community nor captured its imagination in a way that Palestine or Iraq have. For a more detailed sense of the feelings of South Africa's Muslim community, see back issues of the two local Muslim newspapers, *Muslim Views* and *Al-Qalam,* and views aired on the local radio stations *Radio 786* and *Voice of the Cape.* A key point to recall in understanding Algeria's Islamic political movements is

that the radicalisation of Islamic politics was a direct result of the involvement of many *mujahids* in America's battle in Afghanistan against the Soviet Union. Most returned to Algeria and took up leadership positions and adopted extreme positions on gender and politics. The ANC leadership has closely followed religious and Islamist trends on the continent and has developed appropriate policies. The ruling party has a full-time Commission for Religious Affairs at its head office in Johannesburg, and Mbeki meets with religious leaders at least twice a year.

18 The settlement of the Western Sahara question remains on the ANC agenda, despite the South African government's formal recognition of the territory. See the resolution of the ANC's 51st National Conference of 2002 during which it called on 'the South African government to take special initiatives to advance the process to reach an early settlement', at http://www.anc.org.za/ancdocs/history/conf/conference51/resolutions.html.

19 Interviews with South African Department of Foreign Affairs officials, October 2003. This matter was also picked up in ANC discussions on international affairs.

20 Address by the President of South Africa, Thabo Mbeki, at the Pan African Parliament, Gallagher Estate, Midrand, 16 September 2004, http://www.dfa.gov.za/docs/speeches/2004/mbeko917.htm.

21 Telephonic interview with Ambassador Ebrahim Salie, Chief Director of North Africa desk at the South African Department of Foreign Affairs, February 2007.

22 Address by President Nelson Mandela to the Congress of the People, Tripoli, Libya, 19 March 1999, http://www.info.gov.za/speeches/1999/990324546p1001.htm.

23 A recent report commissioned by the US Congress calls on Washington not to normalise relations with Libya until Tripoli stops its support for wars in West Africa. Cited in: The Africa Advisory Panel. 2004. *Rising US Stakes in Africa. Seven Proposals to Strengthen US-Africa Policy.* Report. Washington D.C.: Centre for Strategic and International Studies, Washington, May. During my research in the Horn of Africa, several senior Ethiopian officials complained that Qaddafi's 'cheque book' diplomacy towards Somali militia factions, such as Abdullahi Yusuf and Abdul Qasim Salat, had been counter productive to the region. Somaliland, the peaceful breakaway north-western entity, has repeatedly shunned Qaddafi's diplomatic overtures on principle.

24 Tunisia also played a role in the struggle against apartheid. See, for example, the proceedings of the Conference of Arab Solidarity with the Struggle for Liberation in Southern Africa, Tunis, 7 August 1984, http://www.anc.org.za/un/garba.html#g2.

25 AU press release 2. 2003. 'AU Solicits Closer Links between African and Arab Markets'. 6 December, http://www.africa-union.org/News_Events/Press_Releases/02%20afro.pdf. The 7th Afro-Arab Trade Fair was scheduled to be held in the United Arab Emirates.

26 'State of the Nation Address of the President of South Africa, Thabo Mbeki: Joint Sitting of Parliament', 9 February 2007, at http://www.thepresidency.gov.za/show.asp?type=sp&include=president/sp/2007/sp02091220.htm.

27 'Visit of the Minister of National Defence of Tunisia to the Republic of South Africa'. Speech. 19 September 2006. http://www.info.gov.za/speeches/2006/06092710451001.htm, accessed 5 April 2007.

28 Discussions with African Presidents and foreign affairs ministers in Addis Ababa, Pretoria and Accra from 2000 to 2007.

29 ANC statement on the death of Joe Modise, 26 November 2001, http://www.anc.org.za/ ancdocs/pr/2001/pr1126c.html. See also the statement on Joseph Nduli of 15 August 1995. http://www.anc.org.za/ancdocs/pr/1995/pr0815.html. The only African mission to South Africa, the legation of Egypt, was closed on May 31, 1961, according to UN Press Release GA/AP/523 of 21 January 1976, referenced at http://www.anc.org.za/un/sp-com-3.html.

30 J. Barber. 2004. *Mandela's World: The International Dimension of South Africa's Political Revolution 1990–99*. Cape Town: David Philip.

31 Mahmood Mamdani. 2007. 'Politics of Naming: Genocide, Civil War, Insurgency'. Website of English-language Iranian TV news service *Press TV*, 21 March, http://www. presstv.ir/detail.aspx?id=3330&sectionid=3510303. Also: Gérard Prunier. 2005. *Darfur: The Ambiguous Genocide*. Cornell University Press.

32 Commission of the European Communities. 2006. 'Strategy for Africa: An EU Regional Political Partnership for Peace, Security and Development in the Horn of Africa'. Brussels, 20 October, at http://eur-lex.europa.eu/LexUriServ/site/en/com/2006/ com2006_0601en01.pdf.

33 This is evident from the numerous requests and visits of the region's foreign ministers to South Africa. The latest was the visit of the Ethiopian Minister of State for Foreign Affairs and the Kenyan Minister of Foreign Affairs in January 2007.

34 Iqbal Jhazbhay. 2005. 'Sudan : Renewed possibilities and hope in long walk to peace'. *ANC Today 14(5)*, 8 April.

35 Centre for Conflict Resolution. 2006. 'South Sudan within a New Sudan'. Seminar Report 20 and 21 April 2006, Franschhoek, South Africa. Cape Town: CCR, available at http://ccrweb.ccr.uct.ac.za.

36 See UNISA Sudan capacity building project, http://www.unisa.ac.za/default. asp?Cmd=ViewContent&ContentID=17020.

37 Meles Zenawi is a *nom de guerre*, Zenawi's first name being Legesse. Zenawi is most commonly referred to as Meles.

38 Thabo Mbeki. 2007. 'Somalia needs African solidarity'. *ANC Today 1(7)*, 12 January, http:// www.anc.org.za/ancdocs/anctoday/2007/at01.htm. For more details, see also my response to the US ambassador to South Africa's suggested approach to Somalia: Iqbal Jhazbhay. 2007. 'US Approach to Somalia not worthy to emulate'. *Sunday Times*, 18 February, p. 28.

39 'Notes following briefing by Deputy Minster Aziz Pahad', Media Centre Amphitheatre, Union Buildings, Tshwane, South Africa, Tuesday 4 July 2006. Also see: http://www.dfa. gov.za/docs/speeches/2006/paha0704.htm.

40 African Union Commission. 2005. 'Resumé: AU Fact-Finding Mission to Somaliland (30 April to 4 May 2005)'. Unpublished four-page report. Addis Ababa: African Union. This mission was led by then AU Deputy Chairperson, Patrick Mazimhaka. See also: Tandeka Lujiza. 2003. 'Somaliland's Claim to Sovereign Status'. Six-page report. Office of the Chief State Law Advisor (International Law), Pretoria: Department of Foreign Affairs, April. Also: European Commission. 2005. 'International Donors Support the Democratisation Process in Somaliland'. Delegation in Kenya – Somalia Operations, 1 September. Also: European Commission. 2005. 'Somaliland Parliamentary Elections: International Members of the Steering Committee Commend the Process following Proclamation of the Results'. Delegation in Kenya – Somalia Operations, 18 October.

41 'Statement on the Death of Muhammed Ibrahim Egal, Leader of Somaliland'. South African Department of Foreign Affairs, 3 May 2002, http://www.info.gov.za/speeches/2002/02050609461004.htm.

42 Cited in President Mbeki's weekly letter in ANC *Today* 27(4), July 2004.

43 For further research, see the following: J.J. Cornish. 1999. 'Western Sahara'. In: G. Mills and and E. Sidiropoulos (eds). *South African Yearbook of International Affairs 1999/2000*. Johannesburg: South African Institute of International Affairs, pp. 357–362. Also: F. Kornegay. 'Nigeria, Egypt and South Africa: A Stable Balance of Power in Africa'. In: G. Mills and E. Sidiropoulos (eds). 1999 above. *South African Yearbook of International Affairs 1999/2000*, pp. 61–69. Also: Chris Landsberg. 2000. 'Promoting Democracy: The Mandela-Mbeki Doctrine'. *Journal of Democracy* 3(11), July. Also: S. Makgohlo, I. Jhazbhay and E. Sidiropoulos. 2000. 'North Africa: A Review' in G. Mills and E. Sidiropoulos (eds). *South African Yearbook of International Affairs 2000/01*, pp. 199–218. Also: K. Morais and S. Naidu. 2002. 'Libya's Africa Policy: What Does It Mean for South Africa and NEPAD?' *South African Journal of International Affairs* 9, Winter, pp. 109–118. Also: E. Sidiropoulos (ed). 2004. *South Africa's Foreign Policy 1994-2004: Apartheid Past, Renaissance Future?* Johannesburg: South African Institute of International Affairs. Also: K. Sturman. 2003. 'The Role of Libya as a regional player', *African Security Review* 2(12). Also: F. Aggad. 2005. 'Western Sahara: A Security Risk Analysis'. Occasional paper. Pretoria: Africa Institute of South Africa. Also: F. Aggad. 'Political Reforms in the Arab World: An Analysis of the Egyptian Political Scene'. Occasional Paper. Pretoria: Africa Institute of South Africa, 2/2006. Also: F. Aggad. 2006. 'Future Prospects for the Resolution of Conflict in the Western Sahara: Solution or Revolution?' *Africa Insight* 2(36).

Index

A NOTE ABOUT THE TYPE

This book is set in Minion Pro, a typeface designed by Robert Slimbach for Adobe Systems, California, USA. The first version of Minion was released in 1990, and Minion Pro, a fully developed text family, was released in 2000. Minion was inspired by the classical typefaces of the late Renaissance, and shares characteristics with such faces as Dante, Kis/Janson and Plantin.